ELEMENTS OF HUMAN GEOGRAPHY

TITLES OF RELATED INTEREST

Environmental hazards in the British Isles
A. H. Perry

Earth and man
B. J. Knapp

Man—environment processes
D. Drew

Exploring social geography
P. Jackson & S. Smith

ELEMENTS OF HUMAN GEOGRAPHY
Second Edition

Charles Whynne~Hammond

Still the world is wondrous large – seven seas from marge to marge –
And it holds a vast of various kinds of man;
And the wildest dreams of Kew are the facts of Khatmandhu,
And the crimes of Clapham chaste in Martaban.
Rudyard Kipling, *In the Neolithic Age*

London
GEORGE ALLEN & UNWIN
Boston   Sydney

George Allen & Unwin (Publishers) Ltd,
40 Museum Street, London WC1A 1LU, UK

George Allen & Unwin (Publishers) Ltd,
Park Lane, Hemel Hempstead, Herts HP2 4TE, UK

Allen & Unwin Inc.,
Fifty Cross Street, Winchester, Mass 01890, USA

George Allen & Unwin Australia Pty Ltd,
8 Napier Street, North Sydney, NSW 2060, Australia

First published in 1979
Second edition 1985
Second impression 1986

British Library Cataloguing in Publication Data

Whynne-Hammond, Charles
    Elements of human geography.—2nd ed.
1. Anthropo-geography
I. Title
304.2   GF43
ISBN 0-04-910081-5

Set in 9 on 11 point Melior by
D. P. Media Limited, Hitchin, Hertfordshire
and printed in Great Britain by
Richard Clay (The Chaucer Press) Ltd,
Bungay, Suffolk

Preface to the first edition

Human geography has changed considerably in the recent past. Its character, aims and methods of approach have altered so that a subject that was once essentially descriptive and qualitative has become more scientific and quantitative. The new techniques and terminology involved in this change were first introduced into university degree courses during the 1960s, but they have since percolated downwards through the educational strata. Secondary schools now teach the new approach, and examination syllabuses, especially those at Advanced level, have been modified to accommodate it.

However, human geography is a very wide subject and this has caused certain problems for both students and teachers. They must cover all aspects of a syllabus in sufficient detail for examiners yet should avoid the highly technical information and statistical minutiae of more advanced and specialised levels. At post-Ordinary level I have found these problems to be particularly acute, with sixth-formers falling into that academic middle ground between fairly straightforward and elementary studies up to O-level and highly detailed and intricate degree studies. At present, few textbooks seem to have been published especially for this middle ground. On the one hand there are books that are general readers omitting important information on theories and models; on the other hand there are those aimed essentially at undergraduates. The latter category includes very specialised, often expensive, books, which cover only limited fields of work in human geography and which are, in consequence, often difficult for the sixth-former.

In *Elements of human geography* I have attempted to cover the main aspects of the subject – population, economic activity, settlement and planning – with particular reference to the needs of students in the 16–19 age group. I have specifically aimed to provide sixth-formers with basic information and guidelines for Advanced level and to introduce them to the key topics and principal concepts and theories of the subject. The book is not meant to cover the entire realm of human geography exhaustively – this would not be possible in what is primarily intended to be a standard class textbook. Students are advised and encouraged to supplement the information in this book with more detailed reading from other geography books and academic journals and from their own projects and fieldwork. The exercises, project work suggestions and reading lists included in this book are intended to help students undertake this extra work and to guide the provision of student activity by teachers.

The selection and presentation of the material is based on my own experience in teaching human geography to A-level and on the advice, comments and suggestions given to me by other geography teachers from schools and colleges. I have written the book with particular reference to the requirements of the A-level syllabuses laid down by the major examination boards in Britain, and have attempted to cater for the average sixth-form student. I have tried to remember that the vast majority of post-O-level geography students do not necessarily intend to become specialists in geography; they wish to pass their examinations with as high a grade as possible but are unlikely to pursue the subject to degree level. For this reason I have endeavoured to present human geography in a straightforward way and with a minimum of jargon, verbiage, detailed statistics and technical formulae.

It is hoped that revision and updating will be possible at fairly regular intervals and any comments and suggestions from readers will be most welcome.

C.W.-H.
1979

Preface to the second edition

It is now seven years since I started writing the first edition of *Elements of human geography*. In those days, geography as a subject was still settling down after the 'quantitative revolution': it had become very much a science discipline steeped in mathematical techniques and theory or model analysis. Advanced level syllabuses and teaching reflected this bias, and everywhere geographers were talking of concepts and laws, of patterns and processes, of synthesis and data collection.

But times change and geography has moved on from those heady days. Many geographers have reacted against quantitative techniques and have attempted to bring their subject back to the real world. As a result, geography has become more issue based, more socially aware, more humanistic, more slanted towards the welfare approach. This new edition, it is hoped, mirrors these recent changes in emphasis. The quantitative techniques covered by the first edition are retained, and new societal techniques have been introduced – the two aspects complementing each other. I have continued to keep the style, vocabulary and language as straightforward as possible, thus keeping the book more intelligible to the average student than are many A-level textbooks.

This edition sees some radical alterations to the first edition. The text has been revised, updated and rearranged; much new material (including an entirely new chapter) has been included; and many new diagrams and photographs have been used. Each chapter now begins with an introduction and ends with a summary; it is hoped that this will greatly improve the book's use as a revision and quick-reference aid. A subdivided index and glossary of terms have also been inserted for the same purpose. A new cover and the varied use of typeface and page layout have further produced a different and, it is hoped, an improved appearance.

The end-of-chapter data–response exercises have been restyled and extended. These, together with the project work suggestions at the end of each part (also rewritten), are intended to give students and teachers no more than a guide to further private study. Readers are encouraged to use these sections merely as a base, adapting the questions and ideas for their own specific purposes and in association with their own specialist knowledge, self-obtained data and personal preferences.

Finally, I should like to say that the work involved in the production of this second edition has been both interesting and stimulating. I can now only hope that those students and teachers using it feel that the effort on my part has been worth while.

C.W.-H.

Acknowledgements

The author and publisher of this book gratefully acknowledge the assistance derived from *Economic and social geography made simple* by R. Knowles and J. Wareing (Made Simple Books) in the preparation of the text.

I have spent many pleasurable and interesting hours teaching my students at Southgate Technical College, have learnt a great deal from them in return (not always geographical in nature), and have written this book with the aim of catering for the needs of their successors. In the preparation of the first edition, and in the writing of this second edition, I am indebted to many friends, colleagues and strangers without whose help the successful completion of both editions would not have been possible.

I should like, in particular, to thank Graham Humphrys, John Williamson, Graham Agnew, David Castell, Jennifer Stonhold and Dennis Allen for their assistance in the writing of the original text for the first edition. Their careful reading of the typescript and their suggestions for alterations and additions proved invaluable. John Williamson, Graham Agnew and Jenny Stonhold further helped in the preparation of the second edition, as did Don Agerskow and Allen Astles – all of whom helped tremendously in the diagrammatic and textual changes.

At George Allen & Unwin I should like to thank Roger Jones, Director of Academic Publishing, who has helped guide the editions through the various stages of production, and Geoff Palmer, who worked on the illustrative material.

In addition I should like to convey my appreciation to my friends and colleagues at Southgate (especially those in Room 406), to the very helpful college library staff (including Stephen Mousley), and to Jill Kirtland – who was able to read my handwriting so well and typed so neatly the often complicated text.

Finally, I owe a special debt of gratitude to my family for their support, understanding and encouragement during the writing of the book.

The author and the publishers are grateful to the following for permission to reproduce illustrations:

Aerofilms for Figures 7.1, 7.2, 7.3, 7.4, 7.10, 9.3, 10.1, 13.2, 14.3, 14.6, 14.8, 15.1, 16.4, 16.11, 19.1, 19.5; British Rail for Figure 1.6; J. Allan Cash for Figures 14.5 and 15.4; Central Office of Information for Figure 19.3; Countryside Commission for Figure 19.8; Department of Industry for Figure 20.2; Fox Photos for Figure 19.6; Institute of British Geographers for Figure 15.9; Methuen for Figures 12.1, 19.7, 19.9; and the Borough Council of Newport for Figure 20.1.

C.W-H.

Contents

CONTENTS

CONTENTS

List of tables

xiii

Part I

ASPECTS OF HUMAN GEOGRAPHY

He had bought a large map representing the sea,
Without the least vestige of land:
And the crew were much pleased when they found it to be
A map they could all understand.

'What's the good of Mercator's North Poles and Equators,
Tropics, Zones, and Meridian Lines?'
So the Bellman would cry; and the crew would reply,
'They are all merely conventional signs!'
Lewis Carroll, The Hunting of the Snark

It is a capital mistake to theorise before one has data.
A. Conan Doyle, Scandal in Bohemia

APPROACH TO HUMAN GEOGRAPHY

Quantitative revolution – societal geography – probabilism – systems analysis – concepts – behaviouralism – perception – mental images – relativity – topological maps

---

METHODS IN HUMAN GEOGRAPHY

Spatial analysis – regions – interactions – linkages – laws – matrices – inferential techniques – questionnaires – gravity models – economic man – rationality – theories

1

1 Approach to human geography

Introduction

Human geography is a broad and complex subject. It transcends many other academic disciplines; relates to the operation of physical, economic and social laws; is dependent upon set cultural and behaviour patterns; and determines the character of the world as we know it. To study the subject, a student must possess both a general understanding of the natural environment and a specific knowledge of certain principal aspects of human livelihood.

In the same way that human geography as a whole cannot be detached from other subject areas – and should not be studied in isolation – so it is true that each topic within human geography cannot stand alone. All the various aspects of this book are related to each other and also to the many aspects of physical geography. They link, interconnect and overlap. Thus, readers should cross-reference the information of each chapter with that of other chapters, together with that provided by other geography textbooks, periodicals and the mass media.

This first chapter will provide a foundation upon which an understanding of human geography can be built. It offers an introductory analysis of the thinking, research methods and evaluation techniques of the subject – an examination of how human geographers approach their work. It will attempt to answer the following questions:

- What is human geography and the work of human geographers?
- What are the links between human geography and other subjects?
- How is the approach to human geography changing?
- Which factors influence man's changing relationship with his environment?
- How do human geographers attempt to explain human behaviour?

Human geography today

Geography – the study of the environment and man's changing relationship with it – can be viewed not just as one subject but as many. As can be seen in Figure 1.1, it embraces such a wide field that the study of any one aspect or topic brings the student into contact with another academic discipline. Human geography, by itself, is composed of separate topic areas and the conscientious human geographer needs to acquire a wide knowledge and diverse skills.

But human geography – like most other social science subjects – is dynamic and it changes with time. Over the past 40 years, in particular, it has undergone fundamental alterations in both scope and character. No longer does the human geographer merely identify man's activity and set it against a physical environment. Such work is as simplistic (and as dated) as the traditional regional geography of two generations ago. Today, emphasis in human geography is placed more on a deeper understanding of the forces at work in determining spatial patterns of human behaviour, and on a deeper awareness of the social aspects of human activity. In short, the subject has become less descriptive and more scientific, realistic and sociological.

Since the days when human geography was *qualitative* – geared to the mere recognition of existing world attributes – two major changes have taken place. The first of these changes, dubbed the *quantitative revolution*, had its roots in the 1950s and flourished during the 1960s. This saw a much greater emphasis on the problem of *why* man lives as he does, and less emphasis on *how* he lives. No longer would human phenomena simply be mapped and described, they would be interpreted and diagnosed. This meant the introduction into human geography of methods and ideas imported from other disciplines, notably from mathematics, statistics, physics, biology, chemistry and economics. And with this change came an entirely new vocabulary: soon, geographers were talking of spatial analysis and inferential techniques, of concepts, laws, models and theories, of behaviour, perception and prediction, of ecosystems, linkages, matrices, equations, formulae and paradigms.

However, no sooner had human geography become a scientifically based subject than the second change began to take place. By the 1970s, a reaction had

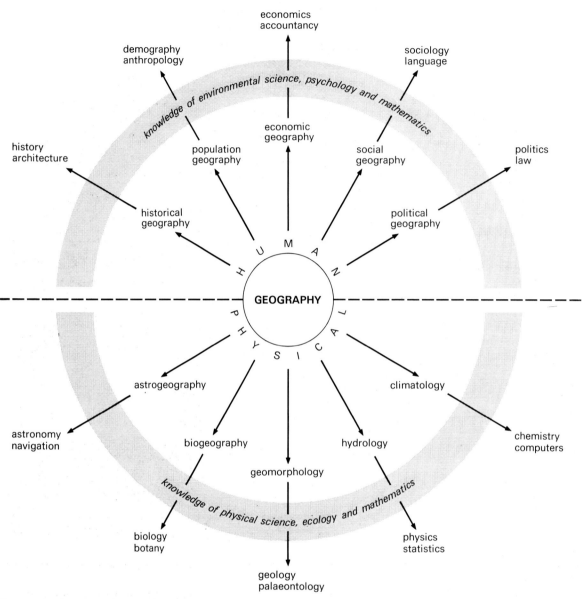

Figure 1.1 The scope of geography
Geography is perhaps the broadest of all academic disciplines. Human geography alone is made up of many and diverse parts, each demanding specialist knowledge.

started against the sterile, inhuman approach of quantitative geographers who had seen the human landscape in terms of set patterns, ordered processes and strict regularities. This reaction ushered in assumptions and ideas taken from such other disciplines as sociology and psychology. Thus, by the early 1980s, an entirely new bias had been introduced into human geography – one which, although not obliterating quantitative techniques, could certainly be superimposed on to them.

This new approach to human geography has been given various names: humanistic, sociologistic, behaviouralistic. Essentially, it is an attempt to set human conditions against a real world background; to accept the complexities of human behaviour and link them with existing socio-economic and political

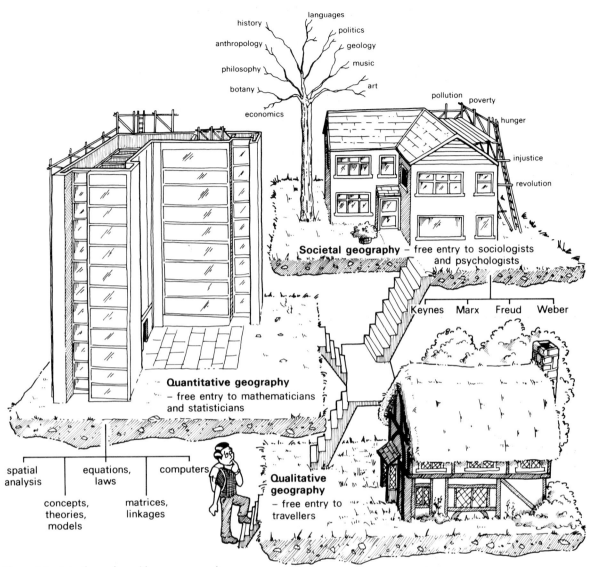

Figure 1.2 Into the realms of human geography
Human geography is a wide, all embracing subject, which can take many forms. It is also an ever changing subject and can be studied from different viewpoints.

conditions; to recognise the faults of man-made systems and place them in the context of global and national problems. 'Radical geography', 'welfare geography', 'societal geography' – whatever its name, this new approach has certainly brought human geography into the mainstream of economic, sociological and political thought. Human geographers, more than ever before, became involved with contemporary issues: pollution, international allegiances, military and psychological warfare, energy misuse, inequalities of wealth, the breakdown of moral values, human contentment, the evolution of political thought, social injustice.

Today, the subject of human geography perhaps has stabilised – at least, for the time being. The three strands of study technique should be seen not as mutually exclusive, but as complementary (Fig. 1.2). There is a place for the qualitative approach, notwithstanding its somewhat superannuated reputation, and both the quantitative and societal approaches can usefully coexist providing the former does not remain too mechanistic and jargon-ridden, and providing the latter does not remain too politically biased. Only together will they add to the general interest, understanding and wellbeing of our environment.

Man and his environment

The study of man's activities over the surface of the Earth combines two themes: how man lives and how he makes a living. The former includes aspects of population, cultural and political attitudes, and settlement; the latter includes agriculture, industry and transport. These aspects cannot be studied in isolation. They are not only linked together, but also to the physical environment in which they are found.

Determinism and possibilism

The strength of the relationship between man and his environment has long been a matter of dispute among geographers. What, for example, determines man's ultimate course of action? Is it his natural surroundings, or does his own will determine how and where he lives? To what extent does man's freedom of choice liberate him from the environment?

Traditionally there have been two viewpoints: **determinism** and **possibilism**. Determinism is basically the idea that the environment is largely responsible for man's behaviour: that human geography is controlled by physical geography. Possibilism takes the alternative view and holds that although the environment offers possible courses of action, man himself determines his own way of life. Certainly both opinions contain some truth.

It is beyond question that physical conditions do affect human conditions and behaviour: racial characteristics, culture, religion and so on. Hot climates have led to the evolution of protective dark skins, and the existence of tropical forests may prolong the hunter stage of development and retard agricultural progress. Inhospitable mountain landscapes, where nature can be harsh and awe-inspiring, may produce superstitious or religious people who are energetic and virile – of the kind that make bold guerillas in wartime (e.g. the Gurkhas from Nepal in World War 2).

Evidence to support the idea of determinism can be gleaned from the fact that human activity is often similar in regions of similar environment, even when such environments are far apart. For example, the lifestyle of the Malays bears a striking resemblance to that of the northern Colombian indians, and the agricultural pattern in northern Mexico is not unlike that in north-west Pakistan.

Conversely, possibilism may be demonstrated with equal conviction. Even in the harshest environment man faces a choice: what crops to grow, where to build his village, and so forth. Indeed, human activity sometimes appears to be totally due to man's own choice; no one would say, for instance, that the dairy farming of Denmark is related entirely to physical factors, since it has been heavily influenced by a definite government policy.

So what is the answer? Of course, reality lies somewhere between the two extremes. Man does have freedom of choice but only within the confines set by the environment. This has been termed **probabilism**, whereby physical conditions determine probable courses of action, but the ultimate decision is left with man's own will.

Man's influence

The balance between man's freedom and nature's controls varies from place to place and from time to time. Sometimes environment is all important, sometimes man's freedom dominates. It is generally true, other things being equal, that harsh surroundings restrict man's choice more than moderate surroundings, and therefore tend to lead to lower standards of living. It is perhaps for this reason that most of the world's technologically developed societies are found in temperate latitudes where climate, relief and raw materials offer the greatest choice of actions. In areas of climatic extremes and high relief, development proceeds more slowly.

The differences between these regions are exacerbated by the tendency for advanced societies to increase their choice of actions still further. With economic development comes a technical know-how capable of overcoming natural disadvantages. The irrigation of dry lands, draining of swampy lands and so forth lead to a reduction of the environment's influence.

However, we should remember that there is a two-way process. Not only does the environment control man's activities to a greater or lesser extent, but man himself may also have an impact on the environment. This impact can be direct or indirect. Man can alter the environment directly by fertilising poor soils, terracing hillsides, constructing reservoirs, roads and railways and generally changing the landscape to suit himself. Indirectly, he can do it unintentionally. Towns, for example, generate urban climates, which are warmer and damper than natural climates over adjacent countryside, and the removal of forests may result in lower rates of transpiration and therefore lower precipitation.

Man and his environment are, then, interrelated (see Fig. 1.3). This interrelationship can be identified as an overall **ecosystem** in which the factors of man,

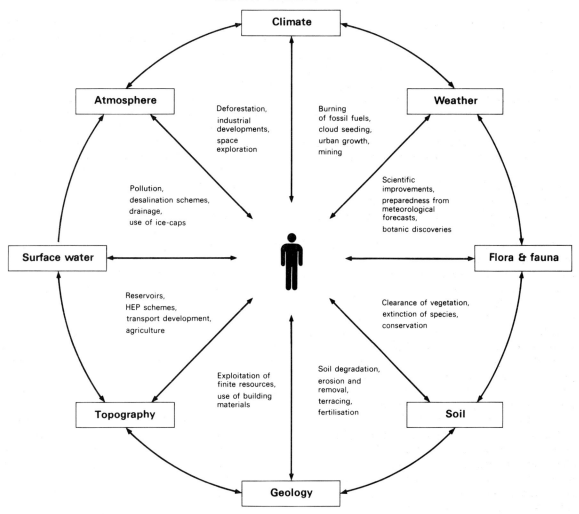

Figure 1.3 Man's relationship with his environment
Man is central to the world's ecosystem, influencing it and being influenced by it. The natural elements of the ecosystem are also interrelated.

animals, plants, climate, rocks and soils have a functional interaction. At any one time, there might be a balance between these, but should just one factor alter, there is likely to be a change in the whole ecosystem. The environment may alter naturally with flooding, sedimentation, earthquakes, volcanoes and other physical phenomena. Man may cause pollution and landscape modification. In either case, the process is usually irreversible.

Of course, as population grows and technology advances, man's influence on his surroundings will increase in both intensity and extent. His power over the world's ecosystem will become more dominant.

For this reason, many geographers employ the concept of a **control system**, whereby an ecosystem is viewed as an instrument of man's control. Through conservation and preservation man can maintain stability in the system, and through positive planning policies he can create changes that are to his advantage.

A new understanding
Part of the work of the human geographer is to identify and understand man–environment interrelationships. In particular, this involves a search for order and regularity in the apparently complex landscapes of the world.

After collecting data, and mapping the findings, certain patterns may become apparent. Key relationships between sets of phenomena may repeat themselves and, from these, predictions can be made. In this way it is possible to develop models and theories that go some way towards placing geography on a scientific footing.

Man–environment relationships can occur on any scale and in any locality. They can also be highly complex in character. Because of this, the work of the geographer is made difficult and certain approaches must be employed if he is to disentangle the relevant factors in his study. Two such approaches are the development of **concepts** and the use of **systems analysis**.

Concepts are basic ideas that can lead to generalisations about real world situations and processes. They are largely based on practical experience and known data relationships. Most aspects of human geography may be viewed through concepts: location, spatial organisation, surfaces, points, movement, distance, scale and direction. The association between sheep grazing and chalk downland may be thought of as a simple (though not necessarily an accurate) concept.

Systems analysis is a method of study. Different aspects of geography may be seen as systems, each being made up of linked elements. In physical geography, for instance, the hydrological cycle may be considered as a system in which the elements of precipitation and ground water are linked through evapotranspiration and condensation. It is through the viewing of systems in this way that relationships may be identified.

An example may help to explain how systems analysis can be applied to human geography. A farm in East Anglia, thought of as a system, would have such elements as crop types, size of fields, number of animals, the economic status of the farmer, climate and soils. From this, linkages between these elements can be considered. Thus, there could be a connection between soil fertility and crops grown or, alternatively, between the status of the farmer and the crops grown. It is by recognising systems and their elements that links can be discovered. Systems analysis

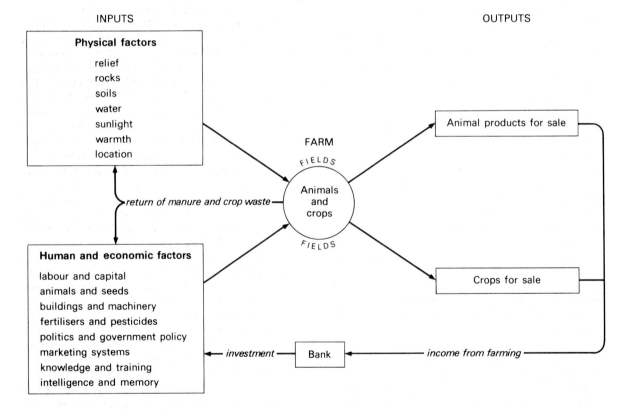

Figure 1.4 Systems analysis applied to a farm
The character of a farm is the product of various geographical factors.

applied to a farm is shown diagrammatically in Figure 1.4 and applied to agriculture generally in Figure 7.6.

Systems analysis is useful since it enables the geographer to understand the wholeness of the environment and the interdependence of its individual components. It provides a logical framework within which to think and allows for the identification and evaluation of environmental changes. The fact that systems can be of any scale means that this approach is useful to all geographers, whatever their principal aims.

Behaviour and perception

Together with the so-called 'quantitative revolution' and the growing interest shown by geographers in man–environment interrelationships, there has also been a movement towards behavioural analysis. Briefly, this involves the study of the factors, other than the environment, that determine human actions: *why* man behaves as he does rather than *how* he behaves.

We have already seen that the environment has a considerable influence on human activity since it limits man's choice. Within these limits, however, man is free to choose. It is here that his personal nature becomes decisive: the way he perceives and evaluates the environment and how he behaves under different conditions. Only occasionally are actions the result of chance or stochastic influences, that is, the outcome of neither physical, nor economic, nor behavioural forces.

What determines human nature is a question only psychologists, philosophers and sociologists are trained to answer. The factors involved are complex and it is not the work of the geographer to disentangle and study them. One aspect, however, does qualify for special investigation, namely perception, which is perhaps fundamental in determining economic, social and political behaviour. Often, what is important is *not* what the environment is actually like but what man *thinks* it is like. The two are not always the same.

Man's image of the environment is conditioned by numerous factors including direct experience, indirect experience, attitudes and value-judgements.

Direct experience is, of course, an actual visit to a place and it forms the basis for the most accurate perception. Indirect experience is based on knowledge acquired from such sources as books, films, newspapers, maps and advertisements and even from the verbal accounts of other people. This kind of information is helpful but not always accurate. Attitudes and value-judgements produce ideas that people acquire about places, and are determined by culture, socio-economic status, age, experience and education, personality, prejudice and temperament. These ideas could be correct but could also be wildly vague and inaccurate.

An interesting feature of perception is that no two people share exactly the same images or ideas. This is because we are all individuals with our own personal tastes, opinions, needs and desires. Thus, two people going on holiday to the same resort might have vastly different views about it. Similarly, a farmer's perception of the countryside is likely to be different from that of a person born and bred in town.

Mental pictures and mental maps
Environmental perception of all types leads people to develop mental pictures and mental maps. Every person has an image of the world inside his head, including even those places he has never visited.

Mental pictures are usually 'representative views' of areas, although they may also include sounds, smells and even feelings. Thus, the term 'Lake District' might conjure up a picture of mountains and lakes, stone cottages, sheep and heather – that is, the visual equivalent of Wordsworth's poetry. In the same way 'Cotswolds' might bring to mind rolling pastures, dry-stone walls, honey-coloured villages and medieval church towers. However, such pictures may be inaccurate. The southerner's view of the North of England, for instance, commonly includes back-to-back houses, slums, smoky chimneys and mills – a picture not dissimilar to the paintings of Lowry. In fact, the North of England contains vast areas of farmland and moors, and Victorian townscapes are rapidly disappearing.

In a similar way, people's perception of foreign countries and their inhabitants may be wildly inaccurate (see Fig. 1.5). Many wars have been prolonged through such misconceptions and many peace initiatives have been hindered. Mental pictures of places, people and things can have a profound effect upon human actions and should not be underestimated as a feature of human geography.

Mental maps are images of spatial relationships. They are quite unlike atlas maps since they vary in accuracy, often distorting both distances and directions, and they may change over time. Generally, people of intelligence with wide experience and

Figure 1.5   The British view of Europe
The old newspaper headline 'fog in Channel, Continent isolated' speaks volumes about the British attitude towards Europe, and the British perception of Europeans is equally condescending. Apart from the physical attributes depicted, Europeans are supposedly endowed with unflattering social graces: the French are selfish, philandering, unreliable, unhygienic and insincere; the Germans are orderly, domineering, clean-cut, disciplined and conformist; the Italians are cowardly, artistic, excitable and passionate; the Dutch are mean, stolid, stoical and unimaginative; the Swedish are neurotic, suicidal, amoral, humourless and pacifistic. The British are also said to have unkind perceptions of other world nationals, and conversely, they have perceptions about the English, Scottish, Welsh and Irish.

knowledge have more accurate, detailed and wider ranging mental maps than do people of lower intelligence and limited experience and knowledge. An example may be drawn from London. An intellectual and wealthy person living in, say, Hampstead is likely to have a fairly exact idea of the shape of Greater London, the location of the boroughs and, probably,

the distribution of the main art galleries, theatres and cinemas. Conversely, a person of limited education living in, say, the East End would know the local streets, the way to work and the main features of dockland, but might not know the general pattern of London as a whole. In the USA, a study of perception in Los Angeles has shown that 'rich whites' from Westwood have a much wider and more detailed mental map of the city than blacks from Avalon, and that Spanish-speaking immigrants from Boyle Heights have the most limited mental maps of all.

Kevin Lynch, in his study of towns in the USA (*Image of the city*, MIT Press, 1960) has identified five elements in mental maps. These are: paths along which people travel; edges or barriers to movement; nodes or centres of concentration; districts of recognised character; and landmarks which provide reference points. Examples of these five in London might be, respectively: Charing Cross Road or Oxford Street; the River Thames; Piccadilly Circus or Trafalgar Square; Soho or Bloomsbury; and finally the Post Office Tower, St Paul's Cathedral or the Albert Hall.

It can be argued that the greater the strength and richness of these five elements, the more coherent and interesting will be an urban area and hence the easier it is to map mentally. Certainly this seems to be true in Britain. Many New Towns and modern suburbs, with their concrete tower blocks and uniform road patterns, have weak, less obvious, elements and thus appear to be formless, monotonous and lacking in character. Old towns, on the other hand, have jumbled street patterns and a variety of architectural styles which produce strong elements and therefore interest for their inhabitants.

Mental maps of country areas are perhaps more difficult to formulate and examine. It seems likely that the same five elements are apparent, but here they tend to be natural rather than man-made and therefore less easy to define.

Mental maps of whole regions were studied by Gould and White during the 1960s (*Mental maps*, Penguin, 1974). In their study, twenty groups of schoolchildren in different parts of Britain were asked to rank the counties of England, Scotland and Wales in order of preference regarding where they would most like to live. As a result it was found that the children most preferred those areas in which they were already living. After these, the English south coast was considered the most popular area, and attractiveness declined northwards. The Lake District was found to be the exception – being fairly popular – no doubt because it is a holiday region and is there-

Relativity

Man's behaviour is, then, largely determined by his perception, and this can distort the truth. Thus, what interests the human geographer is not just the world as it is but also the world as it appears to be. The environment can be viewed at different levels and the student must learn to distinguish between reality and unreality. Accuracy, like beauty, is in the eye of the beholder and what is true to one person is untrue to another, what is infallible to one is fallible to another.

Indeed, such is the nature of geography today that well may one ask 'What is truth?' No longer should we consider facts as objective and faithful exactitudes. They are, more accurately, mere interpretations of the real world measured according to set prejudices and value-judgements. Just as the same news item can be reported differently in different newspapers – the *Daily Telegraph* and the *Guardian*, for instance, giving widely dissimilar slants on political matters – so aspects of geography can be described in many opposing ways. Three people may each describe a Third World village yet give totally different impressions of it – as has been well demonstrated by Roger Robinson of Birmingham University in 'What is truth?', *Times Education Supplement* (3.12.82). Each description would be 'factual' and true but would also be heavily biased according to prescribed viewpoints. All teachers and lecturers provide information that reflects their own preconceptions, and all textbooks (this one included) give facts that are true only within the confines of the attitudes and value-judgements of their authors. Thus, relativity and not absoluteness is the cornerstone of human geography.

The actuality of our surroundings may be considered in terms of absoluteness, with units of measure rated in absolute terms. The perception of our surroundings, on the other hand, may be considered in relative terms – relative, that is, to each individual's personal conditions. Thus, phenomena such as time, cost and distance can be given both absolute and relative values, the former being objective, quantities which are unquestionable to all, the latter being subjective, quantities which are unique to each individual person. Both can be measured, but in different ways.

Absolute and relative time
Absolute time is most commonly gauged in units of calendar and clock divisions: years, months, days, hours, minutes and seconds. Such units are standard

---

... If this study had included ... middle-aged and elderly ...ht have been different. ... of the investigation was ...nt from different places ...al maps is partly deter-...he lives. This fact is of ...here is a great diversity of ...personal impressions are ...ve positive and negative ...iffer in their response to ...s, heavy rain may bring ...t much-needed water to ... would be considered ... wintry Siberia but would probably bring chaos to British Rail.

Hazard perception
There are only a very few universally recognised advantages and disadvantages in nature. Droughts, floods, earthquakes, volcanoes and tornadoes are considered hazards everywhere; they are powerful, difficult to predict, and can kill. In which case it may seem odd to many people that man frequently chooses to live in regions where such hazards are likely. Who has not wondered why the Americans rebuilt San Francisco after the 1906 earthquake? After all, it stands on the San Andreas Fault.

The answer may lie in what geographers call **hazard perception**. This is largely determined by time, experience and extent. The more often a hazard occurs, the greater is man's perception of it; the less often, the more man is likely to forget its disastrous effects. Similarly, a person who has suffered directly from a disaster will be more conscious of that hazard than someone else who has only read about it. This would be especially true if the disaster were very serious, since the greater its extent, the greater would be its perceived impact.

Perhaps a further reason for man's apparent irrationality is that perception is capable of distorting reality in order to rationalise behaviour. Just as people tend to underestimate distances to desirable places and overestimate those to undesirable places, so too might they underestimate hazards in an area where they particularly want to live.

Concepts of behaviour and perception pervade all aspects of human geography. They lead to decisions which in turn generate human actions and these, in their turn, cause further decisions. In other words, behaviour and perception underlie all man's activities and, as such, are of paramount importance.

and universally accepted. Relative time, conversely, can be gauged in all manner of ways that are not uniform: seasons, generations, lifespans and human biological cycles for example. Regions in the Temperate Zone have four seasons each year, areas on the Equator have none (having very similar climatic and weather conditions all the time); winters in northern Canada are considerably longer than winters in Spain. A time span of four generations may be considered about 100 years in the developed world but only about 70 years in the less developed world. Clearly, such relative time measures should be used with caution. Indeed, even absolute time should be used carefully, since it can be judged relatively. A five-year period is considerably longer for a person who only lives 30 years than it is for a person who lives 80 years; to the former it represents nearly 17% of total life, to the latter only about 6%.

Absolute and relative cost

Absolute cost is usually measured in units of currency: dollars and cents, pounds and pence, for example. But such a yardstick is useful only for the assessment of value. For the gauging of real cost, relative measures must be employed. What concerns the human geographer is not, for example, the money wage of a worker but the wage level compared with the price of goods and services. Weekly earnings equivalent to £50 would be a pittance in a developed country where prices are very high, yet would be extremely remunerative in a less developed country where prices are very low. The price of a Rolls-Royce motor car would be cheap to a millionaire but exorbitant to an agricultural labourer.

Absolute and relative distance

Absolute distance is expressed most commonly in units of physical measurement: miles, kilometres, yards, metres and so on. Such quantitative terms are clearly defined and give an exact knowledge of spatial relationships (notwithstanding the drawback that absolute distances may vary even between set points – aerial straight-line lengths differing from surface route-flow lengths, for example). However, in order to study comparative relationships, human geographers may be more concerned with relative distance, measured, perhaps, in terms of time, cost and convenience.

Time distance is measured in hours and minutes. It is not always linked to absolute distance. Terrain and traffic flow may slow down a journey that in absolute

terms is short, or speed up a journey that is physically long. Neither is it true that the time distance from A to B will be the same as from B to A. The air journey from London to New York, for instance, takes longer than in the reverse direction owing to the existence of the westerly, high-altitude, jet-stream winds.

Cost distance is measured in units of currency. It is determined partly by absolute and time distance and partly by such factors as volume and type of goods carried, destinations, and methods of transport used.

Convenience distance measures ease of transport. A town 50 km away could be easier to reach than another only 20 km away, because of a more frequent or faster service, a flatter terrain, or better road conditions.

Relative distances may change over time, absolute distances do not. Time distances can vary even by the hour: everyone will know this who has travelled across an urban area in rush hour and again during off-peak periods. Over the years the difference is even greater. Technological advances have given rise to the cliché that the world is getting smaller. We need only compare stagecoach travel of the Georgian age with modern motorway travel, or transatlantic journeys by sailing ship with those by Concorde to see this to be true.

Absolute distance provides a basic framework for describing location, but relative distance is perhaps more significant in the study of human behaviour. Both are capable of being mapped.

All traditional **topographical** maps show absolute distances since they attempt to represent the landscape accurately. However, **topological** maps are becoming more common – maps designed to show only important relationships. In these, locations are represented by dots, and connections between them by straight lines; distances (and scales) and directions might no longer matter. The London Underground map is topological since it shows only relationships between stations and not actual distances between them. British Rail now produces 'overland' maps on the same principle, these often being based on journey time (Fig. 1.6). The advantages of topological maps are numerous. They are easily understood (since they omit irrelevant detail), lend themselves to rapid analysis, and may be used to predict changes. They are especially helpful in solving transport problems. In short, they are one of the many new tools used by the human geographer in his study of man's environment.

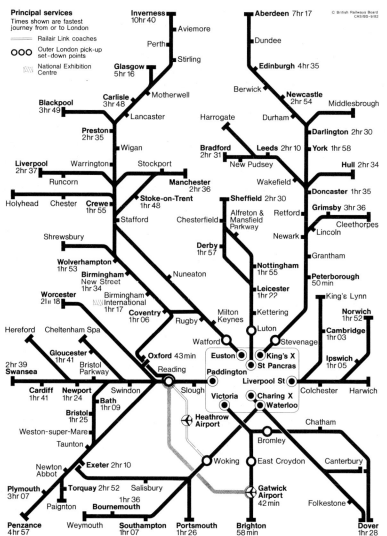

Principal services
Times shown are fastest
journey from or to London

══════ Railair Link coaches

ooo Outer London pick-up
set-down points

〰〰〰 National Exhibition
Centre

© British Railways Board
CAS/BS-9/82

Inverness 10hr 40
Aviemore
Perth
Stirling
Glasgow 5hr 16
Motherwell
Carlisle 3hr 48
Lancaster
Blackpool 3hr 49
Preston 2hr 35
Wigan
Liverpool 2hr 37
Warrington
Stockport
Runcorn
Manchester 2hr 36
Holyhead Chester Crewe 1hr 55
Stoke-on-Trent 1hr 48
Stafford
Shrewsbury
Chesterfield
Wolverhampton 1hr 53
Birmingham New Street 1hr 34
Nuneaton
Worcester 2hr 18
Birmingham International 1hr 17
Coventry 1hr 06
Rugby
Hereford Cheltenham Spa
Gloucester 1hr 41
Oxford 43min
Watford
2hr 39 Swansea Bristol Parkway
Reading
Cardiff 1hr 41 Newport 1hr 24
Swindon
Slough
Bath 1hr 09
Bristol 1hr 25
Weston-super-Mare
Taunton
Newton Abbot
Exeter 2hr 10
Woking
Plymouth 3hr 07
Torquay 2hr 52 Salisbury
1hr 36
Paignton Bournemouth
Penzance 4hr 57
Weymouth
Southampton 1hr 07
Portsmouth 1hr 26
Brighton 58min

Aberdeen 7hr 17
Dundee
Edinburgh 4hr 35
Berwick
Newcastle 2hr 54 Middlesbrough
Harrogate Durham
Darlington 2hr 30
Bradford 2hr 31 Leeds 2hr 10 York 1hr 58
New Pudsey
Hull 2hr 34
Wakefield
Doncaster 1hr 35
Sheffield 2hr 30
Alfreton & Mansfield Parkway Retford
Grimsby 3hr 36
Cleethorpes
Lincoln
Newark
Derby 1hr 57
Grantham
Nottingham 1hr 55
Peterborough 50 min
Leicester 1hr 22
King's Lynn
Milton Keynes Kettering
Norwich 1hr 52
Luton
Cambridge 1hr 03
Stevenage
Euston King's X
St Pancras Ipswich 1hr 05
Paddington
Liverpool St
Victoria Charing X
Waterloo
Colchester Harwich
Heathrow Airport
Chatham
Bromley
East Croydon Canterbury
Gatwick Airport 42 min
Folkestone
Dover 1hr 28

Figure 1.6 Topological map: inter-city services in Britain (by kind permission of British Rail)
This type of map is used by BR since it is easy to read and is visually very effective.

Summary

1 Over the past 40 years, the quantitative approach (using statistical, methodical techniques) and the societal approach (using issue-based, behavioural awareness) have been superimposed on to the more traditional qualitative approach in the study of human geography.

2 Determinism, possibilism and probabilism are traditional theories seeking to explain man's interrelationship with his environment. Man controls the world's ecosystem, for good and ill, and faces the challenge of adapting the natural environment to suit his own ends.

3 Concepts and systems analysis techniques help to simplify the complexities of the man–environment interrelationship. Each may be based on a false premise.

4 Human behaviour is determined by human perception (through mental pictures and mental maps). Truth is subjective; facts are biased towards preset value-judgements; reality is a concept open to question.

5 Relative and not absolute measures are important in the study of human behaviour. Topological maps show the former, topographical maps the latter.

Data–response exercises

1 Convert the flow diagram of man–environment interrelationships (Fig. 1.3) into a real life situation, labelling each square according to actual circumstances. For example, the centre might be a farmer on the Sussex Downs or a nomad in the Sahara Desert.

2 By applying systems analysis to urban areas, redraw Figure 1.4 to show the separate elements to be found in your local town and the links connecting them.

3 Draw a mental map of the world, the size of each country varying according to the number of times it is mentioned in a random ten news bulletins on television or radio. What does the resulting map suggest about the view of the world as given by news programmes? How might such a map based on British bulletins differ from those based on American and Russian news bulletins?

4 Draw concentric circles around a central town to represent absolute distances at 50 km intervals. Plot surrounding towns using straight-line distances as measured on an atlas map. On a similar diagram, plot the same towns using road distances (as quoted in motor organisation handbooks) and travel times (using bus or rail timetables). Compare and account for the differences between the diagrams.

5 Construct topological maps of the rail networks of Ireland and India (using atlases or regional geography books) to show relative positions of all towns and cities served. Comment on how different your maps are from reality and suggest reasons for the differences found.

2 Methods in human geography

Introduction

Human geographers, setting out on a course of specialised study, must first decide which single approach, or combination of approaches, they should adopt towards their subject. Then, armed with the fundamental tools of intellectual activity, they must decide on the methods needed to achieve their objectives. The previous chapter outlined the approaches (qualitative, quantitative and societal) and the tools (concepts, systems analysis, behavioural analysis, perception and relativity). This chapter aims to outline some of the methods that can be chosen by human geographers: spatial analysis, explanation techniques, the use of theories and models. It will also attempt to answer the following questions:

- What particular aspects of the human environment should be considered, and how can these be studied and mapped?
- Where should fieldwork be undertaken, and how can the findings be collected, collated and explained?
- Can the evaluated conclusions of fieldwork be formulated into laws of pattern and process?
- What use can theories and models be in the interpretation of the real world, and how far should human geographers question the basic assumptions of these laws?

Spatial analysis

Geography has always been concerned with landscapes and maps. This is still true, but now the emphasis is changing. Instead of the simple identification of human features, geographers are more concerned with the study of man's spatial organisation: how and why settlements and economic activity are distributed as they are. The question to be answered is whether the spatial structure of human behaviour is purely random or is arranged in a particular pattern. Are there, for example, any regularities in the distribution of man's activities and, if so, are they interrelated? Do certain processes, like the controls of distance and location, produce set or regular human patterns?

Spatial analysis attempts to answer such questions. This is an approach that considers the three elements of geometric space in the context of man's distribution. These three elements are **locations** ('points' or 'nodes'), **interactions** ('lines' or 'flows') and **regions** ('areas' or 'areal units'). In each case, they must be defined, described, classified and, perhaps also, ranked into **hierarchies**, in order that relationships can be identified and patterns can be explained.

Locations
Locations may be viewed as points of activity – such as villages, towns, farms or transport junctions – and can be studied either individually in terms of specific sites or together as general distributions. They may be defined and classified using size, shape, form, visible attributes and functions as units of reference. Thus, taking settlements as an example, a study of specific sites might include an investigation of such phenomena as spring lines, defensive positions or shelter, and a study of distribution might conclude that villages are spaced randomly, clustered (grouped together) or regularly (evenly). They may be defined and classified according to population size or by economic functions.

Locational studies make easier the search for the processes that have produced distribution patterns. Regular patterns may result from the rational action of man over flat homogeneous surfaces (as suggested by Christaller (Ch. 13) and Lösch (Chs 9 & 13), for instance), whereas clustered patterns may result from the process of concentration (as is apparent sometimes in population migration (Ch. 6) and industrial development (Ch. 9)).

Interactions
Interactions take place between points of location: between people, settlements, countries, factories and so on. All such points are linked by physical or functional lines along which economic and social forces are channelled. These lines are usually communication routes (roads, railways, pipelines, for example) and can often display complex interrelationships.

15

Economic interchange takes place, for example, between producers and consumers, and social interchange occurs between peoples of different racial, social or educational backgrounds (or, indeed, between peoples of similar backgrounds).

These spatial interactions may be studied by considering flows and networks. Flows are simply the direction, speed, volume, content, type and frequency of traffic between points. Networks are more complex, being integrated flow structures that link whole groups of points. The study of both allows regularities to be observed and factors affecting interactions to be investigated.

There are flows of mineral and energy resources within and between countries (Ch. 8) and of manufactured goods between industrial areas (Ch. 9). Theories have been expounded on both flows and networks (Ch. 10), and the flow of capital underlies the divisions between rich and poor regions (as suggested by Myrdal (Ch. 12) and various politicians (Ch. 17), for instance).

Regions

As understood by the geographer, regions are everywhere apparent and the study of them leads to a greater understanding of spatial activity. The world is not uniform: it falls into distinct areas, each with its own unique characteristics. Although there is no absolute definition of the term, a 'region' is said to possess homogeny: a cohesion, either physical, functional or cultural, which binds points within an area together and distinguishes them from points elsewhere. There are various types of region (Fig. 2.1). Depending on how they are defined and the aims of a particular study, the criteria used may vary.

Once defined, regions can be examined and, perhaps, ranked into hierarchies. The elements that make them up can be studied, as can the interactions that take place both within and between them. The difficulties of regional classification may also become apparent from their subdivision: geographical proximity is not necessarily a precondition for linkages between points, and distance not necessarily a hindrance to cohesion.

Although regions are commonly thought to be

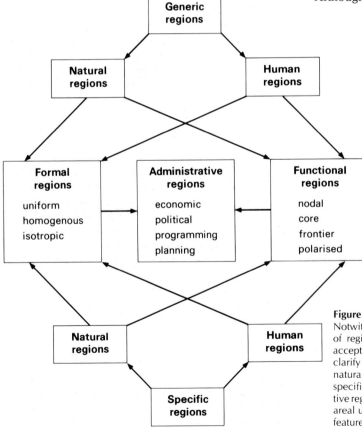

Figure 2.1 Classification of regions
Notwithstanding the difficulties in defining different types of regions, these subdivisions serve as a guide to an accepted classification. Some examples may help to clarify the terms. A river basin would be a generic, natural, functional region, whereas Brazil would be a specific, human, formal region (and also an administrative region). Regions can further be classified into singular areal units and collective areal units, or else into single-feature areas and multiple-feature areas.

larger than local units and smaller than national units, in geographical terms they can be of any size, from a local farming community to an entire continent. The most commonly defined regions are those that have either physical uniformity or functional uniformity.

Physical regions are traditionally discussed in textbooks, and are simply areas that comprise distinct geological or topographical features. In Britain, there are the very obvious physical regions of the Pennines, Dartmoor, the Weald and East Anglia; in Europe there are the Paris Basin, the Black Forest and the Alps.

Functional regions are based on human activity and, unlike physical regions, are more liable to change over time. They may be political, religious or social entities, or areas of common industrial or agricultural structures. In recent years, interest has especially developed in the economic regions associated with urban centres. Around every town there is a region, which both serves and is served by it, providing water, food, raw materials, leisure facilities and labour, and receiving employment and service facilities. These fields of urban influence operate as integrated, but very complex, units and are discussed in greater depth in Chapter 15.

There are, however, problems involved in mapping regions. The first is that their boundaries are often difficult to distinguish and delimit. Even with physical regions, climate, vegetation and relief do not form strict and absolute boundaries; for example, equatorial forests rarely stop abruptly at the edge of savanna grasslands, but gradually become less densely forested over some distance. With functional regions, this merging of elements is more extensive still. The second problem arises out of the fact that boundaries may unite regions just as much as they divide them. For instance, a river may be viewed as a border, yet economic, social and physical unity is often a characteristic of river basins. Thus, a river might actually divide regions that, in fact, are very similar. For example, where the Rhine forms a border between France (Alsace) and West Germany in the southern Rhine Rift Valley, territorial claims have often been disputed.

The third problem is one of potential confusion and is the result of regional overlapping. This occurs not only with regions based on different criteria but also with those based on the same set of rules. For instance, the urban fields of two towns will probably overlap somewhere between the two centres, since people living there might use both towns equally for shopping, entertainment and other activities.

Locations, interactions and regions are, then, the main components of spatial analysis. But all three are continually changing and it is the task of the human geographer to identify, measure and account for these changes. This is done by using set procedures of investigation and various mathematical techniques. In fact, the statistical evaluation of geographical phenomena may be considered a cornerstone of spatial analysis. It aids the identification of regularities in patterns, the understanding of functional processes, the detection of trends and the development of theories and models.

Techniques of explanation

The investigation and evaluation of the data acquired in the initial stages of spatial analysis require set procedures of study. Once the three elements of geometric space, as outlined earlier, have been qualified, they must be explained and quantified. This explanation involves a number of study procedures.

First, a methodical approach must be decided upon; secondly – and based on the chosen approach – a sequence of quantitative techniques must be determined; thirdly, methods of fieldwork and data collection must be designed. Initially, the student must decide between the inductive approach and the deductive approach; subsequently (and determined by this decision) he or she must choose to employ either descriptive techniques or inferential techniques.

Induction
Induction is a method of study whereby the real world is examined, and general, inferred conclusions are made, based on the findings. Particular characteristics of the environment are defined, measured, classified and mapped. They are then sifted, classified and arranged so that a search can be made for patterns and relationships. Based on the findings, general principles and laws are then construed in order to account for the originally observed geographical features. Such laws are called 'inductive laws'.

Deduction
Deduction involves an assumed premise as a starting point, which is then applied to real-world conditions. A logical hypothesis or proposition is made concerning environmental relationships. It is then tested against particular instances so that the truth of the

supposition can be gauged. Depending upon this application to the real world, an original premise can be either proved, modified or disproved. Hypotheses that are proved can be turned into general laws. Such laws are called 'deductive laws'.

Descriptive techniques

Descriptive techniques can be used to simplify data into manageable proportions. They are most commonly employed with the inductive approach but can also speed up or clarify studies using the deduction approach. Inevitably, such techniques may involve the use of definitions, scales and averages.

Definitions can be difficult, owing to the complexity and dynamism of the environment. Industries can be subdivided into primary, secondary, tertiary and quaternary; settlements into 'rural' and 'urban'; populations into social, economic and political groups; but none of these distinctions is wholly satisfactory, owing to interconnections, overlaps, blurred margins and constant change. Where is the exact dividing line between tertiary and quaternary services? When precisely does a village functionally become a town? What accurate measures can be used for 'rich' and 'poor', 'middle class' and 'upper class', 'radicalism' and 'conservatism'?

Scales can be equally difficult to formulate. Absolute measures are simple enough, since they involve the use of fixed, objectively based scale units – kilometres, yards, tonnes, hectares and so on. But what of relative measures? In physical geography, the Beaufort scale for winds and the Richter scale for earthquakes are examples of scales based on relative measures. Is an earthquake of 8 on the Richter scale exactly twice as disastrous as an earthquake of 4? Obviously not. In human geography, the problems of relative scales are greater. Is a town ranked tenth in a country necessarily half as important as a town ranked fifth? Exactly how much more beautiful is a tourist region given a score of seven out of ten by the public compared with another region, which only receives three out of ten?

The measurement of averages is only slightly less problematical. There are three main types of average (mean, median and mode), and these provide different information. The **arithmetic mean** type of average is the total of all values in a list divided by the number of values in that list. The **median** is the point where the number of values in a list above that value is equal to the number of values below it. The **mode** is the most frequently occurring value. Naturally, these three types of average rarely coincide.

But averages, of whatever type, can be misleading. For this reason, geographers may also wish to measure the dispersion of data, thereby finding the extent to which values differ from the average and to what extent averages are typical of the whole array. After all, a mean size of a dead weight 200 000 tonnes of, say, tankers in a range from 50 000 to 600 000 tonnes is far less typical of an array than the same mean with a range from 150 000 to 250 000 tonnes.

Inferential techniques

Inferential techniques are used to test how far samples represent wholes and how far hypotheses fit reality. At the heart of this method is **probability theory**, which brings the geographer into the realms of statistics. As in games of chance, this is concerned

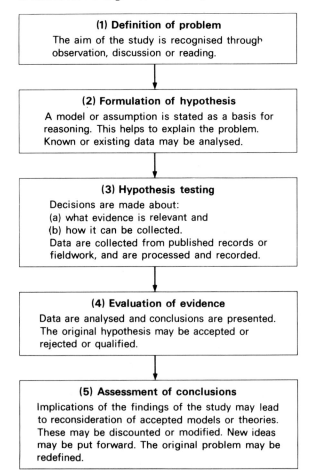

(1) Definition of problem
The aim of the study is recognised through observation, discussion or reading.

(2) Formulation of hypothesis
A model or assumption is stated as a basis for reasoning. This helps to explain the problem. Known or existing data may be analysed.

(3) Hypothesis testing
Decisions are made about:
(a) what evidence is relevant and
(b) how it can be collected.
Data are collected from published records or fieldwork, and are processed and recorded.

(4) Evaluation of evidence
Data are analysed and conclusions are presented. The original hypothesis may be accepted or rejected or qualified.

(5) Assessment of conclusions
Implications of the findings of the study may lead to reconsideration of accepted models or theories. These may be discounted or modified. New ideas may be put forward. The original problem may be redefined.

Figure 2.2 Inferential quantitative analysis
A systematic sequence of steps should be employed in planned fieldwork and data collection.

Design and content

A well written questionnaire should have:

(1) A clear layout with simple instructions and distinct subsections.

(2) Limited terms of reference covering a specific task or a small topic area.

(3) Simple, easily understood questions which invite straightforward answers.

Types of question

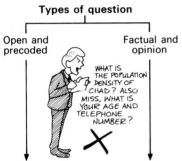

Open and precoded ← → Factual and opinion

Beware

Open questions may give vague and useless answers. Precoded questions may force respondents into categories into which they do not belong.

Beware

Respondents may not know the facts or may not wish to divulge them. Respondents may not have an opinion on every topic; may not have a strong enough opinion to give an immediate answer; may have an opinion that changes from day to day; or may have more than one opinion on a single topic.

Question wording to avoid

(1) Vagueness. Questions that pose general queries or use unspecific terminology will receive indistinct replies.

(2) Directioning. Questions that use leading phrases usually receive answers that have been presupposed.

(3) Incoherence. Questions that are long-winded, complicated, ambiguous and hypothetical will receive no answers at all, answers that the respondents do not mean, or answers that are qualified and conditional.

Figure 2.3 Questionnaire composition
There are right and wrong ways of composing a questionnaire – and the better the construction the more valuable will be the survey findings and conclusions.

with forecasting the outcome of uncertain events. Just as a die has a one in six chance of landing on any one face, so in geography any phenomenon may occur at a particular place by accident. If two different places feature similar human activities, it is up to the geographer to find out if the reason is chance or not.

The undertaking of inferential quantitative analysis involves a logical sequence of steps (see Fig. 2.2).

The first is the definition of the problem. The geographer must ask himself what exactly he wants to know: why wheat is grown in a certain area, for example, or why a particular town is sited where it is.

The second step is the formulation of a basic hypothesis. In other words, a potential solution to the problem should be stated, and this acts as a foundation for study. Most hypotheses are derived from

known or assumed geographical relationships: that wheat growing is related among other things to soil type and climate, or that town sites are linked to water supply.

The third step is to test the hypothesis. This means collecting and processing data obtained either from published records or from original fieldwork. Acquiring data from official sources is relatively simple, but fieldwork is both costly and time-consuming. For this reason, most geographers undertaking fieldwork use sample data, just as those compiling opinion polls question only a small percentage of the total population. One of the most common ways in which data can be collected is through the use of questionnaires – forms of listed questions, which can either be distributed by post or else employed in personal interviews. However, questionnaire composition is far from straightforward (Fig. 2.3). Other methods of collecting information through fieldwork include personal observation, informal interviews and scientific experimentation.

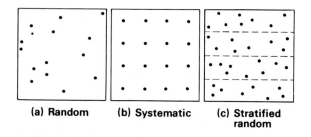

(a) Random **(b) Systematic** **(c) Stratified random**

Figure 2.4   Types of point sampling
Each dot marks a point of investigation – a datum collection spot.

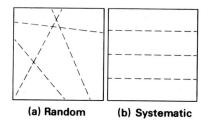

(a) Random   **(b) Systematic**

Figure 2.5   Types of line sampling
Data collection here takes place along distinct routes or lines – a data continuum.

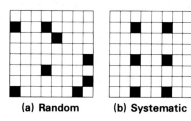

(a) Random   **(b) Systematic**

Figure 2.6   Types of quadrat sampling
Fieldwork and other survey studies can take place in blocks or areas – mini-regional data collection.

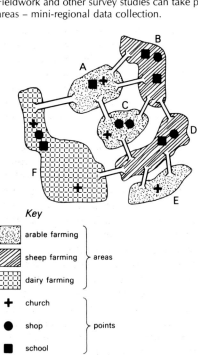

Key

arable farming	
sheep farming	areas
dairy farming	
+ church	
● shop	points
■ school	
═ bridge	— interactions

Conditions (points)

Units of observation	church	shop	school
A	1	0	1
B	0	1	2
C	1	2	0
D	0	1	1
E	1	0	0
F	2	1	1

Conditions (areas)

Units of observation	arable	sheep	dairying
A	1	0	0
B	0	1	0
C	1	0	0
D	0	1	0
E	1	0	0
F	0	0	1

Conditions (interactions)

Units of observation	A	B	C	D	E	F
A	–	2	1	0	0	1
B	2	–	1	1	0	0
C	1	1	–	1	0	0
D	0	1	1	–	2	1
E	0	0	0	2	–	0
F	1	0	0	1	0	–

Figure 2.7   Matrix composition
Spatial conditions or variables can be depicted in numerical charts or matrices. A matrix which identifies points (nodes or locations) can be called an attribute matrix; one that shows areas (regions) an areal classification matrix; one that shows interactions (links) a connectivity matrix. The figures show how the various attributes of a given set of six islands can be shown in matrix form.

To make a sample as accurate as possible, certain methods of sampling have been developed. These include the use of points, lines or areas, and from these information can be obtained at random, in a stratified random scheme, or systematically.

Point sampling involves the simple collection of data from fixed places: houses, farms, hamlets, towns and so forth (Fig. 2.4). Line sampling is more systematic and involves the collection of data from transects: along various cross-sections, taken at random, along rivers or roads or along regular lines of latitude (Fig. 2.5). Area sampling is different again and is undertaken using restricted regions of manageable size. These regions ought to be of similar size and are usually square in shape (hence the term **quadrat sampling**, which is often applied to this method). A good example of the kind of unit used is the kilometre square on Ordnance Survey maps (Fig. 2.6).

The choice of sampling method is determined by the type of data being collected, the size of the region being investigated, the hypothesis being tested (that is, the questions being asked), and, ultimately, geographical judgement. For instance, a region of generally uniform landscape, like the Canadian Prairies, would probably be studied using random sampling, whereas a region of known linear trends, like ridge and vale topography, might be studied using the stratified or line-sampling method.

Once information has been collected, it must be processed into a more easily understood form, such as a numerical index, a graph or a statistical map. In modern human geography, the use of matrices has become especially popular (see Fig. 2.7). It is through processing that data can be examined and relationships found.

The fourth step in quantitative analysis is the evaluation of the evidence. This may lead to the acceptance, rejection or qualification of the original hypothesis. Of course, any sampling, however studiously undertaken, will contain a certain degree of error. It is therefore imperative first to recognise this error and secondly, if possible, to measure it. The smaller the degree of error, the greater will be the validity of the geographer's findings.

The fifth and final step is to assess any implications of the conclusions uncovered by the evaluated evidence. On the strength of the data collected and the response to it, an accepted theory may be proved, partly proved, disproved or modified. Sometimes the original problem may be redefined.

Quantitative analysis has evolved to test accepted relationships in geography, to help with the study of spatial activity and to aid the formulation of theories and models.

The use of theories and models

Spatial analysis attempts to identify, describe and interpret patterns in human activity and to relate any regularities between the elements of point, line and area to the processes producing them. The use of theories and models is an integral part of this study.

But what exactly are theories and models? Many geographers use the terms synonymously and, indeed, it must be admitted that even if they can be defined separately, the two are so bound together that it is often almost impossible to distinguish one from the other. Strictly speaking, theories are sets of statements about established relationships. Those relating to human geography bring together ideas or laws in order to suggest pertinent reasons for socio-economic patterns and processes apparent in the physical environment. In short, they seek to explain, through unproven laws, human phenomena and help to provide a foundation for further investigation. Models have been variously defined as generalisations, frames of reference, programmes of research and explanations of how systems work. In many respects, they are simplified structures, which reduce reality to a generalised form and present standards against which variations can be compared. Models are more descriptive than theories and, as such, are more tied to reality.

The real world appears complex and disorderly. Either this complexity is really chaos or it is complex regularity. The use of theories and models enables the geographer to find out which is the case. Together they remove confusion from reality, isolate major components, make possible predictions and generally provide a theoretical framework for understanding the factors involved in human activity.

In the formulation and examination of theories and models, one aspect should be borne in mind. Patterns recognisable on a local scale may lose their significance at a regional or national level, whereas, conversely, apparently meaningless patterns in a local area may in fact be part of a regularity on a larger scale. It is important, therefore, to keep relative scales in mind.

Many theories and models used in human geography are borrowed from other disciplines, like the **gravity model**. Many others have been conceived within the subject and into this category would fall those of Von Thünen, Weber and Christaller (although, of these, only Christaller was actually a geographer by profession).

Theories can be divided into two types: normative and behavioural. Normative theories represent the world in the most simplified terms: as a flat, uniform plain inhabited by perfectly rational **economic man**. With such theories there is a need to adopt assumptions that are universally recognised as being over-simplified. It is only after the simplified situation is fully understood that some of the initial preconditions can be relaxed. Behavioural theories are more realistic since they take into account human motivation and conduct. They replace the concept of economic man with one of **bounded rationality**. That is, they assume man does not always act rationally and may frequently arrive at economically sub-optimal decisions.

Models may likewise be divided into two categories. **Deterministic models** propose direct cause-and-effect relationships so the consequences are determined by the operation of factors subjected to stated conditions. If A and B occur, then C must take place. Such models often relate to normative theories, and here the work of Lösch is a good example. **Probabilistic models**, like behavioural theories, take into account man as an irrational being. They predict a number of cause-and-effect relationships, any of which might take place. Under this type would come the work of Pred. The models of both Lösch and Pred are discussed in Chapter 9.

Theories and models are useful and have added much to our understanding of human geography. They provide an integral part of environmental study and give a foundation to academic analysis. They form the essence of the quantitative approach to our subject and the basis of the societal approach.

However, such usefulness should not blind us to the limitations of theories and models. They are specialist tools to the human geographer and should be employed only for specific tasks. The problems inherent in both their formulation and their use provide restraints on their scope. They should not be seen as inevitable adjuncts to human geography, neither should their basic assumptions be unquestioningly accepted.

If theories and models are overemployed and used to explain all phenomena, then they are likely to be so complicated that they become either meaningless or impossible to comprehend. If they simplify the real world too much, then they merely succeed in hiding, or even ignoring altogether, the very complexities that geographers wish to comprehend. It is for these very reasons that excessive concentration on quantitative techniques has been criticised and that human geography has seen the appearance of a more societal approach.

Summary

1 Spatial analysis is a method of study that helps the human geographer find patterns and relationships among the apparent complexities of the Earth's surface.

2 The spatial environment can be divided into the three elements of locations, interactions and regions (points, lines and areas). These can be studied separately or together so that links and processes can be identified.

3 Explanation of geographical phenomena involves specialised methodology: induction, deduction, descriptive techniques and inferential techniques. These can involve difficulties in both formulation and use.

4 Inferential techniques entail set sequences of study, these being initiated by a presumed hypothesis. The writing of questionnaires, the taking of samples and the composition of matrices must be undertaken with care and thought.

5 Theories and models attempt to simplify man's relationship with his environment. They may be idealised and deterministic or behavioural and probabilistic. In any case, their usefulness is limited to their own specific functions.

6 The scientific approach to human geography – the use of models, mathematical formulae, computer analysis – should not be used just for its own sake. Issue-based behavioural studies should question the assumptions of quantitative geographers.

Data–response exercises

1 Using Figure 2.3, construct suitable geographical questionnaires to find out:
   (a) shopping patterns of your local inhabitants
   (b) commuter decisions among students and staff at a school or college.

2 From OS map A (Dorset) compare quadrat sampling techniques. Choosing 20 random grid squares and 20 systematic grid squares, compare the estimated percentages of land over 152 m high. Work out the degree of error in each case by

finding the exact proportion of land over 152 m for the map as a whole (which covers 88 km²).

3 On a scale of 1:25 000, draw a base map of the boundaries of voting wards used in your local area for local authority or general elections. On separate sheets of tracing paper show:
(a) the main relief and drainage features
(b) the rail and bus networks
(c) the settlement distribution
Comment on the interrelationships shown between your traced information and your base map. To what extent do the ward boundaries satisfactorily represent geographical entities and local entities?

4 On sketch maps, divide Scotland, Belgium and Switzerland into distinct physical regions. Superimpose on to each of these the administrative regions of each country. Comment upon the correlation between the regions drawn. (Information can be obtained from atlases or regional textbooks.)

Project work

1 Compose matrices to compare the attributes of a given number of (a) towns, (b) farms, (c) villages. Convert these matrices into diagrams (e.g. graphs) and suggest reasons behind the findings. Such project work may be undertaken to test certain hypotheses: (a) towns possess secondary and tertiary functions; (b) agriculture is determined by soil type; (c) villages are located at water sources.

2 Using a questionnaire and a specific method of data sampling, various human perceptions may be studied: distance perception, place perception, people perception. Interviewee answers should be compared with reality: estimated with actual distances, mental pictures with geographical realism, views of human characteristics with what people are really like. The factors determining perception can be investigated by comparing interviewees with accurate perceptions with those with inaccurate perceptions.

3 Compare word descriptions or sketch maps produced by different types of people in order to assess the variations in perception. A village, for example, may be described by (a) a local villager, (b) a tourist, (c) a businessman. Each description would be accurate, yet different. Account for such differences.

Further reading

Bradford, M. G. and W. A. Kent 1977. *Human geography: theories and their applications*. Oxford: Oxford University Press. Well illustrated and concise examination of the major theories and models involved in human geography,

these being backed up by numerous examples. Clearly written and without jargon so that even those not mathematically minded should be able to understand the principal points.

Chisholm, M. 1975. *Human geography: evolution or revolution*. London: Penguin. Slim volume, which outlines the changing nature of human geography – the trends, possible future changes and the subject's place among other sciences. Readable and a good introduction for students meeting 'new geography' for the first time.

Cole, J. P. 1975. *Situations in human geography. A practical approach*. Oxford: Blackwell. A stimulating, well written book which introduces students to new concepts and techniques through exercises, games, project work and case studies. Useful to both students and teachers.

Gold, J. R. 1980. *An introduction to behavioural geography*. Oxford: Oxford University Press. Exhaustive study, which explains the links between man's behaviour and his spatial understanding of the world. Recent research findings are outlined and further investigation into certain topics is both suggested and aided by long bibliographies. The book is of greatest use to teachers and lecturers and to undergraduate specialist geographers.

Gregory, S. 1978. *Statistical methods and the geographer*, 4th edn. London: Longman. A good reference book for those who wish to specialise. Very technical for A-level usage, but useful as a gentle introduction to a difficult subject.

Haggett, Peter 1979. *Geography: a modern synthesis*, 3rd edn. New York: Harper & Row. Voluminous book with an exhaustive coverage of topics, facts and examples. Very well illustrated and easy to digest. Very useful for reference purposes.

Hammond, R. and P. S. McCullagh, 1978. *Quantitative techniques in geography: an introduction*, 2nd edn. Oxford: Clarendon Press. Highly statistical and technical but useful for the mathematically minded. There are many graphs, tables, maps and flow charts which help the comprehension of the text. It covers inferential techniques and hypothesis testing in detail.

Minshull, R. 1975. *Introduction to models in geography*. London: Longman. Slim, readable volume, which gives a useful grounding in 'new geography'. Models are studied in all aspects: need for, definitions, building of, problems and dangers, their place in geography.

Peet, R. (ed.) 1977. *Radical geography*. Chicago: Maaroufa Press (also Methuen). Lengthy book, which aims to give 'alternative viewpoints on contemporary social issues'. Very biased politically to the left, it consists of a number of separate essays most of which expound the anti-capitalist, anti-establishment views common among some modern human geographers.

Silk, J. 1979. *Statistical concepts in geography*. London: George Allen & Unwin. A concise and clear introduction to statistical methods; well written and suitable for sixth-form students. It is so designed that comprehension of later chapters is not dependent upon familiarity with the content of earlier chapters. Worked examples and exercises help reinforce the reader's grasp of the subject.

Smith, D. M. 1975. *Patterns in human geography*. Newton Abbot: David & Charles (also Penguin). A long book, which gives a well written introduction to the numerical techniques now used in human geography. It is aimed specifically at the non-specialist, although some detailed and previous knowledge of mathematics would be a distinct advantage.

Smith, D. M. 1977. *Human geography, a welfare approach*. London: Edward Arnold. One of the first books adequately to cover the post-quantitative-revolution approaches to human geography. A long, well written tome, which considers the social dimension of world developments, economic planning policies and societal changes. Detailed case studies are included to demonstrate the problems (and possible remedies) of human action and inaction. Recommended to the socially and politically alert geographer.

Tidswell, V. 1978. *Pattern and process in human geography*. 2nd edn. London: University Tutorial Press. Highly technical approach studying aspects of farming, industry, settlement and transport networks. Case studies are illustrated and numerous tables aid their understanding. Heavy going for students who are not mathematically minded.

Toyne, P. and P. T. Newby 1971. *Techniques in human geography*. London: Macmillan. This covers the main methods of statistical mapping, the usefulness of maps and diagrams, and how they might be used in fieldwork. Many formulae and tables are used, but their comprehension is aided by exercises and worked examples. Recommended to all those undertaking projects.

Part II

DEMOGRAPHY

For he might have been a Roosian,
A French, or Turk, or Proosian
Or perhaps Itali-an!
But in spite of all temptations
To belong to other nations
He remains an Englishman.
W. S. Gilbert, *H.M.S. Pinafore*

Cold's not cold and hot's not hot
For the Eskimo and the Hottentot.
Owen Roberts

POPULATION DISTRIBUTION AND DENSITY

Racial location – inequality – Lorenz curves – ecumene – non-ecumene – lapse rates – overpopulation – optimum population

---

POPULATION GROWTH

Population explosion – birth and death rates – Malthus – diets and diseases – hunger – overcrowding – zero growth policies – youth cult – radicalism

---

POPULATION COMPOSITION

Age–sex pyramids – social structure – languages – religions – activity rate – plural societies – group interactions – unemployment

---

POPULATION MOVEMENT

Migration classification – push and pull factors – illegal movements – place utility – Ravenstein – Zipf and Stouffer – cosmopolitan societies – ecological change

---

3　Population distribution and density

Introduction

No geographical phenomenon is constantly found, regularly experienced or evenly spread out across the globe. In physical geography there are different climates and weather conditions over the Earth's surface, different rock types and soils, different topographical landscapes. In human geography there are different demographic groups around the world, different ideologies, different settlement characteristics. In short, all environmental factors are locational variables: each particular geographical feature is distributed differently.

Spatial analysis – the study of these locational variables – necessarily involves an examination of the spread of environmental features. Later chapters in this book consider the surface distributions of agricultural, industrial and settlement types.

This chapter will consider the arrangement of demographic types by attempting to answer the following questions:

- Where do the peoples of the world live, and how even or uneven is their distribution?
- Why are people located in certain regions, and can their relative distribution be measured?
- How close do people live together, and what are the results of high population densities?
- Who benefits from unequal distributions, and can the degree of dispersal be linked to the degree of injustice in society?

Reasons for distribution

The location of the human race across the world is the outcome of innumerable geographical reasons and the result of a million years of historical development. Since the dawn of mankind, people have lived – either by choice or necessity – where the environment affords a foothold to livelihood. The greater the potential provided by the natural environment for a successful occupation, the more likely is an area to be populated.

Since distribution is a spatial reflection of environmental advantages, and because the environment itself is locationally variable, it follows that the world's peoples are not evenly spread across the Earth's surface. Some regions are inhabited, others are not (Fig. 3.1); some regions are densely populated, others are sparsely populated. The reasons for this are both physical and non-physical. These are discussed below and can be applied both on a global scale and on local scales.

Physical factors
Physical factors can be viewed as the fundamental causes of variable distributions, and the first to affect man's choice of location. The main factors can be listed thus:

(a) accessibility;
(b) relief and soil fertility;
(c) climate and weather;
(d) natural vegetation and animal life;
(e) water supplies;
(f) mineral and energy resources.

The importance of each of these need not be over-emphasised here since, generally, they are self-explanatory. Within both countries and continents, people will seek out advantageous physical conditions and avoid disadvantageous ones.

More than two-thirds of the world's population still lives directly by farming and, of course, food production is of paramount importance to all of us. Therefore, areas where agriculture is impossible, difficult or expensive to undertake tend to be sparsely settled. These would include areas of mountainous relief and poor soils, together with regions where the climate is too wet, too dry, too cold or too hot. It follows that low-lying areas – especially those in the Temperate Zone – are particularly well populated.

Similarly, since food is essentially perishable and cannot usually travel great distances without loss of quality, large-scale farming can only reasonably take place where there is easy accessibility. Thus, valleys (especially those of navigable rivers) and coastlands are favoured whereas inland areas tend to be ignored.

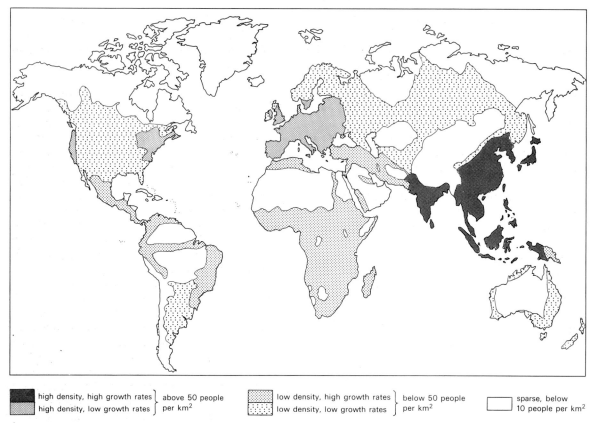

high density, high growth rates ⎱ above 50 people
high density, low growth rates ⎰ per km²

low density, high growth rates ⎱ below 50 people
low density, low growth rates ⎰ per km²

sparse, below
10 people per km²

Figure 3.1   World distribution of population
The world's total population is about 4000 million. Of this total 80% live on only 20% of the land surface; 90% live in the northern hemisphere; 85% in the Old World (Europe and Asia); 70% live in South-East Asia, Europe and north-east North America; 50% live in South-East Asia alone.

This can be seen in South America, North America and Africa. Indeed, in North America there is a heavy concentration of population along the East Coast, doubtless because this coastline is nearer (and therefore more accessible) to Europe and the 'Old World'. Only relatively recently, as a result of the introduction of refrigeration and fast transport, have inaccessible regions been opened up for food production, as in the case of the Canadian Prairies and Manchuria, but these areas remain fairly sparsely settled.

Exceptions to the 'pull' of farming are areas where population has grown up on or near important mineral deposits. Generally, the more valuable the deposits, the more likely is man to overcome harsh natural conditions to exploit them. This can be seen in the Andes, where copper and tin are mined; in northern Canada, where there are nickel, uranium ore and gold mines; and in the Middle East, where oil is drilled.

Non-physical factors
Non-physical factors can be viewed as secondary locational considerations, becoming more important as the population of the world grows and becomes technologically more powerful. The main factors can be listed thus:

(a)   culture and tradition;
(b)   economic preference;
(c)   religion and social beliefs;
(d)   political forces.

As with the physical factors, there is no room here adequately to detail the importance of each of these human considerations. Through conservatism or inertia a group of people may continue to live where the environment has ceased to be conducive to livelihood; for financial gain a group may choose one location rather than another, irrespective of physical conditions.

Sometimes religion has been responsible for settlement in particular regions. Certainly it can be argued that the emigration of the Pilgrim Fathers from Britain in the 17th century, and their subsequent colonisation of New England, helped the American East Coast to develop a high density of population. Similarly, the settlement of the State of Utah and its capital, Salt Lake City, was due to the removal there of the American Mormons during the middle years of the 19th century.

There are also instances of political factors creating new areas of population. Since the 1917 revolution, for example, millions of Russian people have been forcibly removed eastwards by the Soviet government in order to open up and develop the wastes of Siberia. Perhaps we should also remember that south-east Australia was originally developed as a British penal colony and this is probably responsible for that region becoming the most populated part of the entire continent, agriculture and industry having been developed earlier than elsewhere.

The inequality of distribution

So far, discussion about distribution has revolved around the spatial location of people: who lives where and why. But this is a limited view and it involves far too narrow an interpretation of the word 'distribution'. Today, what also concerns the human geographer is the societal nature of distribution: who owns what where, who feeds when where. As we have seen, people are unevenly spread; but so too are wealth, food, medical care, personal contentment, political power and other such socio-economic assets. Both inside individual countries and across the world as a whole there is an unequal distribution of societal privilege: there are rich and poor, the well fed and the hungry, the healthy and the feeble, the dominant and the subjected.

What causes such inequalities? Clearly the answer lies in a complex array of physical and human factors. Environmental disadvantages would certainly lead to social and economic deficiency, and environmental advantages to social and economic affluence, yet the incidences of spatial and societal unevenness do not necessarily coincide. Regions of sparse population are not always inferior socio-economically; regions of dense population are not always superior socio-

economically. The same factors that produce one kind of distribution may also produce an entirely different kind of distribution, based on another criterion. Such are the problems of diagnosing locational variables.

For any given areas, exact levels of distribution, both of the spatial and societal kind, can be given by means of **Lorenz curves** (Fig. 3.2). These can reveal the degree of regularity found in any distribution: the more concave the curve the greater the irregularity. For the location of people, concentration is said to be at a maximum where the total population in a given area is situated at one point, and at a minimum where persons are totally dispersed: that is, situated at an equal distance from all neighbours. For the division of welfare, complete equality is achieved when the ratio between population and assets is proportionally constant and positive; for example, when 30% of people owns 30% of all wealth, 60% of people 60% of all wealth, and so on. Unbalanced ratios mean the inequality of social and economic possessions.

Differences in societal distributions, in relation to developed countries, less developed countries and to the world as a whole, are discussed in greater depth later in this book. There are the problems of economic divergencies to be examined (Chs 7 to 9); aspects of urban population differences (Chs 15 & 16); and divisions between rich and poor regions (Chs 17 to 20). In all these discussions, certain points should be borne in mind. First, spatial population distribution alone tells us nothing about the degree to which an area is suffering demographic, social or economic problems. A country in which population is clustered may have more numerous – or fewer – problems than one in which population is evenly spread. Secondly, human actions can directly and indirectly affect the societal distributions, for better and for worse. Many political geographers believe, for example, that politically extreme policies (both right and left wing) tend to widen the social and economic gulfs within a nation; politically moderate policies tend to reduce inequalities. Thirdly, unequal distributions should not be equated with such concepts as 'efficiency', 'fairness' and 'equity'. A concentrated population spread is neither 'efficient' nor 'inefficient'. Similarly, a totally egalitarian society need not be 'fair' and 'efficient'. Conversely, a society with extremely unequal welfare distribution could well be highly efficient: in Ancient Greece, Imperial Rome, Renaissance Italy and Victorian Britain social and economic assets were unequally spread, yet few would deny their cultural, scientific and political success.

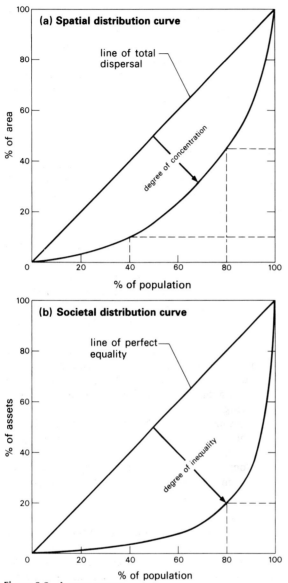

Figure 3.2   Lorenz curves
Lorenz curves diagrammatically express the inequalities of distribution. Graph (a) shows the physical spread of people over a given area. The diagonal represents total dispersal – an even and equal spread. The curve shows the degree of concentration: 40% of the population living on just 10% of the area, 80% on 45% of the area. Total concentration is represented by the horizontal axis. Graph (b) shows the extent of equality found in a given society. The vertical axis may be given various welfare indices or asset units: food, wealth, medical care, political power and so on. The diagonal represents perfect equality: social, economic or political possession being evenly distributed. The curve shows the degree of inequality: for example, 80% of the total population possessing only 20% of the total wealth. This 80% may be viewed as the underprivileged section of society, the remaining 20% as the elite.

Aspects of density

If distribution is the spatial and societal response to the varied conditions of the environment, then density can be seen as an extension of the same relationship. The areas of greatest density are those possessing the greatest net advantage; areas of least density are those of least net advantage.

Density is the degree of compaction in a population; the degree of proximity between people: the closeness of persons living on a given surface, the spatial balance of their social and economic assets. It is the study not of where the butter is spread on a slice of bread but how thickly or thinly it is spread.

Much study on density centres on purely spatial aspects. Some geographers identify two density divisions: **ecumene**, referring to the inhabited areas of the world; and **non-ecumene**, referring to the uninhabited or very sparsely inhabited areas. The former, it is estimated, covers about 60% of the total land surface, and the latter about 40%. However, such a generalised, twofold system is open to criticism; there is, for example, the difficulty of delimitation.

The following threefold division is a more exact method and therefore more useful in the study of population density:

(a)   Areas of very dense population (over 100 people per km²).
Regions of high living standards: England, the Low Countries, West Germany, north-east USA.
Regions of low living standards: South-East Asia, India.

(b)   Areas of moderate population density (25–100 people per km²).
Regions of high living standards: France, south-east Australia, south-east Canada, midwest USA.
Regions of low living standards: Turkey, Ghana, Zimbabwe, Ecuador.

(c)   Areas of low population density (below 25 people per km²).
Regions of high living standards: Sweden, Norway, New Zealand, western Canada.
Regions of low living standards: northern Africa, central Brazil, Patagonia, New Guinea.

Of course, even this method of classification is not without its problems. There are, for example, many areas that are intermediate in terms of both density and living standards – the Middle East and East Indies, for instance. Here rapid growth is causing some countries to pass from low to high density and from poor to rich in a very short time span. Then there is the question of relativity. South-east Brazil and Nigeria are fairly well off compared with other Third World countries, Italy and Spain fairly hard up compared with other developed countries.

Lapse rates

Whichever method of density classification is used, however, one problem remains constant: densities, on both a local and a world scale, do not fall into clear-cut spatial divisions. Towns gradually merge into countryside and industrial regions merge into agricultural regions. Yet this gradation is not totally without order. It is generally recognised that population density declines regularly as distance increases away from a central point of concentration. The rate of decline is called the **lapse rate** (Fig. 3.3).

In developed countries, the lapse rate tends to become more gradual with time as living standards improve (leading to lower densities in cities) and transport becomes easier and faster. In more backward countries, the lapse rate remains steep because of poor transport and few technological improvements. These differences in lapse rates between the

Western and Eastern Hemispheres were first considered by Berry, Simmons and Tennant (*Geographical Review* **53**, 1963 pp. 389–405). They should not, however, be taken as mutually exclusive. Some lapse rates in 'Western' cities may resemble the 'non-Western' pattern and vice-versa. Nevertheless, the basic distance decay trend holds true.

Measurement of density

The density of population is an expression of the ratio between population and a given unit of size. It may be assessed in various ways and using various techniques:

(1) **Crude density** is the most common method. It is a straight measurement of the total number of people per unit of land. For example, Britain has a density of 229 per km², Sri Lanka has 212, Iran 20, New Zealand 11 and Australia only 1.8. This method, however, gives no indication of living standards.

(2) **Nutritional density** is a density based on the ratio between total population and inhabited or cultivated areas (as opposed to gross area). This gives a rather better indication of the standard of living.

(3) **Occupational density** is a density of certain sections of a population over the total area, e.g. of agricultural workers in a country.

(4) **Room density** is most commonly used in urban studies. It is the average number of people per room in a given area.

There are, of course, numerous other measures of density, used to assess different aspects of a population. Protein or vitamin intake, income levels, the possession of luxury or consumer goods, and the length of leisure time are all criteria that might be used to gauge the density of a population's living standards. A country whose car density (number of motor vehicles per square kilometre or per person) is high is likely to be more developed than a country whose car density is low.

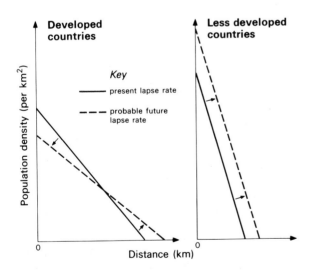

Figure 3.3 Lapse rates
These graphs represent the degree of spatial density change in different parts of the world and probable changes over time. Point 0 may be considered as the centre of highest population density – a town centre or the middle of an industrial region. The differences between the two graphs are the result of economic, social and technological factors.

Population pressure

Distribution maps and graphs, and density measurements, do not in themselves indicate the extent of demographic problems. The estimation of these may only be attempted by the study of population pressure. This can be defined as the degree of impact or effectiveness experienced between people and their environment.

Generally, it can be stated that pressure is a factor that relates population size and density to natural resources. Clearly, a population density of 90 people per km² would result in more problems (have greater pressure) in a region of few resources than in a region of many and varied resources. By 'resources' we mean the advantages of environmental conditions: fertile soils, moderate climate and weather phenomena, mineral deposits, water supplies and so on. It is true to say that the more abundant the resources possessed by an area, the higher is the population it can maintain (assuming, of course, that people can perceive those resources and have the technology to utilise them).

Some geographers have attempted to measure population pressure by the formula

$$I = \frac{P_1 - P_2}{A}$$

in which I is the index of pressure; P_1 is the population size capable of being supported by the resources in a given region within a country; P_2 is the actual population size in that region; and A is the total area of the country. An index below 0 shows negative pressure (causing problems), an index above 0 positive pressure (with no problems). The lower the minus number the greater the problems, the higher the plus number the greater the surplus of resources. However, this method has the drawback of requiring an almost impossible mathematical judgement. How does one estimate the number of people that a collection of resources is capable of supporting?

Indeed, so difficult is this that most geographers resort merely to the use of the terms '**overpopulation**', '**underpopulation**' and '**optimum population**'. Such terms are subjective, debatable and have imprecise definitions, but at least they give a theoretical guideline to the level of population pressure. We may not be able specifically to say what precise level of pressure an area has, but we can certainly recognise whether or not there is pressure and how serious it is.

Overpopulation can be thought to exist where there is too great a population in a given area for the actual or potential resources to support. The symptoms of such a situation might include low incomes, high levels of unemployment, declining living standards and sometimes even famine and malnutrition. Southern India and Bangladesh are examples of such areas. Underpopulation exists where the opposite is true: namely, where there are too few people in a given area fully to utilise the available resources; in other words, where a larger population could be supported by the same resources. These areas may either be regions at a low level of civilisation, like the Amazon Basin, or regions that man has not yet completely developed, like the Canadian Prairies. Optimum population is the theoretically perfect situation. It exists where the size of population in a given area allows the maximum utilisation of resources; where man achieves maximum output per head and the highest possible living standards. A substantial rise or fall in population from this optimum level would lead to a decrease in output and living standards.

However, all three of these terms should be approached with caution. They do not take into account such factors as culture, racial character, levels of technology, differing expectations of life and aesthetic values. Also, it is often difficult to say which resources are actual and which potential, which are important and which are not. Thus, what may be considered 'crowded' and 'poor' in some regions might be the accepted norm elsewhere. Similarly, a resource considered unimportant in one place might be of extreme value somewhere else, and here water is an obvious example. In short, definitions of terms vary from place to place and criteria differ in importance: food, for example, is a prime criterion for overpopulation in developing countries, but space is a prime criterion for overpopulation in developed countries.

In Britain, many people think that the optimum population has now been reached – at about 56 million. However, the pollution, spoliation of the countryside and resource exhaustion that are apparent in modern Britain may suggest that the country has long been overpopulated.

Summary

1   Local and global distributions of population are determined by physical and human factors. The importance of these changes with time. Economic and political forces are becoming more significant.

2   Spatial distribution is the study of 'who lives where'; societal distribution is the study of 'who gets what where'. The unevenness of the former

and inequality of the latter can be measured using Lorenz curves.

3 Crude, nutritional, occupational and room densities are just some of the measures used in gauging population concentration. The spatial change in density is shown by lapse rates.

4 Population pressure is the degree to which the numbers of people in a given area create socio-economic and political problems. The greater the problems, the greater the pressure.

5 All measures are subjective and debatable attempts to link population with resources. Overpopulation suggests symptoms of hunger, unemployment and low living standards; under-population implies symptoms of labour shortage, resource wastage and surplus food supplies. Optimum population is the theoretical ideal of balanced resource use.

Data–response exercises

1 Comment on the distributions and densities of populations shown in Figure 3.1 with particular regard to their relationship with natural environments.

2 Canada, Colombia and Zaïre each have the same population size (approximately 25 million). Analyse these three countries in respect of their densities, their level of development and their degree of population pressure, bearing in mind their differing sizes and economic attainments.

3 (a) Find out the meaning of the terms 'mean centre', 'median centre', and 'modal centre' as measures of population centralisation.

(b) On graph paper, draw an outline map of Wales to cover at least eight squares east to west and 12 squares north to south. Mark the county boundaries and the rough centre of each county. Work out the easting co-ordinate (A) and northing co-ordinate (B) for each county centre, taking your figures to the nearest 0.1 of a square. Calculate and plot the mean centre of population using the formulae:

$$\text{easting} = \frac{\Sigma(PA)}{\text{total population}}$$

$$\text{northing} = \frac{\Sigma(PB)}{\text{total population}}$$

(Σ is the sum of all the counties: $P_1A_1 + P_2A_2 + P_3A_3$, etc.) (Populations of the Welsh counties are given in Table 3.1.)

(c) The same exercise may be undertaken for Europe or any other continent, using data obtained from the *Demographic yearbook*, the population of each country being quoted in millions.

4 Draw Lorenz curves to show the following in-equalities found within the United Kingdom: (a) land ownership, (b) wealth, (c) educational attainment. (Figures obtainable from Government Statistical Offices and publications of HMSO, e.g. the *Annual abstract of statistics*.)

5 Transform the lapse-rate graphs in Figure 3.3 into actual examples, using two countries and accurate scales. Comment on the differences between the two.

6 Draw a choropleth map of the world showing the population densities of the regions listed in Table 5.2. Comment on the densities plotted.

Table 3.1 Population statistics for Wales.

County	Population (thousands)
Clwyd	390
Dyfed	330
Gwent	440
Gwynedd	231
Powys	111
Mid-Glamorgan	538
South Glamorgan	385
West Glamorgan	367

4 Population composition

Introduction

Having studied aspects of population location – where and how people live across the globe – human geographers must pursue demography a stage further. This continuance of study involves, among the other aspects to be considered in Chapters 5 and 6, the analysis of what people are like. To do this we must categorise and subdivide populations into distinct groups.

Just as the physical and human environment can be split into physical units (regions), so the world's peoples can be classified into population units, each unit being distinct from others yet, within itself, uniform in character. These units, or subgroups, can be identified by various means and criteria, based on demographic, socio-political or economic patterns. It is only through the identification of such groups that we can learn to understand human behaviour. Once a population inventory has been made, hierarchies can be recognised, relationships can be identified, past and future changes can be diagnosed. To understand subsequent parts of this book it is important to ask, and answer, the following questions:

- What cohesive force binds population groups together, and how can different kinds of demographic patterns be classified?
- Where are the various subgroups located on local and global scales, and what are the effects of their spatial arrangement?
- How do groups change, and what are the links between group characteristics and socio-economic development?
- What are the cultural and political consequences of composition change and group segregation?

Demographic patterns

Populations can be classified and divided according to physical attributes – that is, to those aspects of human character beyond personal control. Thus, people can be grouped by age and sex structure (as detailed below) and also by such biological distinctions as race, stature, blood group, personality and, perhaps also, mental attributes. Such demographic patterns provide a useful starting point for more detailed study.

Age structure

This is an expression of the number of people in a total population found in each age group. For reasons of simplicity, three age groups are normally recognised: children (usually under 16), adults (usually 16 to 64 inclusive) and the aged (65 and over). It is said that age structure reflects the demographic and socio-economic history of a population over a period of about a century. Certainly it is a result of various and interrelated factors such as fertility, mortality and migration, which have operated during the lifetime of the oldest inhabitants.

Age structures of particular countries are most commonly shown diagrammatically, using age–sex pyramids. Four main types have been identified (Fig. 4.1).

Figure 4.1a shows a **progressive** age structure in which both birth and death rates are high. Children account for 45–55% of the total population and the aged for only 5–10%. Such a structure is common in developing countries such as Bolivia and Angola, where social, cultural and perhaps religious and economic conditions lead to high fertility, and poor living conditions, bad diets and little medical aid lead to high levels of mortality.

Figure 4.1b shows a **regressive** age structure in which birth and death rates are low and declining. Children account for under 30% of the total population and the aged for above 15%. This pattern is common in developed countries (especially those in Western Europe), where high living standards, education and social awareness are accompanied by good food and medicine.

Figure 4.1c shows a **stationary** age structure in which children account for about 35–40% of the total population and the aged for about 10%. This pattern may remain the same for many years.

Figure 4.1d shows an **intermediate** age structure.

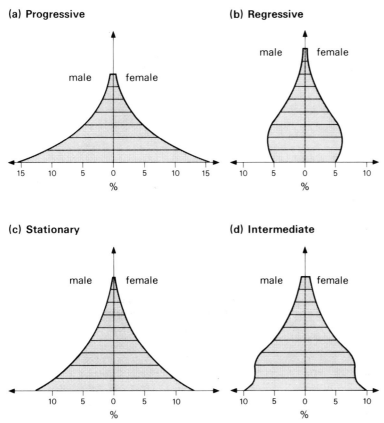

(a) Progressive

male female

(b) Regressive

male female

(c) Stationary

male female

(d) Intermediate

male female

Figure 4.1 Population age-sex pyramids
The horizontal bars in each diagram represent 10-year age groups. Such pyramid shapes are idealised versions of those expected to be found in the different countries of the world. Although every real world example is unique, each pyramid actually found would approach the shape of one of those illustrated.

Such a pattern may vary in character and is most common in countries that are passing through stages of development. Such countries may once have had progressive structures and may, in future, have regressive structures.

Age–sex pyramids like these reflect the social and economic character of individual countries: their state of advancement, the nature of society and even their prospects for the future. They may also show aspects of a country's demographic history: the incidence of wars, plagues, natural disasters and other similar events (see Fig. 4.2).

In practical terms, the first and last age groups may be considered unproductive dependants. Children are mostly at school and people over the age of 65 are usually retired and on pensions. Both these groups must therefore be supported by the middle age group, which includes the wealth-producing working population. Of course, the smaller the adult age group in relation to the other two, the more difficult it is for a country to be economically viable. This is especially a problem where the age structure is either very progressive or very regressive. Generally, the higher the

dependency ratio, the more difficult it is for a country to progress.

Age structure can be affected by social, economic and demographic factors. In developing countries it is more common for children to work at a young age, often being employed before the age of 10. In developed countries the reverse is true: not only are children under 16 non-productive, but so also are many young adults as higher education becomes more widespread. At the other end of the spectrum the aged group is becoming less productive in developed countries as retirement ages fall, and more productive in developing countries as the numbers of those living to over 60 increase while provision for retirement is still not available.

Migration may similarly affect age structure. Generally, the younger people of the adult age group (say, those between ages 16 and 35) are most mobile. Therefore, a country experiencing a net inflow of migration would have a slight bulge in its age–sex pyramid, whereas a country with a net loss would have a slight indentation at that point.

Changes in population growth also lead inevitably

35

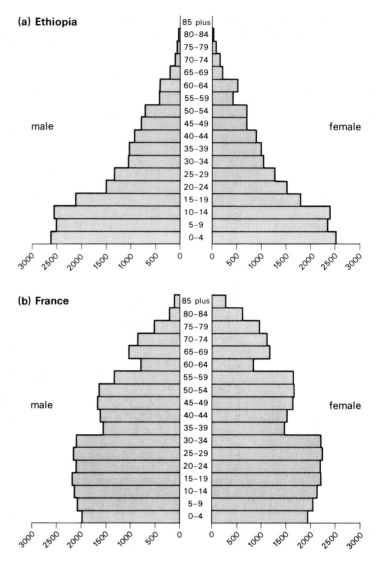

(a) Ethiopia

male

female

(b) France

male

female

Figure 4.2 Population age-sex pyramids of selected countries
Pyramids like these demonstrate not only the overall level of development that a country has reached but also the course of events over the past century. For example, birth rates tend to decrease during wartime and increase immediately after wartime. (Source: figures taken from UN *Demographic yearbook* 1982.)

to changes in age structure. A falling growth rate results in an ageing population, and a rising growth rate in a youthful population. In either case a population becomes unbalanced with a proportionally small adult age group having to finance the livelihood of the rest.

Sex structure
This is an expression of male–female proportions in a total population. The figure quoted may either be the ratio between the number of males and every 100 females or that between the number of females and every 100 males.

It is to be expected that, in broad terms, the two sexes are evenly balanced in numbers, and certainly this is largely true. In nearly every country the ratio varies only between 90 and 110 females to 100 males. In Britain, for instance, the sex ratio is 106:100 and in India 98:100. However, these overall ratios can hide differences within individual age groups. For example, male births always exceed female births although, at the other end of the age structure, women tend to outnumber men. In other words, the excess of males at birth is slowly cancelled out as time goes by so that beyond about the 30–40 age group females increasingly dominate in numbers (see Table 4.1).

In Britain, which may be taken as typical of developed countries, the sex ratio amongst newborn

Table 4.1 Age and sex structure of the United Kingdom 1980.

Age group	Sex (thousands)	
	Males	Females
under 5	1 751	1 660
5–14	4 323	4 094
15–29	6 409	6 158
30–44	5 410	5 334
45–64	6 077	6 400
65–74	2 250	2 936
75 and over	1 008	2 135
total	27 228	28 717

Source: *Annual abstract of statistics* 1982. London: HMSO.

babies is about 94 females to every 100 males. In the over-60 age group it is 110:100. On average a man has an expectation of life of 70 years and a woman 76 years. In developing countries male mortality exceeds female mortality even more obviously. In the Ivory Coast the excess of male births is cancelled out within the first year of life.

Natural mortality in every age group is biased against males for a combination of biological, environmental and socio-economic reasons. Men are the 'weaker sex' in the sense that they contract a greater number of illnesses than women and therefore tend to die younger. The fact that they also work longer on average and are thought to bear greater responsibilities adds to their mortality rate. Only in very few countries do female deaths exceed those of males. South-East Asia and parts of Africa are examples, perhaps because women there have a lowly status and are set to undertake heavy work.

The effect of war has also been significant in the preponderance of male deaths. Even in recent times, when fighting has more directly involved civilian populations, more men die during hostilities than women. They do, after all, make up the vast bulk of the armed forces. The age–sex pyramid of every European country still shows the disastrous results of the two World Wars (see Fig. 4.2).

Migratory patterns can affect sex structure just as much as age structure. Generally, men are more mobile than women (especially in the adult age group). Thus, areas experiencing net immigration are likely to have more males than females, and areas experiencing net emigration will have more females than males. Examples of the former are the 'pioneer' regions of Alaska, the Northern Territory of Australia and, until the beginning of this century, the American Mid-West. Examples of the latter are such places as Ireland and the West Indies. Even on a relatively small scale, this tendency is apparent. In India there is a steady movement of people from countryside to towns, and Calcutta now has 175 men in its population to every 100 females.

Socio-political patterns

Socio-political patterns can be identified when populations are divided according to superficial and personal attributes – that is, to aspects of individually acquired characteristics. Thus, people can be grouped by religion, language and nationality (as detailed in the next section) and also by such diverse cultural distinctions as class, health, marriage status, political affiliations, living conditions and even allegiance to sports teams.

Religion
Religion may be defined as an attempt to explain nature and the mystery of life. Most religions involve procedures of faith and worship, normally of a god, and usually encompass sacred observances and codes of behaviour. They are important since they can exercise all types of restraints on human activity: controlling diets, farming practices, trade, marriage and family life, and even economic prosperity. The deeper the religious convictions, the more extreme their impact on the world.

Ethereal or heavenly beliefs go back to earliest times and have developed in different ways. Today, distinct groups can be identified, the principal ones being Christianity, Islam, Judaism, Buddhism, Hinduism and Shinto. There are spatial differences between these religions and each tends to have its own special location in the world. Christianity is most common in Europe, America and other regions of European settlement; Islam covers Arabia, northern Africa and western Asia; Buddhism is found in central Asia. This spatial pattern suggests that environment has some effect on religious beliefs. Certainly, there is little doubt that representations of the gods, ideas of heaven, objects of worship and even styles of temples vary according to physical surroundings. In countries of seasonal or uncertain precipitation, the rain god is a common deity; in societies dependent upon fishing there is often a god of the sea. In deserts, heaven is thought to be a place of fountains and cool running streams; in the extreme north it is a place of warmth; to most Englishmen it is a Garden of Eden not dissimilar in appearance to an idealised image of rural England. Hindu temples and images seem to reflect the exotic vegetation of Asia, and Islamic mosques are dark and cool to keep out the heat of the sun.

But to imagine that religion and environment are inextricably linked is to oversimplify. In fact, religious beliefs have increased as a result of various physical, cultural, social and political forces. They can transcend all other groupings, like racial and national divisions, and may thus unite peoples of diverse origins.

This can be seen by the fact that the spread of religions has been bound by neither geographical nor political barriers. Instead it has been due partly to the innate attractiveness of the individual beliefs, partly to historical circumstances, and partly to the vigour of missionaries. Islam filtered out from its birthplace in western Arabia as a result of the growth of the Turkish Empire, and Christianity has become worldwide as a result of the growth, in the last 2000 years, of the Roman, French, Spanish and British empires.

However, just as religion may unite otherwise different populations, it can also arouse antagonism between otherwise similar populations. Disunity is found not just between different religious ideologies, but often within them. One need only think of the division in Islam between Sunni and Shia or the deep cleavage between some Roman Catholics and Protestants to see that religious differences can be serious. Some of the most terrible wars in history have resulted from deep-seated religious conflicts. Such differences produce human barriers so that zonal patterns exist on both a world and a local scale. In West Germany there is a tendency for Catholicism to be common in the south and Lutheranism common in the north (see Fig. 4.3). In Northern Ireland there are spatial religious patterns even within towns; for example, in West Belfast the Falls Road district is peopled by Catholics, the Shankhill district by Protestants.

Linked with religious divisions are intellectual and psychic differences between peoples. It is often thought – mistakenly – that these are associated exclusively with economics, education and technological know-how. In fact, intellectual or mental achievement may be related to religious beliefs, institutions, intuition and insight rather than to any material progress. It may well happen that economically backward societies have great natural intelligence. The ancient Celts in Britain built Stonehenge, which still baffles modern man. In present-day India

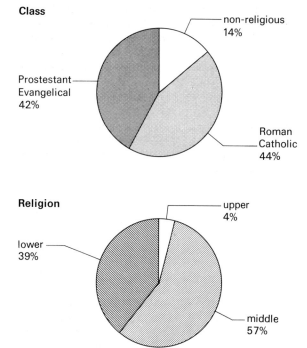

Class

non-religious 14%

Prostestant Evangelical 42%

Roman Catholic 44%

Religion

upper 4%

lower 39%

middle 57%

Figure 4.3 Societal patterns in West Germany
Religious divisions in West Germany result from cultural and environmental differences between the north and south of the country, protestants living generally in the former, Roman Catholics in the latter. Some evidence also suggests a link between religion and class, Catholics tending to fill the higher end of the social hierarchy. The above class division is subjective, based on incomes and lifestyles.

there are holy men or 'fakirs' who seem to possess mystic powers unknown in the civilised West.

Language
Language is an inherent characteristic of human culture. Like religion, many types have developed since earliest times. It is estimated that well over 3000 different languages still survive in the world. Many are linguistically linked and can be traced through common sources, but many others are of unknown origin.

Certain linguistic families can be identified, such as Indo-European, Ural–Altaic and Hamitic–Semitic, and within each of these there are variations. Under Indo-European, for instance, there are the Romance languages (Italian, French, Spanish and others), the Germanic languages (German, English and Swedish, for example) and the Slavonic languages (like Polish, Czech and Russian).

Some languages are global, being spoken by people all over the world; others are local and spoken by very few. The fourteen most important are used by 60% of the world's population. Numerically, Mandarin Chinese is the most common for it is spoken by 600 million people. It is not, however, worldwide. In practical terms, English is of prime importance since it is widespread, spoken by well over 350 million people, and is known as a second language to millions more.

Superimposed on to every language are dialects and accents involving differences of pronunciation, idiom and tone within a single tongue. So diverse are some dialects that it is possible for two people speaking the same language to misunderstand one another. A Cornishman, for example, may find difficulty understanding someone from even another part of England – a 'Geordie' from Newcastle upon Tyne, for instance.

Both languages and their dialects are linked to race, environment, culture and history. But since these factors are never constant, owing to human migrations, intermixture and natural change, the worldwide patterns of languages are continually altering. The proportion of the world's population speaking each language is changing; so are their spatial distributions. Some languages are spreading and becoming more common, others are dying out.

As world commerce and communications grow and education increases, the number of bilingual people increases. Generally, those whose native language is global are less likely to learn another than those who speak a local one. A great many Dutchmen can speak English fairly fluently, but can the same be said of Englishmen speaking French or German, let alone Dutch?

It is perhaps a pity that the predominance of certain tongues leads to the death of others. In Britain, Cornish vanished two centuries ago and Gaelic is spoken by ever decreasing numbers. Even dialects are on the wane as a result of national mass media, and in particular radio and television. Many people who acquire a higher standard of living and social status actually make a deliberate attempt to lose their original accent.

In the same way languages themselves are being modified. New words are incorporated, sometimes from other tongues, and other words go out of use. Just as many Frenchmen are concerned at the growing number of English words used in their language, so many Englishmen are concerned about the growing number of Americanisms in their mother tongue.

Like religions, languages can both unite and divide the peoples of the world. Those areas that share a common tongue feel a sense of kinship, even if their cultures are very different. Conversely, linguistic feelings can engender considerable conflicts, especially where minority tongues are at risk. The recent revival of Welsh nationalism is perhaps indicative of this. It is not just simple humour behind the saying that the USA and Britain are divided by a common tongue.

Nationality

It is natural for man to convene into groups, and nationality may be viewed as an expression of group identity. It is a concept that reflects the national political status of the country to which a person belongs. Of all divisions of mankind, nationality is perhaps the most convenient since it forms a direct link between man and the place where he lives.

A state or country is essentially a political unit. Those living within its borders normally share the same laws, civil service, police and armed forces. They probably also share a common way of life, common experiences and owe allegiances to a common government or ruler. They do not necessarily share the same race, language or religion; uniformity in these is not a prerequisite for nationality (see Fig. 4.4). Among indigenous Britons there are Celtic and Saxon races, four languages (English, Welsh, Manx and Gaelic) and numerous religions, and today there are numerous immigrant peoples as well, yet all are united under British nationality. Belgium has two distinct groups (Flemings and Walloons), and Switzerland has four (those speaking German, French, Italian and Romansh). Such instances should not seem surprising. Nationality reflects human nature. Most people possess a basic sense of patriotism, a love for their own country, which binds them to others who share the same personal ties, traditions, history and outlook. The support for one's own territory and the desire to see it remain independent is a very deep and real human sentiment, which has often led to political and physical conflict.

It is thought that the stability and prosperity of a country lies partly in the quality of its nationalism: the degree to which the various groups can live in harmony and put loyalty to the state before more personal considerations. Uniformity of race, language and religion would, of course, help to produce this feeling, but it is not essential.

Often a state has some natural or geographical unity. An island or peninsula may become an independent country because of its physical setting, in which case it would probably be relatively stable in

I WAS BORN IN AFRICA, AM ROMAN CATHOLIC, SPEAK SWAHILI AND AM A BRITISH SUBJECT

I WAS BORN IN INDIA, AM HINDU, SPEAK URDU, AND AM ALSO A BRITISH SUBJECT

I WAS BORN IN CHINA, AM BUDDHIST, SPEAK MANDARIN AND NOW LIVE IN THE UNITED STATES OF AMERICA

I WAS BORN IN MEXICO, AM AN ATHEIST, SPEAK SPANISH AND I TOO LIVE IN THE UNITED STATES OF AMERICA

Figure 4.4   The embracing nature of nationality
The country in which one lives and the government to which one owes allegiance may have little to do with race, language, religion or any other division of society.

shape, size and character. Elsewhere, boundaries between countries may be constantly changing and this could lead to national instability. One need only compare three political maps of Europe to see how national territories may alter: one drawn before World War 1, one drawn between the two World Wars, and one drawn recently.

Some countries may group themselves into a union for political or economic reasons. This might be an empire in which a single country holds sway or a federation in which separate states combine under a common central government, as in the case of the USA and USSR. In Europe many people hope that the economic union of the European Economic Community will, some day, grow into a political union based on a single European Parliament.

Socio-political patterns can be viewed on global, continental (see Fig. 4.5) and national scales. They are the result of numerous physical and human

phenomena and are of fundamental importance to the study of human behaviour.

Economic patterns

Economic patterns can be identified when people are divided according to attributes of living standards – that is, to aspects of *achieved status* characteristics. Thus, populations can be grouped by occupations and employment (as detailed below) and also by such livelihood criteria as wealth, income, working hours and spending decisions.

Occupational structure
Only part of the total population in any one country may be classed as being *economically active*. This working population is engaged (or is seeking to be engaged) in gainful employment, that is, in work that produces an income. Generally excluded are children

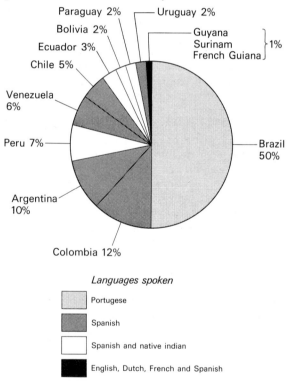

Languages spoken

Portugese

Spanish

Spanish and native indian

English, Dutch, French and Spanish

Figure 4.5   Socio-political patterns in South America
The total population of South America is about 250 million and this is divided into 13 nationalities. The languages spoken reflect the colonial history of the continent. Although various native indian tongues are used by minorities within all the countries, only when the number speaking these is over 25% is a country shown as having a mixed language composition. In Bolivia, native indian is spoken by the majority (60%).

and full-time students, the aged, housewives and those living off private means. The size of this working population is affected not only by demographic considerations – fertility, mortality, migration and so on – but also by various economic, social and political factors. It is normally quoted as a proportion of total population and called the **activity rate**.

In developed countries, like those in Europe, the activity rate is likely to be high (say 50%) since the number of young people tends to be low and, today, female employment is more common. In developing countries, the activity rate will tend to be low (perhaps as low as 20%) because of the high percentage of children and the tradition of non-employment of women. This is especially the case in Muslim societies where women still have a sheltered existence. In Communist countries political ideology has caused a significant rise in the activity rate. There, women have been so emancipated that they work even in jobs thought elsewhere to be the preserve of men. In Russia the proportion of population being employed is as high as 55%.

The working population can further be divided into individual occupations, thus giving a more exact occupational structure. This also is determined, to a large extent, by socio-economic factors. Usually the percentage of workers in primary industries (like farming, fishing, mining) is very low in developed countries and very high in less developed countries. Conversely, the proportions employed in secondary, tertiary and quaternary industries (manufacturing and services) increase with economic progress. Thus, in areas like Western Europe and the USA, only about 5%, or less, of the working population is in agriculture, whereas in China and India well over 80% may be found on the land. Indeed, it is believed that in the most advanced countries the importance of tertiary and quaternary occupations tends to increase even beyond that of manufacturing owing to such factors as automation, increased leisure activities and the process of deindustrialisation. In the USA, Britain and West Germany, 50% of the working population is employed solely in service activities. (See Table 4.2.)

Unemployment

All countries, even the richest ones in times of prosperity, have a certain amount of unemployment. This is caused by a variety of factors: changes of residence, natural changes in industrial output, disability or infirmity, unwillingness to work, and so forth. So inevitable is this that any unemployment level below 3% is normally regarded as indicating full employ-

Table 4.2 Occupational structure of the United Kingdom.

Analysis of industry based on Standard Industrial Classification of the UN	Thousands	
	1971	1981
total working population	25 123	26 070
of which: males	16 220	15 984
females	8 903	10 086
unemployed	723	2 681
employed labour force	24 399	23 388
HM Forces and women's services	368	334
employers and self-employed	1 909	1 856
total employees in employment	22 122	21 198
of which:		
agriculture, forestry, fishing	434	360
mining and quarrying	396	332
manufacturing	8 056	6 038
construction	1 262	1 132
gas, electricity and water	377	340
transport and communication	1 568	1 440
distributive trades	2 610	2 635
insurance, banking, finance and business services	976	1 233
professional and scientific services	2 988	3 695
miscellaneous services (including catering and entertainment)	1 945	2 414
public administration and defence (national and local government services)	1 510	1 579

Source: *Annual abstract of statistics* 1974 and 1983. London: HMSO.

ment. At such a time the number of vacant jobs tends to exceed the number of persons seeking work. However, very often, unemployment rises above this level and it is then that the position becomes serious. Types of unemployment vary:

General unemployment affects all groups of workers. In the USA, during the Great Depression of the 1930s, about 15% of the labour force was out of work; in Britain the recession of the 1980s led to 12% of the labour force being jobless. This type of unemployment is often associated with the 'trade cycle' in which there is a continual alteration between the extremes of 'slump' and 'boom'.

Seasonal unemployment occurs at specific times of year. Normally it happens in occupations that are dependent upon the weather, such as those connected with tourism, agriculture and construction.

Structural unemployment affects only certain industries and is often the result of falls in demand for particular products or services, as in the European steel industries and the British teaching profession.

POPULATION COMPOSITION IN SOUTH AFRICA

Such is the extent of South Africa's demographic diversity that the Republic may be viewed – in economic and social terms if not in political terms – as a microcosm of the world. It combines the elements of both the developed and the less developed world: a feature undoubtedly the result of the country's unique position on the globe and of its patterned history.

Racially, the population of South Africa can be divided into four anthropological sections: Whites (16%), Blacks (72%), Asians (3%) and Coloureds (9%). Between and across these sections are superimposed various linguistic, religious and cultural subgroups – thus giving the Republic one of the most plural societies to be found anywhere in the world. The Whites derive from Europe whence colonial migration took place from the 17th century onwards. Most of the migrants came from the Netherlands and Britain so that, today, the Whites can largely be divided between the Afrikaners (speaking a form of Dutch) and the English-speakers. However, other European languages are still spoken by minorities – French, German, Italian, Portuguese and Greek especially. The Blacks originate from parts of Africa further north whence settlers moved southwards during the Middle Ages. This group has nine major ethnolinguistic divisions, including North and South Nguni, Tswana and Sotho (all these divisions speaking various Bantu, Bushman and Hottentot tongues). The Asians derive from peoples from India and China who moved to South Africa during the 19th century when extra labour was required to work on the colonial sugar plantations. They speak a number of oriental languages – Tamil, Hindi, Urdu, for example. The Coloureds are people of mixed racial blood who speak mainly Afrikaans. (It should be noted that these racial divisions are those defined by the South African Government.)

Differences in religions (various Christian churches, Jewish, Islam, Hindu and numerous native beliefs); educational levels; standards of living; employment and occupational achievements; and political power serve only to compound the inherent racial and linguistic divides. For example, the White population, alone, possesses a fairly regressive age–sex pyramid with a relatively low ratio of children (30%) and a relatively high ratio of aged people (11%). Conversely, the Black and Coloured populations, individually, have fairly progressive pyramids (50% children, 4% aged). Among the Whites, monogamy is enforced, contraception is common and the growth rate is low. Among the Blacks and Coloureds, polygamy is allowed, birth control is little practised and the growth rate is high. Levels of literacy, wealth, medical care and civic responsibility are also far higher among the Whites than among the Blacks and Coloureds.

The apartheid laws of South Africa (though now being modified) are much opposed both within the country and across the world. These laws maintain a system and philosophy that separates peoples of different ethnic origins. Strict segregation takes place, so that racial identities are preserved – cultural, economic, social and political development continuing within distinct groups, at different paces and in different ways. South Africa is a multiracial or plural society *par excellence*, but it is neither a mixed nor a mixing society.

Concealed unemployment is a term used when joblessness is not apparent in labour statistics. Workers may be on 'short time' or otherwise not working fully, being underemployed or overleisured. In the former, employees may be forcibly kept on reduced hours; in the latter, workers may voluntarily have taken part-time or job-sharing employment.

All these types, with the possible exception of seasonal unemployment, are the outcome of numerous factors such as labour and management problems, government policy, world trade and price fluctuations, changes in production and other factors beyond human control.

Of particular concern, not just to human geographers but also to planners, sociologists, administrators and others, is the fact that unemployment, together with its associated problems (economic decline and social depression), is often distributed unevenly. Such unevenness occurs because those factors that create unemployment vary spatially in their significance. Over long periods, some countries, like Italy, suffer more from joblessness than other countries, like West Germany. Even within countries distinct spatial patterns can be identified. In Britain, for example, regions like South Wales and north-east England experience considerably higher rates of unemployment than do London and south-east England. Some of the ways in which the government can try to correct this imbalance are considered in Chapter 20.

Composition and demographic change

Population subgroups are neither stable nor permanent. They change in character and in size, in distribution and in importance. Some sections of society are growing less cohesively uniform as a result of increased interaction with other sections: certain racial minorities are being diluted through mixed marriages; certain religious groups are having to modify their own distinctive beliefs in order to relate more constructively with other religions (as exemplified by the Muslims and Roman Catholics); certain social classes (such as 'the aristocracy' in many developed countries) are becoming less recognisable. Some groups are growing in number (such as the middle classes in the Third World), others diminishing (such as the Jews in Europe).

Apart from changing themselves, by their very nature subgroups can also influence changes in other respects. Some population structures are associated with economic stagnation, others with progress; some forms of composition have a negative effect on political effectiveness, others a positive effect. Certain subgroups (the young, the literate, the healthy) are more inventive, energetic and development oriented; certain others (the old, the superstitious) are more conservative. Indeed, it may be possible to link all kinds of human activity with the nature of population composition: socio-economic instability, philosophical ideology, political success, cultural advancement. Human behaviour is determined largely by the human environment, and population structure is a reflection of that environment.

Summary

1 Populations can be subdivided according to demographic, socio-political and economic attributes. Such divisions produce distinct and recognisable groups. These can be studied separately as units or collectively as interrelated sectors of society.
2 Demographic structure can be shown on age–sex pyramid diagrams. Progressive pyramids indicate underdevelopment, having high birth and death rates; regressive pyramids indicate development, having low birth and death rates. The dependency ratio shows the relative sizes of the unproductive and productive sections of a population.
3 Socio-political structure includes subdivision by religion, language and nationality. These reflect environmental and historical phenomena. Differences between these subgroups can create social tension and, sometimes, war.
4 Economic structure divides a population into working (active) and non-working (passive) groups. It also subdivides the active population according to occupation. The more advanced a country, the more likely it is to have a high percentage working in service activities. Unemployment (general, seasonal, structural, concealed) can result in social and political discontent.

Data–response exercises

1 On the triangulation graph (Fig. 4.6) plot the regions listed in Table 5.2 to show their relative age structure. Suggest the types of age–sex pyramids these regions would have.
2 Construct an age–sex pyramid for the United Kingdom based on Table 4.1. Comment on the shape of that pyramid and suggest how it might change over the next 50 years.
3 Show diagrammatically the occupational structure of the United Kingdom using the information in Table 4.2. Discuss the changes that have taken place, and are likely to take place in future, in this occupational structure.
4 To what extent can the standard industrial classification of occupations (Table 4.2) be regrouped into primary, secondary, tertiary and quaternary activities? In what ways might the regions of the UK differ in occupational structure from the national pattern?
5 Comment on the shape of the age–sex pyramids for Ethiopia and France (Fig. 4.2) bearing in mind the economic and geographical characteristics of these countries and their history over the past hundred years.
6 Suggest reasons for the socio-political patterns in South America (Fig. 4.5) and outline the possible consequences of these patterns.

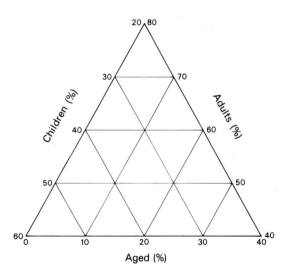

Figure 4.6 Triangulation graph
Points can be located according to three variables.

5 Population growth

Introduction

As we have seen, the composition of a population is an aspect of demography that has a profound bearing on the character of human activity and on its ability to change. The correct interpretation of population structure and the study of demographic subgroups can help us understand socio-economic or political change. Perhaps the most important change of all now facing the world is population growth and its consequences.

Population growth is a topic far too wide to be covered fully by a single chapter. Thus, within the limited confines of this book, only a brief outline can be given of the main aspects. Indeed, such is the nature of population growth that all the topics covered in this book can be linked to it, for growth has direct and indirect, long-term and short-term effects on all human activity.

The questions to be answered in this chapter can be listed thus:

- What factors cause population growth, and how important are they?
- Why do growth rates vary from place to place and from time to time?
- What are the consequences of growth, and how can these be measured?
- What problems may arise from growth, and how can these be solved?
- Can the understanding of population growth help in the study of political, medical, agricultural, industrial and settlement changes?

The nature of growth

Today's great problem is not so much the size of the world's population – it stands at about 4500 million – but its rate of growth. This is accelerating faster than ever before.

It has been estimated that at the time of Christ the population of the world was below 300 million; by the 18th century it had reached 600 million and by 1820 the first 1000 million was passed; at the beginning of this century it was about 2000 million, and in 1960 about 3000 million; it is likely to be well over 7000 million by the end of this century. In other words, whereas it once doubled in 1700 years, it now doubles in just 30 years. It is perhaps hard to imagine such growth in real terms. It may help to remember, therefore, that every day there are an extra 300 000 mouths to feed; more than 12 000 are added every hour (Fig. 5.1).

The average annual growth rate of the world's population is now around 2%. This sounds little, but it involves huge numbers and a rapid expansion. Yet this growth is not evenly spread throughout the world. In some regions it is sluggish, almost to the point of being non-existent, in other regions it is fast.

In general, the developed countries have far lower growth rates than developing nations. Western Europe has average rates of around 0.6% p.a. whereas most parts of Asia, Africa and Latin America have rates of 2.5% p.a. (see Fig. 5.2). The significance of this difference may be far reaching indeed. At present there are some 1000 million people in the developed world compared with some 3500 million in the developing countries. In the future the former will probably remain fairly constant and the latter will double if present trends continue.

Determinants of growth

In earlier times, man was a hunter and gatherer or else existed solely by agriculture. Even in regions now considered developed, he lived from hand to mouth and survived at the will of nature. Checks on population growth were for ever in operation: plagues and diseases, famine, floods, fire and tribal wars. Only the fittest survived.

Of course, a few parts of the world are still like this. In general terms, however, the last 400 years have seen fundamental changes. Britain experienced the birth of agrarian and industrial developments that were to have untold effects on economic, technological and scientific progress the world over. On the one

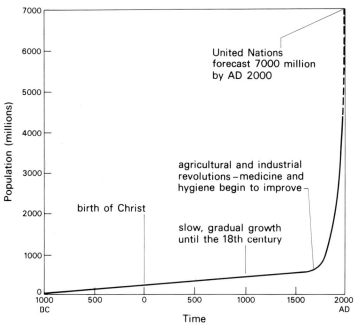

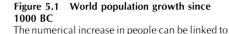

Figure 5.1 World population growth since 1000 BC
The numerical increase in people can be linked to economic and social conditions; the 18th century can be viewed as a demographic turning point.

hand, increased economic productivity could support ever increasing numbers of people; on the other hand, improvements in medicine and hygiene, flood control, and fire precautions lessened the effects of natural population checks. The result was that more children were being born and, since the chances of survival were increased, fewer people were dying.

As long as birth rates remain higher than death rates on a global scale, world population grows. The wider the gap, the greater the growth. Yet what are the many and complex factors that determine fertility and mortality? Both are the outcome of a combination of economic, religious, social and political considerations.

Birth rates
The most commonly used index of fertility is the **crude birth rate**. This ratio between the number of births in a single year and the total population is expressed as a number per thousand. Generally, birth rates in developed countries are low, below $20^0/_{00}$, and in developing countries are high, being up to $40^0/_{00}$ or even higher. Thus, West Germany's is $9.7^0/_{00}$, Japan's $17.2^0/_{00}$ and Togo's $50.6^0/_{00}$ (see Fig. 5.2).

It is tempting to assume that birth rates are linked to economic advancement. Certainly it is true that fertility tends to decline in countries where living standards improve, and remains high where technology

is backward. Over the last hundred years, for instance, the developed world has seen a dramatic fall in birth rates and the developing world has not (although there are a few recent signs that this may be changing). But to rely too heavily on this correlation is to ignore a plethora of other factors: various moral, intellectual and financial motives together with such social issues as the status of women in society, attitudes towards marriage and children, the power of religious or superstitious beliefs and the extent of material ambition in modern living. A summary of the main influences on birth rates is given below:

(1) *Demographic structure*. The character of a population's age–sex composition is of fundamental significance. It is to be expected that regions with a high proportion of young adults will tend to have high birth rates. New towns, pioneer settlements and areas of high immigrant numbers would fall into this category. Conversely, regions with a high percentage of children or aged, or areas with a dearth of females, will tend to have low birth rates.

(2) *Education*. Generally speaking, the more advanced the level of education reached, the smaller will be the average size of families. With education comes a knowledge of birth control, greater social awareness and a wider choice of

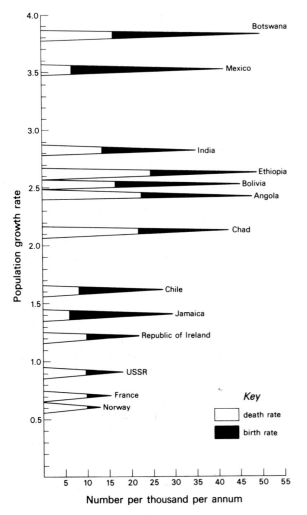

Figure 5.2 National growth rates
Birth and death rates are the most important determinants of population growth. In all the countries shown in the figure, birth rates exceed death rates but by different amounts. Levels of births and deaths can be linked to levels of development: those countries towards the top of the diagram tend to be the least developed.

action. This factor may also be linked with class, since it is often the case that knowledge correlates with social standing. Lower classes are, on average, less educated and have larger families than the middle classes, who may be more keenly aware of material wealth and have greater financial aspirations.

(3) *Religion.* Many of the world's churches, like the Muslim and Roman Catholic, encourage large families in order to safeguard the continuance of their beliefs. Some actively oppose any form of contraception. Thus countries and areas within countries where these religions are dominant have considerably higher birth rates then elsewhere. Italy, the Republic of Ireland and the Latin American countries are examples in point. In Canada, Quebec province (Catholic) had, until recently, a birth rate three times higher than neighbouring Ontario (Protestant). Algeria (Muslim) has a birth rate of $47^o/_{oo}$. Many of these regions are also economically backward and this only exacerbates the problem.

(4) *Social customs.* Concepts of marriage vary between social and cultural groups. In some places, polygamy is practised and this adds greatly to levels of fertility. In other places, like India where most people are Hindu, the average age for girls to marry has traditionally been only 16. They have their first child at 18 and up to nine other children in the next 25 years. Even with the introduction of new marriage laws in India, large families are likely to remain the norm. Certain cultures attach great importance to a male heir so that large families are common in order to ensure the survival of at least one boy.

(5) *Diets and health.* The poorest and most undernourished people of the world tend to have the highest birth rates. The reasons for this are not altogether clear, but sociologists believe a correlation exists between diet and sexual appetite. Unfortunately, high birth rates often lead to poverty, which maintains malnutrition and thus maintains a vicious circle. It is also noticeable that countries with high levels of mortality also have high levels of fertility. This suggests that parents in these regions deliberately have many children in order to ensure that at least some reach adulthood.

(6) *Politics.* The effect of war as a natural limit to population growth has been much written about. The two World Wars, for example, resulted in the loss of over 60 million lives. However, their importance in this respect should not be overstressed. Wars usually reduce populations for one generation only; demographic recovery sets in soon afterwards with an increase in the birth rate. During hostilities the menfolk are away fighting and the number of births naturally falls. After the war the troops return home and the birth rate suddenly rises. Most European countries experienced such a 'fertility bulge' in the years 1918–1920 and again in 1946–1949.

Occasionally, birth rates are even more closely linked to politics. During the 1930s, both Germany and Italy encouraged the procreation of children by offering state bounties and even medals to prolific mothers. The British system of giving child allowances could also be construed as encouraging a higher birth rate.

Death rates

Crude death rate is the ratio between the number of deaths in a single year and the total population, and is expressed as a number per thousand. It is the most common measure of mortality despite the fact that its simplicity is likely to hide important details such as the occurrence of death in different age groups.

As with fertility, there appears to be a link between death rates and economic development. The lowest (around $5^0/_{00}$) are associated with regions of generally high living standards, whereas the highest (around $30^0/_{00}$) are characteristic of economically backward areas. In other words, countries with low birth rates tend also to have low death rates and those with high birth rates have high death rates. Western European countries have death rates of about $10^0/_{00}$, India's is about $15^0/_{00}$ and some African countries (notably Malawi and Ethiopia) have death rates of around $25^0/_{00}$ (see Fig. 5.2). Yet it is dangerous simply to relate death rates to economic prosperity. Many small countries with limited technology have surprisingly low mortality levels: Fiji has $4^0/_{00}$ and Puerto Rico $6.5^0/_{00}$. Perhaps this is partly because these places have all been subject to the influence of major Western countries.

There are numerous factors influencing death rates and the main ones are summarised below:

(1) *Demographic structure.* Countries or areas within countries where the age structure is top-heavy – where there is a high proportion of aged people – will have generally high death rates. In Britain, the retirement resorts of the south coast are examples of such areas. Regions with a preponderance of men over women will have higher death rates than areas where the proportion is the reverse.

(2) *Medicine.* The better the medical services and supplies, the lower will be the death rates. A general guide to the extent of medical facilities is the ratio of doctors to patients within given areas. On average, developed countries have fifty times more doctors to patients than do developing countries. Several countries in Central Africa are so badly off that there is only one doctor to every 70 000–80 000 people.

(3) *Social class.* Poorer sections of population usually have higher death rates than do richer sections. This is doubtless because they are less privileged, perhaps living in substandard housing and insanitary conditions and being unable to afford a balanced diet or adequate medical treatment. In the USA the mortality rate of the black population is significantly higher than that of the white population.

In countries where social security and state-financed welfare schemes are in operation, the connection between social class and mortality levels is reduced. In Britain, for instance, the Welfare State ensures that everyone has a comparatively high standard of housing, nutrition and medical care.

(4) *Occupations.* Certain occupations are more dangerous than others and therefore lead to a greater number of deaths. Coalminers are vulnerable to a high accident risk as well as being prone to such respiratory diseases as pneumoconiosis and tuberculosis. Indeed, it is possible (although there are few statistics available to prove this) that any occupations which involve harsh conditions lead to relatively high death rates. These might include jobs in quarries, mines, building and construction, and those dealing with asbestos. Other occupations lead not to physical deterioration, but to mental strain. These also may result in early death and would include all jobs that carry high levels of responsibility.

(5) *Place of residence.* Generally, death rates are higher in urban areas than in the countryside. This is probably related to such factors as crowded living conditions, high traffic densities, atmospheric pollution and nervous strain, all of which are the hallmark of modern urban life.

A model for population growth

The fact that both birth and death rates tend to decline with economic and technological progress goes some way to explaining why developed countries have considerably lower population growth rates than do developing countries. It also helps to explain why such growth rates in any single region may change over time.

Over the last thousand years or so, the expansion of population in Europe has developed through a set

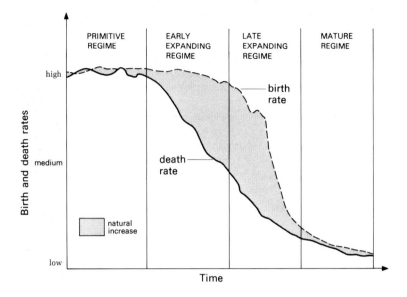

Figure 5.3 Demographic transition model
A possible fifth stage could be added to the diagram, in which death rates fall below birth rates and population growth becomes negative.

pattern of change. The recognition of this pattern, together with the known characteristics of population growth in other parts of the world, has led to the identification of a general model for demographic transition. This is shown in Figure 5.3.

Stage 1. *Primitive regime.* Both fertility and mortality levels are high and subject to short-term fluctuations. This stage is characteristic of undeveloped or uncivilised societies in which a large number of births is accompanied by natural population checks and a low expectation of life. The increase in numbers is gradual. Until about 1750, Western Europe was in this stage and many parts of tropical Africa and South-East Asia remain so.

Stage 2. *Early expanding regime.* Economic growth and improvements in sanitation, medicine and diet bring about a significant fall in death rates, but sociological factors continue to cause high birth rates. Under these circumstances population growth is rapid. Western Europe exhibited the characteristics of this stage from 1750 to about 1870 and many parts of the developing world still do, like Egypt, Uganda and Brazil (although these countries are unlikely to remain the same for long).

Stage 3. *Late expanding regime.* Further economic development and education bring about a fall in birth rate, which results in a slowing down of population growth. Old traditions and taboos may weaken, and contraception may become more widespread. North-west Europe was in this stage until fairly recently (around 1950) and some countries still show

these characteristics, for example Spain, Portugal, USSR, New Zealand and Canada.

Stage 4. *Mature regime.* Both fertility and mortality levels are low and the rate of population growth is consequently small. This situation is indicative of economic wealth and high standards of living. As such it is exemplified by north-west Europe today, where growth rates are below 1%. In a few instances death rates may rise above birth rates, thus causing a natural population decline, as in the case of West Germany.

Of course, the fact that countries like Britain have experienced this type of demographic transition does not necessarily mean all countries will do likewise. Countries in Africa, Asia and Latin America have differing racial, cultural and historical backgrounds

Table 5.1 Demographic transition in India 1880–1980.

Year	Crude birth rate (%oo)	Crude death rate (%oo)
1880	48	41
1890	45	44
1900	47	43
1910	48	46
1920	46	38
1930	44	32
1940	45	29
1950	44	24
1960	45	18
1970	43	17
1980	34	12

and will probably undergo different population growth patterns. Some may experience the four stages very quickly, others may develop their own unique stage characteristics. A few – those that possess political and social planning policies – may omit one stage altogether. In India (see Table 5.1) the introduction of family planning may result in the reduction in the length of the early expanding regime, thus accelerating the movement towards the eventual stability of stage 4.

Notwithstanding such modifications, this model of population growth provides a useful basis for further study.

Problems of population growth

The world's population is growing at an alarming rate and the problems to be faced are many and serious. On the one hand there is the overriding problem of space, on the other there are the problems of food and resource provision. Will the world be able to house and feed the extra numbers? Will there be enough minerals and energy supplies to provide for sufficient industry, trade and social services?

These problems are not new – the ancient Greeks and Egyptians were concerned about the results of there being too many people – but they are, perhaps, more serious than ever before. This is because the world's population is not so much expanding as exploding.

Of all the theories of population growth and its effects, the two most famous are those of Malthus and Marx (see Fig. 5.4). Of these the former is more relevant to the present discussion. In 1798, Malthus wrote his *Essay on the principle of population*, in which the difficulties arising out of population growth were discussed. In this, the author argued that the number of people always increases faster than food supplies and that eventually the world would be unable to feed its multitudes. When that point is reached, nature would impose her own checks on further growth in the form of diseases, famines and wars.

The fact that world starvation did not come about appeared to disprove Malthus's theory. He did not foresee the tremendous agricultural and industrial changes made during the 19th century. Crop yields in the developed world more than doubled; the great wheatlands and ranching areas of North America were opened up; new mineral resources were discovered in regions hardly known in Malthus's time; and better transport allowed for more efficient trade.

Figure 5.4 Theories about population growth
Thomas Malthus (1766–1834) said that population tends to increase geometrically (2, 4, 8, 16, 32, . . .) whereas food supply tends to increase arithmetically (2, 4, 6, 8, 10, . . .). Eventually this would mean that population would grow in excess of food and the world would consequently suffer natural constraints. Karl Marx (1818–83) argued that population increases only in response to social and economic inequalities within society: the more unfair the distribution of wealth between classes, the greater would be the growth in numbers. Eventually, excessive inequalities would lead both to a population explosion and to the overthrow of the capitalist system.

Because of these improvements, Malthus's ideas were either neglected or rejected; only recently have they been resurrected. Economic progress has begun to slow down, populations have continued to rise and once again warnings of future disaster are being heeded. Many regions are already overpopulated and millions of people, especially in South-East Asia and parts of Latin America, are now living under conditions similar to those that Malthus predicted. In retrospect it seems that the changes Malthus failed to forecast did not refute his argument but merely postponed the inevitable.

Today, then, the world is facing some harsh ecological facts. Man is pressing hard on his environment and the imbalance between the world population and material resources is becoming greater. Unless radical action is taken, the social, economic and political problems now being experienced will grow to gigantic proportions.

There is a myth that, since the world's population might find standing space on the Isle of Wight, there must be plenty of land to go round. This is not true. There are vast stretches of land that are likely to remain unproductive, and therefore underpopulated

– areas that are too mountainous, too forested or marshy, too hot, too cold, too wet or too dry. It is estimated that only about 20% of the Earth's land surface is capable of being used for agriculture and habitation (at least in the foreseeable future). There-fore, overpopulation is liable to remain a very real problem.

In developing countries this pressure of numbers results in hunger, poor sanitation and poverty. In developed countries it leads to concern about the pollution of land, water and the atmosphere, the deterioration of social facilities (caused, for example, by the overcrowding of hospitals and roads) and the spoliation of amenities and natural beauty.

The economic problems of overpopulation are also serious. That of too many people in relation to resources is likely to lead to a general fall in per capita output. The factors of production are put under pres-sure as land and capital grow relatively scarce, and the law of diminishing marginal returns begins to act in respect of industrial and agricultural output. Beyond a certain level, increased labour leads not to an increase in per capita output, but to a decrease as workers begin to work in congested conditions and below their full capacity. The outcome might be a general fall in the standard of living and a general rise in the cost of living. This is especially true in econom-ically backward nations, so much so that the gap between developed and developing countries is widening. The advanced regions are able to offset their own deficiencies by utilising the resources of the less advanced regions. The backward regions have no such means of reducing their problems.

Political difficulties are no less real than economic difficulties – indeed, they could well be more acute. With enormous social and economic problems, few governments will be able to cope and political insta-bility may result: riots, demonstrations, high crime rates and proliferation of political parties. This is already becoming apparent in Latin America and Africa.

Scientists, experimenting with rats, have found that animals tend towards self-destruction when their own numbers endanger the survival of their species. Man, it is thought, behaves in a similar fashion. Thus, with increasing population and overcrowding, there is a growth of violence. Inside cities this is being reflected already in vandalism and crime. Nationally it may be reflected in wars, as people compete for the same resources in order to survive.

In conclusion, then, we see that the environment does have an ultimate 'carrying capacity', a ceiling

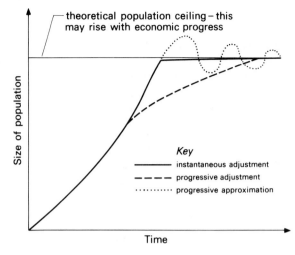

Figure 5.5 Exponential growth model
Nature can adjust to circumstances: population growth cannot for long continue beyond the level of maximum resource capacity.

beyond which extra numbers of people cannot be adequately housed, fed or employed. The possible implications of this have been incorporated in the **exponential growth model** (Fig. 5.5). This suggests ways in which population growth can adjust to circumstances.

Instantaneous adjustment, in which population growth suddenly becomes zero, is highly unlikely to occur in real life. Progressive adjustment, whereby growth slows down before the ceiling is reached, is more likely, although this still assumes that there is great control over birth rate. Progressive approxima-tion, whereby numbers rise and fall about the ceiling, is most likely. This results in periodic checks on growth by famines, diseases and wars, and as such is not dissimilar to the prophecies of Thomas Malthus.

Possible remedies for the population problem

If man is not to experience the various problems of overpopulation, he must formulate policies to deal with the situation. Broadly there are two courses of action he can adopt: the first is to accommodate the expanding population by developing new tech-nologies so that living space and food can be found for the growing numbers; the second is to limit popu-lation growth, thereby obviating the need for alterna-tive remedies, in the long run at least. But whichever policies are introduced, man must act quickly for time is running out.

Providing for growth

Improving agriculture. Certainly the production of more food is of paramount importance since, without sustenance, life is impossible. This may be done both by opening up new lands for farming and by increasing yields on land already under agriculture.

It is estimated that only about half of the land in the world with agricultural potential is actually being cultivated; the remainder is largely made up of regions of limited accessibility which could be brought into cultivation only at great expense. Even so, some large areas are now being farmed for the first time, in central Russia, north-east Brazil and southern Africa, for example.

It is also possible to extend farming into regions formerly thought **marginal** or even totally unproductive. Using new machinery and improved crop strains, both Canada and the USSR are now extending agriculture northwards, and elsewhere farming is being pushed much further up mountains than was once the case. In the same way, irrigation and fertilisation are bringing certain desert areas into food production. In the Sahara there are even experiments in the use of oil as plant food. Deforestation is common in many countries for extension of farmland, and in Brazil work is under way to turn part of the Amazon jungle into an important producer of tropical commodities.

The extension of farming regions is important, but greater possibilities lie in policies that increase yields on land already farmed.

Turning extensive agriculture into intensive, or intensive into highly intensive, is largely a matter of money and planning. The use of fertilisers, selective breeding of animals, improved methods of pest and disease control, seed selection and greater crop rotation all have the desired results. Greater efficiency can also be achieved by the wider use of machinery, rationalisation of farm holdings and field sizes, and by the increased use of energy (although this sometimes leads to inverse efficiency – farming using up more energy than it produces). The attainment of higher yields is especially necessary in the densely peopled peasant lands of Asia, Africa and Latin America, where serious food shortages already exist.

In many places, new crops are adding considerably to food production. Soya beans, in particular, are now grown in vast quantities, their advantage being that they give extremely high yields, provide nutritional food with high protein value and can even be used for other purposes, such as textile manufacture. In the USSR a new strain of edible wild lupin has recently been developed and this also may have great potential for the future.

Finding other foods. In order to supplement the extra food supply provided by agricultural progress, it is also hoped that new foods will be obtained from sources previously underused or ignored. A much wider use of sea farming, for example, has been recommended by food scientists. This would mean a greater consumption of fish, the introduction of types of seafood once thought inedible and perhaps also the eating of seaweed. There have also been developments in the production of synthetic foods – artificial foods of high protein value. Some American dieticians have even considered the consumption of earthworms as an addition to our daily diets!

Industrialisation. Some economists think that the further development of mineral resources and the expansion of industry would help solve the population problem. In developing countries, industrialisation would absorb surplus rural labour and, through greater exports, provide a source of income. This extra wealth might then be used to import food supplies.

Unfortunately, such a remedy has drawbacks. By definition, industrial expansion needs capital, raw materials, power and technological skill – all of which developing countries often do not possess. Even if industrialisation were possible, it is questionable whether this policy is economically or socially desirable. It is liable to postpone rather than cure the problems caused by overpopulation and could lead poor nations to become even more dependent upon the rich. After all, few developing countries are able to develop without external help.

Migration. It has been suggested that the population problem is not so much concerned with total numbers as with the uneven distribution of the world's peoples. If this were so, then migration on a massive scale would clearly solve the problem. However, as we have seen, resources are maldistributed and a more even spread of people than exists today is therefore impracticable – populations are unlikely to live where fertile soils and mineral deposits are absent.

Nevertheless, individual countries that suffer from serious overpopulation may well be helped by emigration. This was certainly true in both Britain and Italy last century and today is true in many of the Commonwealth countries. To what extent it con-

DIETS AND DISEASES

There has been considerable research recently into the patterns and nature of diets in the world and their correlation with the incidence and distribution of diseases. The idea that food consumption is linked with illness is, of course, not new, but studies are now beginning to show that the relationship is much stronger than was once imagined.

Over half of the world's population is underfed. In Asia and Africa, particularly, undernourishment is common and thousands of people there suffer from kwashiorkor, a disease caused by hunger, which results in malformation, body swelling and eventually death. Yet malnutrition is not just a question of shortage. It is often a matter of unbalanced diets and poorly prepared food.

Diets ought to contain carbohydrates and fats to give energy, and proteins, minerals and vitamins to maintain the fabric of the human body. A balanced diet should have about 60% carbohydrates, 20% fats and 20% protein. But nature does not distribute food supplies in these proportions, neither do uneducated people understand dietetics. (See Fig. 5.6.)

Although carbohydrates are very common, proteins are scarce. Most regions have a natural abundance of staple crops: wheat in Europe, maize in America, rice in Asia and various products like millet, yams, and cassava in Africa. These foods are starchy and peasant cultivators lack either the know-how or the incentive to supplement them with meat, milk and fruit. The situation is especially serious where population is expanding rapidly. In these areas, quantity becomes even more important than quality and dependence upon the staple foods increases accordingly. It costs more to breed livestock for food than to grow vegetables or cereals, and only relatively wealthy countries can afford to produce animal products for human consumption.

It should also be remembered that a fairly large proportion of the world's population restricts its diet for reasons other than those of availability and cost. Buddhists are vegetarian, Jews do not eat pork and Hindus are forbidden to eat beef. In India, cows are reared but, being sacred, are never slaughtered.

About 60% of the world's population has a diet that contains 80% or more vegetable starch. This state of affairs is not only unfortunate but is likely to be difficult to change. Malnutrition leads to physical weakness and lethargy. This means that undernourished people are able to work less, production is held back and food shortages result. Lack of food leads to malnutrition and the vicious circle starts again.

A deficiency of proteins and vitamins will eventually take its toll. Not only are some diseases, such as rickets and goitre, a direct result of this, but general debility leads to a lower resistance to diseases of all kinds. In areas where unbalanced diets are common, the expectation of life is considerably below that of developed and wealthy regions. In Bolivia it is 49, in Somalia 38 and in Angola it is just 33, compared with the European average of 70. Moreover, in underdeveloped countries the occurrence of infant mortality is extremely high.

Illnesses fall into two groups: exogenetic, which result from external factors, and endogenetic, which result from the natural exhaustion of the body. Into the first category would come infectious diseases, some respiratory diseases and a few diseases of the nervous system. The second category would include diseases of the curculatory system and cancer. Both types may be caused or aggravated by various environmental, epidemiological and socio-economic influences.

Some environments are especially hazardous in terms of the diseases they can cause. Tropical areas, for instance, have the heat and dampness to harbour insects and vermin. Malaria, yellow fever, leprosy and hookworm are common in these regions, and river blindness can be caused by the flies that infest watery places like the Red Volta River area in Ghana. Polluted water may lead to hepatitis and polluted air to lung cancer.

Epidemic diseases are those that spread rapidly from the spot where they first appear. Of course, surroundings might encourage this spread, but generally environment is not responsible for their original occurrence. The Black Death, which swept across Britain in the 14th century, was first introduced by the black rats that came off ships from the East. The Plague of London in 1665 and the cholera epidemic in the USA in 1849 are similar examples. Frequently, natural hazards such as earthquakes and flooding provide the essential conditions for the rapid spread of diseases like typhoid, cholera, dysentery and smallpox since poor sanitation and overcrowding in relief settlements can foster germs, and the hazards themselves can bring destruction and disruption to sanitary systems and social welfare facilities.

The dominance of almost any disease is determined by socio-economic patterns. Overcrowding, lack of good sanitation, poverty, illiteracy, the unavailability of medical treatment and, of course, unbalanced diets all bring about a higher incidence of illness and premature death. It is not surprising, therefore, that developing countries suffer more than developed countries. Neither is it surprising that there is a correlation between diseases and social class, rich people suffering less than poor people within nearly every country in the world.

What is surprising is that certain diseases seem to affect some races more than others. The Chinese are driven from the mountains of South-East Asia because of malaria, but the Lolo, Moi and other local tribes continue to live there, apparently unaffected by the disease. The reason is probably that certain peoples build up an immunity to particular diseases. White people in Africa suffer illnesses that the blacks do not. Conversely, Africans in Europe have a particularly low resistance to influenza. Clearly, nature is able to adjust human biology to suit the circumstances of life.

Notwithstanding this fact, it remains true that diseases are reduced in both number and seriousness with social, economic and technological advancement. Increasingly, illnesses once thought fatal are being conquered, such as smallpox, polio, tuberculosis and whooping cough. More people die of 'natural causes' and at a greater age than ever before.

Yet there is an upper limit to the advantages of progress. Tobacco smoking can cause bronchitis and lung cancer, lack of exercise can cause thrombosis, and the modern rush of life can cause nervous disorders. So-called improvements in diets may actually increase the death rate. The addition of chemicals into foods may cause cancer, and the consumption of too much animal fat (in butter, milk and meat) may lead to heart disease. It is perhaps not surprising that the present movement towards 'health foods' in Europe and North America is accelerating.

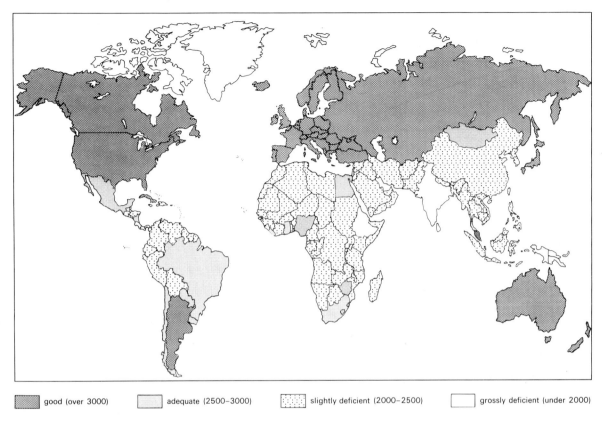

good (over 3000)   adequate (2500–3000)   slightly deficient (2000–2500)   grossly deficient (under 2000)

Figure 5.6 World nutritional standards, daily per capita calorie intake (from information supplied by FAO)
Levels of diet are the result of environmental, historical and cultural factors.

tinues to be true remains to be seen. Many countries no longer allow large numbers of foreigners to settle within their borders, and many others, like most Communist states, do not allow mass emigration. These restrictions limit world migration and largely reduce the importance of this particular remedy.

Finding more space. In recent years technological research has also centred on the development of new forms of living accommodation as a solution to the lack of space. Future towns could consist of large towers holding thousands of people and rising as much as a kilometre into the sky (as suggested by Corbusier), or alternatively be built on stilts in the shallow waters around the continents. Looking even further ahead, some scientists see the world's excess population being accommodated in space satellites or on other planets. Of course, whether these visions are realistic or not is debatable.

Limiting growth
Despite the number and success of the above remedies, it is realised that, together, they may still be insufficient to solve all the problems of too many people. Increased food supplies are unlikely ever to catch up with population growth, and natural resources continue to be used up faster than new sources are developed. Perhaps the only real solution is to limit population growth itself.

Zero population growth is achieved when birth rates and death rates are roughly equal and the average number of children per family is 2.3 (an average of just 2 would be insufficient to replace each generation: not all couples have children, not everyone marries and some children die before reaching reproductive age). Yet policies aimed at limiting growth will not be easy to introduce. Birth control, either by voluntary restraint or by contraception, will be especially difficult to accomplish since all manner of religious, social, economic and even political obstacles must be overcome.

The Roman Catholic, Hindu and Muslim religions are all opposed to family planning, and in many poor areas of the world large numbers of children are seen by parents as a source of cheap labour and therefore an economic asset. Education will be a slow process and incentives may have to be offered to encourage people to have smaller families. Some countries have, like India, already instigated sterilisation pro- grammes, but these have met with much public resentment and opposition. Any policies aimed at restricting population growth are likely to be unpopular with some groups of people, yet such policies are essential if the world, as we know it, is to survive.

Population growth and societal change

Clearly, rapid population growth, for the world as a whole, is creating serious and far-reaching problems, with economic, social and political dimensions. Yet, the repercussions of population growth for indi- vidual countries are less obvious. Some nations will cope more efficiently with a fast increase in human numbers than will others; some will face more serious difficulties than others. Some countries may actually benefit from population growth.

Economists differ in their evaluation of the effects of population growth within individual countries. On the one hand, it can be argued that growth will hinder agricultural and industrial advancement: more people means more mouths to feed, more families to house, more workers to employ. This will overstrain the social and economic facilities of a country, leading to hunger, homelessness, unem- ployment, lower work efficiency and, eventually, a fall in economic productivity. On the other hand, population growth may stimulate economic development: more people means a larger workforce, increased demand for goods and services, a more youthful and mobile labour market. This will encour- age agricultural improvement, industrial and tech- nological invention, greater efficiency and, in due course, a rise in per capita production. Which opinion is correct rather depends on which countries are being considered, together with all manner of physical and human factors – resource potential, climatic limitations, culture, political stability and so on. It also depends upon which economic ideology one supports: after all, there are wide divergencies between free and planned market economies, be- tween the views of Maynard Keynes and those of Milton Friedman.

The effects of population growth on socio-political change are similarly diverse and debatable. Accord- ing to some academics, increased human numbers

can lead to a rise in intellectual achievement and technological invention, a greater understanding of man's behaviour, and a positive development of humanism as an ideology. Conversely, more people could merely increase tensions between races, classes and nations and, ultimately, destroy civilisation itself.

Three changes that have been apparent in society during the past hundred years – and which may or may not be a direct result of population growth – are the rising cults of youth, women and radicalism.

Paradoxically, as the world's death rates are falling and populations are growing older, there has been an increase in 'youth culture'. This takes many political and social forms. History this century has been cre- ated by the young. The Bolsheviks of the Russian Revolution, the Republicans of the Spanish Civil War, and the German Nazi party of the 1930s and 1940s all had an average age of about 30; world lead- ers have grown younger – many heads of state are now under the age of 45 – and active scientists rarely exceed the age of 50. Even on a lower level, this 'youth cult' is visible – in advertising, education, religious teaching and entertainment.

At the same time, there has been the rise of the women's liberation movement, especially in the developed world. This 'feminism' owes its origins to the two World Wars of this century (when women first went out to work); to the increase in materialism and automation (causing women to be more keen to earn money and less bound to domestic duties); and to the liberalisation of intellectual reasoning (result- ing from higher female education standards). No longer are women in many developed countries dependent upon men; they can pursue academic and career opportunities without the strict family respon- sibilities and can enjoy the pleasures of life without the domesticities of motherhood. Certainly, the links between 'feminism' and birth control (and, indeed, abortion) should also not be overlooked.

Finally, both on a world scale and within countries, there has been a distinct change in political and sociological thinking, perhaps as a result of popula- tion growth. This can best be seen through the rise in radicalism: the general movement of ideologies from right to left, from feudalism and capitalism to social- ism and communism. Since the Russian Revolution there has been the constant spread of Marxist thought across the world and within public opinion. Even free democratic countries have not been impervious to this change as their capitalist systems are modified by government planning, welfare policies and egalitarian reforms. Liberal beliefs in human rights, equality and tolerance are replacing the older beliefs in human responsibility, social selection and discipline, and are becoming the tenets of society.

Population growth, then, may have incalculable effects on the social, economic and political environments of the world and its individual countries. Just how great are the effects, however, and exactly the extent to which population growth can bring about societal change, are open to question.

Summary

1 Population growth proceeds at greater speed in the less developed world (average rate 2.5%) than in the developed world (average rate 0.5%). Growth rates are determined largely by birth and death rates and partly also by migration.

2 Birth and death rates reflect social, economic and political phenomena in human society. It is generally true that, as a country makes economic progress, birth and death rates fall.

3 Changes in population growth over time can be identified through a demographic transition model. This has four stages and can be applied to individual countries. Time spans spent in each stage vary from country to country.

4 Increasing population can lead to severe problems – of food supply, space, employment and health. Malthus foresaw such problems 200 years ago. There are remedies to these problems, but time is running out.

5 Population growth may have profound yet subtle effects on society since it can influence people's behaviour and ideologies. The rise in liberalism and socialism, and the cults of youth and feminism, may be attributed in part to increased numbers. It remains to be seen whether near-zero growth in some countries (such as Britain) will be accompanied by a reversal of these trends and a return to more conservative and traditional values.

Data–response exercises

1 Construct a demographic transition graph of India based on Table 5.1. Suggest reasons for the nature of this graph and comment on the possible changes likely over the next 20 years.

Table 5.2 Demographic statistics for selected world regions.

Region	Population (millions)	Rate of increase %	Crude birth rate ‰	Crude death rate ‰	Density (persons per km²)	Age structure (% of total population)			Sex ratio (males per 100 females)
						Under 15	16–64	Over 65	
Eastern Africa	141	2.6	46	19	21	45	52	3	98
Southern Africa	34	2.5	37	11	12	42	54	4	98
North America	248	0.9	16	9	11	25	64	11	96
Latin America	397	2.5	35	9	18	42	54	4	100
East Asia	1 156	1.5	24	9	96	34	60	6	103
South Asia	1 428	2.4	40	15	89	43	53	4	105
Western Europe	154	0.6	13	10	155	23	63	14	94
Southern Europe	143	0.9	17	9	108	26	64	10	95
Australia and New Zealand	18	1.7	20	8	2	28	62	10	101
USSR	268	0.8	17	8	12	26	65	9	87

Source: *Demographic yearbook* 1982. UN.

2 Account for the differences in natural growth rates shown in Figure 5.2. Why is there no exact correlation between growth rates and birth rates — India, for example, having a higher growth rate than Ethiopia and Angola, but a lower birth rate?

3 On an outline map of the world, show by means of a suitable method the rate of increase, the crude birth rate and crude death rate of each of the regions shown in Table 5.2. Comment on the information plotted with regard to the links between population data and physical and social factors.

4 Outline the possible environmental, economic and social consequences of the three ways in which population growth adjusts to the natural ceiling (Fig. 5.5). In which countries is each of the three most likely to occur and why?

5 Discuss the world nutritional standards shown in Figure 5.6, bearing in mind the environmental and human conditions found in different parts of the world.

6 In some developed-world countries, the birth rate is falling. Examine the implications of this for education, industry and leisure activities.

6 Population movement

Introduction

The movement of people from place to place can be viewed as a spontaneous human effort to achieve balance between population and resources. It is a natural phenomenon, which produces demographic, social and economic interactions that, together, reduce some of the irregularities of nature. Without these interactions, the spatial imbalance of such factors as wealth, food consumption and industrial output would be extreme.

Migration, seen in this context, is therefore both the result and the cause of the physical and human environment. Certain environmental conditions encourage movements of people and these movements, in turn, can alter environmental conditions. By studying migration we can better understand the nature of and the changes in these environmental conditions.

This chapter is to consider the following questions:

- What kinds of population movement can be identified, and how do these occur?
- What factors determine the patterns of migration on local and world scales, and how important are those factors?
- Can any set processes in population movement be analysed or measured, and, if so, can they be formulated into models?
- What are the results of migration, in terms of physical and human environments?
- What are the causes and consequences of multiracial societies?

Classification of migration

Migration can be subdivided according to motive, distance and duration (see below) or else by volume, direction and organisation. Such classifications are necessary so that we can highlight and clarify the issues and characteristics involved in human movements.

However, no single classification is perfect. This is because each type may overlap and interrelate with other types and also because each type is not uniformly characteristic. For example, internal migration (within a country) suggests relatively small distances, whereas international (between countries) suggests large distances. This is not always the case, of course: movement across the USA requires much greater effort than movement from, say, Belgium to the Netherlands.

Notwithstanding such problems of classification, a summary of migration types (see Fig. 6.1) follows.

Motive

Unconscious drifts. Man has always wandered and drifted across the face of the globe. In earliest times this movement was perhaps without obvious reason or objective and it took place over thousands of years. One after another, tribes penetrated into the unknown, many originating from the cradle of civilisation in Mesopotamia. Anthropologists can trace most races back to Asia, even the American Indians, who, it is thought, crossed to that continent via the Bering Straits.

Compulsory movements. These have always been largely associated with unhappy and often violent periods in history. Much compulsory migration has resulted either from religious and political persecution or from economic need. Throughout history the Jews have been oppressed and since the early Middle Ages have, at some time, been expelled from most of the countries in Europe. The Huguenots were forced to leave France by the harsh policies of King Louis XIV, and in the 17th century Puritans sought refuge away from Stuart England.

The slave trade was a striking example of enforced population movements. Begun by the Portuguese in the 15th century and continued by the Spanish, Dutch, French and British, this trade involved the removal of black Africans to work in the plantations of the New World. It has been estimated that by the time slavery was finally abolished at the beginning of

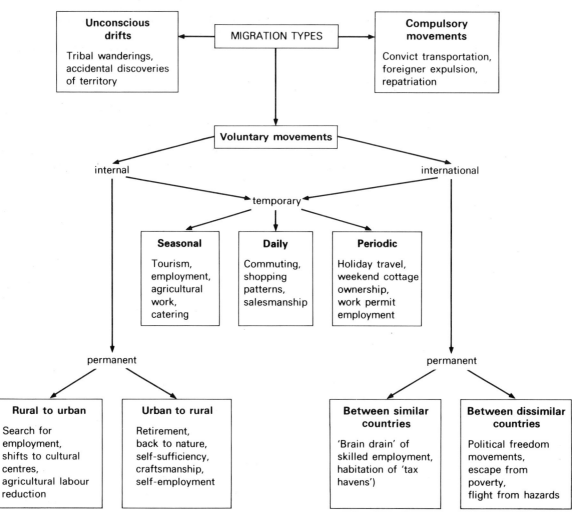

Figure 6.1 Types of migration
Diverse classifications are difficult but pertinent to study in the context of understanding individual elements.

the 19th century, as many as 10 million black people had been transported across the Atlantic.

In recent times, upheavals of population have followed large-scale warfare. As a result of World War 1, about six million people migrated across Europe, mostly away from the defeated countries. Of far greater significance was the effect of World War 2, which resulted in the displacement of well over 60 million people. Many left Germany during the 1930s to escape the persecution of the Nazis; many more evacuated the areas under heavy fighting once the war had begun. With peace came the migration of still more millions as labour movements were instigated and ethnic or linguistic groups were resettled: Poles were deported from Germany and Russia, for example, and Slavs were moved into Czechoslovakia.

Even today, some forced movements occur. During the past 50 years the Russian government has operated a colonisation programme and several million people have been moved into Soviet Asia in order to open up its waste lands for agriculture and industry. In China, migration is taking place towards the interior as part of a government policy to balance the country's economy and secure a strategic advantage over possible attack. In Uganda, Asians have been expelled (1970s); in Lebanon, Palestinians have been evicted by the Israelis (1982); in Nigeria, illegal immigrant Ghanaians have been ejected (1983).

Voluntary movements. Migration that results from unenforced motives is perhaps of greatest interest. The study of voluntary movements brings into consideration the diverse geographical factors that determine human choice. For man to move on his own accord, he must have very real physical, economic, political and social reasons, together with the required degrees of knowledge, ambition and energy. He needs strong motives indeed for leaving his home environment and settling in a chosen new environment. Of course, no two people will share exactly the same reasons for moving. Neither will those reasons stay the same over time. Depending on external as well as human forces, some motives may lessen in importance and other motives may grow.

In the same way, the extent of voluntary migration might change over time. Movement is now far more frequent and widespread than it once was and this is probably the outcome of improved communications, increased wealth and a greater human desire for increased living standards. Of all types of migration, voluntary movements are now the most important.

Distance

Internal migration. Movements can take place across all distances from the very shortest to worldwide. Many people may simply move from one house to another within the same neighbourhood or town. Others may move further afield, to another town or from countryside to town. Some, usually the more adventurous, may move across national boundaries or even between continents.

By definition, internal movements involve relatively short distances. They do not require fundamental upheaval since migrants remain within a familiar cultural environment and therefore have few problems of adjustment to language, social customs, ideology and institutions. The only constraints on these movements are economic and human: an inadequate number of jobs and houses, low incomes and strong personal ties with family and friends.

In many countries **pioneer advance** has long been a feature of population mobility. In the USA, for instance, the 19th century was marked by the spread of settlement across the Mid-West, and in the 1930s thousands moved from the 'Dust Bowl' in the High Plains region to better farmland on the West Coast. In fact, California has remained the American 'promised land' and over six million people have moved into that state during the last 25 years. Elsewhere pioneer advance has been associated with mineral deposits: in Brazil there is a steady flow of people into the

Amazon Basin and in Canada a similar movement occurs into the Laurentian Shield area.

For the most part, however, internal migration in nearly all countries is characterised by the movement of people from countryside to towns and from poor areas to rich areas. In Britain, there is both rural depopulation in most regions and an overall drift of people to southern England. Northern Scotland and central Wales in particular are experiencing a net loss of population, East Anglia and the Home Counties a net gain. In Norway, migration is generally coastwards on a local scale and southwards on a national

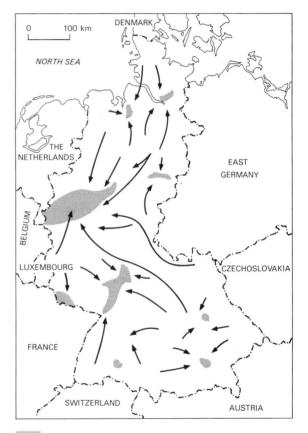

centres of high population concentration

Figure 6.2 Population movements in West Germany, 1960–80
Internal migration within West Germany has been the result of environmental, economic, social and even political pressures. However, today the West German government has undertaken policies aimed at reversing the trends of the last 30 years: regional policy is helping to stem depopulation from the upland areas and to relocate industry away from Hamburg, Munich and the Ruhr valley.

scale. In West Germany (see Fig. 6.2) migration is mainly towards the interior on a local scale and westwards on a national scale. In recent years, a further pattern of internal migration has become apparent in the more advanced countries – in Britain, for example. Here, people are tending to leave the very largest cities such as London and Birmingham and move into smaller urban settlements such as Norwich and Nottingham.

With economic progress and rising affluence, people become more mobile and internal migration increases accordingly. In the USA as many as 20% of the population changes addresses every year, giving that country the highest migration rate in the world. In Britain it is about half that level and in many developing countries it is below 4%.

The character and destinations of internal movements are also differentiated by age. The young move after marriage, or to new jobs, the middle-aged move to better housing (often in suburbs or New Towns), and the aged retire to the countryside or coast. In many countries, like those in Western Europe, the young tend to migrate inwards towards the central part of the country, the old (free of job constraints) tend to migrate outwards to the periphery. Certainly in Britain this movement can be witnessed – young adults towards inland towns such as Oxford, Northampton and York, and retired people to coastal resorts like Eastbourne, Worthing and Weston-super-Mare.

International migration. Movement between countries generally involves far greater distances than is the case with internal migration. It also entails far greater upheaval. People leaving their home country for a foreign one often have to face a totally different physical and social environment – a new climate, culture, institutions, political system and perhaps also a new language. Adjustments are consequently more difficult to make and integration is slower than is usual with internal migration. Because of this, we can assume that the factors leading to international migration are much stronger or more numerous than those leading to internal migration.

Over the last five centuries, by far the most important international movement has been the migration of people from Europe to North America. This first began in the 16th century when a few Western Europeans colonised the opposite side of the Atlantic: in Nova Scotia, New England, New York and New France. But the trickle became a flood and soon people from all over Europe, from as far east as the

Table 6.1 Migration into and out of the United Kingdom 1980.

Country of last or next residence	Immigrants into UK (thousands)	Emigrants out of UK
Australia	12	35
Canada	5	19
New Zealand	6	10
Africa (excluding South Africa)	11	12
Bangladesh, India, Pakistan, Sri Lanka	14	4
West Indies	4	3
United States	7	19
European Economic Community	14	18
total migrants	109	181

Source: *Annual abstract of statistics* 1982. London: HMSO.

Urals and Balkans, were making the long trek westwards. Between 1800 and 1924 over 60 million people crossed the North Atlantic, more than half these settling in the United States.

Other significant international movements in the past include the migration of Europeans to Australia, New Zealand and southern Africa, and the outward movement of Chinese to Burma, Malaysia and many of the islands of the South Pacific. In more modern times, migrants from India and Pakistan have settled in parts of central Africa, and migrants from all over the Commonwealth have settled in Britain. (See Table 6.1. and Fig. 6.3.)

The reasons for emigrating include overpopulation, poverty and hunger (termed **push factors**), and for immigrants (who are often the same people arriving at their destinations) the natural human wish to improve the personal standard of living: higher wages, better social facilities and improved opportunities (termed **pull factors**). These motives still remain today, but it seems as though the major world movements are over. Many countries can no longer absorb large numbers of aliens into their existing economic and social systems, so immigration is restricted. Some countries are highly selective indeed in their acceptance of foreigners, Australia, USA and Canada being prime examples.

Duration

Periodic and seasonal migration. Unlike permanent migration, which results in lasting resettlement, some population movements involve only temporary settlement. Temporary migration is certainly as old as

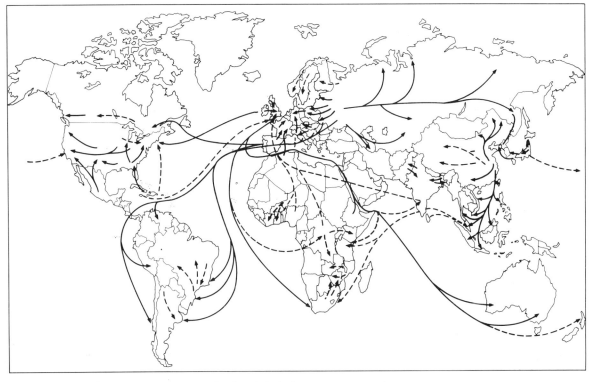

```
——————  principal migrations        ◄— — —  other important migrations
```

Figure 6.3   World migrations of the 20th century
Certain patterns of international migration may be identified: people tend to move from 'poor' to 'rich' countries and from Tropical to Temperate Zones. Today most governments operate laws to control immigration or emigration.

any other type of movement. It takes place everywhere and is the outcome of various economic, cultural, traditional and physical factors. Lengths of stay may be anything from a matter of days to several months. Sometimes many years can elapse before migrants return to their place of origin.

Migration on a seasonal basis is normally associated with agriculture and is determined largely by climate and the need for people to earn a living. In developing regions shifting cultivators (as found in the Amazon Basin) may be viewed as seasonal migrants; so may desert nomads who are attracted by the wet seasons to the north and the south (as found in the Sahara).

Transhumance can also be viewed as a type of seasonal migration. This usually entails the removal of animals (and farmers) to high mountain pastures in summer, leaving lower land free to be cropped with cereals or fodder, and their return to the valleys in winter. This is especially common in Scandinavia, the Alps and the Himalayas.

The employment of extra labour at harvest times similarly may lead to seasonal movements. Such temporary labour is commonly used on the plantations of many developing countries in cultivating cacao, coffee, sugar cane and other crops normally found in **monoculture**. In developed areas like Europe, fruit and hop picking, potato gathering and grape harvesting involve autumnal migrant labour. To some poor people in nearby towns these activities may represent the only chance of having an annual holiday away from their urban surroundings.

Other kinds of transient migration are more concerned with industrial employment. People living in economically deprived regions frequently seek temporary work in areas where conditions, opportunities and wages are better. After a specific period they are able to return home having saved enough money to secure their survival until the next migration.

There are millions of workers of this type in southern Africa where the gold mines and industries provide substantial opportunities to earn a respectable living. They move down from countries like Zambia and Mozambique, stay for several months in Zimbabwe and South Africa, and then return to their families in the Bush. Similarly, many Irish workers migrate periodically to England and, being exempt from income tax, are able to save large sums of money before returning to their own country.

Periodic migration has become very common in Europe, partly because here also there are spatial inequalities of wealth and partly because the terms of the European Economic Community allow for free movement of labour between member countries. In France the total number of immigrant workers averages 2½ million every year, coming mostly from northern Africa, Spain and Italy. A similar number has formerly been found in West Germany, originating from Eastern Europe (especially Turkey). In Switzerland one in three workers is foreign, the highest proportion in Europe.

Another form of temporary migration is that associated with tourism, this involving both foreign travel and holiday movements within countries. At present such migration is to be found on a large scale mainly within, between and from developed nations where wealth, leisure and individual aspirations encourage people to move for pleasure as well as for economic necessity.

Seasonal and periodic migrations of all types are normally advantageous to all concerned. On the one hand the workers themselves are able to earn more than they could at home; on the other hand, the countries or regions that employ temporary labour benefit in that their economies are kept stable and healthy. The distribution and intermingling of national currencies may create certain monetary difficulties but, overall, temporary immigration rarely causes the serious problems associated with permanent immigration.

Daily migration. Movements of very short duration – say, a number of hours – are usually concerned with journeys for shopping, recreation or daily employment. The last named is perhaps the most significant numerically. This type normally occurs twice a day and has really only appeared on a large scale during the last century and a half. The coming of the railways gave rise to large-scale commuting, but it was the invention of the motor car that made it more widespread. It is, of course, in the developed countries that daily population movements have particularly grown in importance.

Transport improvements and higher living stan-

dards have obviated the need for people to live near their place of work surrounded, perhaps, by industry, commerce and heavy traffic. Instead, people can choose more pleasant residential areas and commute to work. With economic progress, journeys to work are becoming faster and people are willing to travel greater distances. Who would have thought, even 30 years ago, that Southend, Margate, Brighton and Bournemouth would now be commuter towns for London?

A city centre acts as an industrial and commercial heart. In the morning it exerts a centripetal force as commuters converge from all directions; in the evening it exerts a centrifugal force as commuters radiate outwards and homewards. Every day over a million people travel into central London, over 200 000 of these coming from outside the Greater London area. The resulting problems are immense. Overcrowding on buses, trains and roads during rush hours alone can lead to all manner of economic, physical and psychological repercussions. Such problems are at least partly responsible for many firms moving out from city centres and relocating in less congested surroundings.

Reasons for migration

Migration involves effort, planning and expense, and the motives behind it include physical, economic, social and political factors. But before these are discussed in greater depth, we should remember that the decision to migrate is two-sided. First there are the push factors, which encourage emigration and comprise all those reasons why certain areas or countries repel people. Secondly there are the pull factors, which encourage immigration and comprise all those reasons why certain areas or countries attract migrants. The stronger and more widespread these factors are, the further will migrants be prepared to travel.

Migration (except in the case of refugees) is essentially the outcome of a complex number of personal decisions: whether or not to move, when to move, how to move and where to move. All these decisions will be based on a perception of the interactions between many pushes and pulls. Each prospective migrant weighs the several advantages and disadvantages of his present house, job and surroundings and compares them with what he believes a new house, new employment and new surroundings might offer. Unfortunately, man's 'perceived environment' does not always conform with the real

ILLEGAL MIGRATION

One aspect of migration that is likely to be of major concern in the future is the illegal movement of people. This is either when persons leave a place (normally a country, but sometimes a region or town) or else enter another place without permission. Countries most likely to suffer illegal emigration are those with rigid social or political systems where freedom is limited and life unpleasant. Countries most likely to suffer illegal immigration are those with prosperous economies, social and political freedom, an easily learned language, and a liberal society in which financial, medical and occupational aid is provided. Thus, there are illegal movements (defections) away from Communist, totalitarian and dictatorial nations and into more stable and democratic nations. The most serious and largest movements include those from Mexico to the USA, from China to Hong Kong, from the New Commonwealth to Britain, from Eastern Europe to Western Europe.

It is generally true that land boundaries are more easily crossed illegally than river or ocean borders. Mountain frontiers are especially favoured by illegal migrants (as are deserts and swamplands) since these are more difficult to patrol. There are three main methods of illegal movement. The first, by surreptitious means (by night perhaps, and by human endeavour and bravery); the second, by forged papers and passports or by marriages of convenience; the third, by overstaying a legal visit on holiday or work permit. To counter such illegal acts, countries take various precautions. The most extreme precautions can be witnessed along the Iron Curtain through Europe, where the Communist bloc has erected barbed-wire fences, set minefields, built watchtowers and kept guard dogs.

world. Not a few British people have emigrated to Australia only to return disappointed because life was not as they had imagined it would be 'down under'.

The main factors leading to migration are summarised below:

(a) *Physical conditions*. Harsh climates, difficult relief and poor soils can all make livelihood precarious, and therefore act as strong push factors. Natural hazards such as earthquakes, volcanic eruptions, floods and hurricanes may likewise encourage emigration. Physical pull factors are

Figure 6.4 Decisions to migrate
In many cases the decision to move is taken on a personal basis and for entirely personal reasons.

obvious since people usually want to move to areas where the climate is agreeable, the land fertile and hazards are unknown.

(b) *Economic factors.* These may provide very strong push–pull incentives. For the most part, people move away from poor areas and into rich areas where living standards are high. Unemployment, low wage levels, high rates and rents, poverty and malnutrition all create potential emigrants, and the promise of wealth elsewhere can act as a magnet. It is not hard to see why Commonwealth citizens come to Britain or why many British professional workers leave for the USA.

On a more local level, people will move to a new area solely because their employer has moved. They would rather look for a new house than a new job.

Another possible pull factor is the existence of rich mineral deposits, which attract rapid inflows of population. Many migrate as prospectors hoping to 'get rich quick', and many others may follow to serve the pioneer communities. In 1851 a gold rush in Australia brought in 250 000 people over the subsequent five years. Similar rushes occurred in California (1849–51), and in the Canadian Klondike at the end of last century.

(c) *Social factors.* These are often linked with economic considerations since material wealth and social wellbeing tend to correlate. A very common push factor is a change in family size and status. Newly married couples hope to set up new households away from their 'in-laws', and families with growing children may wish to move out of a small house and into a large one. Nowadays it is becoming more common for offspring to leave their parents' homes even before marriage and rent flats or bed-sitting rooms.

The lack of entertainments and other social activities in country districts may often account for rural depopulation, and the social, cultural and educational centres found in towns may cause urban population growth by attracting migrants. Conversely, some people move away from the noise, pollution and ugliness of towns to live in the peaceful and attractive surroundings of the countryside. In other words, the strength of social push–pull factors depends on the outlook of the individual.

(d) *Political factors.* Voluntary movements do not usually result from political motives. Occasion-

ally, however, some people do migrate because they disagree with the political persuasion of the local, regional or national administration. Many Russians, for example, have defected from the USSR to seek refuge and political asylum in the West.

These physical, economic, social and political factors create migration decisions. Such decisions can be taken individually or collectively. Individual decision-making results from personally observed conditions and experiences and is undertaken in isolation (see Fig. 6.4). Collective decision-making results from shared and acquired perceptions (inside an extended family, for example, or a tribe) and is undertaken in groups. In the former case, the reasons for and results of migration can be self-inspired, in the latter case they can be group-imposed. A person may move with a tribe or firm against his or her own personal wishes – a common feature of collectively formed migratory decisions.

Place utility

Consideration of the reasons behind migration leads inevitably to a study of the wider implications of the whole concept known as 'place utility'. This can be defined as the net acceptability of a location. Each place offers people set geographical conditions, some good, some bad. If the advantages of a place outweigh the disadvantages, that place is said to possess positive place utility – a person is likely to remain there. Conversely, when the disadvantages outweigh the advantages, negative place utility results and a person is liable to leave. A migrant will also choose to relocate where place utility is likely to be positive (either actually or by perception).

Naturally, this concept brings us into the realms of sociology and psychology. What determines an individual's view of place utility? To what extent can a person behave according to his instincts and desires? How does place utility change over time?

Human beings are creatures of habit, and migrants thus tend to be conservative. Most people dislike moving and, when they do change location, tend to pick areas where they will feel 'at home' – that is, areas of similar conditions to their original homes, utility here being rated by degree of social and economic constancy. Also, of course, people differ in their subjective judgements and are likely to give different utility ratings to set environmental conditions. Elderly people, for example, may rate a warm climate as a much higher plus factor than would young people.

Finally, it should be remembered that populations have differing mobility levels. For social, economic or political reasons, certain sections of the world's peoples may be restrictively mobile. A working-class person or an immigrant may be stationary through a lack of social acceptance elsewhere; a poor person may not be able to afford to move; a member of the general public in a Communist country may not be allowed to migrate. Each of these can recognise positive place utility at other locations but is made to accept negative place utility. In strictly segregated societies – Whites and Blacks in South Africa or tribes and sects in other African states – migration to locations of positive place utility locations can be almost impossible.

Theories of migration

Although the decision to migrate is essentially unique to each individual, people frequently act in groups and share in group decisions. When this occurs, patterns may be identified in population movements, and these have led some geographers to formulate theories that attempt to explain the principles underlying migration.

The first to hypothesise on patterns of movement was E. G. Ravenstein who, in the 1880s, proposed the *Laws of Migration*. The most important laws were as follows:

(1) Most migrants travel short distances and numbers decrease as distance increases.
(2) Migration occurs in stages so that one short movement from an area leaves a vacuum to be filled by another short migration from beyond. In this way, population progresses in waves towards an eventual goal.
(3) Migration is a two-way process. Each movement has a compensatory movement in the opposite direction. Net migration is, of course, the difference between the two.
(4) Where migration occurs over a long distance, it tends to terminate in an urban area. The longer the journey, the greater the likelihood that movement will end at a large city. Extremely long journeys will probably end in large metropolitan areas or conurbations.
(5) Town dwellers are less migratory than country dwellers.

(6) Women are more migratory than men over short distances.

Since Ravenstein's day, many others have modified these laws, partly as a result of changing circumstances and improved technology, and partly through the use of more exact mathematical techniques.

G. K. Zipf, for example, has developed a sophisticated version of the first law listed above. This is the *Inverse Distance Law*, which states that 'the volume of migration is inversely proportional to the distance travelled by the migrants'. This can be expressed in the formula

$$N_{ij} \propto \frac{1}{D_{ij}}$$

in which N_{ij} is the number of migrants from town i to town j and D_{ij} is the distance between the two towns (see Fig. 6.5).

However, this does not recognise the pull exerted by the population of each settlement. In order to measure this pull, various gravity models have been introduced into the study of migration. One of these is based on the assumption that a town's attraction is proportional to its size. In other words, the larger the town, the greater the pull, and one town twice the size of another will have twice the pull – that is, will attract twice the number of migrants.

Another migration theory looks not at the size of

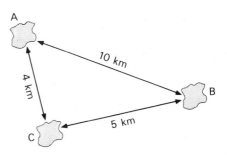

Figure 6.5 The inverse distance law
The number of migrants from town A to town B (N_{ij}) will be represented by $\frac{1}{10}$ or 0.1 (since D_{ij} = 10). The number of migrants from A to C will be $\frac{1}{4}$ or 0.25 and from B to C $\frac{1}{5}$ or 0.2. Thus, twice as many people travel between B and C than between A and B. Yet more people travel between A and C. Hence, the greater the distance between places, the smaller the migration flow. This is an inverse relationship.

settlements nor at the distance between them, but at perceived opportunities between them. This was first proposed by S. A. Stouffer in 1940 and is known as the *Theory of Intervening Opportunity*. It states that the amount of migration over a given distance is directly proportional to the number of opportunities at the point of destination, but inversely proportional to the number of opportunities between the point of departure and the destination. 'Opportunities' may be defined as vacant houses, employment prospects, social facilities or any other similar pull factors. If a town develops a greater number of such opportunities, it will attract a greater number of migrants than before, even from the same area.

All these theories have a basis in reality, as can be seen from the known migratory patterns in England and Wales. Of all moves made annually, slightly more than half are within local authority areas and many of the remainder are between adjoining local authority areas. Relatively few are between distant places. This supports the first of Ravenstein's laws and Zipf's theory.

Another characteristic of migration in Britain (although now less obvious than formerly) is that the largest urban centres receive a higher proportion of migrants than smaller urban centres, which, in turn, receive a higher proportion than still smaller towns. This progression downwards seems to validate the gravity model outlined earlier.

A study made during the 1950s of migration patterns in south-east England has brought to light a further characteristic of population movement. This consists of a cyclical movement. The majority of incoming migrants to the south east are young adults, many of whom are single and settle in central London. When these people marry and start families, they tend to move to the suburbs. In time, increased wealth causes a further move outwards, this time to the urban periphery, commuter belts and satellite towns. Ultimately, upon retirement, couples move out of the London area and sometimes out of the south east altogether. As each generation moves outwards from the city centre, new migrants enter to take its place, thus keeping in motion the migration cycle. Whether this cycle is common in all urban areas, and whether it is therefore a basis for a theory, remains to be seen.

MULTI-RACIAL SOCIETIES

For various social, economic and political reasons man has become more mobile and the distribution of races is no longer fixed spatially. This has led to countries having mixed demographic compositions – known as **plural** or multiracial societies.

In some instances, racially mixed societies have their origins in past periods of European colonisation. As a result of imperialism and foreign intervention, many colonies or former colonies contain four distinct ethnic groups: the indigenous population, the descendants of the European colonists, a non-indigenous coloured population brought in as slaves, and people of mixed racial origin resulting from interbreeding between the other three groups.

Both North and South America have plural societies of this kind. In the USA, for example, there is a relatively small number of native Red Indians, a great many people of European stock, a fairly high percentage of 'black' Americans and a few racially mixed peoples like the Creoles of New Orleans.

In Britain, a multiracial society has emerged for quite different reasons. After World War 2, this country was economically depressed and needed to revitalise its industry. This required a larger labour force than was available in the country at that time. In addition, many low-paid jobs, such as those in the transport sector, were undermanned and needed an injection of new labour. During the 1950s, therefore, the British government started to encourage Commonwealth peoples to settle and work in the 'Mother Country'. Persuaded by advertisements and financial incentives – and by the relatively poor conditions in their own countries – many took advantage of the scheme. The result was a steady flow of immigrants from the West Indies, Asia and Africa. Since these immigrants have come from such diverse parts of the world, there has been a mixing of several races, languages and cultures. This intermingling of ethnic minorities has created problems, not the least of which are those of reduced opportunities for economic advancement (owing to excessive labour supplies), restricted freedom and racial prejudice.

These problems are exacerbated by the tendency for new immigrants to settle in particular areas, living together almost as closed communities. Such communities may offer advantages for their inhabitants – cheap housing, close cultural ties, gradual transition to a new way of life – but can lead to disadvantages for an indigenous population. Urban **ghettos** are found in many of the big cities and are characterised by substandard housing, overcrowding, neglected amenities and high levels of delinquency, crime and violence. In many cases, the ghettos grew in areas that were already run down and squalid, and in which house prices and rents were low enough for the new immigrants to afford. In London's Brixton, for example, streets of modest terraced houses quickly became West Indian homes during the 1950s. Each successive group of immigrants may replace a previous group so that, once a ghetto develops, it tends to continue in existence even though the cultural character alters. Thus the East End of London was once a Jewish quarter and is now an Asian quarter.

Results of migration

Migration can have significant effects on population distribution, composition and growth. Areas of net emigration become depleted of young adults whereas regions of net immigration show an increase in the proportion in that age group. In the former, reduced growth generally results, owing to reduced birth rates; in the latter, growth is encouraged, owing to an increase in birth rates. Where retirement migration occurs, pension zones might develop in which the influx of a large number of elderly people can have serious consequences on an area's social services and employment structure.

Yet the consequences of migration are far wider ranging and more complex than just these population changes, for it involves, in addition, the movement of culture, technology and way of life. Entirely new landscapes may be created in alien environments, either by design or by accident. The Spanish introduced sheep and horses to North and South America, and Europe received, from across the Atlantic, tobacco, tomatoes and potatoes. American towns are full of examples of European architecture, from the Spanish baroque to the British neo-classical. Place names the world over reflect past migrations.

Even the apparently unchanged features of nature have been altered. The rabbit is a native of neither Britain nor Australia, but today it is a common rodent in both. The Lombardy poplar and Lebanon cedar are trees found almost everywhere and the horse chestnut originates from Eastern Europe. Many of Britain's wild flowers arrived with the Roman invaders 2000 years ago; the rhododendron comes from the foothills of the Himalayas and has only been in England for about 200 years.

The economic results of migration are more difficult to identify and evaluate. Nevertheless, the movement of people undoubtedly leads to a flow of capital, which may give rise to economic expansion in areas of net immigration and economic contraction in areas of net emigration. There has also been an apparent centralisation of financial power. Western-style economic systems have been superimposed on to areas where Europeans and North Americans have infiltrated so that, nearly everywhere, financial control has remained in the four great commercial centres of Wall Street (New York), the City of London, the Paris Bourse and Zurich.

The social problems that may be created by migration are not new. Wars in Canada during the 18th century and in South Africa at the end of the 19th century resulted from the intermingling of diverse migrants. Yet the mixing of races and cultures is not an inevitable source of friction. Sometimes it can engender greater understanding between peoples and so help preserve peace. Certainly it could be argued that the universality of the English tongue, English standards and English institutions has done much to provide a bond of friendship between nations all over the globe.

Summary

1 Different kinds of migration can be identified, motive, distance and duration being the main criteria. Pioneer advance occurs when people move into formerly unoccupied territory – it can be encouraged or hindered by political factors.
2 Emigration is determined by push factors, immigration by pull factors. Most people move in order to improve their way of life and are influenced by their perception of the world.
3 Place utility is a concept which gauges the acceptability of a location. People are conservative by nature and tend to move to areas where they will be easily assimilated.
4 People have differing mobility levels: the young tending to move further and more often than the old. In some cases, high migration desirability leads to illegal movements across national boundaries.
5 Ravenstein, Zipf and Stouffer have formulated laws and theories concerning migration. Movements occur in waves, are more common between near places than between distant places, and are inversely related to the number of intervening opportunities.
6 The results of migration are varied and diverse. It can lead to cultural mixing and problems of racialism and prejudice; it can have an adverse effect on a region's economic structure. Migration can also change such aspects as architecture and wildlife.

Data–response exercises

1 Suggest reasons for the patterns of internal migration in West Germany shown in Figure 6.2. What could the West German government do to reverse rural depopulation?
2 Draw a topological flow-line map of the world to show the population movements tabulated in Table 6.1. In what ways might these movements change over the next 20 years? Which factors have been largely responsible for migrations into and out of Britain over the past 30 years?

Table 6.2 Populations of selected towns (based on district council area statistics).

Town	Population (thousands)
Leominster	37
Swansea	186
Norwich	122
Maldon (Essex)	48
Berwick-upon-Tweed	26
Carlisle	101

3 Examine the world pattern of 20th century migration as shown in Figure 6.3 and discuss the consequences of these movements.

4 Using the gravity model formula

$$N_{ij} \propto \frac{(P_i \times P_j)}{D_{ij}}$$

measure the comparative extent of movement between the pairs of towns listed in Table 6.2. N_{ij} is the number of migrants from town i to town j. P_i and P_j are the populations of each town, given in Table 6.2. D_{ij} is the distance between the towns (km), to be worked out from an atlas map.

5 Examine the migrationary push and pull factors suggested by the cartoons in Figure 6.4. How can such migration decisions be (a) supported rationally, and (b) condemned as irrational?

6 Many developed and less developed countries (e.g. Britain and Venezuela, respectively) no longer suffer from great rural depopulation. Suggest reasons why this should be the case and discuss the consequences of this rural permanence.

Project work

1 Population densities, their variations and degree of spatial change, may be studied through fieldwork and the acquisition of data from official sources. Lorenz curves may be drawn for specific areas and for different times. For example, the population densities of the Greater London boroughs can be mapped and a Lorenz curve drawn for the whole GLC area. The extent of change can be gauged from the borough densities 10 and 20 years ago. Are cities like London becoming more concentrated or more dispersed in terms of density? Lapse rates may also be drawn for specific regions, using official statistics, and these can be compared.

2 Patterns of population movement can be found from personal fieldwork through interviews, the use of modes of transport and the study of stress times on the roads (rush hours, Friday and Sunday evenings, summer weekends, and so on). Alternatively, bus, train and ship timetables, or information obtained from local estate agents' offices, might enable migration pattern study. Different kinds of movement can be compared in respect of causes and consequences.

Further reading

Beaujeu-Garnier, J. 1978. *Geography of population*, 2nd edn. (translated by S. H. Beaver). London: Longman. Very readable, well illustrated and not too technical in approach; recommended for general reading. Chapter 15 is interesting on economic aspects of underdevelopment and the attempts to improve conditions.

Borgstom, George 1973. *Food and people dilemma*. Belmont (California): Wadsworth. A forthright and critical study of overpopulation and the hunger problem which, in parts, is politically biased. Interesting and informative.

Clarke, John 1972. *Population geography*, 2nd edn. Oxford: Pergamon Press. Slim paperback giving a concise, readable and not too detailed outline of the main aspects of population. By the same author is a companion volume, which studies just the demography of the developing world. Recommended.

Cox, P. R. 1976. *Demography*, 5th edn. Cambridge: Cambridge University Press. A comprehensive and very readable study of population, though rather lengthy. Technical in parts but useful for reference purposes.

Henry, Louis 1976. *Population analysis and models* (translated by van de Walle and Jones). London: Edward Arnold. All aspects of population are covered through quantitative techniques. Useful for reference only.

Jones, H. R. 1981. *A population geography*. London: Harper & Row. A detailed book, which concentrates on evolving patterns of fertility, mortality and migration and the spatial character of these processes. For background reading and reference purposes.

Kammeyer, K. C. W. 1971. *An introduction to population*. San Francisco: Chandler. An introduction to the ways in which population is studied – data, conceptual frameworks and population processes. As a reference book it provides a useful foundation for deeper study.

Pressat, Roland 1974. *A workbook in demography* (translated by E. Grebenik and C. A. M. Sym). London: Methuen. This demonstrates how methods and techniques used in demographic theory can be applied in practical ways and to real world examples. A collection of case studies is examined with detailed precision. Mathematical in parts; a reference book rather than a good read.

Stanford, Quentin (ed.) 1972. *The world's population: problems of growth*. Toronto: Oxford University Press. Thirty-three articles and extracts from various authorities, together with essays by the author. Well written and straightforward introduction to population. Part 3 studies solutions to the population problem.

Woods, Robert 1979. *Population analysis in geography*. London: Longman. This studies demography from a spatial perspective – through data patterns, census statistics, migration matrices, national projects and so on. Heavy-going for the non-specialist but a useful reference book for the technically minded.

Part III

ECONOMIC ACTIVITY

For the mine ran dry, and there wasn't
An ounce of gold left in the vein,
But my greed was so great that I left it too late
To accept there was nothing to gain.

And I made my mineworkers, poor devils,
Work twelve-hour shifts every day
In the bowels of the earth, but their labour was worth
Precious little in product or pay.

And I was still spending my money
At quite a ridiculous pitch.
If I'd come to my senses and cut my expenses
I might have remained fairly rich.
    Alex M. Donham *The Man with the Two Tin Spoons*

Work is the curse of the drinking classes.
Oscar Wilde

AGRICULTURE

Farming classification – monoculture – consolidation schemes – Common Market – innovation and diffusion – Green Revolution – Von Thünen – Sinclair

NATURAL RESOURCES AND ENERGY

Raw materials – minerals – power – nature spoliation – pollution – fuel-mix economies – new energy sources – conservation

INDUSTRY

Activity classification – functional linkages – locational quotients – inertia – concentration – Weber, Hotelling, Lösch and Pred – satisficer concept – deindustrialisation

TRANSPORT AND COMMUNICATIONS

Transport systems – containerisation – cost curves – Ullman – distance decay – flows and networks – connectivity – deviations – climax – prediction – planning

TRADE AND COMMERCE

Trade classification – entrepôts – freeports – free trade and protection – trading links – GATT – trading blocs – the trade trap

ECONOMIC DEVELOPMENT

Inequalities of wealth – Myrdal – multiplier effect – growth poles – poverty cycles – colonialism – environmental hazards – political instability – growth policies – intermediate technology – Rostow

7 Agriculture

Introduction

Of all economic activities, it can be argued that agriculture is the most important. It engages two-thirds of the world's population and supplies the primary products essential for life. Foodstuffs such as cereals, vegetables, fruit, meat and dairy produce are provided; beverages like tea, coffee and cocoa; and industrial raw materials like rubber, vegetable oils, cotton, wool and hides.

Agriculture underlies many other activities in the human environment and is functionally related to many other topic areas. It is influenced by population characteristics as well as by the physical environment; it influences the patterns in industrial location and settlement; it determines social and economic changes in human behaviour. In short, agriculture provides a cornerstone to the study of human geography; it is a crucial piece in the jigsaw.

Agriculture is a wide and diverse subject and in this book there is room for no more than a brief outline of the principal aspects. Thus, this chapter will attempt to answer the following questions:

- What kinds of agriculture are found in the world, and how do they differ in character and location?
- Where are distinct agricultural landscapes found, and how are these determined?
- What determines the nature of farming, and how do farming operations vary?
- How do we classify agricultural regions and for what purposes?
- Which agricultural changes are taking place and where?
- Can land-use patterns be identified, and do they relate to any theories or models?

Types of farming

Farming goes back a long way but not to the dawn of history. In earliest times man neither cultivated the land nor bred animals. He lived, instead, entirely on the bounty of nature: he was a gatherer and a hunter, a subsistence wanderer. Farming as we know it developed only gradually over thousands of years of economic and social progress, as man learnt to tame the natural environment. In the Old World, prehistoric times saw the first appearance of farming; in the New World it came in medieval times with native indian cultivation and European colonisation; in parts of the Third World it has come relatively recently. (Indeed, in some pockets around the world the gathering and hunting stage still persists to some extent – among the Eskimos in North America, the Yaghans in Tierra del Fuego, the pygmies and bushmen of Africa, the aborigines of Australia.)

Yet agriculture, where it has developed, has not appeared uniformly in character. For many human and physical reasons, different types of farming have evolved. Some types are 'backward', some 'advanced'; some produce food for local needs, others for national, or even international, markets; and some provide raw materials for industry. Some are highly mechanised, others preserve elementary methods of hand ploughing and manual reaping. Some types involve a variety of crops and animals, others are devoted to a single main product. In fact the variations are such that any attempt at classification is fraught with difficulties. Nevertheless, certain basic distinctions can be made. There are, for example, fundamental divisions between types: arable and pastoral, shifting and sedentary, subsistence and commercial, intensive and extensive.

Arable and pastoral agriculture

Arable farming developed when man first learnt about seed collection and selection. It includes all types of crop cultivation, but cereals and root crops are the usual products and farmers either grow a combination of these or specialise in just one. Horticulture – the growing of fruit, vegetables and flowers – and viticulture – the cultivation of grapes – may also be placed in the 'arable' category. All these activities are normally found on flat or undulating land where soils are deep and fertile (see Fig. 7.1).

Pastoral farming involves the grazing of animals that can provide food, raw materials or carriage. The common types are cattle, sheep, goats, horses and camels, all of which are herbivorous (that is, can survive solely on grass or other herbage). Pastoral farming tends to be found in areas that are either physically unsuitable for arable farming or well away from urban markets. This is because it is more tolerant of inhospitable environments than crop cultivation and its produce is generally less perishable. One exception is dairying, which specialises in the pro-duction of milk, cream, butter and cheese; another is pig keeping. Both are often carried out on an intensive basis and are found near areas of dense population, which provide easily accessible markets for their perishable produce.

In many countries, farms combine arable and pastoral production. Various crops are grown, partly for sale, partly to be used as fodder, and more than one type of animal is reared. This mixed farming has the advantage of spreading capital investment over a greater number of activities and safeguarding the enterprise against adverse fluctuations in both supply and demand, and against hazards of weather or disease.

Shifting and sedentary agriculture

Shifting agriculture may be viewed as a primitive system signifying the first step away from the gathering and hunting stage of early man. It was common in Europe during the Stone Age and still exists in many tropical and tundra regions of the world. It involves the continual movement of people in search of new lands to farm. The time spent at each spot depends on the nature of the products farmed and on the quality of the ground. Shifting arable cultivators may be able to remain in one place for up to three or four years before the soil becomes exhausted or leached; shifting pastoralists (like nomads), on the other hand, may need to move daily to find new grasslands.

Sedentary farming results from a further stage of agricultural progress. Once farmers have learnt about crop rotation, fertilisers and seed selection, the need to search for new land disappears. With this know-how they will farm one spot, build permanent settlements and remain indefinitely. Settled agriculture of this kind may also be seen as a response to higher population densities. It has been estimated that shifting systems are only feasible in regions where the population density is below 55 per km². Once densities rise above this level, sedentary farming becomes imperative.

Subsistence and commercial agriculture

Subsistence farming produces only enough food for the farmer's own needs. He and his family live from

Figure 7.1 Farming types in Japan
Irrigation in the Aichi region of Japan has transformed an area of poor subsistence agriculture into highly commercial arable farm-land. Fruits and vegetables are grown intensively to satisfy the high demand for food. The distant hills continue to be used for extensive pastoral farming.

hand to mouth, eating well in good years and going hungry in bad years. Should a surplus be produced at any time, it is sold in the local market, but to produce such a surplus is not the farmer's aim. The income from its sale is viewed not as an expectation but as a bonus. This system is associated with poor or backward regions and continues to be commonplace in large parts of Africa, Asia and South America.

Commercial agriculture involves the deliberate production of surpluses, and farmers work specifically for a profit. The produce is sent regularly to the markets and the money obtained is essential for this method of farming to continue. Without profits farmers would lose the incentive to cultivate, and money would not be reinvested in agriculture.

A particular form of commercial agriculture is monoculture, a system in which farming is given over exclusively to a single product. This has the advantages of increasing efficiency and quality of produce (by means of specialist techniques, scientific innovation and labour specialisation) while at the same time reducing the costs. The disadvantages of this system include a susceptibility to fluctuations in prices and weather conditions, an increased likelihood of soil exhaustion and possibly rapid spread of plant diseases. Although going back to at least Roman times, monoculture today is largely thought of in connection with tropical plantations, in which form it has developed through European colonisation. Elsewhere it can be observed to a certain extent in the maize and cotton belts of the Mississippi Lowlands, the vineyards of Europe and even the large-scale pastoral economies of the New World.

Intensive and extensive agriculture
Intensive agriculture aims to obtain maximum profits by using either large amounts of capital and/or large amounts of labour per unit of land. Yields per hectare are high and little land of agricultural potential is wasted. Only certain crops tend to be cultivated this way – high value or perishable crops, for instance, which would not be economical unless grown under this system. Intensive farming is commonly found in regions where population density is high and land scarce. In Western European countries, and especially in Denmark, the Netherlands and southern England, intensive farming involves carefully planned crop rotations and the absence of fallow, much use of fertiliser, specialised seed selection and scientific breeding and feeding of animals. In parts of South-East Asia and in Japan (see Fig. 7.1), high agricultural output is obtained with irrigation, terracing and the sowing of **catch crops**; that is, crops that provide a secondary yield, often sown between the rows of the main crop.

Extensive agriculture aims to obtain maximum production per unit of manpower. Yields per hectare may be low and land may be 'wasted', but farming is undertaken with minimum attention and expense in relation to returns. It is found where land is abundant, where technology is limited or where high profits are unnecessary. In Canada and the USA, wheat growing has been extensive, the high degree of mechanisation allowing for a particularly economical use of manpower, and the great capital outlay being expended on vast quantities of land. The grazing of cattle and sheep in Argentina and Australia is also extensive in nature. So poor are the pastures in parts of Australia that there is, on average, only one sheep to every 2 ha.

Agricultural landscapes

Every farming locality in the world has its own unique appearance. This is because the factors that make up agricultural landscapes – farm sizes, field patterns, field boundaries, building materials and farmhouse styles – are determined by phenomena which themselves vary from place to place: geographical conditions, the history of farm settlement, the types and methods of production, the economic aspirations of farmers, and the customs and traditions of the past.

Farm size
Farm size is often the result of the natural environment, economic requirements and traditions of inheritance. Areas of poor physical conditions – infertile soils, rough topography and inhospitable climates – may be associated with large farms since only large farm units would provide sufficient returns for livelihood. Small farms in such areas are unlikely to be economically viable. This is especially true where extensive agriculture is practised. On the drier parts of the Great Plains, USA, a farm of 200 ha is scarcely big enough to support a family since yields per hectare are so low. In areas of good physical conditions, or where intensive farming is undertaken, much smaller farm units are usual; in South-East Asia, 1 ha under rice is sufficient to support a family of six or seven. There is also a link between farm size and living standards: the higher the standard of living in an area, the larger tend to be the farms. This is partly because increased wealth

enables a farmer to expand his landholding to a more efficient level – especially if extra finance is available for expansion (as in the case of farms in the Common Market).

Farm shape

Associated with the size of a farm is its shape and degree of compactness. Some farms are elongated, perhaps along or across a valley floor, others are more circular or square, perhaps where many are spread out across a uniform land surface. Many, especially those in less developed areas (both in the developed and the Third World) are fragmented into numerous, small, and often widely scattered, plots. This may be caused by all manner of social and economic conditions.

Field patterns

Field patterns, also, vary spatially and are no less indicative of the type of agricultural development. Large fields are most common in areas of flat relief and fertile soils, and suggest highly mechanised arable farming. Small fields, conversely, are common in hilly or mountainous country where pastoralism is practised. One need only compare the fields of northern and southern Germany, or those of the Paris Basin with those of the Central Massif to see this to be true.

An irregular overall pattern of fields may suggest a long history of farming, perhaps where land has come under cultivation in a piecemeal fashion and agriculture has evolved gradually over generations: such a pattern can be seen, for example, in the Yunnan region of China. Regular, rectangular patterns have on the other hand tended to result from more recent agricultural developments and, in particular, from systematic farm planning. The square fields of Illinois and Iowa date back to early last century when the United States Survey laid out the unoccupied territories of the Mid-West on a grid pattern. A similar pattern can be seen in the Canadian Prairies (Fig. 7.2), the Murray–Darling Basin in Australia and on the reclaimed polders of the Netherlands. In eastern Canada, pioneer French settlers laid out their fields at right angles to existing rivers and roads so that, even today, long narrow parallel fields are a feature of the St Lawrence Valley.

Farmhouse styles

The building materials used in farmhouses commonly reflect local geology. Regions of high relief have farmhouses constructed of local stone; granite or limestone walls with slate roofs, for instance. This is because such rocks are readily available and provide sturdy structures, which are needed in areas of inhospitable climate. In lowland or clay areas, building materials are more likely to consist of timber or rushes, wattle and daub, or brick, and roofs may be of thatch or tile.

Climate is also reflected in architecture. Flat roofs are common in hot, dry regions; steeply pitched roofs in wet regions. In savanna lands, wide verandas often protrude from farmhouses to act as open-air sitting rooms shaded from the sun. In equatorial regions where flooding is likely, many buildings are erected on stilts.

Economics, culture and fashion may determine farmhouse styles too. In poor areas farmhouses are not only small and mean but are frequently joined to animal sheds or grain barns within the same building. Either the human quarters and farm buildings are side by side under a single long roof, or else living accommodation is built above the barn and is reached by a flight of steps. In prosperous areas, farmhouses are large, solidly built and usually stand alone, well away from other farm buildings.

Landscape differences in Britain

Agricultural landscapes differ even across relatively short distances and no richer variety is to be seen than that found in Britain. So great is the diversity of British geology, climate, culture and historical development that each locality has its own peculiar character.

Long before the time of Christ, the Celts farmed large parts of this country. They were subsistence cultivators who extended their farmlands as population grew. New fields were claimed gradually out of the forests and moorlands, and field boundaries were adjusted to the topography. The resulting irregular pattern of small fields, divided by dry-stone walls, remains to this day the essential characteristic of south-west England, Wales and much of Scotland. (See Fig. 7.3.)

During the Dark Ages, England was invaded by the Anglo-Saxons, who brought with them new agricultural methods. They cleared areas of forest and developed what has become known as the open-field system. Around each nucleated settlement the land was partitioned into two or three large fields and within each of these lay the unfenced strip holdings of individual farmers. Each farmer worked many strips, and these were usually scattered about the open fields in order to ensure a fair distribution of good and poor soils. All strips in a single field grew

Figure 7.2   Field pattern in the Canadian Prairies
The large rectangular fields in this part of Manitoba reveal the area's recent history of settlement (19th century). The Prairies are used for extensive monoculture, wheat being the major crop. Around each isolated farmstead are windbreaks and pockets of intensive horticulture.

Figure 7.3   Field pattern in south-west England
Although many have been enlarged in recent years, the fields around St Teath in Cornwall still show the small, irregular shapes of Celtic origin.

the same crop in any year and animals were grazed on the common pastures beyond the field limits.

The open-field system became especially common across Midland England in a wide band stretching from Yorkshire to Hampshire. In several places it can still be seen: in the Isle of Axholme (Lincolnshire) and at Laxton in Nottinghamshire. Elsewhere this ancient farm pattern can be seen superimposed upon a later landscape: across many pasturelands a ridge-and-furrow regularity can be picked out, especially when the sun is low in the sky and shadows are lengthened. (See Fig. 7.4.)

Figure 7.4   Field pattern in Oxfordshire
The regular fields here date back less than 200 years to the time of Parliamentary Enclosure. Across the landscape, however, can be seen the strips that once formed part of the Saxon open-field system of agriculture.

Saxon strip cultivation lasted, with little modification, throughout the Middle Ages. It was not until fairly recently that its fragmented character was rationalised and its strips were combined into small fields. Between 1750 and 1850, in particular, the English countryside was transformed. By successive Enclosure Acts of Parliament the open fields were almost entirely wiped out. Everywhere Enclosure Commissioners surveyed the land and laid out new fields in a regular square pattern. Today, long straight stone walls or hawthorn hedges are still a feature of the English Midlands.

Since the mid-18th century, the steady increase in the use of farm machinery has led to further modifications in the British landscape. In lowland areas, especially, hedgerows have been removed and fields enlarged. In East Anglia a single field of corn may extend, uninterrupted, over the distant horizon, perhaps covering several hundred hectares. Even so, the essential variety of the British agricultural landscape survives.

Farming operations

Other geographical variations in agriculture may not be reflected in the landscape. One of these is the way in which farming is organised, covering such aspects as land tenure, marketing systems and co-operative undertakings.

Ownership
Systems of farm ownership vary according to economic, social and even political interactions. Among primitive peoples, private ownership is unknown since all land is both held and worked by the community as a whole, the community usually being a tribe. Such communal ownership also still survives in some religious sects, in Israel and in parts of Asia. In advanced societies individual ownership is more common, either as freehold or in various forms of leasehold.

Freehold ownership involves the farmer owning the land he cultivates, finding his own capital and keeping the profit he makes. It dominates farming in most developed countries, although in Britain various political and historic factors have caused this system to be less important and less widespread.

Tenant farming divides into two kinds: **cash tenancy** and **share cropping**. Cash tenancy is simply where a cash rent is paid by a farmer to a landowner. Normally a farmer holds a lease for a stipulated number of years and, in many countries, his rent would be controlled (perhaps by the government). This system is common in Britain where the land may be owned by members of the aristocracy, large companies, the National Trust, the Oxford and Cambridge colleges, or the Church Commissioners. Share cropping involves a tenant farmer giving the landlord an agreed proportion of his farm produce by quantity or value. This has the advantage of safeguarding a tenant from years of bad harvest (since he loses only a percentage of his reduced income), but has the disadvantage, if the percentage is set rather high, of providing him with only a meagre income. The system has resulted in some impoverished agricultural communities, as exemplified in many developing countries as well as in parts of France, Italy and the USA. In these areas tenants may have little control over the running of their farms and little say in the sale of their produce. They may earn only small sums of money and be prevented from making improvements because of the fear of eviction.

State ownership is a form of tenancy set up in the Communist world. All land, capital equipment and agricultural production is owned and controlled by the state, which is thereby able, at least in theory, to rationalise and modernise farming practices. All farmers are the tenants of the government and have little or no freedom to act as individuals. Whether such a system works is debatable. Perhaps the failure of the USSR to produce enough food to support its own population is indicative of the drawbacks inherent in state ownership of this kind.

Marketing

Except in purely subsistence economies, marketing is of prime importance to farmers. The more efficient the marketing system, the higher will be their profits. Marketing methods vary from place to place as do

---

LAND CONSOLIDATION SCHEMES

In many parts of the world, farming is inefficient – with low yields per worker or per hectare – largely because of the division of land. Farms may be undersized, fields may be small and irregular in shape, landownership may be fragmented. There are many reasons for such uneconomic land-use patterns: cultural, historic, social and political. In Europe there are many areas of fossilised medieval strip-cultivation units; here and elsewhere, fragmentation is also caused by the piecemeal reclamation of land from forest and bog, the tradition of equal land inheritance (**gavelkind**), or the need to give farmers equal shares of good and bad soils.

In order to bring such anachronistic agricultural landscapes up to date, and to encourage modernisation and technological innovation in farming, many countries have introduced land consolidation schemes. Some of these schemes are simple, small and piecemeal; others are massive programmes whereby farm and field amalgamations are linked to general infrastructure improvements – drainage or irrigation, water and soil conservation, road and rail construction, increased training and education for farmers. Such comprehensive programmes are found in both the developed and less developed world, and result in greater farm output, a decline in subsistence agriculture and substantial rural depopulation as fewer workers are required on the land and displaced farmers move to the towns.

France

General consolidation schemes were first introduced towards the end of the 1939–45 war before which the average size of French farms was only 20 ha. Land fragmentation was especially acute in the Central Massif and in the south, so it was in these areas that further, and more specific, consolidation programmes were set up after 1960. Prior to this date a typical upland farm would be just 10 ha in size and be divided into more than 200 field plots. Today, over 600 000 ha of land in France are being consolidated annually and the average size of farms has increased to over 50 ha. In the Central Massif the farms now average 30 ha in size, and less than 20 field plots (largely given over to vines, fruit, maize, rye and beef cattle).

India

Land fragmentation is a problem throughout the subcontinent. But it is especially problematical on the Himalayan foothills in the states of Punjab and Uttar Pradesh where farms average less than 25 ha in size and as many as 30 plots. Consolidation schemes, financed from central government funds, began after 1960 and were accompanied by large-scale irrigation programmes, farm modernisation and technological innovation projects and the introduction of new high-yielding seed varieties. Generally, farm size has remained the same but plots have been amalgamated (see Fig. 7.5). The number of tenant farmers has been greatly reduced and the land produces larger quantities of rice, wheat, gram (a type of bean), millet, barley, cotton, oil seeds and sugar cane – the last three grown as cash crops.

Before   **After**

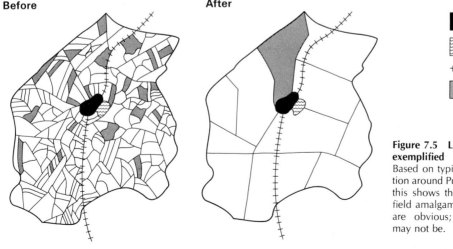

Key

■ village

≈ pond

+++++ railway

▦ land owned or rented by a single farmer

Figure 7.5 Land consolidation exemplified
Based on typical schemes in operation around Punjabi villages in India, this shows the impact of farm and field amalgamation. The advantages are obvious; some disadvantages may not be.

other aspects of agriculture. In relatively poor countries, it is usual for farmers to be their own merchants: they will take their produce to the local market and sell direct to the customer. With economic progress, however, and the distribution of farm produce over large areas (perhaps across the world), wholesalers and retailers begin to emerge. Generally, the more advanced the society, the more comprehensive and complex are the marketing systems used.

Agricultural produce that deteriorates rapidly, or requires expensive processing, is often marketed through national agencies. In Britain, for instance, the Milk Marketing Board, Egg Marketing Board and Sugar Corporation all exist to transfer produce from farm to customer. Similarly, large companies (often those owning supermarket chains) may act as both wholesalers and retailers. Sometimes such companies even maintain their own farms and act as landlords to tenant farmers, as in the case, in Britain, of the retail associates of the Co-operative Wholesale Society.

In many countries, marketing is undertaken through co-operatives: associations of farmers which exist to increase efficiency and reduce costs. Often co-operation is extended to include other agricultural pursuits. In Denmark and the Netherlands, co-operative schemes are so well developed that farmers take advantage of them in almost every part of the food production process – purchasing and using capital equipment, buying seeds, fertilisers and fodder, and converting produce into marketable goods, as with cream separation, butter making, packaging and canning. Elsewhere, as in West Germany, Britain and most developing countries, co-operation is not as widespread nor as well organised as this. Even so, its advantages are obvious and it seems likely that co-operatives will become more common in future.

Influences on agriculture

The character of agriculture is the result of the interaction of a complex array of physical and human factors. These combine to produce possible courses of action, some of which are acted upon by farmers who make their decisions on the strength of behavioural and chance elements (Fig. 7.6). However, there is a tendency for certain factors to produce set agricultural characteristics, and these are now discussed.

Climate
This is a fundamental determinant of agriculture

since all plants need warmth, sunshine and water in order to survive.

Heat is necessary for the germination of seeds and, although requirements vary from plant to plant, it is generally true that a minimum temperature of about 6°C is needed for crop growth. This naturally rules out high latitudes as potential agricultural regions – little farming of any kind is possible inside the Arctic Circle. Wheat needs warmer temperatures than barley (one of the least demanding grain crops) and cannot be grown above the 60° parallel. The latitudinal limit in both hemispheres is about 50° to ripen maize and about 35° for cotton. In some instances these limits can be extended by the scientific improvement of plant strains, but its high cost often makes such an extension impracticable.

The occurrence of frost may cause damage to some crops such as fruits, coffee and cotton, at times in their growth when they are vulnerable, but its ability to kill pests and break up the soil at other times can be an advantage (as in winter on the wheat-growing Prairies of North America).

Sunshine and dry summers facilitate ripening and early harvesting and it is not surprising that regions of persistent cloud cover tend to have poor-quality yields. Water, too, is essential for plant growth, but it must be available at the right times of the year (differing with different crops). Prolonged aridity can be as disastrous as continual rainfall in causing crop losses. Some plants are particularly demanding in their water requirements. Cotton cannot be grown where the rainfall is either below 550 mm a year or above 1150 mm (unless, of course, irrigation is adopted as in Texas and southern California). Rice usually needs at least 1500 mm of rainfall each year and rubber grows best where annual rainfall exceeds 1700 mm.

The length of the growing season is important not just for the ripening process but also for the variety of agricultural produce. Where the growing period is short, as in tundra regions, there is a limited range of plants. In equatorial regions, where growth takes place all year round, there is a great range of plants.

Wind is another element of climate that affects agriculture. It increases transpiration, thus reducing the effectiveness of rainfall, and loosens root systems, making tall plants difficult to grow in exposed places. Very strong winds can cause extensive damage, both by flattening crops and by causing soil erosion. In dry regions this is a serious problem, as was shown by the Dust Bowl of the American Mid-West. Cold local winds like the mistral of southern France can bring

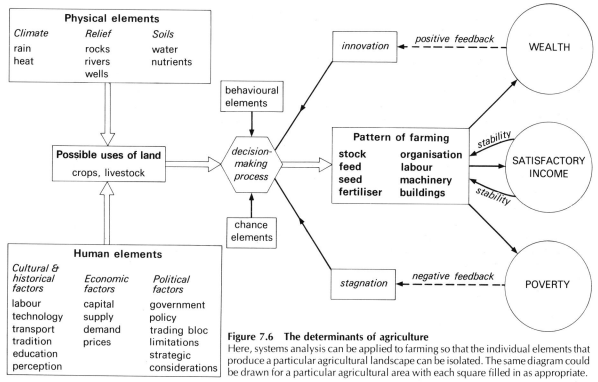

Figure 7.6   The determinants of agriculture
Here, systems analysis can be applied to farming so that the individual elements that produce a particular agricultural landscape can be isolated. The same diagram could be drawn for a particular agricultural area with each square filled in as appropriate.

about crop losses, and hot dry local winds, like the sirocco of southern Italy and Malta, can have a desiccating effect upon plants.

Relief and rocks
Agriculture is also influenced by topography. Increased altitude brings colder temperatures (by about 1°C every 200 m), greater precipitation and stronger winds, and thus tends to limit farming in some of the ways mentioned above (especially in regions outside the Tropics). The steepness of slopes similarly imposes a significant control. The steeper the gradient, the greater is the risk of soil erosion and the more difficult and dangerous is the use of machinery. It has been estimated that efficient cultivation is impossible on gradients of more than 11° and all cultivation is impossible on 18° slopes (Fig. 7.7).

Rock type helps to create both topography and the nature of the soil, and therefore may be seen as having an indirect effect on farming. Generally speaking, hard igneous acid rocks like granite are associated with areas of low agricultural potential, often being regions of mountains, moorland or forest useful only for the rough pasturage of sheep, beef cattle or goats.

Limestone, chalk, sandstone and other similar permeable rocks underlie thin soils, which lack surface drainage and may be covered by short grass or heathland. Here, too, rough pasturage is common (except where heavy fertilisation has taken place).

Because of these relief and rock factors, large-scale cultivation is mostly restricted to lowland or flat regions in the Temperate Zones.

Soils
Apart from being heavily influenced by rock type, soils are the result of past and present climatic conditions, vegetation, soil organisms and man's activities. They vary widely in their structure, texture, depth, workability and fertility, and consequently lead to wide variations in agricultural activities.

Soils which are either too acid (like sand deposits) or too alkaline (like fen peat) tend to be poor for farming. Heavy clays are difficult to plough and are easily waterlogged, and light, porous soils tend to be dry and lacking in nutrients. Some of the finest natural soils for cultivation are alluvial deposits, glacial till, loess and loam, each of which tends to be fertile and friable. In temperate regions these are

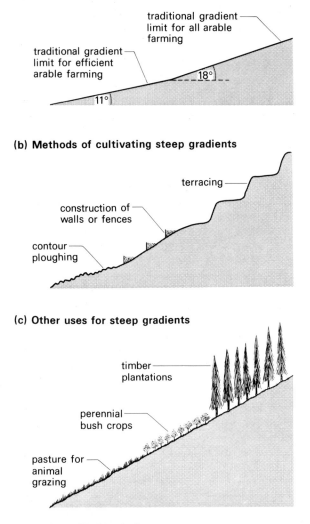

(a) Natural limits to cultivation

traditional gradient limit for all arable farming

traditional gradient limit for efficient arable farming

18°

11°

(b) Methods of cultivating steep gradients

terracing

construction of walls or fences

contour ploughing

(c) Other uses for steep gradients

timber plantations

perennial bush crops

pasture for animal grazing

Figure 7.7 Hillside agriculture
The steeper the gradient, the more difficult is cultivation. For this reason, arable farming tends to be found on flat or gently undulating ground and pastoral farming on upland areas. Some animals, such as sheep and goats, are especially well suited to mountain terrain. If demand for crops is sufficiently high, farmers will adapt hillsides for cultivation.

usually turned over to rich arable land, fruit growing or market gardening.

Culture
Within the constraints set by nature there is little doubt that social customs influence the character of farming in many regions. The veneration of cattle in the African savanna lands, and among Hindus, is a well known and somewhat extreme example of this. Similarly, there seems to be a strong link between the tribal system and shifting cultivation since the two are invariably found together. On the other hand, countries where a strict social order exists are likely to maintain systems of tenancy farming, and freehold farming is only common where there is a long history of democracy and individual freedom.

Culture may also be reflected in farm and field patterns. The custom of **gavelkind** whereby land is distributed equally among heirs, leads to the continual fragmentation of farming units. **Primogeniture** (the inheritance by the eldest child only) tends to maintain farm size and compactness. Tenancy systems of all kinds may lead to the expansion of both farms and fields since it is often only landlords who can raise the capital needed for farm unit amalgamation and rationalisation.

In some parts of the world, agricultural incomes are so meagre that farmers must engage in secondary occupations. In Scandinavia many supplement their earnings in winter through fishing or forestry, and in France, the Low Countries and West Germany, many hold full-time jobs in nearby towns and farm their smallholdings only during their 'leisure' time.

Demand
Wherever commercial farming is practised, economic factors are rapidly becoming the most important influence of all on agriculture. Clearly, a farmer will only produce those commodities that bring in sufficient profits to make his labour worth while. In effect, the area under arable and pasture fluctuates with changes in market prices: should demand for cereals rise more than the demand for meat or milk, then the area under arable crops would increase and that under pasture decrease. For example, barley is currently replacing sheep pasture over large tracts of chalk country in southern England, doubtless because it is more profitable than either wool or mutton.

Transport
Farmers need efficient transport both to link them with their markets and to obtain seeds, fodder and fertiliser. There has, therefore, always been a significant connection between communications and agricultural production. In North America the building of the railways converted ranching lands into rich grain-producing areas because the transport of inputs and produce became easier, and in Argentina and Australia the invention of refrigerated transport

greatly extended the potential grazing regions for sheep and beef cattle, since meat could be carried over greater distances without deteriorating.

In advanced economies especially, the cost, speed and frequency of transport services are all dominant factors in determining farming systems. Bulky and heavy products, like potatoes and sugar beet, are expensive to transport and are therefore often grown close to urban markets, or processing factories. Highly perishable commodities, such as peas, lettuces, soft fruit and dairy produce, must also be produced near towns. High-value commodities, on the other hand, may be able to withstand high transport costs and might profitably be produced at great distances from their markets. For example, air transport is used to take expensive early-season fruit, vegetables and flowers from the Channel Isles and Isles of Scilly to the London, Birmingham and Manchester markets. On a larger scale, international transport is used to take exotic fruits and vegetables such as oranges and avocado pears from the mediterranean regions to temperate regions where they do not grow.

Labour
Agricultural systems have varying labour requirements. Some crops need little labour, others need constant attention, and others may need labour only during harvest times. For the most part, animals require a greater number of man hours than crops, although even here variations do occur. Upland sheep can be left untended for months on end, beef cattle need but scant attention, yet dairy cattle require constant care.

The availability, cost and type of labour will also influence a farmer's choice of crops and livestock. A shortage of labour may lead to extensive, highly mechanised methods, whereas a labour surplus could favour labour intensive forms of production. This can be seen in both developed and developing countries. The highly mechanised, intensive grain farming of Western Europe reflects the small agricultural labour force in that area, whereas the paddy-rice cultivation in South-East Asia indicates cheap and abundant labour supplies.

The seasonal labour requirements of certain commodities naturally cause problems. Either farmers must employ part-time or casual labour at harvest time or must subcontract work out. In periods when little work needs to be done, a regular labour force may be underemployed and reduced to short-time working.

One particular problem being faced in many European countries is the depopulation of rural areas. Low wages, dissatisfaction with working conditions and the better opportunities offered by industry are together, leading great numbers of farm labourers to move off the land. Improved mechanisation and the modification of farming systems have allowed increased output with the decreased workforce, but there is a limit to such change, and diminishing agricultural production is a very real danger for the future in certain areas such as northern Scotland and the Italian Mezzogiorno.

Capital
In primitive agricultural systems, financial capital is absent since farmers live largely from hand to mouth and from day to day. Little or no machinery is used and little effort is made to improve the land with fertilisers. With agricultural progress, however, capital does become important.

Capital availability, especially, can determine the character of farming. The greater the amount of money and equipment required, available and used, the more efficient agriculture can be, with larger farm units. Inefficient farming and small farms are common where capital is limited. The capital needed to set up plantations is so great that only companies and governments can usually afford such agricultural enterprises.

In economically advanced countries, there are many ways of raising capital. Banks, insurance companies, industrial organisations and governments are all able to supply loans to farmers and, in this way, improvements and experimentation can take place. In less advanced countries, however, funds are generally less readily available. Peasant farmers are sometimes forced, in years of poor harvest, to borrow from money-lenders, and successive bad years may increase their debts to levels from which they can never free themselves. Such are the exorbitant interest charges on these debts that profit margins are severely reduced and the farmers cannot afford essential agricultural improvements. In parts of South-East Asia, the Middle East and southern Europe, this rural indebtedness is so serious a problem that agricultural progress is almost non-existent.

Politics
In most countries today, governments exert both direct and indirect controls over agriculture. In Communist states, of course, this control is direct and

absolute, but elsewhere it is normally operated indirectly through subsidies, land taxes, food prices, wage levels and various trading policies. In many cases, a central authority instigates land reclamation schemes, farm consolidation, agricultural research and education, and these also may have an effect on farm patterns and development.

The extent and strength of government control varies from time to time and from place to place. Between the two World Wars many European countries introduced policies that compelled farmers to produce certain commodities as part of a drive towards self-sufficiency. In other countries, governmental interference has always been minimal and farmers can generally grow what crops they like.

The problem of farm fragmentation can, by its very nature, only be tackled by a central authority, and for many years consolidation programmes have been instigated in several countries. In France, such a programme began in 1941, since when over 7 million ha of farmland have been reorganised. Similar schemes are under way in West Germany and the Netherlands.

The nature of international trade, and especially the existence of trade barriers, is a further influence on agriculture. Around the European Economic Community there is a high tariff wall, which controls the import of cheap food supplies from countries in the rest of the world. This protection results in the continuation within many European countries (particularly France) of inefficient farming methods, which would disappear under conditions of greater competition. Indeed, the EEC has a double effect on farming: not only does it maintain present systems, but it also determines the nature of production. In Britain, policies adopted as a result of joining the Community have led to a significant reduction in fruit growing and dairying and a concomitant increase in the cultivation of cereals. In Europe as a whole there has been, over the past 20 years, a significant increase in the production of grapes, wheat, barley, sugar beet and maize as a direct result of the Common Agricultural Policy.

EEC COMMON AGRICULTURAL POLICY

Objectives

(1) To increase farm efficiency and productivity by subsidising agricultural modernisation and land consolidation schemes.

(2) To standardise produce-quality levels by imposing rigid marketing systems and product controls.

(3) To ensure a standard of living for agricultural workers comparable with industrial workers by guaranteeing fixed prices and high profitability.

(4) To provide adequate and constant food supplies to the populations of member countries by presetting farm prices, irrespective of the laws of supply and demand.

(5) To establish, ultimately, common price levels for all agricultural goods by replacing trade barriers with levies to offset internal price differences.

Effects

(1) High fixed food prices have caused falls in demand and supply surpluses, leading to the well publicised 'butter mountains', 'beef mountains' and 'wine lakes'. Such surpluses involve high storage costs for warehousing and administration. Frequently, surplus produce is sold outside the EEC at prices far lower than those available to Community consumers.

(2) Guaranteed prices and profit margins have discouraged agricultural improvement, inefficient farmers (e.g. in France) being given little incentive to modernise.

(3) The high tariff wall around the EEC restricts member countries in their purchase of cheap food supplies from elsewhere in the world (e.g. Britain buying lamb from New Zealand). This also leads to excessive price rises in food shops.

(4) Differential price levels for foods have caused some undervalued commodities (e.g. English cooking apples) to disappear since they are no longer profitable.

(5) Unfair systems of farm price controls and of financing the EEC budget lead to political disagreement and acrimony between member countries (e.g. between Britain and France).

(6) About 75% of the Community budget has been used in the interests of a very small proportion of the EEC population (e.g. the politically powerful French farmers). Consequently, there is little money available for non-agricultural projects such as urban, industrial, commercial enterprise improvements.

Agricultural classification

Agriculture is, then, influenced by numerous factors and it is not surprising that within even small regions there will be differences in farm types, landscape and organisation. Even so, many geographers have attempted both to classify and to map agricultural areas.

In the 1930s many attempts were made, basing agricultural regions on climatic divisions. Grigg (*Economic Geography* **45**, 1969, pp. 95–132) was more scientific in approach and tried to distinguish farming types using such criteria as the degree of commercialism, type of tenure and scale of enterprise, intensity of agriculture, crop and livestock combinations and method of farming. These aspects provide a logical framework but pose certain problems. How, for example, can intensive farming be defined? British dairying and Asian rice growing are both intensive but can hardly be called similar. Even the apparently simple pastoral/arable division contains complications. India has about 20% of the world's cattle but can scarcely be termed a country of pastoral economy since those animals are sacred and not used for human consumption.

Perhaps the most satisfactory attempt to classify world agricultural regions was that made by Whittlesey in 1936 (*Annals of the Association of American Geographers* **26**, 1936, pp. 199–240). He adopted five criteria: crop and livestock combinations, intensity of land use, processing and marketing methods, degree of mechanisation and types of agricultural buildings. The resulting classification involves 13 main types of agricultural region together with a further category of land virtually unused for farming.

However, a fundamental problem arising out of all classifications is that farming tends to change over time. For instance, greater wealth and increased aid given by developed to developing countries are blurring the distinctions between commercial and subsistence farming and between intensive and extensive practices. Monocultural systems are being modified by diversification of production (as in the case of the coffee *fazendas* in Brazil) whereas some mixed farming areas are becoming more specialised (as in the case of arable farming in England). Even the diversity of tenurial methods is being reduced as there is a spread of state ownership on the one hand and greater freehold farming on the other.

Methods used to distinguish and categorise agricultural regions, by land use, intensity or mechanisation levels tend to be objective but the initial concept of classification is subjective. All divisions of the human landscape into categories are arbitrary since they are valid only for the purposes for which they are designed. A classification based on farming methods would be of little use in the study of crop and livestock characteristics; regions based on agricultural land use would be useless in the study of farm organisation and ownership. The same is true of agricultural hierarchies: their utility is limited to their own objectives.

Notwithstanding the shortcomings of agricultural classification, the investigation of the spatial nature of farming patterns is useful because it highlights the processes involved in land-use distributions. Many geographers conclude that existing agricultural patterns are the outcome of two principal processes, **innovation** and **diffusion**. The first produces a land-use pattern, based on the interrelationship between the physical environment and man's behaviour. The second produces land-use changes in both character and location, resulting from the rate of adoption of new techniques and the spread of farm patterns.

Innovation determines an initial or original agricultural landscape, which can usually be mapped. From this, three kinds of farming regions can normally be identified: uniform, core and multicore. Uniform agricultural regions exist where land-use types are spread evenly or where the intensity of farming is homogeneous throughout an area. A core agricultural region exists where farming is set around a central point or focus (often a town or market place). Such a core acts as a centre of gravity from which farm output or the intensity of production decreases outwards through concentric zones. In England the traditional core of hop growing in Kent is the Maidstone area; the core of market gardening in the south-west Midlands is Evesham (see Fig. 7.8). In the USA the core of the Tennessee tobacco region is Greenville. A multicore agricultural region exists where a farming zone possesses a number of separate focal points. The old 'cotton belt' of the southern USA was set around the cores of New Orleans, Houston, Galveston and Dallas. The coffee region of south-east Brazil is set around Londrina, Marilia and Ribeirao Preto.

Diffusion introduces alterations in agricultural landscapes, as a result of either expansion or relocation. For various physical and human reasons, a farming region may either grow or diminish in size. It might even shift entirely. In Britain the sugar beet regions of East Anglia have expanded considerably over the past 20 years; the sheep grazing regions of Wales have contracted. In Ghana, the cocoa belt has

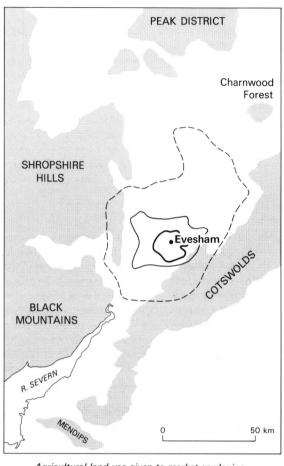

Figure 7.8 Agricultural core region in the English south-west Midlands
The Severn Valley and Vale of Gloucester are famous for the growing of plums and cherries and of such salad crops as asparagus, lettuce, cauliflower and tomatoes. Such agriculture becomes more intensive – and covers a greater proportion of farmland – towards the core at the town of Evesham. This is where market gardening first began.

moved inland and westwards from its original focal point 50 km north of Accra (Fig. 7.9).

World agricultural regions

Despite the problems and subjectivity of agricultural classification, certain global zones of land use can be identified. The following agricultural regions are based on simple environmental criteria and they help to identify the links between physical geography and land-use characteristics.

Equatorial regions
These areas are hot and wet, may have a natural vegetation of dense evergreen forests and tend to be far removed from civilisation. Primitive subsistence farming is common, especially shifting cultivation, as practised for example by Indian tribes of the Amazon (like the Boro) and African tribes of the Congo (like the Ubangi).

The natives clear areas of forest, often by the slash and burn method, and grow foodstuffs such as yams, manioc, beans, millet and sweet potatoes. They may also hunt wild animals and gather various useful products from the surrounding trees such as cacao, rubber, palm oil and wax. After a time, perhaps two or three years, the soil becomes exhausted or leached and the cultivators are forced to move on and clear

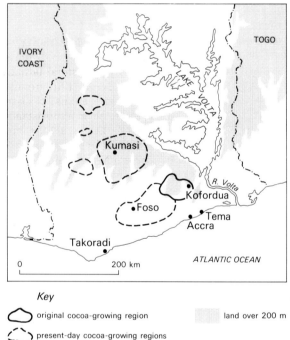

Figure 7.9 Diffusion of cocoa-growing regions in Ghana
Colonial cocoa-growing developed in the Akwapim area, around the core of Kofordua, where the soils and dense rainforests were most conducive to the cultivation of the crop. The region was close to the port of Accra (connected by rail) and had a large surplus labour market. Today this region has declined in importance as a result of overproduction, insect damage, disease and the increased age of the trees. New cocoa regions have appeared elsewhere and around new cores, reflecting the greater penetration of communications.

new areas of forest. In recent years there have been attempts to encourage more sedentary methods, but these have met with only limited success so far. The tribal system, lack of education and suspicion of new techniques are partly the cause of this failure.

Commercial agriculture is found in equatorial regions, often where foreign investment has created plantations. The main crops grown under this system of monoculture are rubber (Malaysia and Indonesia, Sri Lanka and Liberia), and cacao (in Ghana and Zaïre). Plantations may cover several thousand hectares and, since heavy investment is required, are usually owned and run by large companies or governments. Cheap labour is normally employed and both transport and marketing are efficiently organised. For political and social reasons, some plantations, like those in Ghana and Malaysia, are now being subdivided into smaller holdings and native growers are being given some degree of tenurial freedom.

Savanna regions

In these areas hot temperatures and heavy summer rainfall are experienced over a vegetation of grassland. This lends itself naturally to pastoral farming although, since land is generally plentiful, populations sparse and uneducated and animal diseases prevalent, such farming tends to be on a subsistence, shifting and extensive level. Beef cattle are the most commonly reared animals and can be found grazed by nomadic herdsmen in northern Nigeria and Zambia, and by sedentary pastoralists in the northern interior of Australia where grazing is more successful owing to the absence of the tsetse fly.

As with equatorial regions, plantations are common here where foreign intervention has occurred. The main types are those growing coffee (southern Brazil), sugar cane (West Indies) and groundnuts (West Africa).

Hot desert regions

The extreme aridity of these areas prevents the growth of much natural vegetation, except patches of poor grass and desert plants like cacti. Shifting subsistence pastoralism is most common, as exemplified by the nomadic Bedouin tribes of the Sahara. Herds of goats, sheep and camels are continually moved, from oasis to oasis, water-hole to water-hole and from north to south with the changing seasons, towards the Mediterranean in winter and towards Central Africa in summer, seeking the seasonal rains. The herders live largely on meat and milk with occasional supplies of vegetables and fruit from the oases they pass. Their homes are tents and their clothes are made of hides and skins.

Sedentary farming is found only where water is available. Here labour-intensive methods and irrigation allow for the growing of maize, rice, cotton, sugar cane and date palm. Sometimes winter crops are possible and cereals may be cultivated. Oasis farming was once only a subsistence activity but today it is becoming more commercial as transport improves and the demand for its produce increases. Even so, it remains on a small scale and farms rarely exceed 20 ha.

Monsoon regions

Hot temperatures and heavy seasonal rainfall in monsoon regions have given rise to a natural vegetation cover of deciduous forest, grassland and thorn bush. In South-East Asia – the principal monsoon region – an extremely high population density has led to oriental intensive agriculture. Rice, the dominant crop, is grown in paddy fields using primitive labour techniques. Farms are small and often fragmented, but high yields can be achieved by constant applications of fertiliser, crop rotation, the practice of double cropping, the widespread use of irrigation and intensive use of labour.

The local demand for food is so high that this oriental farming rarely provides a marketable surplus, and is therefore operated as a subsistence system. Dry seasons often permit the cultivation of a second crop (barley, millet, beans or vegetables), but this too is consumed by the farmers and their families. Only a few animals are kept, mostly pigs and poultry, and these are usually left to forage for themselves. Even so, they may provide the cultivators with a welcome supplement to their otherwise starchy diet.

Mediterranean regions

Warm to hot summer temperatures, and rainfall confined mainly to winter, lead to a natural maquis vegetation of evergreen trees, grassland and shrubs. Nearly all types of farming are found in these mediterranean regions. In the poorer areas, peasant subsistence cultivation is common, and pastoralism is found on uplands and where soils are infertile. The main advantage for commercial agriculture is that farming is possible all year round. In summer, with the aid of irrigation, citrus fruits, peaches, figs, olives and grapes are harvested. In winter, cereals, deciduous fruit (such as apples and pears) and vegetables can be cultivated.

undertaken intensively in generally small agricultural units. There is a bias towards dairying in wetter parts, towards cereals in drier parts, and towards horticulture around urban markets.

Other forms of commercial farming include extensive pastoralism and extensive grain production. Livestock ranching utilises the natural grasslands of temperate interiors and hence is a feature of the North American Mid-West, the Russian steppes and parts of Argentina. Geared to the rearing of beef cattle and sheep, it is undertaken on an immense scale. Most American ranches are over 1000 ha and many are over 4000 ha. Animal densities are very low, but the quality of meat is high as a result of specialisation, high capital expenditure and efficient breeding techniques.

Extensive grain farming emerged after the Industrial Revolution when the demand for food rose and the development of machinery permitted the conversion of natural grasslands to arable land and the cultivation of formerly marginal land. Farms and fields tend to be large and the use of labour is minimal. In many areas such grain farming takes the form of monoculture: wheat in the Canadian Prairies, northern central USA and the Russian steppes, and maize in the central Mississippi Lowlands.

Tundra regions

Long, cold winters and short summers in tundra regions are conducive to little agriculture beyond primitive subsistence methods. Pockets of fertile soil, especially near coastlines, may support small sedentary mixed farms, but over vast areas nomadic pastoralism is most common. Tribes like the Lapps, Samoyeds and Tungus of northern Eurasia herd reindeer on the summer mosses and lichens, or in the forests, and supplement their livelihood with hunting, fishing and forestry.

Mountain regions

Mountainous areas generally have shorter growing periods than are usual in surrounding lowlands, and the number and types of crops that may be grown are therefore restricted. This is especially true in mediterranean and temperate regions. In southern Scotland, for example, the length of the growing season decreases from 240 days at sea level to 180 days at 330 m and to only 135 days at 600 m. Only occasionally, where nearby lowlands are too hot for cultivation, can mountains actually be advantageous to agriculture – as is the case in tropical areas. In Java the best tea is grown at heights of 1200–1800 m and in

Figure 7.10 Alpine farming
In this part of Switzerland (Chirfirsten-Wallenstaat) the importance of topography in determining agriculture is well exemplified. We are looking towards a south-facing slope.

Farms in mediterranean regions, with the exception of the large estates (**latifundia**) found in Spain, tend to be small, and agricultural methods fairly labour intensive. Even vineyards, which exemplify highly commercial monoculture, rarely exceed 50 ha.

Temperate regions

Most of the world's major agricultural areas are found in the Temperate Zone, partly as a result of the existence here of the most advanced countries and partly because of the moderate nature of the climate. Mixed, commercial farming is common in maritime regions, like north-west Europe and north-east USA, and is

Kenya the main coffee crop is grown between 1400 m and 1800 m.

In temperate areas of high relief, pastoralism is most commonly practised and arable farming is found only in valleys. Transhumance is a particular feature of these regions – a system whereby cattle are moved seasonally, grazing on the high mountain pastures during summer and being stall-fed in the valleys during winter. The valleys in summer are turned over to fodder crops, vegetables and, where climate permits, vines. Mountain agriculture is exemplified in the Alps, where farming also extends higher up the south-facing (adret) slopes than the north-facing

(ubac) slopes since aspect produces significant differences in both the strength and duration of sunshine. In areas of high population density, or where farming is profitable, many hillsides are terraced. (See Fig. 7.10.)

Occasionally, crops are grown not on valley floors but upon valley sides because of temperature inversion. Under certain conditions, cold air slumps to the lowest levels, forcing warmer air to rise above it. Coffee is susceptible to frost and for this reason is grown on the slopes of southern Brazil rather than in the valleys.

THE GREEN REVOLUTION

Since World War 2, great efforts have been made to improve agriculture and, in particular, to increase crop yields by a more intensive and efficient use of the land. These efforts have collectively been called the Green Revolution and examples of their development can be found in all parts of the world.

The intensification of agriculture can be undertaken through various processes. Modern technology and know-how enable the effects of soil erosion to be reduced, irrigation to be extended and made more effective, mechanisation, storage, handling and processing methods to be improved, and pests and diseases to be controlled. In addition, land ownership and management systems are being rationalised and new strains of crops and animals are being developed (see Fig. 7.11).

Much of the work involved in the Green Revolution takes place under the auspices of the FAO (the Food and Agriculture Organisation, of the United Nations) but individual countries also have their own programmes and experimental institutes. For instance, in the Philippines there is the Los Baños research institute (financed by the Ford and Rockefeller Foundation); in Italy much research is undertaken at Borgo under Shell Italiana; and in Britain the government runs the Rothamsted Experimental Station (Hertfordshire).

Hybridisation – the creation of plants with new genetic combinations – is an especially important aspect of the Green Revolution. This makes possible the evolution of new strains, faster growing crops and higher yields. It is largely as a result of hybridisation that the USA has been able to double its total food production over the last 30 years on a total cultivated area that has diminished by 13%. There are many hybrid plants today – maizes, wheats, fodder grasses and rices. The new improved 'miracle rice' (such as IR31) has been particularly successful and 10% of India's total paddy land is planted with this variety.

Another promising development is the use of synthetic hormones, which regulate plant sizes and growth rates. Many of these hormones are so potent that just a pinch is sufficient for a hectare of crops to grow larger and faster. Hormones can also make possible the extension, contraction or shifting of the growing season.

Other significant aspects of agricultural change include the increased use of fertilisers, pesticides, insecticides, herbicides and fungicides. World chemical fertiliser consumption has risen by about 10% per year since the early 1960s. The types used are mainly nitrogen, phosphate and potash, and in tropical areas their application has resulted in a doubling of crop yields. Pests and diseases affect both crops and animals, of course, and their eradication is fundamental for higher yields. New organic chemical pesticides are now used and these alone have increased yields in many developing countries such as India by as much as 30%. A particular menace in tropical areas is the locust, and swarms of these insects are now being combated with aldrin. One swarm sprayed with aldrin in northern Somalia in 1960 was estimated to weigh 30 000 tonnes.

The most common herbicides (weedkillers) now being used are those of hhe phenoxy group of chemicals, which kill weeds by stimulating their growth to such an extent that they 'burn themselves out'. Fungicides are often used to disinfect seeds prior to sowing and some chemicals are being used as defoliants to bring about a rapid collapse of the leaves and stems of plants so that their tubers attain high quality.

The Green Revolution is not without its problems: of cost, social upheaval, education, employment changes and, perhaps also, of danger to human health. But its success so far has certainly been staggering. In particular it has brought benefits to less developed countries and is helping the world cope with the population explosion.

AGRICULTURE

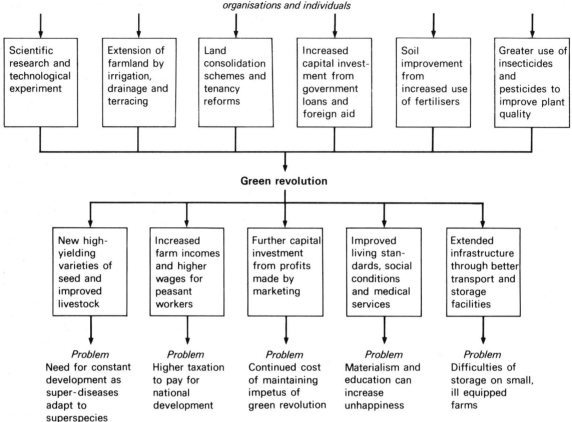

financial, political and technological encouragement from national governments, United Nations, independent aid organisations and individuals

| Scientific research and technological experiment | Extension of farmland by irrigation, drainage and terracing | Land consolidation schemes and tenancy reforms | Increased capital invest-ment from government loans and foreign aid | Soil improvement from increased use of fertilisers | Greater use of insecticides and pesticides to improve plant quality |

Green revolution

| New high-yielding varieties of seed and improved livestock | Increased farm incomes and higher wages for peasant workers | Further capital investment from profits made by marketing | Improved living stan-dards, social conditions and medical services | Extended infrastructure through better transport and storage facilities |

| *Problem*
Need for constant development as super-diseases adapt to superspecies | *Problem*
Higher taxation to pay for national development | *Problem*
Continued cost of maintaining impetus of green revolution | *Problem*
Materialism and education can increase unhappiness | *Problem*
Difficulties of storage on small, ill equipped farms |

Figure 7.11 The inputs and outputs of the Green Revolution
There are positive and negative aspects to the Green Revolution – farming progress is not necessarily advantageous to everyone.

A theory of agricultural location

The pattern of agriculture is the result of various physical and socio-economic factors, and set conditions tend to produce set agricultural landscapes. This has led many geographers to hypothesise about the general principles that may determine land use, and from these to develop theories or models for agricultural location.

The most famous model of all is that first proposed by Von Thünen in 1826. Von Thünen owned an estate near Rostock in northern Germany and his major work, *The isolated state*, was largely based on personal observations and deductions. The processes making for land-use patterns in that area, Von Thünen argued, might equally apply elsewhere and

with similar results. In other words, the model can be expanded into a general theory of land-use patterns.

The model in question is illustrated by the example of a single town in the midst of a uniform land surface where physical factors such as climate, relief, geology, soils and drainage remain constant and transport costs are directly proportional to distance. Each farmer would sell his surplus produce only in that town, would bear the total cost of transport himself, and would always aim to undertake that type of farming which yields maximum profits.

A cornerstone of the theory is the principle of **economic rent**, whereby different types of land use produce different net returns per unit area (Fig. 7.12). Of the three commodities, potatoes yield the largest bulk per hectare and require the highest transport

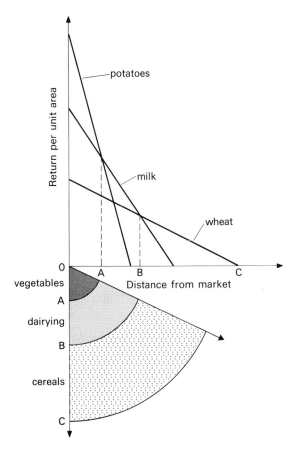

Figure 7.12 Economic rent for agricultural produce
These three commodities have different profit curves and are thus found at different distances from the market.

costs. The income from potatoes therefore falls sharply away from the market, making them profitable only around the urban fringe. Milk is less bulky per hectare than potatoes but still needs to be fairly near the market because it is perishable. Wheat is the least perishable and also the cheapest to transport. It can therefore be grown at a profit, even at some considerable distance from the central town. The result is that potatoes will be grown most profitably between O and A, dairying will take place between A and B and wheat (together, perhaps, with other cereals) will be grown between B and C. By rotating the axis OABC through 360°, a concentric zonation of land use will be produced.

Such a concentric pattern of agriculture was drawn by Von Thünen around his own theoretical isolated urban centre (Fig. 7.13). Market gardening is located closest to the town since it requires the most intensive use of labour, involves the highest transport costs and

produces the most perishable goods. Being the most profitable land use, it is also undertaken most intensively. As distance from the market increases, however, the return per unit area from one form of agriculture falls to a point where it becomes more profitable to substitute another land use. There is a steady progression outwards of farming types which are successively less profitable and less intensively undertaken. Extensive cattle grazing was seen by Von Thünen as requiring least human attention and generating least transport cost, and is therefore found on the periphery.

The existence of wood production near the centre of Von Thünen's rings seems strange at first but it must be remembered that, in his day, timber was essential for fuel. It returned higher profits per hectare than cereals and was costly to transport.

Much has happened since the early part of the last century to modify the arrangement of crops in Von Thünen's original pattern. The carriage of goods is no longer slow, laborious and dependent upon animal transport, and the invention of refrigeration has largely diminished the importance of the perishability factor. In addition, the theory is open to some general criticism. Crop yields vary from year to year according to weather conditions, market prices may fluctuate according to demand and returns per unit area are not as easy to estimate as Von Thünen suggested. Also, in the real world, uniform land surfaces are rarely if ever found, and farmers seldom act rationally. Few farmers share the same evaluation of the land or the same ideas of what is a just remuneration for their work.

Thus, we must realise that when Von Thünen's hypothesis is applied to real world conditions, distortions are likely to occur in the ideal concentric ring patterns he envisaged. This does not detract from the usefulness of the model, however. Studies of selected regions in the world show that, as a model, it has stood the test of time remarkably well. In many places, both on a small and large scale, concentric agricultural patterns may still be found. In the Netherlands, the model can be linked to labour costs. Plots of land less than half a kilometre from farmsteads receive, on average, about 400 man-hours per hectare annually. At a distance of 2 km this figure falls to about 300 man-hours and at 5 km to 150 man-hours. In Cyprus, villages are surrounded by successive rings of vegetables, olives, grain, vineyards and, beyond these, goat pastures.

Even in highly developed countries, where technology might be expected to dispel Von Thünen's

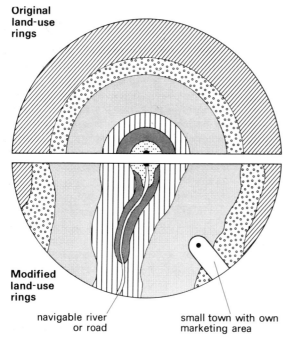

Original land-use rings

Modified land-use rings

navigable river or road

small town with own marketing area

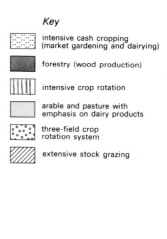

Key

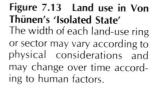

intensive cash cropping (market gardening and dairying)

forestry (wood production)

intensive crop rotation

arable and pasture with emphasis on dairy products

three-field crop rotation system

extensive stock grazing

Figure 7.13 Land use in Von Thünen's 'Isolated State'
The width of each land-use ring or sector may vary according to physical considerations and may change over time according to human factors.

principles completely, land use can be seen to correlate with unit returns. The fact that market gardening remains a feature of rural–urban fringes is more than coincidentally similar to the original isolated state concept. It is of further interest to note that agriculture in Western Europe becomes progressively less intensive in zones radiating out from a centre in the Low Countries.

A model for agricultural land values

One aspect of agricultural land use that seems not to have concerned Von Thünen is the way in which it can be determined, and can change, in response to urban growth. This fact has led many geographers fundamentally to modify Von Thünen's original hypothesis and to suggest alternative land-use patterns. One such geographer is R. Sinclair (*Annals of the Association of American Geographers* **57**, 1967, pp. 72–87).

Sinclair has developed a model in which agricultural land-use patterns are, to a certain extent at least, the reverse of those of Von Thünen. Instead of agriculture becoming less productive and less efficient away from a town, it actually becomes more productive and efficient (see Fig. 7.14). The reason for this, according to Sinclair, is the blight effect that urban sprawl has on land values.

As a town spreads outwards over the surrounding countryside, so farmland is eaten away by rural–urban fringe uses – waste tips, recreation grounds, cemeteries and so on. At the same time, there is greater interference from urban man: more pollution, road building, the infringement of 'country code' regulations and the arrival of building speculators who anticipate the further expansion of the town's limits. The sum total of this is to cause land values for purely agricultural purposes to fall, few farmers being willing to cultivate land over which suburban blight hangs. On such land, farmers are reluctant to invest money in agriculture. Instead, they allow their fields to deteriorate into 'demi-farming' (half-hearted agricultural activity) or else let them become vacant altogether with the intention of selling, at the most profitable time, to the speculative newcomers. Further afield, as the blight effect of urban sprawl diminishes, farmland values increase, as do the efficiency and productivity of agricultural practices.

Evidence to suggest that this Sinclair model is realistic can be obtained around certain Mid-West cities in the USA and around some British county towns where there is no 'Green Belt policy. Notwithstanding such evidence, it should also be remembered that this model is subject, as are all models, to the geographical variability of the real world.

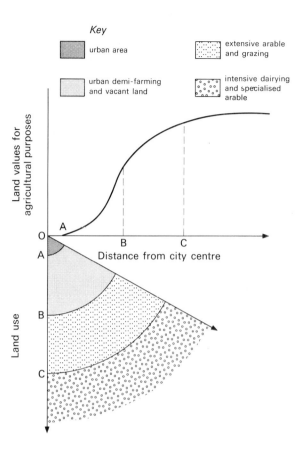

Key

urban area

extensive arable and grazing

urban demi-farming and vacant land

intensive dairying and specialised arable

Land values for agricultural purposes

O

A

A

B

C

B

C

Distance from city centre

Land use

Figure 7.14 The agricultural land value model (after R. Sinclair)
The efficiency and intensity of agriculture increase with distance from a city centre since farming activity is related to land values: the higher the values, the more productive will be the farming.

Meeting increased food demands

Mention has already been made in Chapter 5 of some of the ways in which man can improve agriculture. He can extend farming over a wider area and can increase yields on land already cultivated.

More than ever before, man, with his technological knowledge, is able to control the natural environment to suit his own ends. In areas of insufficient warmth, greenhouses, cloches or convector machines can be used; in areas of insufficient rainfall, irrigation can be practised. Contour ploughing and terracing enable steep slopes to be cultivated, and fertilisers can correct mineral deficiencies in soil. Areas of marshland or waterlogged soils can be ditched, drained or pumped dry. The invention of the Ottomeyer deep

plough has brought formerly leached soils into farming, as in the heathlands of the Netherlands and northern Germany, and the 'stump jump plough' allows for the cultivation of areas not completely cleared of tree-stumps, as in Australia.

The development of special plant strains and the careful breeding of animals can similarly extend agricultural limits. Short-maturing varieties of wheat and hybrid maize have done much to bring marginal areas under the plough and in South America new potato strains are now permitting the use of Andean slopes and tropical rainforests for food production. Zebu cattle, which have been specially bred for arid conditions, are now common in many developing countries and today other animal breeds are being introduced. In Peru new grazing and breeding methods are resulting in the faster reproduction of alpacas and this may well revolutionise mountain farming. Instead of being reared solely for milk and wool, alpacas might in future be reared in large herds for meat on an extensive and commercial basis.

Changes now taking place in agricultural infra-structures are no less fundamental and important. Many countries today have set up development pro-grammes aimed at rationalising and modernising farm techniques. In some of these, the consolidation of fragmented land holdings is of prime importance; in France and West Germany, for instance, where some farms cover over 20 scattered plots. Elsewhere the merging of small farms into larger units is taking place – in Pakistan and India, for example, where over 90% of all farms are under 10 ha, a fact that has cer-tainly restricted agricultural improvements in the past.

As progress continues, many old and established systems of land tenure are disappearing. Although freehold ownership is becoming more common in the 'Free World', state ownership is spreading through those areas increasingly dominated by the Commun-ist nations. Share cropping is vanishing in places where it was once the norm and cash tenancy is becoming more secure for the farmer with increasing governmental control.

In short, the need for man to increase food produc-tion has set in motion a series of changes, which are reflected in agricultural geography at every level.

Summary

1 Agriculture can be classified into four pairs: arable/pastoral; shifting/sedentary; subsistence/

commercial; intensive/extensive. All continents have examples of each type, although both shifting and subsistence farming are beginning to disappear.

2 Many plantations in the less developed world have been repossessed by national governments from foreign ownership. Some are being subdivided and returned to peasant farmers, others are being turned into collective farms.

3 Agricultural landscapes include aspects of farm size and shape, field patterns, farmhouse architecture and field boundary characteristics. Such features reflect the environment and constantly change with economic necessity.

4 The physical influences on agriculture (geology, topography, climate, soils) are becoming less important compared with human influences (economics, politics, new technology).

5 Political influences on farming can be positive (leading to land consolidation schemes and higher yields) or negative (causing stagnation and inefficiency, as in the case of the EEC Agricultural Policy consequences).

6 Agricultural classifications are difficult to quantify, subjective in concept and limited in use. Even generally accepted agricultural region terms and characteristics – shifting cultivation, commercial pasturage, desert farming – are disputed by some geographers.

7 Farm regions can develop as a result of innovation (initial introduction of land use) and diffusion (change as a result of expansion or relocation). Core regions are common, in which farming specialisation decreases outwards from a central point.

8 The Green Revolution (through scientific improvement) is helping to feed the world's growing population, but is resulting in economic and social problems. In Third World countries, debts are being incurred to finance the continued search for new crop strains.

9 Agricultural land-use patterns may be quantified through theories and models. Von Thünen suggested that intensity of activity and perishability of farm produce decrease away from towns. Sinclair suggested that the towns give rise to 'demi-farming' on their peripheries.

10 Laws concerning land use appear to have substance, on both a local (among farms) and a continental scale (across national boundaries). However, behavioural factors influencing agriculture should not be ignored.

Data–response exercises

1 Account for and compare the distributions of woodland in Figures 7.1 (Japan) and 7.2 (Canada). To what extent would it appear that these woodlands help farming practices?

2 Examine the possible advantages and disadvantages that may result from such a land consolidation scheme in the Punjab suggested in Figure 7.5. What might be the consequences to the social and economic character of the village itself?

3 With the aid of regional geography textbooks, draw a diagram based on Figure 7.6 to show a particular agricultural area (e.g. East Anglia, Paris Basin, Argentine Pampas) as viewed through systems analysis.

4 Suggest reasons why market gardening developed first around the town of Evesham (see Fig. 7.8) and outline the advantages to be gained from agriculture being based on such a core region.

5 Draw an annotated sketch view of Figure 7.10 to show the relationship between physical and human geography. What evidence is there to suggest that the Alps have reached their maximum agricultural capability?

6 Figure 7.11 shows the reasons for and results of the Green Revolution. Expound upon the negative aspects of this advancement in farming techniques and suggest how thay might be reduced.

7 Place tracing paper over a land-use map and draw concentric rings around a chosen town or village. Colour in the agricultural types in each circular zone and calculate the percentage of each zone covered by each agricultural type. To what extent does the resulting pattern resemble Von Thünen's hypothesis? Is there any evidence to suggest the existence of demi-farming (as suggested by Sinclair)? Account for the pattern you find.

8 Outline the possible consequences for the value of agricultural land around a town (Fig. 7.14) of (a) population decrease; (b) stricter controls on urban growth.

8 Natural resources and energy

Introduction

Natural resources provide the products essential for human life: food, clothing, possessions, power and machinery. These resources are found under, on and above the surface of the Earth; as such, they can be regarded as the one link between man and his environment. The greater their exploitation, the stronger is the man–environment relationship; the more thoughtful and considerate their exploitation, the more intelligent and lasting the relationship.

The study of natural resources – as this chapter will demonstrate – goes far beyond the simple identification of the world's minerals and energy sources. Since resources form the essential link between man's behaviour and the physical landscape, they can be viewed as the pivots of human geography. To have a greater knowledge of natural resources is to understand more fully man's actions and the Earth's character; to have a deeper comprehension of behavioural patterns and the Earth's morphology is to understand more fully the importance of natural resources. In short, the world's resource capacity is central to the geographical scope of this book, and its study is as broad and wide ranging.

The questions to be answered by this chapter are as follows:

- How do we define and classify natural resources, and what are the problems of classification?
- What are the main resources, and where are they found?
- How and why are resources exploited, and what difficulties must be overcome in their exploitation?
- What is the impact of resource exploitation on the environment?
- How fast are resources being consumed, and can conservation help to prolong man's dependence on known supplies?
- Which new resources might be discovered and used in the future?

Resource classification

So diverse are the characteristics of natural resources that no classification or subdivision is easy. They can be grouped and categorised according to different sets of criteria, or can be listed, ranked and put into a hierarchy according to their innate attributes. Some of the ways in which classification can be made are shown in Figure 8.1. Here, separate subdivisions can be made within each criterion. In addition, we can identify organic and inorganic resources (based on their physical properties); and physical, economic and social resources (based on their environmental character). Physical resources are those inanimate attributes that produce basic wealth (such as rocks, climate, soils); economic resources are those productive attributes that lead to human advancement (such as labour supplies, energy sources, minerals, communications); social resources are those acquired attributes that advance societal wellbeing (such as welfare services, academic structures, living-space provision).

The term 'natural resources' is all-embracing. If it is defined as 'the geographical features of the world that enable man to realise his initiative', then almost everything can be called a natural resource. Apart from the more obvious elements, such as minerals, rocks, soils, water, plants and animals, we can include air, location, climate, man's skill, dexterity and intellect, even human resourcefulness. Air is vital for life and also for the various gases that it contains, which can be used industrially (oxygen, nitrogen, argon, hydrogen, helium, krypton and several others). Location – for example the degree of accessibility – can be important in the encouragement of economic development: an advantageous position, for instance, can be the main reason for the development of a port (such as Singapore). Climate is not only important for agriculture and the tourist industry, but it can also indirectly influence industrialisation through the use, for example, of wind and solar energy for power or through the use of rain and surface water in manufacturing processes. Man's intelligence and physical ability are certainly a

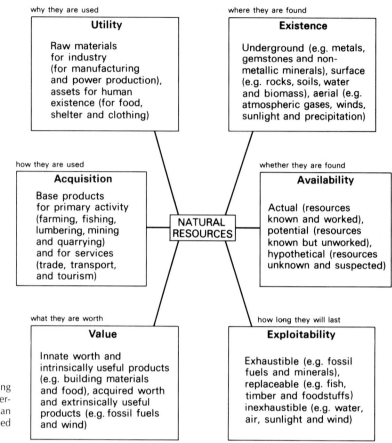

why they are used

Utility

Raw materials
for industry
(for manufacturing
and power production),
assets for human
existence (for food,
shelter and clothing)

where they are found

Existence

Underground (e.g. metals,
gemstones and non-
metallic minerals), surface
(e.g. rocks, soils, water
and biomass), aerial (e.g.
atmospheric gases, winds,
sunlight and precipitation)

how they are used

Acquisition

Base products
for primary activity
(farming, fishing,
lumbering, mining
and quarrying)
and for services
(trade, transport,
and tourism)

NATURAL RESOURCES

whether they are found

Availability

Actual (resources
known and worked),
potential (resources
known but unworked),
hypothetical (resources
unknown and suspected)

what they are worth

Value

Innate worth and
intrinsically useful products
(e.g. building materials
and food), acquired worth
and extrinsically useful
products (e.g. fossil fuels
and wind)

how long they will last

Exploitability

Exhaustible (e.g. fossil
fuels and minerals),
replaceable (e.g. fish,
timber and foodstuffs)
inexhaustible (e.g. water,
air, sunlight and wind)

Figure 8.1 Classifications of natural resources
There are six main criteria for classifying resources. These, of course, overlap and inter-relate. Further subdivisions and categories can be made within each box for more detailed study.

resource, and a country inhabited by an innately inventive or hard-working population will tend to progress at a faster rate economically than one inhabited by a population that is predominantly ignorant or slow. Even the indefinable resource of luck or serendipity – in a country, a group of people or an individual – can make all the difference between success and failure: chance occurrences might identify economic possibilities in one country, yet not in another, even though the resources of the two might be the same.

Another aspect that becomes clear in the study of resource classification is the variable quality of natural resources. Some are very limited in quantity, others seem limitless; yet others appear to grow more abundant as new discoveries extend human knowledge. Some resources are being utilised fully, some are underused, some are latent and unused, some are still to be found. Even renewable resources that are limited in supply at any one moment; even those that are inexhaustible, may be affected by pollution or

ecological change. For no long period of time are the resources of the world stable in either quantity or quality, neither is their usefulness constant nor their importance the same. Moreover, it must be remembered that the value of resources is subject to human perception – an element only becomes a resource when its essential quality is perceived. The same factor may be termed a resource at one place or time but not a resource elsewhere.

World resource supplies

Excluding energy supplies (which will be discussed in the next section), the world's resources can be quantified and classified according to their degree of usefulness. For reasons of space, only the more important resources are studied below. Those having a direct bearing on agriculture were indicated in the previous chapter; those with a direct bearing on industry will be discussed in the succeeding chapter;

those that have a direct bearing on settlement will be considered in Part IV.

Fish

Of all the resources obtained from water, fish are by far the most important. They are a major source of food and various by-products (such as glue, fertiliser and liver oils) and there are numerous occupations involved in their extraction and processing.

Although nearly all countries possess freshwater fish such as carp, trout and roach, these are not generally of commercial significance. The saltwater varieties are much more important, and some countries, like Iceland, are almost entirely reliant on these for their existence.

Figure 8.2 shows the chief fishing grounds of the world. Their predominance in the temperate zone of the northern hemisphere is the result of geographical factors. Fish tend to prefer cooler (temperate) to warmer (tropical) waters; continental shelves, in whose shallow seas plankton are common, are better developed around northern continents; and coastal regions in temperate areas tend to be heavily populated, giving rise to the need for fish as a food resource. Japan, USSR, China and Peru possess the largest fishing industries, together accounting for over 40% of the world's total catch.

The main fish caught include **pelagic** varieties such as herring, sardine and mackerel, which live near the ocean surface, and **demersal** kinds such as cod, haddock, plaice and sole, which live at greater depths. Other marine animals caught include Crustacea (crabs, lobsters, crayfish), molluscs (oysters, cockles, mussels) and sea creatures such as dolphins, seals, turtles and whales.

Only about 40% of the world's total commercial fish catch is marketed fresh. Of the remainder, some is processed for human consumption by being canned, packaged, dried, cured or frozen; some goes to make fertilisers; and some is used in the manufacture of fish glue, petfood and liver oils. The ancillary industries dependent on fishing include boat building, the manufacture of nets and other fishing tackle, the making of cans and boxes, and the production of ice.

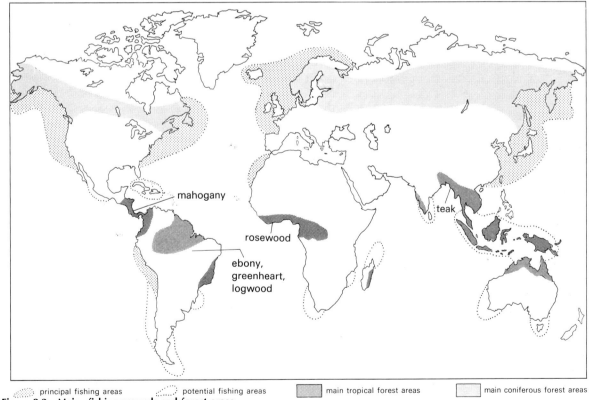

principal fishing areas ⋯ potential fishing areas ▓ main tropical forest areas ☐ main coniferous forest areas

Figure 8.2   Major fishing grounds and forest areas
These resources are limited in supply and must therefore be replenished. Their exploitation should be controlled and their replacement carefully planned.

95

Timber

With over a quarter of the Earth's land surface covered by forest, it is to be expected that timber remains an important natural resource. As such it falls into two main groups: softwoods obtained largely from fast-growing coniferous trees (e.g. pine, spruce and fir) and hardwoods derived either from temperate deciduous trees such as oak, elm and maple, or from tropical evergreen trees such as teak, ebony, mahogany and greenheart.

The locations of the main forest areas of the world are shown in Figure 8.2. About 40% of all coniferous timber comes from North America and over half the remainder from Scandinavia. Burma, Thailand and Indonesia, together, produce well over a third of the world's tropical hardwoods and are especially noted for teak.

About 40% of total wood production is used directly as fuel (firewood). The other 60% has a variety of uses but is chiefly utilised as a raw material for industry. Softwoods far outweigh hardwoods in importance in this respect and supply more than 70% of global demand for industrial timber. They are relatively inexpensive, strong and easily worked, and are thus used for building construction, cheap furniture, box making and match making. Their most important use is in making wood pulp from which are made paper, cardboard, fibre boards, plastics and even synthetic textiles such as rayon. Hardwoods are more expensive and heavier than softwoods and tend to be used when very tough, resistant timber is essential, as in the case of dock gates, harbour piles, railway sleepers, sports gear and marine crafts. Much good quality furniture is also made of hardwoods, although today only veneers tend to be made of such costly and heavy timber.

Rocks

There are numerous types of rocks to be found in the Earth's crust and many have become extremely useful to man. Some are quarried solely for construction and road building purposes, others solely for industrial raw materials, and a few for a variety of uses.

All hard rocks can be used directly as building stone. These include nearly all igneous and metamorphic rocks (e.g. granite and slate), as well as many hard sedimentary rocks (e.g. limestone). For obvious reasons, such rocks usually form mountainous or hilly country, and it is in these regions that they are most easily accessible for quarrying. In Britain, granite is quarried in Scotland, Wales and south-west England, and gritstone in the Pennine

hills. In chalk downland areas, flint often provides a useful local building material. Marble, a metamorphosed limestone usually beautifully marked and coloured, is extensively used for ornamental construction work and is quarried in central Italy, Greece and western Ireland.

Those rocks used in manufacturing processes include chalk (for cement), gravel (for concrete), clay (for bricks), and sand (for glass). Kaolin (china clay) is a white residual clay from decomposed granite and is used in the pottery industry, and for paper making and pharmaceuticals. The finest deposits are in Cornwall, but large quantities are also obtained in Bornholm (Denmark), France, Germany, China and the USA.

Of all rocks, limestone is perhaps the most versatile. It can be used for buildings, for cement and concrete manufacture; as a flux in iron and steel production; as a water purification agent in sewage works; as a fertiliser; and as a component in such industrial processes as sugar refining, glass making and chemical manufacture. For this reason limestone is extensively quarried wherever it is found. In Britain it is extracted from the Pennines (Carboniferous Limestone), the Cotswolds (Jurassic Limestone) and southern Dorset (Purbeck and Portland Limestone). Abroad there are large areas of limestone in southern Africa, southern China, eastern USA and northern Canada.

Minerals

Apart from being used as a resource themselves, rocks also contain valuable materials. These can be divided between metallic minerals, including iron, precious metals and non-ferrous metals, and non-metallic minerals including industrial substances (such as mica and graphite) and natural fertilisers (such as nitrates and potash).

Metallic minerals are usually found either in ancient 'shield' areas and plateaux where the underlying rocks are igneous in origin or have undergone metamorphosis, or else in some young fold mountains which have experienced complex earth movements. The Baltic and Canadian Shields and the plateaux of Brazil, Africa, India and Australia are examples of the first types of area; the Andes and Rockies are examples of the second.

Iron is the most ubiquitous of all minerals (making up about 5% of the Earth's crust), but is normally only worth exploitation if the ore has over 30% iron content. It is now indispensable to civilised life since it is needed for the manufacture of machinery, for making

FISH RESOURCES IN THE NORTH SEA

The shallow waters of the North Sea once provided Britain with her most important fishing grounds (see Fig. 8.3). Along the east coast of England and Scotland, numerous small trading and fishing settlements grew up and many of these developed into major centres for the fishing industry after the arrival of the railways in the middle of the 19th century. Until recently, Grimsby was the world's greatest fishing port, and boasted the largest trawler fleet.

Since World War 2, British fishing ports have experienced a drastic decline. There has been a steady depletion of fish stocks as a result of overfishing generally and, in particular, because fishermen from many European countries use small-mesh nets, which catch even the very small and young fish. The introduction of factory ships and freezer trawlers has also been detrimental to the North Sea's fish resources. There have been repeated attempts to secure international agreements to prevent overfishing but, so far, little success has been achieved. Today, the east coast fishing ports are in serious economic difficulties, with trawler fleets laid idle and fishermen made redundant. The larger and more traditional fishing centres, especially, are feeling the pinch of reduced catches – Great Yarmouth, Aberdeen, Grimsby and Peterhead. Kingston-upon-Hull, perhaps, has been the most seriously affected of all, since this port depended on the Icelandic and Norwegian fishing grounds where political restrictions have put an additional limit on catches.

In recent years there has been considerable opposition by British fishermen to the Common Market and its effect on the North Sea fish industry. EEC quotas on catches, together with severe discrimination against the larger fishing vessels, have led to a drastic fall in the amount of long-distance fishing. Low-tonnage catches are imposed, and modernisation and improvement grants have been confined to vessels under 24 m in length. Thus, while the 'inshore' fishing industry continues to prosper (together with the small ports), the offshore industry flounders. Even a Common Fisheries Policy agreement raising the grant limit to vessels up to 33 m does little to help such ports as Hull, where most vessels exceed 50 m in length.

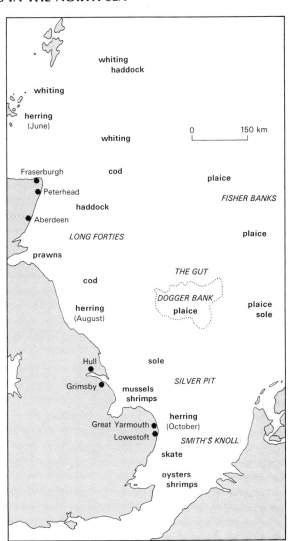

Figure 8.3 Fishing in the North Sea
Overfishing by foreign fleets has greatly diminished the fish stocks of this region and caused great economic depression in Britain's major fishing ports.

transport equipment and, in many cases, for building materials. Precious metals such as gold, silver and tungsten, are characterised by their resistance to chemical change and their high density, and are used for both industrial and domestic purposes. Non-ferrous metals include copper, lead, zinc, tin and bauxite. These, too, are essential commodities: copper for the electrical trade; lead for cables, batteries, ammunition and roofing; zinc for the printing industry; and bauxite for making aluminium used for transport and domestic equipment.

Non-metallic minerals are found in nearly all geological formations and are used either for industrial purposes or for agriculture. In the former category are asbestos, mica, graphite, sulphur and salt. In the latter are nitrates, phosphates and potash. Asbestos and mica are both resistant to heat and are thus important for various fireproof purposes; graphite is used for carbon brushes in electric motors and atomic 'moderators'; sulphur and salt are essential in the chemical industry. Nitrates, phosphates and potash are rich fertilisers. Potash, in addition, is used in the manufacture of explosives, glass, paper, soap and medicines.

Finally, not to be forgotten are the precious gemstone minerals mined largely for jewellery and other domestic ornamental work: diamonds (also for industrial purposes), emeralds, rubies, sapphires, opals and others.

World energy supplies

In earliest times, man possessed only primitive sources of energy. Apart from his own personal toil, he used animals to carry and haul, the wind to blow sails and turn windmills, and running water to rotate wheels. It was not until he had learnt more about his environment and had developed new technology that man began to use fuels in order to obtain power.

Wood and peat were perhaps the first fuels to be burned, both being easily available. Forests were cut down and moorland wastes were excavated, and even today in many parts of the world these are the main fuels used. Steam power was first harnessed during the 18th century and it was not long before coal, the burning of which helped produce steam, had become the most important industrial fuel in the world. The developed countries grew to be industrial largely on coal power.

Over the last hundred years, further energy supplies have evolved, especially in advanced regions where technology has been sufficiently progressive to adapt to new methods of power generation.

Petroleum had a slow beginning as a source of energy. It first came into use during the middle years of last century when, in the USA, it was introduced to the white man by the Seneca indians. Originally used as a medicine, it was not until 1850 that its combustible quality was discovered. Even then its full potential was not realised. It was to take the invention of the internal combustion engine to transform petroleum into a major global source of energy.

Natural gas – which is often found with or near petroleum deposits – had an even more hesitant beginning as a fuel. It was once considered a nuisance by oil drillers and, in consequence, was usually burned off or allowed to disperse into the atmosphere. Its commercial use began in North America early this century, but only since World War 2 have people everywhere seen natural gas as an important source of energy in its own right.

The discovery and subsequent development of electricity revolutionised the nature of world power supplies. Unlike other forms of energy, this can be transmitted but not easily stored (except on a small scale by batteries). Its production originally depended exclusively on the use of fossil fuels (coal and oil), but recently other methods of generation have been employed. First came the use of running water (to make hydroelectric power) in the late 19th century, and later, in the 1950s, came nuclear fission whereby radioactive substances like uranium and thorium are 'split' to release energy.

Today, all these sources of energy are still important since without them neither commercial agriculture nor industry would be possible on a large scale. Even so, the significance of each source varies from country to country. This is because they are unevenly distributed geographically and each is suited to different purposes. They each have distinct characteristics and each requires specific levels of technological know-how.

Coal

Coal is unevenly distributed since it is commonly found only in geological formations laid down during the Carboniferous period. The major deposits are in the northern temperate latitudes on the flanks of Hercynian mountain regions. The most important worked fields are in Europe (running through England, Belgium, Germany and Poland), the USSR (in the Ukraine), south-eastern Asia (in southern Manchuria) and North America (along the Appalachian mountains). World production is around 3000 million tonnes per annum.

Coal varies in quality and therefore in both importance and uses. Anthracite (containing over 90% carbon) burns slowly but without waste, and is mostly used in central heating plant. Bituminous coal (70–90% carbon) burns freely but leaves ash behind, and is used for producing coke, coal-gas or steam. Lignite (under 70% carbon) burns with a smoky flame, leaves abundant waste and thus has limited uses, being largely confined to domestic use or for producing electricity. In addition, coal can be made to yield many valuable products including ammonia, dyes, perfumes, disinfectants, plastics and artificial fibres.

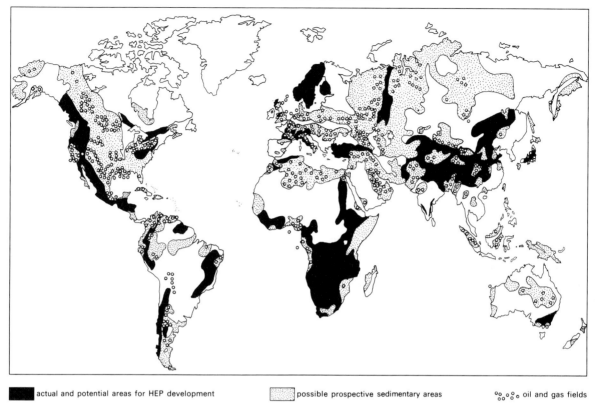

■ actual and potential areas for HEP development	▨ possible prospective sedimentary areas	° ° ° oil and gas fields

Figure 8.4   The world's energy supplies from oil and water
The world has great potential for supplying its increased energy needs but physical and human difficulties hinder the realisation of this potential: extremes of relief and climate, lack of capital and insufficient technology.

Petroleum
Petroleum is derived from organic matter and is normally associated with sedimentary rocks that have been folded; generally the more gentle the folding, the larger the deposits. The most important regions for oil drilling are the Middle East, North America (including Alaska), the Caribbean, the Ural–Caucasus area of Russia, West Africa, and South-East Asia. Sizeable deposits are also found in Europe: in northern Italy, southern France and, of course, the North Sea. Over 2700 million tonnes of crude petroleum are produced annually in the world. (See Fig. 8.4.)

The chief advantage of petroleum is that it has numerous and diverse uses and is easily transported. Through the fractionating process, different liquid products result, each of paramount industrial significance: heavy fuel oils, lubricating oils, diesel oils, paraffin and petrol. Petroleum is also used in the manufacture of detergents, synthetic textiles, plastics, paints, insecticides, fertilisers, pharmaceuticals, toiletries and synthetic rubber.

Natural gas
Natural gas – gaseous hydrocarbons in the form of ethane and methane – is often found in the same geological structures as petroleum: in the USA (which accounts for about 50% of the world's total output), the USSR, Canada, Romania, Mexico, Italy, the Netherlands and in the North Sea. The annual world production is around 1 298 000 000 m³.

After purification, natural gas can be used for domestic and industrial heating, its advantage here being that it is clean, easily controlled and economically transported. It also provides a raw material for the petrochemical industry; by means of the polymerisation process a wide range of synthetic substances can be made. Today about 16% of the world's energy is derived from natural gas, a percentage that is likely to increase in the future.

Hydroelectric power
Hydroelectric power (HEP) has greatly expanded the economic potential of many countries and, in particu-

99

lar, has given promise of industrial development to regions lacking either coal or oil. Nevertheless, it is a possible source of energy only where geographical conditions permit. For example, there should be fairly heavy and regular rainfall or else a constant water supply from rivers or lakes. Also, steep slopes are preferable to aid the fall of water (which drives dynamos), together with narrow, deeply incised valleys and impermeable rocks to facilitate the construction of dams to impound the water. In addition a large fairly local demand for electricity is necessary since the transmission of generated power, without the use of costly boosters, is only economical below distances of 800 km. These geographical restrictions mean that the major hydroelectric regions of the world are to be found in the uplands of developed countries: the Rockies, Scandinavian mountains, Central Massif of France, the Alps and, in Britain, the Scottish and Welsh mountains (Fig. 8.4). In some cases, where the volume of available water is limited, pumped storage schemes are used to generate hydroelectric power, as with the Ben Cruachan plant in western Scotland.

Only occasionally are large HEP plants found in flat areas (e.g. the St Lawrence Valley in Canada and the great basins of Siberia) and this is usually only because of unique local factors: for example, where lakes can be harnessed for power. In many countries, for reasons of cost, hydroelectricity tends to be produced in conjunction with other schemes, such as irrigation and flood control projects. Such multipurpose schemes include the Aswan High Dam on the Nile and the Volta scheme in Ghana. Sometimes, also, HEP plants are built to serve industries needing a large input of electricity, like those for timber and pulp processing, electrochemicals, electrometallurgicals and the electrolytic refining of certain metals.

Nuclear power

Nuclear power is, at present, of limited significance in world energy supplies, accounting for less than 5% of the total output. Its potential importance, however, is great since, at a time when demand for electricity is rising, there is a very real danger of more conventional fuels becoming exhausted. The main advantage nuclear power has over its rivals is the relatively small weight of fuel required. Only 28 g of uranium or thorium are able to produce more electricity than 100 tonnes of coal. What is more, there seem to be abundant supplies of these minerals in northern Canada, western USA, South Africa, Australia and Czechoslovakia so the chances of them running out in the near future are remote indeed. The only likely constraint on the extraction of these minerals could be future political events – in South Africa, for example, where much conflict exists between the various racial groups.

The development of nuclear power is not without its problems and it is likely to be many years before this form of energy is generally accepted. Indeed, in many countries this power source may never be accepted, owing to the strength of the anti-nuclear lobby. The mining of radioactive minerals is dangerous, as is the process of transforming them into electricity. Apart from the risk factor, power stations have the further disadvantages of being expensive to build, needing high levels of scientific know-how to operate and having the problem of radioactive waste disposal. Not surprisingly, only very advanced countries possess nuclear power stations in any great number – the USA, Britain, France, West Germany, Japan and the USSR – and even here their construction is often met by public opposition. Some developing countries (for example, India) are now beginning to acquire them but, in most cases, this is the result of external aid and foreign investment.

The nature of resource exploitation

It is a fallacy that the world's resources are 'free'. Certainly they do not have to be 'made', but man does have to collect and process them if he is to reap their full benefit. This collection and processing can be both expensive and difficult, and man may have to pay highly – in financial, social, political and ecological terms – for the privilege of using them.

The factors determining the nature of resource exploitation – where and why man exploits certain resources, how he undertakes collection and processing techniques, the degree of man's exploitation success – are listed below.

(1) *Physical accessibility*. The topographical location of the deposits concerned; their extent, depth and size; the distance between their location and their market; the climatic conditions prevalent at this location.

(2) *Resource characteristics*. The quality of the deposits concerned; the varied uses to which they can be put; the coexistence of several resources together; the scope of their future importance.

(3) *Economic feasibility*. The existence of a suitable labour supply; the availability of capital and the type of capital being used; the size of the market and profitability of the resources concerned.

(4) *Cultural feasibility.* The technical know-how of those undertaking exploitation; the need to acquire minerals and energy sources which provide social wealth; the political will, stability and incentive to develop resources; the extent of knowledge of resource location.

(5) *Political necessity.* The desire by some countries to be independent of traditional resource supply countries; the need for strategic security through self-sufficiency; the demand for guaranteed future supplies in a politically divided and unstable world.

Resources that are easily accessible and are found in great quantities will be exploited before those in inaccessible locations or in small quantities. The resources of the developed world are better known and more intensively worked than those in the less developed world.

Farming

This particular form of resource exploitation is examined in Chapter 7. There are different types of farming – mixed agriculture, monoculture, horticulture, viticulture and so on – and these vary in methods, extent, degree of success and intensity throughout the world. Agricultural characteristics, as already mentioned, are the outcome of physical geography and human behaviour.

Fishing

When the demand for fish is small, or where technology is limited, fishing is practised primitively with spears, rods, lines and traps. Only in more advanced regions, where fish provide important food supplies or industrial raw materials, is it undertaken more systematically. Netting, by trawl, seine or drift nets, is especially common although baskets are more usual for shellfish, as with lobster and crab pots. A still more advanced method of fishing is exemplified by **pisciculture** (fish farming). This involves rearing and breeding fish under controlled conditions, thereby providing for regular and assured catches. It is common in South-East Asia, where a large population of high density demands a large supply of fish, and is being introduced in many developed countries, often in conjunction with irrigation or drainage schemes which result in new man-made lakes.

Lumbering

Techniques of exploiting timber resources also vary. In regions of difficult relief or inaccessibility, or where forests are dense and individual tree species widely scattered, lumbering (cutting and preparing

timber) is fraught with problems. This is particularly true in the Tropics, where climatic conditions make tree felling even more arduous. In such places, native labour still may be used for cutting and stripping, using handsaws, and in the East Indies elephants are only gradually being replaced by machinery for haulage. Rivers can make transport easier and in high latitudes softwood logs are normally stacked in winter on frozen waterways to be floated down to the pulp and paper mills in the spring thaw, as happens in Norway, Sweden and Canada (British Columbia and Ontario).

In many parts of the world, timber plantations have been established. These represent the most advanced method of exploitation and are common in all major timber producing countries of the world. In Scandinavia, Canada and Russia, vast coniferous plantations may be found where cutting, transport and processing are all highly mechanised. In Britain, the Forestry Commission (set up in 1919) owns nearly 1 million ha of productive woodland, in 250 separate forests, although some of this total is now being sold off to the private sector.

Provided that fishing and forestry are controlled, they may continue indefinitely since they are renewable resources. The same cannot be said of quarrying and mining. Once rocks and minerals have been excavated, they are gone for ever.

Quarrying and mining

The quarrying of rocks must have begun in earliest times, since the process is a relatively simple one. Rocks are found on the surface and, with adequate tools, there are few physical difficulties that prevent them from being exploited. For the same reason, the first minerals mined – metal ores, coal, salt and others – were obtained from open pits. It is only after the Earth's surface has been excavated, and the minerals exposed at the surface have been exhausted, that man abandons open-cast mining to work underground. And as demand for raw materials has increased, so subterranean workings have become even deeper and more extensive.

Most solid mineral resources can be mined by fairly simple techniques. Shafts and tunnels are constructed, and extracted material is conveyed to the surface. For liquid or gaseous resources, however, more complex methods must be employed. Petroleum is obtained by drilling, whereby a circular cutter bores through the overlying rocks. The trapped oil then gushes out naturally (as a result of pressure) or is pumped to the surface.

RESOURCE WEALTH IN THE NORTH SEA

It had long been suspected that the geological structures of the North Sea Basin were possible oil traps, but it was not until 1959 that any important discoveries were made. In that year a major gas strike occurred in Gröningen, Holland. This find stimulated further exploration beneath the North Sea itself, and the early 1960s saw an 'oil rush'. Numerous licences to drill were taken out, mainly in the British sector, and it was soon realised that the whole area was a major source of both oil and natural gas (see Fig. 8.5).

The first gas pipeline ashore was built in 1967 to Easington, Humberside, and a second was built to Bacton, Norfolk, in the following year. These, and subsequent pipelines, are linked to the trunk pipeline from Canvey Island to Leeds. The total gas reserves in the British sector are estimated at 7 000 000 m³.

The extraction of oil followed soon after the discovery of gas. The first oil to be drilled was shipped from the Ekofisk field to Norway in 1971, and today pipelines link the main oil fields with the United Kingdom. The largest oil field is the Brent, 160 km from the Shetlands, where the sea is 140 m deep. The pipeline along the sea bed carries the oil to the Sullom Voe terminal where it is refined. By 1982 the North Sea was supplying Britain with most of her oil needs and also provided some for export. However, rich as these reserves are, they are unlikely to meet more than about 12% of Western Europe's total energy requirements. Since the early 1980s, further oil and gas exploration has continued elsewhere around British waters, notably in the Celtic Sea – off the Hebrides, Wales and Cornwall. One major find was in Morecambe Bay, where vast reserves of natural gas may lead to developments along the Lancashire coast similar to those around Aberdeen.

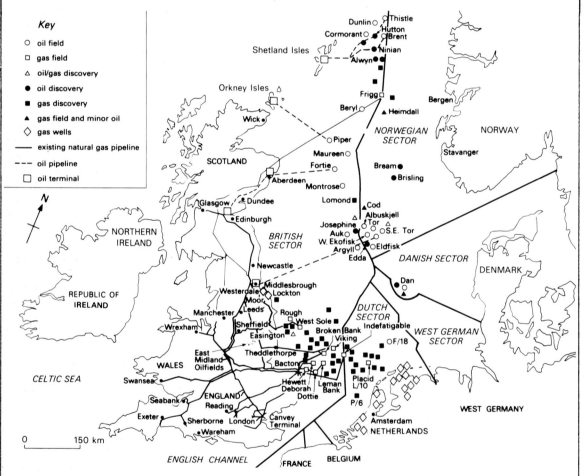

Figure 8.5   Resources in the North Sea
As oil and gas output from the North Sea begins to decline towards the end of the 1980s as supplies are used up, so the need to find other sources around Britain's coasts increases. New gas fields have already been discovered in the Irish Sea.

Problems of resource exploitation

Both the extraction of a resource and its subsequent use or processing may involve problems. Such difficulties may increase the cost of exploitation substantially and may greatly hinder a country's economic development. The main types of problem can be listed thus.

(1) *Environmental difficulties*. High altitudes, steep gradients, rugged topography, meteorological hazards, climatic extremes, frequent earth movements, deep or contorted deposit seams, surface instability (e.g. on oceans, marshes, ice floes), natural diseases and illnesses, wild animals.
(2) *Economic difficulties*. High cost of labour and difficulties of attracting workers, high cost of machinery and transport development, instability of world demand and market fluctuations, weak economic planning or currency, poor labour relations, capital unavailability.
(3) *Social difficulties*. Wide divisions in wealth and social class leading to fear, mistrust and anger between socio-political groups; racial tensions, high birth and death rates, low levels of literacy and intelligence, high incidence of disease or lethargy owing to poor medical aid.
(4) *Political difficulties*. Government inefficiency and corruption, artificial trading barriers caused by nationalism and tensions between countries, political instability or the existence of military regimes, ideological dogma, strategic expediency, disputed boundary location.

It is generally true that the greater and more numerous the problems faced by a country intent on exploiting its own resource potential, the slower and more inefficient will be that exploitation. The Third World certainly experiences more of the difficulties just mentioned than the developed world and, consequently, has a generally poorer record of resource development (although in the past some resource exploitation took place under colonialism).

Some energy sources create difficulties even after they have been removed from the ground or otherwise acquired. Coal can be used directly as a fuel but is heavy and bulky and so is costly to move. Winds, tides and waves can be harnessed for electricity but this can be expensive and technologically difficult. Petroleum must be processed before it can be used as a fuel but the refining process creates enormous social and economic difficulties. The location of oil refineries is a problem in itself. They require solid rock surfaces and large open spaces and, above all, easily accessible oil supplies. In many countries this last requirement normally results in deepwater coastal locations so that the crude liquid can be drawn off direct from ocean tankers.

In the same way, nuclear materials must also be processed to create electricity. Thus, in many regions the exploitation of nuclear power involves, not the mining of uranium, but the building of nuclear power stations. Their location is even more restricted than that of conventional power stations. They must be near the sea, a large lake or a broad river (preferably no more than 15 m above water level) since vast quantities of cooling water are needed (up to 90 million litres per hour); on firm ground to take the weight of the plant itself (up to 26 tonnes per m²); and away from centres of dense population because of the danger of radioactivity.

If a particular resource is in great demand and its profitability is assured, man will try to overcome almost any difficulties in order to exploit it. In Bolivia and Peru, the Andes present especially difficult mining conditions, not only because of the coldness but also because of the altitude, steep gradients, inaccessibility and contorted mineral seams. Even so, tin and copper are so precious that such problems are worth tackling. In the same continent, the wet, hot, humid conditions of the Amazon Basin have not prevented the exploitation of recently discovered deposits of iron ore and petroleum. In the Canadian Shield, radium, uranium, iron ore and gold are mined, despite temperatures well below −20°C and long dark winters. Oil drilling in Alaska takes place in even worse conditions, and even in Britain the rigours of life on North Sea oil rigs should not be underestimated.

The impact of resource exploitation

The physical consequences of resource exploitation can be widespread, fundamental and serious. Not only can it have devastating effects on human life and the human landscape, but it can also cause irreversible damage to the natural environment.

The exact impact of natural resource development is, of course, debatable. This is because many of the results of exploitation are not just direct but also indirect, they are not only short term but also long term. By definition, indirect cause and effect relationships are difficult to quantify and qualify; by

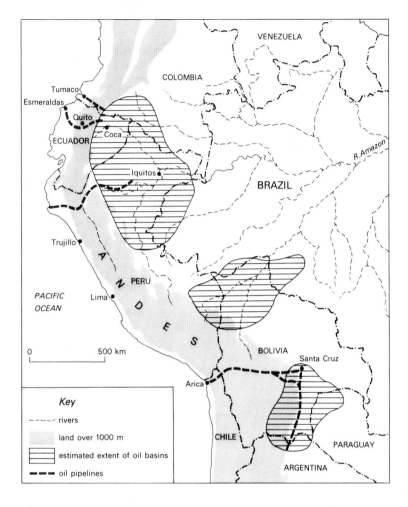

Figure 8.6 Oil reserves in the Amazon Basin
At present the full extent of oil reserves in South America is not known – for reasons of inaccessibility, environmental restrictions and insufficient exploration. However, it is known that the oil fields shown here probably constitute some of the largest reserves in the world. Apart from the pipelines shown, transport routes include waterways: oil is being taken by tanker down the Amazon network to Manaus and beyond.

definition, long-term cause and effect relationships are impossible to gauge. It should also be borne in mind that environmental impact analysis is only partly objective. Experts can say for certain how much sulphur dioxide in the air can damage the mental health of human beings, or how much radioactivity will cause deformity in animals. But no experts would agree on the extent to which a new coalmine will damage the aesthetic quality of an area of attractive countryside, or the extent to which the culling of seals off Canada might eventually alter the ecosystem of the North Atlantic.

The human environment
It can be argued that man's impact on the human environment, as a result of developing natural resources, is almost total. The landscapes of the world

are essentially man-made: vast areas are farmed or covered by industrial and urban use; regions have been denuded of their natural forest cover or their wildlife; hills and mountains have been hacked away for the wealth they contain. Even deserts and savanna grasslands may be the result of overcultivation and overgrazing. Perhaps only the few natural forest areas of the world – parts of the Amazon and Zaïre Basins, for example – are untouched by man's impact; and even these are now rapidly disappearing. On a more detailed, intimate scale, the results of resource exploitation are no less obvious.

In many instances, settlements such as fishing ports, lumbering villages and mining towns are very much a feature of natural resource development and often exist for that sole purpose. Yet these places (mining towns in particular) tend to be ephemeral,

OIL RESERVES IN THE AMAZON BASIN

One of the world's largest oil deposits is now being worked in the upper Amazon Basin (see Fig. 8.6). Three major oil fields are thought to exist, stretching across so many national boundaries as to benefit no fewer than seven countries: Brazil, Colombia, Ecuador, Peru, Bolivia, Paraguay and Argentina.

Although the presence of oil in these areas has been suspected since the 1920s, only recently has its quantity and value become apparent. As other world oil sources began to dry up – and became more expensive – so an impetus was given in South America for new explorations. The first major discovery was made along the Amazon in 1971, since when not only South American nationalised oil companies but also many foreign companies (mainly from USA, Britain, West Germany, France and Spain) have taken out exploration options and started drilling.

The problems of oil exploitation in the Amazon Basin should not be underestimated. Indeed, it has been said that tapping oil in this terrain is the most difficult in the world: far harder than in, say, Alaska, the North Sea or the Sahara. In hot, wet, humid, climatic conditions – with temperatures well above 35°C and rainfall reaching 0.3 m a day – the sun rarely penetrates through the dense jungle to the Earth's surface. In these forests there are numerous diseases and wild animals, frequent storms and floods – all of which make human habitation extremely uncomfortable. Furthermore, there is the problem of inaccessibility: to the west of the oil fields are 5000 m high mountains; to the east the Atlantic coast is 3000 km away.

Notwithstanding such difficulties, oil and its accompanying natural gas are successfully being carried out of the oil-field areas. One pipeline is 500 km long (from Ecuador's field to Esmeraldas), reaches altitudes over 400 m and negotiates 70° slopes. Much oil is refined locally near the fields themselves, for example at Sucre, Cochabamba (Bolivia) and Iquitos (Peru), and is then piped out; some is piped crude to be refined at the coast.

The results of oil exploitation are far reaching indeed. Oil has become the biggest single money-earner in Ecuador, Peru and Bolivia. New roads and oil-rush towns have opened up new lands for farming and forestry; increased trade has generated greater industrial activity; higher incomes and profits have led to new housing projects and social services schemes. Indeed, this part of South America may have reached a boom the like of which will probably not be seen again for generations.

growing when the resources are abundant and declining when they become exhausted. Before the discovery of oil, Kuwait was a poor, sparsely settled country of desert and camel herders. Today, it is among the richest states in the world and boasts two thriving cities. In the USA some resources ran out long ago and only scattered 'ghost towns' in the Rocky Mountains remain as reminders of 19th century mineral extraction. In the Klondyke (Canada), the gold rush transformed the tiny frontier post of Dawson into a city of 35 000 people. By 1900, just three years after the first gold strike, it had dwindled to a village of just a few hundred inhabitants. Even in the British uplands there are numerous derelict villages to be found, which were once prosperous on quarrying or mining.

Air pollution (Fig. 8.7) and the spoliation of the countryside are also grave consequences of resource exploitation. Quarries, open-cast pits and slag heaps all leave very obvious scars on the landscape and many people see HEP dams as equally ugly features. Power stations are no less damaging to the visual aspect of the environment. The fact that nuclear power plants have limited lifespans and cannot be demolished after their usefulness has finished (except at great risk and expense), is a further cause for concern. Future generations may have to suffer the existence of empty, highly dangerous nuclear buildings scattered around the country, their deadly shapes indicative of past mistakes. It is true that some attempts are being made to reduce this spoliation. Derelict quarries and mines are being filled in or landscaped, and many slag heaps are being levelled and planted with grass. Oil storage depots, like those at Milford Haven and Shetland, are sometimes built into the contours of the land, and power stations may be shielded by trees. Even so, much environmental destruction continues to take place.

There is also the possibility of earth movements as a direct result of mineral extraction. Underground

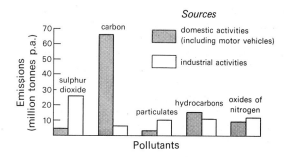

Figure 8.7 Sources of air pollution in the USA
These pollutants have far-reaching consequences, affecting not only humans but also the whole ecosystem. They can cause cancer, bronchitis and heart disease and can destroy animal and plant species.

mining causes subsidence, and ill-planned quarrying and waste disposal may lead to landslides (as in the case of the Aberfan disaster of 1966). There is even evidence to suggest that crustal upheavals can be a product of deep mining, drilling and reservoir construction. In 1973 an international conference confirmed that the building of a 100 m dam and the impounding of water behind it is able to trigger off an earthquake registering up to 6½ on the Richter scale, enough to demolish buildings. This might be because the weight of a large body of water produces additional stress on the underlying rock, which must be relieved elsewhere. It is perhaps significant that earth tremors occur frequently in the Tashkent region of Russia, an area much dammed for HEP schemes.

The ecological environment
The world's ecosystem is a delicate and finely balanced whole in which nature's elements are linked in equilibrium: climate, weather, geology, landscape, soils, living things, water and man all existing in a state of even interrelationship. By altering the physical and human landscape, resource exploitation can disrupt this entire ecosystem.

The removal of forests and other natural vegetation cover could cause climatic change of a fundamental nature. Less transpiration would lead to less condensation and less precipitation, resulting in drier climates. Compounding this change, atmospheric pollution (the emission of gases and dust particles) can create a 'greenhouse effect', whereby the world warms up owing to the blocking effect of a thicker atmosphere on the solar radiation reflected from the Earth's surface. It has been estimated that the burning of fossil fuels can increase the carbon dioxide content in the atmosphere by 0.2% per annum, possibly causing a rise in the surface temperature of the world by an average of 0.5°C by the end of the century.

An alteration of the Earth's climatic conditions could have all kinds of repercussions on the biological nature of the planet. So too, and more directly, can the disposal of waste from resource exploitation. The discharge of toxic heavy metals (including mercury), nutrients and oil into the world's oceans can damage marine life severely, destroying plants and fish, cutting food chains and causing excessive bacterial decomposition, which will, eventually, create 'dead water' (a process known as **eutrophication**). Such changes would naturally have a knock-on effect on the rest of the world's ecosystem.

Resource consumption

The variety of uses to which resources are put often means that those that are dissimilar may in fact compete for the same market. Fish, nitrates, potash and phosphates are all used as fertilisers, and stone, timber, sand and gravel (in concrete) and iron all provide building materials. Heat can be obtained from gas, oil, coal or electricity, and the last mentioned can even be generated in different ways. This competition means that the consumer must choose between different resources. Sometimes the choice is easy since, for certain uses, only one mineral or energy supply is available or suitable. Only timber can easily be made into newsprint and only electricity can smelt aluminium. At other times the choice is more difficult and man must weigh up the relative advantages and disadvantages of each resource. His final decision will probably be determined by such diverse factors as price, type of market, availability, efficiency, flexibility, amenity considerations and government policy.

The price of a resource is determined by the cost of extraction and processing, the quantities available, transport and delivery costs and, sometimes also, taxes and royalty payments. Naturally, cheap resources will compete successfully against expensive resources and demand for a particular product is likely to fall as its price rises. However, the difficulty in forecasting future trends poses a problem; what is cheap now may not always remain cheap. For a long time, oil was favoured to the detriment of coal, yet this is no longer true. Who could have foreseen the action of the Organisation of Petroleum-exporting Countries (OPEC) in raising oil prices by 500% in a single year (1973/4)? How many firms and individuals installed oil-fired heating only to regret the move later?

Both the size and nature of the market may also be significant in resource choice. Large markets may warrant the use of one resource, purchased in bulk and at reduced costs, whereas the same resource might not be used for a small market for which only small quantities are needed, purchased at high costs. Coal, for instance, can be cheap when used for large markets but expensive when used for small markets. For some purposes, only a limited number of resources are suitable anyway. A moving vehicle, for example, must carry its own fuel or else run on electricity along fixed tracks. For reasons of bulk and

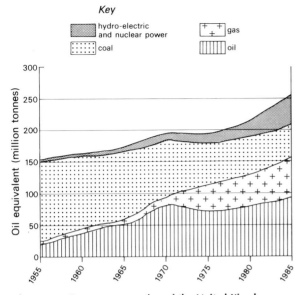

Key

hydro-electric and nuclear power

coal

gas

oil

Figure 8.8 Energy consumption of the United Kingdom
The relative importance of each energy source changes with time and in response to various economic, social and even political factors. In the future, other energy sources may also enter the country's fuel-mix economy.

conscious and the introduction of 'smokeless zones' is just one example of the policies now being instigated. Indeed, such is public concern for the environment that the use of coal is now limited largely to power generation, in which its residues can be controlled, and even the burning of oil and petrol is viewed with alarm because of the carbon monoxide and other noxious gases that it produces.

On a national scale, the final quantities of each resource consumed are often determined by government intervention. This is especially true in the case of energy. For various economic, political and social reasons, most developed countries now operate power policies, in most instances based on diversity or **fuel mix**. Under these, energy is obtained from several sources (coal, oil, gas, HEP and nuclear power) so that, at all times, some power is guaranteed (Fig. 8.8).

Clearly, resource consumption on a world scale is not evenly distributed, neither is it linked strongly with resource extraction. Developing countries consume a disproportionately small quantity per capita and developed countries consume a disproportionately large quantity, despite the fact that large amounts of resource wealth are produced in the former. So what does determine the overall pattern of consumption?

A comparison of the possessions and consumption of food, power, materials and newsprint of the average American with those of, say, an Ethiopian, may suggest that the use of resources is related to the standard of living. Certainly this is true to a point: as people become wealthier, their demand for goods rises. However, this is not the whole story; population size and density, the level of technology, social structure, culture and education all play a part as well. Two countries may share the same standard of living but have a different per capita consumption of resources because their socio-economic circumstances are dissimilar.

Every country aims to improve the quality of life for its people. The use of local resources may help to achieve this aim but it is not essential to economic development. Hong Kong and Singapore bear testimony to this, both cities having grown as a result of trade and industries based on imported raw materials.

The pattern of resource consumption, then, is the result of various and interdependent factors. It is dynamic and may change in both time and space. It may also itself determine the nature of human activity.

weight alone, such fuels as coal and firewood can be ruled out for the powering of motor cars.

Availability is a matter of geography and technology. Some countries may lack certain mineral deposits, others may possess them yet may not be able to exploit or process them. Coal may be found but, for want of capital, may not be used as a fuel to generate electricity. In the Republic of Ireland there is an abundance of peat, but until recently it was useful only as a domestic fuel. Today peat-burning power stations supply large amounts of electricity to Irish industry.

Efficiency and flexibility differ between resources. Some forms of energy, such as coal power, can only be used at the operational site (where the power is actually produced), whereas others, such as electricity, can be produced at one place and used at another. Conversely, fossil fuels can be stored, which is convenient for markets in which demand is liable to fluctuate, whereas electricity cannot be stockpiled and so is best suited to markets of constant demand. Some minerals require specialised machinery, for either processing or utilisation; others may need only simple equipment, which can also be used for substitutes.

Over recent years the amenity factor has grown increasingly important in determining resource consumption. At last, society is becoming more pollution

Resource conservation

Perhaps the most serious of all the consequences of resource consumption is that it may result in the eventual exhaustion of the Earth's natural wealth. Population increase, technological progress and rising standards of living lead to the consumption of more fish, timber, minerals and energy than ever before. Within the next generation, the demand for energy supplies alone is likely to double and it has been estimated that the world's petroleum supply will be exhausted within the next hundred years. Neither is the problem simply concerned with the so-called non-renewable minerals: even renewable resources are being depleted.

It is, therefore, not surprising that conservation – the careful, rational, intelligent use of resources – is fast becoming a cornerstone of resource utilisation. Its roots lie in North America at the end of the last century, when people first observed the devastation caused by careless exploitation of minerals in the Appalachians and the Mid-West. Since then, the conservation movement has gathered momentum, especially in the developed world, as people grew more aware of the gap between the 'haves' and 'have-nots' and began to react against the planned obsolescence common in affluent countries and the so-called 'throw-away society'. Pollution and the loss of aesthetic amenity brought the problems to a head and caused the general public to realise that environmental destruction, resource shortages and the creation of waste are all linked to the senseless exploitation of the Earth's natural gifts.

Conservation policies can be instigated in various ways. For renewable resources they largely revolve around controlled exploitation and planned replenishment. Whaling still continues and the whale is still in danger of extinction, but at least efforts have started to limit both the size of the catch and the length of the hunting season. Member countries of the International Whaling Commission, for example, have self-imposed quotas for their own catches. Unfortunately, conservation policies require total co-operation, and international agreements are often difficult to reach. The North Atlantic is becoming seriously depleted of fish but, sadly, only a few countries have introduced fishing controls. France and, especially, the USSR, East Germany and Poland seem to care little for conservation. They are interested only in bulk fish supplies and they net even the smallest and most immature fish. Such action naturally reduces the capacity of the fish population to reproduce and replace itself.

The threat to timber resources is being combated in most countries by vigorous afforestation. In addition, many have adopted stringent forestry laws, as in Norway and Sweden, to reduce waste, and elsewhere experiments are taking place to find alternative materials for making paper. In Britain, as in other countries, waste paper is recycled, although this is still undertaken only on a relatively small scale.

The conservation of non-renewable resources involves much stronger measures. The wasteful use of minerals must be strictly reduced, more efficient extraction methods must be adopted and greater efforts should be made to recover minerals and, perhaps, to reuse them. Also, the use of substitute materials should be encouraged wherever possible.

Conservation makes sense both morally and economically. On the one hand it protects resources against reckless exploitation, waste and wanton destruction; on the other hand, it leads to their preservation so that they will last longer and be of benefit to future generations. Even so, successful conservation policies are not easy to set up. They are only possible if human ignorance and carelessness are reduced, if a measure of governmental control is instigated, and if the countries of the world agree to co-operate. The United Nations is beginning to play a key role in conservation by setting up international standards for resource extraction, but it is up to individual governments – and indeed up to individual people – to ensure that such policies succeed.

Future resource supplies

Notwithstanding the conservation of natural resources, the world is still likely to need more resources in the years to come. Even if the world's population does not grow, per capita resource consumption is liable to increase dramatically as people obtain higher standards of living and demand greater material wealth. With a rapidly increasing human population as well, the demand for resources will inevitably accelerate.

There are two ways in which man can attempt to satisfy this growing demand for resources. First, he can search for new reserves of existing resources. Secondly, he can investigate the potential for entirely new resources – finding ways of profitably utilising those aspects of nature which, up to now, have been considered worthless.

Into the first category come such developments as the reworking of old deposits with new techniques and the spread of geological surveying. Oil is being sought in the Celtic Sea off Britain, in the South Atlantic (around the Falkland Islands), and across the major hot desert regions of the world. Antarctica might well supply major resources in the future, once the problems of working in such harsh conditions have been overcome. Such companies as Rio Tinto Zinc are searching for metals in Wales, and the Brazilian government is searching for new sources of raw materials in the Amazon Basin and on the interior uplands.

New sources of power should, if possible, be both reliable and inexhaustible. So far, various experiments have taken place and success has been mixed, but there is certainly hope for the future. At present the most promising sources for the years to come are biomass conversion, waste heat, solar radiation, wind force, tidal power, geothermal energy and the harnessing of hydrogen.

Biomass conversion includes the production of methanol from waste cellulose and lignin in the pulp and paper industry. This could then be used for power, either directly, or indirectly through further transformations. The conversion of agricultural and municipal waste would offer similar possibilities. The use of biomass for energy is already being investigated in such countries as Japan, the USA and the USSR.

Waste-heat harnessing is merely the production of extra power from existing thermal power stations, nuclear plants and factories. The heat given off from such structures – through the dynamos or chimneys – can be harnessed so that no excess energy is given away into the atmosphere. Experiments in this are well advanced in Canada (Quebec and Ontario), the USA (Oregon) and the Netherlands.

Solar radiation involves the use of the sun's rays to produce both heat and light. Its chief advantage is that it is inexhaustible. However, there seems to be doubt as to whether such energy could be used for large-scale purposes: to date it is only being employed for domestic uses and at high unit costs. Only if technology advances is solar energy likely to be convenient and cheap enough for industrial uses.

The harnessing of the wind would mean the building of massive towers to be run on a similar principle to windmills. The drawbacks to this method include the difficulty of construction and of finding suitable sites. Nevertheless, some prototype experiments into areogeneration have taken place – for example in Wales and Scotland.

Tidal power seems potentially more feasible in terms of both cost and technology, although current estimates suggest that some major schemes may entail costs running to thousands of millions of pounds. Indeed, development of such power is already underway. In north Brittany (France) the Rance Barrage tidal scheme near St Malo has operated successfully since the late 1960s and on the eastern Canadian coast a plant is now being built to produce electricity from the Newfoundland bore. In Britain there are suggestions for harnessing the Severn Bore for a similar plant.

Associated with tidal power is wave energy, but this is still in the experimental stage; so far research by British scientists has resulted only in the construction of successful models.

Geothermal energy can be obtained from the intense heat below the Earth's crust, but the technical complications involved make it expensive as well as dangerous. At present some relatively small geothermal power schemes are in operation, for example the Krafla station in northern Iceland, but many larger plants are now being developed.

Of all possibilities, hydrogen is perhaps the most likely source of energy for the 21st century. The electrolysis of water to obtain hydrogen is already being done on a small scale and scientists see no reason why the system cannot be enlarged. If it is, the world's oceans could be transformed into power reservoirs capable of supplying more energy than the Earth is ever likely to need. But we must not be uncautiously optimistic. Scientists disagree, and hydrogen power may not be as successful as some of them imagine. The truth is that no one knows for sure how the world may be provided with energy in the future. In the meantime we must come to terms with the steadily decreasing availability of present fuels – what has been called the 'energy crisis'.

Summary

1　Natural resources help people achieve their economic potential. Location, labour skills, climatic advantage and water can be termed 'resources' and not just geological elements (e.g. fossil fuels and rocks) and living things (e.g. fish and timber).

2 The usefulness of resources is subject to human perception. People must know how to recognise and understand a resource as well as be capable, technologically, of using it. Over time, more of the world's elements are being identified as resources.

3 Some resources have innate uses and are valuable in their natural state (fish, wood, rocks); others have acquired utility and are only valuable after they have been processed (coal, oil, gas). Most of the exploited resources are situated in the developed world for reasons of perception and technology: in more advanced countries minerals and the elements of nature are more likely to be valued as resources than in less advanced countries, and more likely to be harnessed.

4 Nuclear (fission *and* fusion) power is perhaps the most promising energy source for the future, but is also the most opposed. Nuclear fission is dangerous, because of radioactivity and the risk of nuclear bomb production by unscrupulous political regimes. There are also very long-term risks associated with nuclear waste disposal.

5 Resource exploitation takes place where conditions are physically easy, where the product is especially valuable, where sufficient technical knowledge exists, and where political necessity demands.

6 The impact of resource exploitation is far reaching. Natural landscapes and wildlife may disappear, human health may deteriorate, and the Earth's atmosphere and climates may change.

7 The conservation movement has grown rapidly over the past 20 years – leading to the appearance of such groups as Greenpeace, Friends of the Earth and various ecology parties. In some countries (e.g. Sweden and West Germany) such groups have significant political power.

8 New energy resources for the future include geothermal, wind, solar and biomass-conversion power supplies. Geothermal energy is, perhaps, likely to be the most important of these.

Data–response exercises

1 Comment on the distribution of the world's major fishing grounds and forest areas as shown in Figure 8.2. Why are no areas of deciduous woodland shown?

2 Examine the indication from Figure 8.4 that areas of greatest energy supplies of oil and water are not necessarily areas of greatest energy demands, and vice versa. Does the distribution of energy sources in the world have any political consequences?

3 What problems have been encountered in developing gas and oil reserves in the North Sea (Fig. 8.5), and how have these been overcome? Why does no gas or oil pipeline run from the fields to the Norwegian mainland? Where else on the map is exploration for gas and oil proving successful?

4 Discuss the economic and political problems that may arise in the exploitation of oil in the Amazon Basin (Fig. 8.6).

5 With reference to Figure 8.7, list the chief effects of air pollution and state how changes in weather caused by air pollution may be harmful to mankind.

6 Redraw Figure 8.8 to show possible future trends in UK energy consumption up to the end of this century. Are any new energy sources likely to appear on the graph? Comment on the future trends you have suggested.

9 Industry

Introduction

As with all the other subject areas covered by this book, industry is merely a piece in the jigsaw – a component part of the whole: it is interrelated with all other topics. It is determined by – and itself largely determines – aspects of population, agriculture, transport, settlement, socio-political development and even the wider fields of human behaviour patterns.

All that this chapter can attempt is a relatively brief and comprehensive summary of industry. In doing this, it will address the following questions:

- How can different types of industrial activity be identified, classified and studied?
- What are the links between different kinds of industry, and – indeed – between industry as a whole and the rest of the environment?
- Which factors influence industrial location, and what is the relative importance of each?
- Why do industrial groupings occur, and where are these agglomerations found?
- What changes are taking place in industry, and with what effects?
- Can locational analysis propound set models and theories, and are these relevant to real world situations?

Classification

The term 'industry' covers a multitude of meanings. In its narrowest sense it may only refer to manufacturing: the making of goods. This conjures up visions of factories and mills and is, in consequence, rather limited in scope. In its broadest sense it refers to all stages and types of economic activity, including extraction, construction and services. This latter definition is the more common in economic geography. It is, therefore, quite acceptable to speak not only of, say, the steel industry or textile industry but also of the 'tourist industry', the 'music industry' and even the 'education industry'.

Today, the most usual classification of industry is fourfold and is based on the nature of the work undertaken and the stage in the production process. This runs as follows:

Primary industry is any activity in which natural resources are acquired from the Earth's surface. It includes agriculture, fishing, forestry, mining and quarrying. In other words, such industry is where naturally occurring commodities are collected but not physically changed in any way.

Secondary industry is where the resources collected at the primary level are made into other products, thereby involving a certain amount of manufacturing. Goods are made either for other manufacturers or for the general public. In either case raw materials undergo change.

Tertiary industry may be summarised as the distributive trades and as such it includes the commercial services of transport, wholesaling and retailing. It deals only with goods and forms a link between primary and secondary industries and between these two and the customer.

Quaternary industry comprises all personal services. Unlike tertiary industry it deals not with goods but with people, and requires generally higher levels of skill, expertise and specialisation. Activities in such fields as education, research, administration and financial management may be termed quaternary.

Most of the goods we buy have passed through, or have been affected by, all four types of industry. The motor car can be taken as an example. Mining for iron ore and coal, quarrying for sand and collecting tree rubber are all primary activities. The making, from these raw materials, of steel, glass and tyres and the subsequent manufacture of the car itself may all be classed as secondary activities. The removal of the car to the showroom and its sale to the customer are part of tertiary industry. Quaternary activities are necessary for all these processes to take place since they include the management of the individual firms, the supply of finance and the design of the final product. The customer also requires quaternary services in the form of motor insurance and, possibly, a bank loan with which to purchase the car.

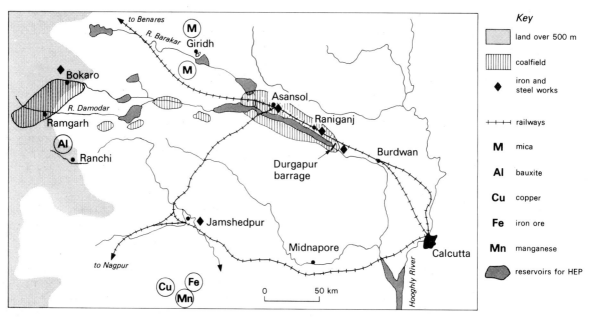

Figure 9.1 Industry in the Damodar Basin, India

The Damodar Basin, in north-east India, is today one of the most important heavy industrial areas in Asia. Large deposits of easily worked iron ore, limestone, copper, manganese and chrome, together with three productive coalfields, have given rise to major raw-material and power orientated industries. At Jamshedpur is the largest integrated iron and steel works in the Commonwealth, and other steel works have been built at Asansol, Durgapur and Bokaro. A wide range of rolled and sheet steel products are produced, much of which is used in the shipbuilding and heavy engineering industries of Calcutta. Other industries in the Damodar Basin include cement, aluminium smelting, chemicals, textiles and electrical engineering. The development of India into an industrialised country is largely a result of the economic expansion of this region and the financial and technical aid supplied by Britain and the USSR.

An alternative and much more detailed classification is that used in official British statistics and is derived from the International Standard Industrial Classification employed by the United Nations (see Table 4.2).

Such is the complexity of modern life, however, that economic activities are more diverse than ever before. This means that all classifications are open to criticism: invariably they group activities that are almost but not exactly alike. Neither do they make a clear distinction between the very important difference between industry (based on the product of the activity overall) and occupation (the job an individual might do). A carpenter working in a steel works would be a carpenter by occupation but a steelworker by industry. Notwithstanding these drawbacks, industrial classifications continue to be used. One used commonly in economic studies is that based on economic balance and locational pull. Seldom, if ever, are the four factors of raw materials, power supply, labour and market equally weighted in importance. In most cases, one or two of these override the others to exert a dominant influence not only on an industry's location but also on its general character, prosperity and growth. This classification is as follows:

(1) *Raw material orientated.* By definition, this includes all industries in the primary group. In the secondary group it is generally true that 'heavy manufacturing' (e.g. heavy engineering and chemical industries) is of this type. Those industries that use large amounts of raw materials – especially if these are heavy or bulky – will be dependent upon the location, extent and value of those natural resources. Where many mineral deposits are found in close proximity, large-scale manufacturing industries may cluster, as is the case in the Damodar Basin, India (Fig. 9.1).

(2) *Power orientated.* These industries are mostly found in the secondary group. The larger the power requirements of a manufacturing firm, the greater will be its dependence on power supplies. Most of the first industries to grow beyond the 'craft' stage were of this type, relying on such

112

power supplies as water (to drive water wheels) and timber (for charcoal). After the Industrial Revolution, coal overrode all other factors in determining the growth of Britain's major industries. Today, other sources of energy such as oil, hydroelectric and nuclear power may dominate, and thus many firms are now locating near these sources.

(3) *Labour orientated*. These industries rely either on a large labour force or on particular skills. Many large manufacturing companies such as car manufacturers have traditionally been of the former kind, whereas many small specialist companies such as chinaware producers are of the latter kind. Many high-technology companies now locate in areas of advanced educational or training facilities – for example in New England (USA) near Yale and Harvard, and in Britain around Cambridge, Oxford and the south Berkshire belt from London to Newbury.

(4) *Market orientated*. Tertiary and quaternary industries are almost exclusively of this type since services nearly always involve direct contact with the customer. In manufacturing, market orientated industries are becoming more common. They include those depending on sales direct to the public (e.g. tailoring) together with those with highly perishable or elaborately packaged products (e.g. food manufacturers and cosmetics firms). Such industries are generally located in and around towns.

The nature of manufacturing

Since most of this chapter is concerned with secondary industry, let us consider the nature of manufacturing in a little more detail.

We have already seen that manufacturing involves the conversion of raw materials, or the assembly of parts, to make new products. Yet between raw materials and the final goods there may well be several stages of production, each involving an alteration of the materials being used. Firms produce either finished or semi-finished goods. Thus the finished product of one industry may be the raw material of another. For example, one firm will turn wool into cloth, but it takes another firm and another process to turn that cloth into clothes. (Incidentally it is for this reason that the term 'raw materials' is necessarily vague in definition. Such materials would be viewed differently by different industries. To an iron and

steel firm, 'raw materials' would include iron ore, limestone and coal; to a car manufacturer they would include finished steel, glass, plastic and other vehicle components.)

There is a general principle in manufacturing that the more processing and alteration a material undergoes, the more valuable will be the final product. This is an important point since it is largely the length and complexity of the manufacturing process that determine the cost of the final product and therefore the income of producers.

Secondary industries fall into three broad groups: craft manufacture, domestic manufacture and factory industry. Craftsmanship is characterised by a worker who buys his own raw materials, fashions them and sells the finished products himself. Domestic industry sees the appearance of the merchant who would deliver the raw materials and control the sale of the finished goods. Factory industry is the most advanced form of manufacturing since it usually entails the use of large premises, large numbers of people, powerful and sophisticated machinery and specialised production.

For the most part, craft and domestic industries characterise secondary industry in the less developed nations of the world, whereas factories tend to appear in the course of economic progress. This is true despite the fact that many Third World countries do possess large-scale manufacturing, and many industrialised countries retain craftsmen and cottage workers. In Japan, domestic and factory industries are found side by side.

However, the identification of different groups of manufacturing activity does not solve the problem of how industries can be studied in economic terms. For example, what criteria may be used to measure the efficiency, output and nature of industry? How can the relative social and economic advantages and disadvantages of industries be judged?

There have been various attempts to solve such questions. The following four are the most important.

Size of unit
This method is based on a simple count of the number of factories found within each industry and an assessment of the size of each production unit. Naturally, sizes may vary greatly from industry to industry and from firm to firm. This is caused by a number of factors including differences in the types of goods made, the number and complexity of the techniques involved in their production, the volume of demand·

for the goods, and the financial and managerial organisation of the industry. Thus, bulky products are usually made in large factories. For products with a very large demand there may be a large number of factories, but for those with limited demand only a few factories. Similarly, centralised control (as with a nationalised industry) often leads to the concentration of production into a few large plants.

Number of employees
This method, like the one just mentioned, is easily calculated since it, too, is based on numbers. It suffers, however, from the same basic drawback in that an industry's size (either in physical terms or in numbers employed) rarely correlates with its efficiency and gives few clues to its economic structure. Furthermore, the number employed is no real evidence of the extent to which industries are beneficial to their employees or to their localities. For instance, a factory employing large numbers may help to alleviate unemployment but could also create overcrowding problems and social stress.

A factor to be considered in this method is that not all employees are alike. Some workers may be productive, others non-productive; some may be skilled, others unskilled. There are male and female workers, full-time and part-time workers, and those on piecerates and those on time-rates. A bias towards any one of these might well lead to unbalanced economies in the areas concerned.

Cost structure
This is based on the proportions of total costs spent on each factor in the manufacturing process – raw materials, power, labour, transport, taxes and capital charges. Some industries such as printing and publishing spend the greatest single proportion of their costs on labour, whereas others such as chemical manufacture spend the largest proportion on fixed capital: that is, on manufacturing plant.

Value added by manufacturing
This is perhaps the best approach since it is most likely to indicate the overall benefit given by factories to their surrounding areas. The greater the gap between the value of the raw materials used and the value of the finished goods, the higher will be the wages given in a particular industry and, hence, the greater the benefit to the community. In the EEC this measure is used as a basis for tax payment. In the USA a more common VA index used is **value added per employee**, a figure which takes into account the

size of the workforce. For both VA figures, petroleum and tobacco products rank highly and textile goods rank lowly.

There are, of course, other measures, including the assessment of the total value of output and a measure of the impact an industry has on the environment. Even so, with any of these approaches, economic comparisons between firms within the same industry remain simpler than economic comparisons between industries.

Functional linkages

No industry is entirely independent or self-sufficient. It has links with other industries and, possibly also, links with the general public. Generally, the more technologically advanced the industry, the greater will be the number of linkages. Such functional linkages may be termed either 'input' or 'output'. In other words, firms will either receive goods or services from, or supply them to, other firms (Fig. 9.2).

Examples of these links may be taken from the building and construction industry. An individual house-building firm would have input linkages with those producing building materials (bricks, cement, timber) and output linkages with estate agents who undertake the sale of the completed houses. There would also be links with such service activities as banking, accounting and transport.

Functional linkages may vary in their complexity, scale and strength. Some might be simple movements of a single product or service from one factory to another, others might consist of a large number of inputs and outputs between numerous factories. Similarly, some links may be small in scale, say between one workshop and another, whereas others are very large, being between major industries. If a certain link is considered important or essential to a firm, it is termed a 'strong linkage', if it is not essential, it is a 'weak linkage'. For example, the links Lucas, Goodyear and Triplex have with Fords and BL are strong, but the same firms may have weak links with, say, stationery or catering firms.

Links may also vary with regard to distance. Some exist over very short distances, within the same locality or even the same street, whereas others may cover enormous distances – some linked firms being continents apart. Generally, local linkages are more numerous than non-local linkages and they usually lead to industrial agglomerations. In some industries – for instance motor manufacturing – linkages are becoming more international.

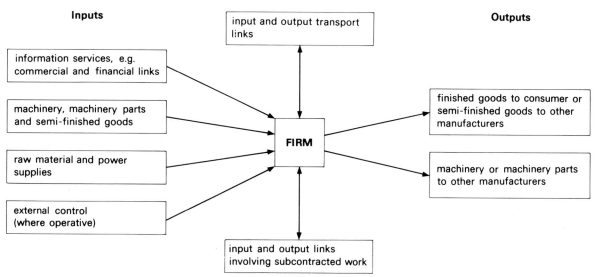

FUNCTIONAL LINKAGES

Inputs

Outputs

input and output transport links

information services, e.g. commercial and financial links

machinery, machinery parts and semi-finished goods

raw material and power supplies

external control (where operative)

FIRM

finished goods to consumer or semi-finished goods to other manufacturers

machinery or machinery parts to other manufacturers

input and output links involving subcontracted work

Figure 9.2   Functional linkages
These links may vary in complexity, scale and strength and can change over time. Generally the larger the firm, the more involved are its links with associated activities.

DEINDUSTRIALISATION

Over the recent past, a significant change has occurred in the industrial structure of many countries within the developed world – namely, a drastic fall in the number of workers employed in manufacturing. This process has been termed 'deindustrialisation' and has had a profound impact on the economic structure of those nations where it has been most apparent.

Britain, in particular, has experienced a net and absolute loss of jobs in secondary activities. Since 1960, the proportion of the working population engaged in manufacturing has fallen from 35% to under 25%. In other words, over 1.8 million jobs have been lost in the manufacturing sector within the past 30 years.

What have been the reasons for this deindustrialisation? Certainly the technological revolution is accountable for some of it: the coming of automation, robotics, computers and microsystems has reduced the need for many unskilled jobs and has made the production of goods less labour intensive. Then there has been government policy. During the 1960s and 1970s, successive British governments increased expenditure on non-marketable output: manpower in Civil Service departments and local authorities rose sharply, investment in financial, tourist and retail services increased, national government funding of infrastructure projects went up. After 1979, the 'monetarist' policies of the Conservative government – together with world economic recession – squeezed investment out of manufacturing production and reduced capital availability for new industrial

developments. The general problem of unemployment in the late 1970s and early 1980s especially hit secondary activities – many firms shrinking or going out of business. Finally – in the case of Britain's deindustrialisation – there were many external causes: the steep rises in the cost of oil in the 1970s; the increased competition from Third World countries such as Taiwan, India and Korea; the changing values of sterling against international currencies.

However, it should not be assumed that deindustrialisation is necessarily disadvantageous. In the short run it may well lead to unemployment, balance of payments deficits and social hardship. In the long run it may lead to improved working conditions (as fewer employees are needed in unpleasant, unhealthy, tedious or dangerous manual jobs); greater leisure opportunities (since average working-hour weeks fall); and more prosperous service activities (as workers move into tertiary and quaternary employment). The manufacturing workforce might decline but output does not necessarily follow suit. Production per worker will go up and even total manufacturing production might rise. In Britain during the 1980s, for instance, output from secondary activities continued to rise even though employed manpower fell.

Deindustrialisation, it can be argued, is a natural development in highly developed countries. It enables an economy to move away from a manufacturing base and into a services base. It may also bring closer the age of leisured consumer society.

Of course, links create chains that bind firms together: the more numerous the links, the more complex the chain. The advantages of chains include reduced costs, greater efficiency and improved quality. The main disadvantage is that, as with every chain, they are only as strong as their weakest links. Each firm's production is reliant upon the production of other firms, so that inefficiency in one firm has repercussions throughout the chain.

The study of linkages is important since it may lead to a greater understanding of the factors determining industrial location and prosperity.

Industrial location

There are two important approaches to the study of industrial location. One is regional and attempts to assess the reasons why certain locations are attractive to industrialisation generally. This may be viewed on any scale from local (within, say, a single town or county) to international (between countries, continents and latitudes). The other approach is industrial in perspective and seeks to explain why individual industries or firms are attracted to particular locations. This involves the study of the particular needs of different industries and why those of one industry may differ from those of another. Of course, these two approaches complement one another. For example, on the one hand, we must consider why South Wales and south-east England exert a pull on industries; on the other, we must find out why, say, the Spencer steelworks is located in South Wales (rather than in any other area) and, also, why it is situated east of Newport and not west or north of it.

The factors to be considered are manifold. They include aspects of physical geography, economics, human and social considerations and politics. However, to generalise about the relative importance of each of these factors is dangerous. This is partly because they act not in isolation but in complex inter-relationships, and partly because their significance may change over time, between areas and from industry to industry. Even so, it is probably true to say that although environmental factors determine the overall regional pattern of industrialisation, economic factors are more likely to direct industries to particular sites.

In deciding upon a final location, the industrialist must weigh up the relative merits of all the potential locations and then select that site which best suits the particular needs of his firm. This does not necessarily mean he will choose the location with the most advantages. Usually, areas possess advantages *and* disadvantages, and manufacturing plant is likely to be located where the favourable factors outweigh the unfavourable ones. It should also be remembered that the best location for one firm may not be the best for another, that the advantages as perceived by one industry may be viewed as disadvantages by another, and that perception varies from individual to individual. Often the choice is a simple one. If an industry has a particular economic bias, it will tend to be located near the factor on which it is dependent: primary industries must be found at the natural resources, and tertiary and quaternary industries, being market orientated, will normally be found in urban areas. But what about secondary industries, which are not especially orientated towards any one economic factor? The optimum location may be near raw materials, or near labour supplies, or again near markets. Some industries, such as light engineering, seem not to be tied to any special kind of location and are called **footloose**. Even those that appear to have similar economic structures and requirements are frequently found in different types of location.

Locational factors

Physical geography. The importance of relief and climate is often overlooked in the study of industrial location. This is unfortunate since these physical factors exert an overriding influence on the pattern of industrialisation. People tend to work only where living conditions are congenial. Any atlas will show that industrial regions are usually associated with areas of low relief and moderate climate, even within relatively small areas. In some cases, industries have particular environmental demands – tourist activities in areas of pleasant climate or spectacular scenery, for instance. The sunny conditions of California certainly encouraged the development of the film industry at Hollywood earlier this century, and, more recently, the location of computer companies in the famous 'Silicon Valley'.

Land. Although strictly 'physical', land may be considered separately in the economic sense since it contains wealth in the form of raw materials and potential power supplies. Generally, industries that lose either bulk or weight in the manufacturing process, or use highly perishable primary products, tend to be located near their raw materials. This is because it is undesirable to transport either waste or materials that may become unusable, the former for reasons of

Figure 9.3 Industrial location on an English coalfield
Seaham, on the Northumberland and Durham coalfield, has grown up as an important industrial town. Local iron and steel works and port facilities led to urban expansion last century – around new factories and mines – and many manufacturing firms still survive here despite the recession of the early 1980s.

cost, the latter for reasons of the efficiency and standards of production. Into this category would come copper smelting, the iron and steel industry, cement making and most types of food processing.

Power supplies may act similarly as a pull. Many types of energy source are either immovable or may be transported only at immense cost; heavy or bulky fuels especially are of this kind. Thus, industries based on coal or oil tend to be tied to particular locations, the former to coalfields (Fig. 9.3), the latter (if oil is imported) to the coast. The same is true where large quantities of energy are needed. The electro-metallurgical industry, for instance, requires large amounts of hydroelectricity and is thus located where such power is cheaply obtained. This can be seen in both Canada (Kitimat) and Norway (Rjukan), where HEP is used to extract aluminium from bauxite.

It should be mentioned at this point that the importance of both raw materials and power supplies is now declining. This is as a result of improved transport and technology, greater sophistication and complexity in modern industry and the relative increase in the importance of other locational factors. This change is well illustrated by the textile industries of the UK.

Water supplies may also be considered under the heading of land. As would be expected, industries that use large quantities of water, either for cooling purposes (e.g. steel making and power generation) or for processing (e.g. brewing), will be found at rivers or wells if fresh water is needed, or at the coast if salt water is needed. In Britain, brewing takes place along the River Trent, in the London Basin and in the West Midlands (where local sandstones provide important underground reservoirs), and most nuclear power stations (e.g. Dungeness, Bradwell and Oldbury) are sited on the coast.

There are some basic land requirements demanded by all firms, such as sufficient space and a flat surface, both of which reduce the cost of building. In addition, some firms require land where waste disposal is both easy and cheap. Recently, amenity considerations have exerted themselves. In many areas, as in the case of national parks, firms are expected to blend their buildings and processing plant into the surrounding landscape. This inflates the cost of construction and therefore discourages industrialisation generally.

Capital. This includes both fixed capital (buildings and machinery) and financial capital (money); both may be of importance to the location of industry. The cost of acquiring fixed capital varies from place to place, and areas where costs are low will have a greater pull than those where they are high. This is

---

TEXTILE INDUSTRIES IN THE UNITED KINGDOM

Woollens

Britain's woollen industry was originally accommodated in numerous cottage workshops scattered throughout the country, prospering during the Middle Ages in areas where sheep grazing was widespread: in Wessex, East Anglia, the Pennines and the Welsh and Scottish hills. West Yorkshire especially became important; here there were the added locational advantages of soft water and power from the Pennine streams and the skilled labour of the Flemish weavers from the Low Countries who settled here. With the introduction of coal as a source of power and the development of machinery to replace hand labour, those woollen manufacturing areas on or near coalfields expanded at the expense of others. Today, well over half Britain's woollen cloth is made in West Yorkshire. Small woollen industries survive elsewhere (in Somerset, Wiltshire, the Tweed Valley and on Skye), but these concentrate on high quality, limited markets and specialised products. In West Yorkshire there is now an industrial agglomeration developed on the linkages between various woollen manufacturers which together have achieved economies of scale. The original reasons for their location no longer apply, but these firms remain in the same locality and are an example of 'industrial inertia'.

Cotton

Once a centre for woollen industries, Lancashire turned to cotton in the late Middle Ages. When raw cotton was first imported, workers already skilled in textile production were needed for its conversion into cloth. The Yorkshire guilds (craft unions), however, were more powerful than their Lancastrian counterparts and refused to handle the new fibre. The less effective Lancashire guilds could not so refuse. Other locational advantages for cotton manufacture included soft water and power from the local rivers, a damp atmosphere (which prevents the snapping of cotton fibre), a west-coast position (facilitat-

ing raw cotton imports from the USA) and, later, the close proximity to the coalfield and the invention of spinning and weaving machines. Along Clydeside a smaller cotton industry grew up for similar reasons and in the East Midlands a small lace-manufacturing industry developed as a result of the local invention of lace-making machinery. In the old county of Lancashire, the various linkages between cotton manufacturers and other firms have led to the growth of a large industrial area. Textile machinery is made at Oldham, chemicals are produced at Widnes (to aid the bleaching and dyeing of cotton) and a whole variety of engineering firms have grown up over the entire region.

Linen

Northern Ireland was, up to the 1960s, one of the most important linen-manufacturing areas in the world. This industry grew up originally on abundant supplies of home-grown flax and cheap labour. Coal was imported from Ayr and flax imported from Belgium.

Man-made fibres

Not shown on Figure 9.4 are the locations of Britain's artificial fibre manufacturers. Man-made cloth can be derived either from cellulose (wood pulp), as in the case of rayon, or from petroleum, as with nylon, polyester and acetates. The makers of these are mostly linked to the chemicals industry and are generally located around the coast where raw materials can easily be imported – for example on Teesside, Merseyside and Humberside.

Foreign competition

Over the past 30 years, British textile manufacturers have suffered badly from the import of cheap foreign materials. A great many mill closures have resulted, and many firms have had to shed labour in order to become more competitive.

Figure 9.4 Textile industry location
There is evidence to suggest – especially with the production decline of natural fibre and increase of artificial fibre – that the importance of coalfields in the location of textile industries is declining. Other locational factors are becoming more important.

mon examples of this. Such places are now used commonly for small-scale electrical engineering and specialist textile manufacture.

The availability and cost of investment capital exerts no less a pull and this could explain why centres of finance such as the City of London and New York have also become industrial centres.

Labour. The cost and availability of labour, together with its quality and quantity, vary spatially. Areas with skilled or versatile labour will tend to be attractive to automated or specialist firms, whereas areas where there are vast quantities of unskilled, and possibly cheap, labour will attract large-scale, labour-intensive firms. It is, for example, the relative cheapness of labour in Britain compared with other parts of the EEC that brings the Japanese Nissan car company to this country. Other considerations to be taken into account include the stability and efficiency of labour, absenteeism and labour relations. In the past there have been suggestions that the Ford Motor Company might leave Britain, such is the country's poor record for strikes.

It must be borne in mind, however, that the importance of the labour factor is governed to a certain extent by its mobility. Labour can be either geographically or occupationally mobile: that is, can move between places and regions or between jobs. Generally, the less mobile it is, the greater will be the significance of labour as a locational consideration.

Management. Once considered part of labour, managerial and entrepreneurial enterprise is now more often discussed separately. The success of any industry is dependent upon the ability of its management. Yet such skills are not evenly distributed. In Britain, for instance, south-east England is believed to possess a larger number of high calibre executives than other regions and therefore it has a correspondingly stronger industrial pull.

Transport. Transport facilities are essential to all firms. Therefore areas well provided with efficient transport routes will attract more industries than those where such facilities are lacking. This is why firms are situated along roads and canals, and around harbours, railway stations and airports. It should be pointed out that firms aim to reduce 'economic distance' rather than actual distance. In other words, they aim to reduce transport costs. The only firms that do not appear to seek lowest transport costs are those that make goods with high value:weight volume

particularly significant in the location of small or new firms, which often find existing buildings attractive propositions since converting and using them will save time and money. For this reason, buildings erected for one purpose might now be used for another: cotton mills, wartime ammunition factories and even old railway stations or post offices are com-

ratios (jewellery and advanced computers, for instance). Small but highly priced articles can be transported long distances almost irrespective of cost.

Markets. As we have seen, a firm's market can be either the general public or another firm, can be in the immediate vicinity or abroad. In all cases, its importance as a locational factor is growing, even for firms not formerly considered to be market orientated. This is because technological advances and improved transport have reduced the importance of other locational factors – even coal can be transported much more easily and cheaply now than formerly. Also, in developed countries there has been an increase in luxury consumer goods which, by their very nature, are market orientated. In addition, markets are usually found in towns where labour and capital are available, thereby making the market appear more important than it really is as a locational factor.

Human and chance factors. Occasionally, industries and firms have been located and have grown in areas for no apparent physical or economic reason. These may be considered chance locations. Sometimes firms have started up by accident, sometimes because a manager or owner has chosen a site which he personally likes. One of the most famous examples of such a location is the motor vehicle industry at Oxford. This began when William Morris, a repairer of bicycles, bought the old school where his father had been educated, and converted it into his first factory.

Politics. It has been assumed that industries are free to develop anywhere, depending on a combination of physical, economic and personal factors. Yet, in reality, this is not always true. Often industrial location is the result of government intervention. For various social, political and strategic reasons, most countries today have policies whereby industries are persuaded or forced to locate in particular areas. For example, in the USSR, industries have been moved eastwards into the Urals, Tashkent and Ukraine, and for the same defensive strategic reasons the USA has relocated its aircraft industry away from the eastern seaboard.

Even on a small scale, local authorities may influence location. Land-use zoning policies, for instance, can prevent firms moving into residential areas or regions of beautiful countryside, and high rate levels can discourage industrial growth.

The ways in which location in Britain has been influenced by government policies is discussed in Chapter 20.

Locational changes
An important feature of industrial location is its dynamism: the factors outlined earlier are constantly changing. New sources of supply are discovered, new methods of production and transport evolve, and new demands develop (see Fig. 9.5). Such changes may only have a small or gradual impact on the relocation of old firms; they can have an immediate impact on new firms and their distribution.

In many developed countries, the old supplies of raw materials and power have become, or are becoming, exhausted, and new supplies – often from less developed countries – must be imported. This may encourage industry to move to coastal sites. Similarly, new technologies and inventions may reduce the importance of one locational factor and increase that of another. Such innovations might also lead to a general expansion of factories, which itself could result in a greater need for flat, cheap and open land on which to build.

As standards of living rise, the relative importance of industries producing necessities declines while that of those making luxuries increases. Since these industries have different locational demands, this tendency could have far-reaching consequences. This is especially so if there are also changes in output. Many old industrial regions have declined in importance (e.g. Manchester and Merseyside), whereas areas formerly considered agricultural are growing into major industrial regions, such as parts of southern France and southern Germany.

Industrial agglomerations

Industrial concentration occurs when an area offers the greatest relative advantages to a variety of firms and different firms share the same locational requirements. In each agglomeration may be found all types of industries located side by side. These, and the firms that make them up, may have strong functional linkages that bind them together, and will probably achieve financial savings or **external economies of scale** by sharing transport facilities, research, administration, social services, training and educational services, and so forth. A concentration also provides pools of labour, capital, managerial

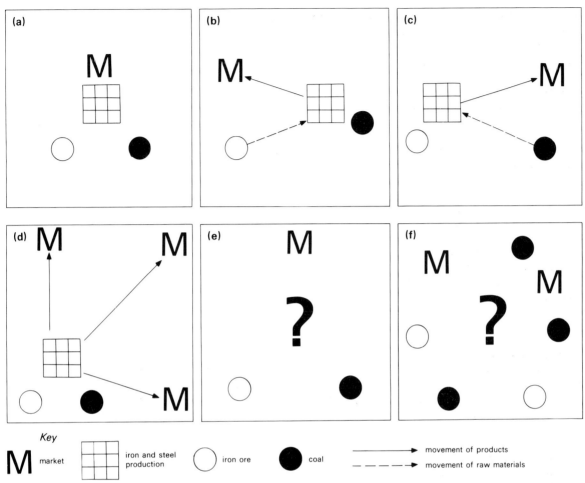

Figure 9.5 Locational change in the iron and steel industry
In diagram (a), both raw materials and the market are situated together so that iron and steel production takes place locally. Should the existing coal reserves become depleted and new reserves be found elsewhere (b) or existing iron ore deposits become worked out and new deposits be found further afield (c), the location of iron and steel production might change (especially if the new resources are low grade). Should, alternatively, the existing market disappear and several new markets open up (d), an iron and steel firm might find it advisable to remain at the same site (near to the resources). Should the location of both resources and market become more dispersed (e) or more numerous (f), the choice of new sites for iron and steel production becomes more problematical. Such a choice might be affected by the quality of the resources concerned, transport facilities and government policy.

expertise and customers, and hence will attract still more industries from outside.

Once in existence, therefore, agglomerations tend to grow. Every factory movement or expansion sets in motion a chain reaction called the **multiplier effect**. Each new industry will lead to the development of connected industries and transport facilities, which, in turn, will have further effects of a similar nature.

Generally, the extent of industrial concentration increases with economic progress: the more advanced the country, the greater will be the size of its agglomerations. Thus, the largest agglomerations are found in the developed world, for example in South Wales, West Yorkshire, the Ruhr coalfield (West Germany) and the Great Lakes industrial belt of North America.

The degree to which industries are concentrated, on both a local and a national scale, may be measured using the **locational quotient**. To measure the relative importance of a single agglomeration, the percentage of industrial workers in that region is divided by the average percentage for the country as a whole. Thus, if a town has 60% of its working population employed in manufacturing, when the national average is 40%, the quotient for that town is 60÷40=1.5. A quotient above 1.0 shows that an area has more industrial concentration than does the country as a whole; a quotient below 1.0 shows that industry is less developed in a region than might be expected from the national average. Thus, the higher the quotient, the more important tends to be an agglomeration.

More complicated quotients, using other formulae, may be calculated for particular industries and using other criteria, including the number of factories, the wages paid and the number of man-hours worked. The choice would depend upon the purpose of the analysis.

Thompson's *Concentration theory* has identified a hierarchy of agglomerations whereby each level of industrial development is linked to the next (Fig. 9.6). For every two units there is one at the next stage up. The smallest is the individual industrial plant. For

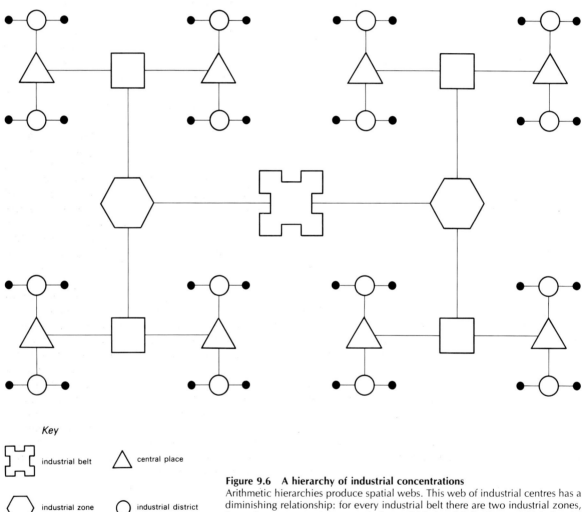

Key

⬒ industrial belt   △ central place

⬡ industrial zone   ◯ industrial district

▢ urban system   ● individual plant

Figure 9.6 A hierarchy of industrial concentrations
Arithmetic hierarchies produce spatial webs. This web of industrial centres has a diminishing relationship: for every industrial belt there are two industrial zones, four urban systems, eight central places, 16 industrial districts and 32 industrial plants. A large, developed country – or perhaps a developing continent – might have two such webs. A small country might only be part of an international web – having, perhaps, five central places.

every two of these there is one industrial district. Two districts are linked to a central place (usually an industrial town such as Swindon). This hierarchy continues up to an urban system (usually a small conurbation such as Sheffield–Rotherham), an industrial zone (usually a large urban region such as Clydeside) and finally an industrial belt (e.g. that which crosses north-west Europe or the Great Lakes region in North America).

Agglomerations can bring to firms not only benefits but also drawbacks. Frequently, heavy concentrations lead to overcrowding, congestion, higher land prices and pollution. There may even come a time when firms will actually benefit by moving away from an agglomeration, a process often called **deglomeration**. Such a movement became apparent in many British cities (such as London) and was encouraged by the government's regional policy. In the USA many companies are now moving away from conurbations and into smaller towns, where industrial growth is easier and cheaper.

Industrial inertia

Industries may remain in a particular location long after the reasons for being there have disappeared. This **inertia** is the result of two main factors. The first is that physical capital is fixed. Once land has been acquired, a factory built and machinery installed, there is a great incentive for a firm to stay where it is. The enormous cost of relocation would far outweigh any financial savings made at a new site. The second is that, once located, a firm may acquire secondary advantages. The benefits of agglomerations already mentioned would exert a magnetism from which a firm may find it both difficult and expensive to break away.

Examples of industrial inertia are numerous. In the Don Valley (South Yorkshire), the original iron industry was based on charcoal supplies for power and local iron ore deposits. Today, other fuels are used (mainly coking coal) and scrap or iron ore must be imported, yet Sheffield remains an important steel town and Doncaster remains an important iron and steel town, in both cases, partly as a result of the concentration of education and training facilities. Similar inertia is found in the woollen textile industries of West Yorkshire and the cotton textile industries of Lancashire.

Industrial regions of the world

The distribution of manufacturing, and especially of large-scale heavy industry, is very uneven around the world. Figure 9.7 shows that industrial development has been generally associated with temperate latitudes, coalfields, port facilities and regions of European settlement.

Factory-based industrialisation may be said to have started in Britain during the 18th century. Population growth, agricultural improvements, increasing trade with the Empire, technical inventions, and the large-scale use of coal all led together to the Industrial Revolution. With this came the growth of towns and industries over coalfields. From Britain, industrialisation spread first across Europe and later to the United States. More recently still, it emerged in Russia, Japan and many parts of the developing world. In many of these cases, coalfields, or easy access to coal supplies, have been the most important single locational factor.

Today, the industrial use of coal is declining and a new generation of industrial regions is growing up. New, easily transmitted, power supplies are being used and light industry is becoming more important as higher living standards generate a greater demand for luxury goods. The location of these industries shows the increasing importance of transport facilities and markets. In consequence, large industrial areas have appeared around the capital cities and metropoli of the world: London, Paris, New York, Moscow, Sydney, Tokyo and Buenos Aires.

In many developing countries, where primary production was once exclusively important, manufacturing is growing rapidly. Sometimes new industry is based on imported raw materials and fuel and, often, even imported technology. There are two reasons for this industrial expansion. The first is that the supplies of finished goods which developing countries obtained from Europe and the USA were cut off during the two World Wars, causing them to produce their own. The second is that many economically backward countries see industrial growth as a means of making themselves more self-sufficient and politically more independent.

Theories of industrial location

As with many other aspects of human geography, the

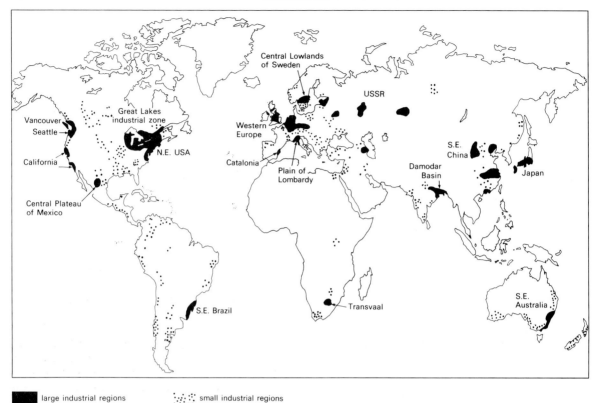

large industrial regions   small industrial regions

Figure 9.7   World industrial regions
The 'Power Belt' from the Mississippi to the Ural Mountains accounts for about 80% of the world's total value of manufactured output and about 90% of the world's total energy consumption.

study of industrial location has moved away from being descriptive and towards a more scientific approach. In particular, theories and models (representing order and regularity) have been formulated in an attempt to explain real world locations.

The central aim of such theories is to find, for each firm or industry, the **optimal location** – the economically best location. What this actually means and how it might be measured are, of course, open to question. Most economists, however, agree that 'best' locations are those that give maximum profits. Highest profits are obtained when costs are at their lowest and revenues at their highest. Yet rarely, if ever, are these two situations found at the same time or place. For this reason, locational theories divide into two groups: those that consider **least-cost locations** and those that consider **maximum-revenue locations**.

The Weber theory
The most important theory based on least costs is that proposed by Weber in his book, *Theory of the loca-*

tion of industries, published in 1909 (English translation published in 1929 by University of Chicago Press). This is based on transport costs (as opposed to processing costs) and, like all theories, assumes certain preconditions. These are: some raw materials are fixed in location whereas others (such as water) are ubiquitous (found everywhere); markets are fixed at certain points; transport costs are determined by weight of product and distance; perfect competition exists; and man acts rationally. Fundamentally, Weber imagined that least costs obtain highest profits.

To find the least-transport-cost location, Weber used simplified locational triangles, assuming two points where raw materials are found and a single market. In Figure 9.8a it is assumed that transport costs are equal for the finished goods and for both raw materials: that is, the firm pays the same for bringing its raw materials into the plant as it does for taking its products to the market. Point **P** – where the factory would be built – is therefore located at the centre, so

124

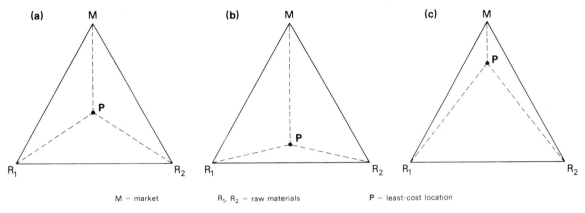

Figure 9.8 Weber's locational triangles
These hypothetical instances can be applied to real world examples.

that the total distance to be covered by transport is at its minimum. Figure 9.8b illustrates a 'weight-losing industry', in which the total weight of raw materials is higher than that of the finished goods. Here, the transport costs for raw materials are far higher than for finished goods (because the raw materials contain waste). Point **P** is located nearer to the raw materials. Figure 9.8c illustrates a 'weight-gaining industry', in which the total weight of raw materials is lower than that of the finished goods. Here, transport costs for the raw materials are much smaller than for the finished goods (because they weigh less or, possibly, because they are less fragile). Point **P** is located nearer the market.

In order to find out whether industries are market orientated or raw-material orientated, Weber devised a simple *Material Index* formula:

$$\text{material index} = \frac{\text{weight of raw materials}}{\text{weight of finished goods}}$$

For example, if it takes 4 tonnes of raw material to make 2 tonnes of finished goods, the material index would be $4 \div 2 = 2$. Conversely, 1 tonne of raw material making 2 tonnes of finished goods would give an index of $\frac{1}{2}$. Naturally, an industry with an index of more than 1.0 would be raw-material orientated (e.g. heavy steel manufacturing) and an index of less than 1.0 would indicate a market-orientated industry (e.g. baking).

A basic fault in this approach is its overemphasis on transport costs. Weber realised this and therefore considered possible modifications to his locational triangles. One possible cause for modification is differing labour costs – a pool of cheap labour may act as a locational pull factor. In other words, firms may be tempted to locate away from the point of least transport costs and towards a point of least labour costs (provided, of course, that such a move resulted in a fall in total costs). This would especially be the case for firms employing great quantities of labour. Figure 9.9 shows this diagrammatically. A similar modification may be caused by the existence of an industrial agglomeration, which also acts as a magnet to industries and firms.

Many geographers have tested Weber's hypotheses on modern industry and found that several of his conclusions remain valid. Smith (*Transactions of the Institute of British Geographers* **21**, 1955, pp. 1–18) applied the material index formula to a variety of British industries, and Isard used the transport cost concept in his work on the United States steel industry. Both achieved some degree of success. Notwithstanding these studies, however, Weber's theory is open to criticism. In particular it can be argued that his preconditions are unrealistic. Transport costs do not rise commensurately with weight and distance, perfect competition rarely exists, and man does not always act rationally. Some theorists have criticised Weber for being too concerned with costs and assuming that demand comes from a single point. For this reason, further locational models have been based on a maximum profit approach. The most important of these are the models of Hotelling and Lösch.

The Hotelling theory
An early attempt to explain industrial location through the profit motive was made by H. Hotelling (see 'Stability in competition', in *Economic Journal* **39**, 1929, pp. 41–57). In his theory the impact of

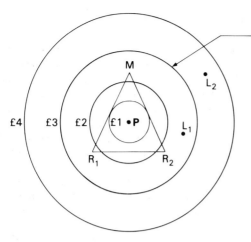

£4   £3   £2   £1 •P

M

L₂

L₁

R₁   R₂

Each isodapane represents a unit of £1 – industrial location on the £4 line would be £4 more costly in terms of transport costs than location at point **P**

Figure 9.9   The effect of labour and transport costs on location
Isodapanes are lines of equal total transport costs. Two points (L₁ L₂) offer cheap labour, which will reduce total costs by £3 per unit. Location of the factory at L₁ is likely since it is within the £3 isodapane – more is saved by the move than is lost. Location at L₂ is unlikely.

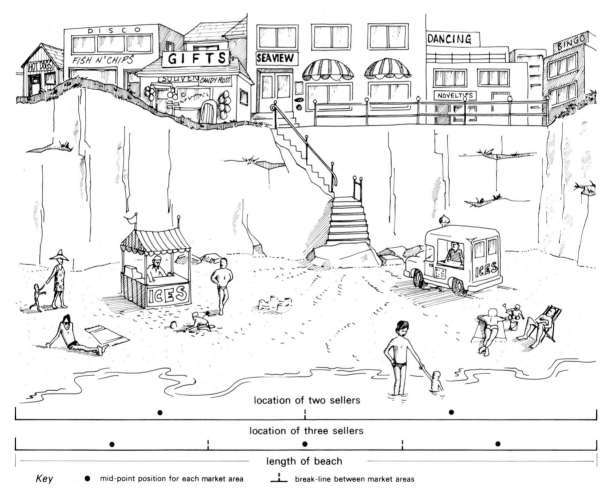

location of two sellers

location of three sellers

length of beach

Key   ● mid-point position for each market area   ⊥ break-line between market areas

Figure 9.10   Location according to mutual interdependence (after Hotelling)
The break-line between market areas will be halfway between each pair of sellers. This means that market areas will be equal in size and sellers will be equally spaced. This ensures economic equilibrium and the survival of all sellers at a mutually beneficial level. If one seller moved to one end of the beach, he would reduce the size of his own market area and would thus lose custom to his competitors.

demand was considered together with the idea of locational interdependence, whereby firms in perfect competition arrange themselves spatially for mutual sales benefits.

In order to simplify the workings of his theory, Hotelling devised a model composed of two ice-cream sellers in competition for custom on a busy holiday beach, these representing firms or industries situated on a uniform market area. Upon this beach, people (potential customers) are evenly distributed, have totally inelastic demand (inexhaustible at any price) for ice-cream and rationally would purchase ice-cream from the nearest seller. The sellers themselves have the same financial overheads, sell the same quality ice-cream, can each relocate without extra cost and would each be able (if allowed) to supply the whole market. In addition, Hotelling presupposed that costs of production are equal everywhere and that conditions of local monopoly exist (whereby each seller totally dominates his own market area).

The conclusions of this theory are outlined in Figure 9.10. For a while each seller would try to beat his competitor, by reducing his prices or by moving his position on the beach in order to outsell the other. Eventually, after failing to oust each other (since both ice-cream sellers are equally able to compete), they will reach a compromise solution. An agreement of equilibrium would be struck: they would agree on a common price and would locate at such points that each would control the same share of the market (50%). For their own convenience – and the spatial and financial convenience of their customers – they would locate at the centre of the two market areas. Theoretically, three ice-cream sellers on a beach would each agree to control one-third of the total market and locate themselves accordingly at regular intervals.

Naturally, Hotelling's theory of locational interdependence has been criticised, not least because of its unreal preconditions of perfect competition and uniform demand. However, the idea that firms and industries might find mutually beneficial terms and might locate in conscious response to their neighbours and competitors is an interesting concept and, notwithstanding the constraints of the natural environment, economics and political forces, has a certain degree of validity.

The Lösch theory

Long after Hotelling first suggested a link between industrial location and profitability within separate market zones, another academic devised a more comprehensive theory based on the same premise. This theory (see A. Lösch, *Economics of location*, Yale University Press, 1954) is based on demand, and it presupposes that the optimal location of a firm or industry is that which commands the largest market area and so produces the greatest revenue. Assuming a flat, uniform land surface, constant supply, and demand spread out evenly throughout a region, Lösch set out to explain the size and shape of market areas. To do this he imagined that the delivery price of all products is determined solely by transport costs: as distance from a factory increases, so the price charged for a product rises since the industrialist must cover the extra cost of transport involved. Since price tends to rise with distance, demand tends to fall. At a certain point, therefore, demand for a particular product will disappear entirely. This being so in all directions around a factory, the market area will be circular (Fig. 9.11). Each factory owner will look for a location that can command the largest possible market area. He would not wish his market area to overlap that of another factory making similar goods, since this would reduce his revenue. The result would be a region in which factories are spaced evenly with their market areas adjacent to each other, each being hexagonal in shape (Fig. 9.12).

On a much larger scale, the factories in the diagrams may be viewed instead as industrial estates or even as industrial towns, each with its own hex-

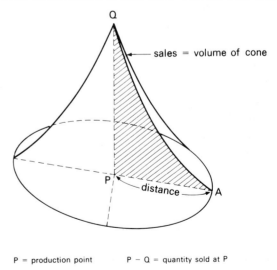

P = production point   P − Q = quantity sold at P

Figure 9.11 The theoretical shape of the market area
Circular market areas are to be expected on isotropic surfaces and in perfect competition. They are therefore only theoretical.

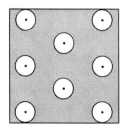 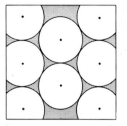

(a) Series of small circular trade areas centred on production points

(b) Enlarged circular trade areas with unserved areas shaded

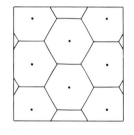

(c) Hexagons represent the most efficient shape of trade areas

Figure 9.12 The development of market areas
The hexagonally divided surface is a common phenomenon in geography since it represents an ideally tessellated division of an area.

agonal **hinterland**. Of course, every product will have its own demand and therefore its own market. Thus different factories will have different sized market areas, as would different industrial complexes.

The value of locational theories

Various geographers have tested the usefulness of industrial location theories by studying actual examples. There is no space here to consider these tests in any detail, but some comment can be made about their findings. For example, certain conclusions become apparent when comparing hypothetical with actual industrial situations. The first is that all three theories so far considered are valid, to a limited extent, everywhere and that each has its strength among particular industries and in particular countries. Thus, Weber's theory seems to be more accurate with heavy manufacturing firms using a small number of raw material supplies and inside

developed countries, whereas the theories of Hotelling and Lösch seem to be more accurate with consumer and service industries and inside less developed countries. The second conclusion is that all three theories can usefully be modified and adapted in order to improve their value in explaining real world phenomena. Such alterations do not necessarily devalue their acceptability as theories. The third conclusion is that all attempts to formulate spatial models for an industrial environment are restricted by their own hypothetical limitations. The further reality grows away from theoretical perfection, the less valid are the hypotheses enshrined within the theories.

Two other considerations to be borne in mind when comparing locational theories with the real world are those concerning historical accident and human perspectives of reality. Theories and models often tend to ignore the constant changes taking place in the location of industry and in the relative importance of the determinants of location. They fossilise those factors which originally determined industrial distribution and, in so doing, fail to reflect the transient nature of locational elements. Weber's theory was probably more accurate at the beginning of this century than it is now; Hotelling's theory was probably more appropriate in the years between the two World Wars than today; Lösch's theory was probably more true in the 1950s than in the 1980s. As the years have gone by, other newer theories have had to be devised to fit the changing circumstances. Then there is the personal dimension. Theories and models are the result not just of research and detailed study but also of the characteristics of their formulators. Two geographers might discover the same findings yet formulate different theories, since their perceptions of the world, their sociological and cultural characteristics, their personalities and behaviour patterns and their political persuasions are different.

All theories have faults: Weber overemphasised costs, Hotelling overstressed interdependence, Lösch gave too much attention to demand. Because of this, the past 30 years have seen the formulation of many new theories to suit the altered circumstances of industrial location. Greenhut and Isard, for example, attempted to combine the two approaches of Weber and Lösch, with a consequent increase in complexity.

M. Greenhut (*Plant location in theory and practice*, University of North Carolina Press, 1956) based his study on the maximisation of profit, and W. Isard (*Location and space economy*, MIT Press, 1956) linked location theory with other branches of

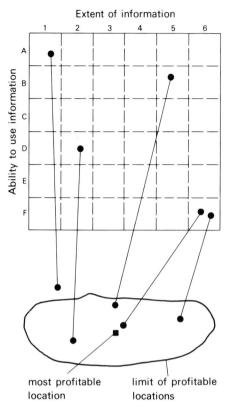

Extent of information

Ability to use information

most profitable location

limit of profitable locations

Figure 9.13 Locational decisions based on a behavioural matrix
The matrix square shows the levels of knowledge and intelligence of decision-makers (managers or entrepreneurs); the sketch shows the locations chosen for industrial development by those decision-makers. The least able and informed businessmen (A1) may choose a non-profitable location and build a factory doomed to failure. More intelligent or more informed businessmen will probably choose more favourable locations. The best and most informed businessmen (F6) are most likely to choose the best location – but might not, as a result of other factors: chance or political restraint, for example.

economics, especially with the **substitution principle** – the idea that firms try to minimise costs by looking for cheaper substitutes for a location.

More recently still, locational theories have been concerned more with the **behavioural approach** in an effort to bring models closer to reality. The work of A. Pred is of particular interest in this respect (see *Behaviour and location*, Gleerup, 1967). He devised a **behavioural matrix**, which can be used to analyse various locational decisions. This is based on the realistic assumption that industrialists have varying levels of knowledge and ability. For example, a businessman with limited knowledge but great abil-

ity would choose a different location from another with extensive knowledge but limited ability. The worst location would probably be chosen by the businessman with little knowledge and limited ability. (See Fig. 9.13.)

It is easy to prove that locational models like those of Weber and Lösch do not conform exactly with the real world. But they are not meant to – if they did, they would not be models. Theories and models serve not to demonstrate or describe what happens in reality but to help our understanding of how the real world works. Oversimplifications are usually necessary in order to understand complexity.

Even so, let us consider some of the ways in which locational theories do not correspond with reality. In particular it should be emphasised that real man, as opposed to 'economic man', does not act rationally. Even if he knew where maximum profits could be obtained, he is unlikely to choose an economically optimal location. More probably he is likely to choose that location which gives sufficient profit at least effort. This is called the **satisficer concept**: a businessman is prepared to accept a satisfactory location rather than the economically best location. Many industrialists place more emphasis on their share of the market than on maximum profits, and would therefore be quite happy to achieve profits which are merely higher than those of their competitors.

Taking the satisficer concept a stage further, we should remember that even the greatest share of profits is not always a businessman's sole aim. He may prefer to forgo some profits in order to locate in a place that is especially amenable – in a pleasant climate, for example, at the coast or near a favourite golf course. Such social benefits might equal economic benefits and exert a comparable pull. Conversely, of course, environmental or social disadvantages may actually discourage industrial location in a certain area. In Britain the traditional image of northern England as a place of 'dark satanic mills' is undoubtedly a factor in the movement of light industry to the South.

Other factors to be considered when applying theories to the real world are levels of rates and taxes, entrepreneurial skills and political systems. Whereas higher rates and taxes may result in higher costs, subsidies may have the reverse effect. The former would reduce the number of potential least-cost locations and the latter would increase them. Similarly, a more efficient firm will have more of a locational choice than a less efficient firm. Very skilled entrepreneurs could make a profit almost anywhere within reason; entrepreneurs with limited skill might need

THE LOCATION OF THE MOTOR VEHICLE INDUSTRY IN THE USA

A study of a major manufacturing industry and its location within almost any large country can show the relevance of those factors which determine industrial location and can, also, demonstrate the validity of accepted locational theories. In this respect, the United States motor vehicle industry is no exception. The spatial characteristics of this particular industry not only show the importance of both physical and human factors but also help to prove that the theories of both Weber and Lösch have some claim to realism.

Figure 9.14 shows the principal centres of the motor vehicle industry. We can distinguish the traditional motor vehicle manufacturing areas on the one hand (where components are both made and assembled) and the recent motor vehicle assembly-only areas on the other.

Traditional motor vehicle manufacturing centres

These are located according to the following criteria:

(1) *Physical advantages.* The landscape hereabouts is devoid of steep gradients and difficult terrain; this has always allowed for relatively easy industrial and urban development.
(2) *Local raw materials.* In the early days, firms making furniture, wagons and horse-drawn carriages grew up around the Great Lakes since this belt formed the dividing line between hardwood and softwood timber-growing regions, making all varieties of wood accessible. Later, iron ore from the Vermilion and Mesabi Ranges (near Lake Superior) and coal from Pennsylvania and West Virginia were sufficiently close for use in the early car industry.
(3) *Transport facilities.* The Great Lakes themselves, and adjoining canals, provide a cheap form of water transport for both raw materials and finished goods. Chicago is, in addition, a major rail junction, with train links all over the continent.
(4) *Labour supplies.* This region is sufficiently close to the East Coast and its conurbations to be accessible to large numbers of cheap and unskilled workers. Many immigrants were attracted from their eastern landfall to the Mid-West car factories by the certainty and regularity of work.
(5) *Capital availability.* Much money filtered into motor vehicle manufacture from the excessive profits of early coalmining at Pittsburgh and from the economic boom which accompanied political patronage at Washington and New York.
(6) *Market proximity.* On a local scale there has always been a large market for motor cars in north-east USA, the most densely populated region in the continent. On a national scale, the Great Lakes are sufficiently central to be reasonably close to all parts of the country, giving them a large potential market hinterland. Also, since the USA is such a large land mass, travel involves great distances and this increases the need for transport facilities.
(7) *Skill tradition.* In earlier days, metal-working firms were set up to supply this most agricultural of regions – with farm machinery, carts and trucks, springs, rubber tyres, paints, varnish and numerous other pressed-steel and brass implements. Such firms could easily adapt to supplying the motor vehicle industry.
(8) *Chance factors.* Henry Ford (1863–1947) – who pioneered mass-production methods and set up some of the first car factories – was born in Michigan and brought up in the countryside just outside Detroit. It is largely owing to his efforts that Detroit became the automobile capital of North America. At the beginning of this century, the Great Lakes belt and New England both contained a vehicle industry. The former survived and the latter failed because New England industrialists mistakenly concentrated upon the design and manufacture of steam-driven and electric vehicles, whereas the Mid-West industrialists concentrated upon petrol-powered models, which subsequently became most popular. Once the major car companies around the Great Lakes (especially Ford and General Motors) had beaten off early competitors, their monopoly strengthened and industrial inertia set in.

Recent motor vehicle assembly centres
Although the Great Lakes region has remained the chief car manufacturing zone – the agglomeration bringing with it advantages of economies of scale – recent years have seen a geographical dispersal of car assembly plants. This process can be viewed both through Weber's theory of industrial location and through Lösch's theory.

The Weber theory applied   The transport of car parts is considerably cheaper than that of completed cars: a railway wagon being able to carry the unassembled parts for 12 cars compared with the finished versions of only four cars. In addition, complete vehicles require more care and packing (at greater cost) than do vehicle parts. Thus, motor vehicle assembly represents the equivalent of Weber's weight-gaining industry and is therefore located close to the market. Since the market for motor cars is widespread across the USA, it follows that assembly plants should also be located at widespread points.

The Lösch theory applied   The demand for motor cars is evenly distributed throughout the USA in proportion to population density. Since all the vehicle assembly plants are owned by only a small number of companies, locational planning is easy and inter-company agreement is feasible. Thus the locations of assembly plants conform closely with the geographical distribution and population throughout the country. An automobile assembly plant is never far away!

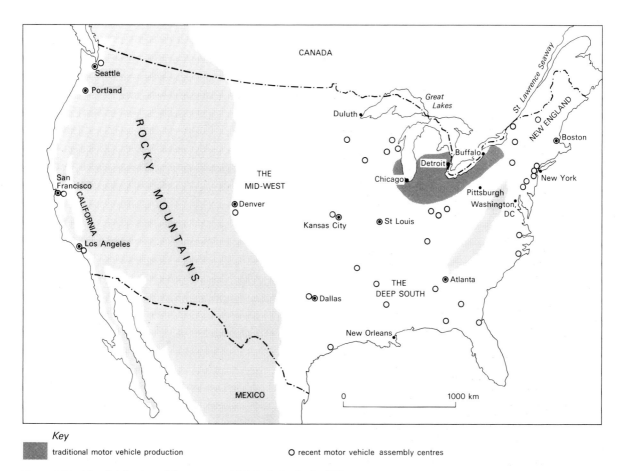

Key

▨ traditional motor vehicle production   ○ recent motor vehicle assembly centres

Figure 9.14   The distribution of the motor vehicle industry in the USA
The movement of car assembly plants southwards from the Great Lakes can be attributed to the locational pull of cheap labour supplies in the traditionally poor 'Deep South'. Such an instance was recognised as a theory modification by Weber. Even today, motor car companies find assembly costs are significantly cheaper in Georgia and Alabama than in Pennsylvania. This fact is now especially important. Ever since the recession of the early 1980s – when sales fell and over 300 000 auto-workers were made redundant – motor companies have been hypersensitive about efficiency and low cost locations.

the very best location in order to make any profits at all.

The ways in which politics can lead to suboptimal locations have already been noted. Generally the more 'capitalist' a country, the more significant are economic factors in the location of industry. Thus in the USA it might be argued that economic factors still exert the greatest pull on the siting of new plants, whereas in countries of more mixed economies like Britain, economic, political and social factors are weighted more evenly in importance. In totalitarian regimes, such as those in Communist countries, the very idea of maximum profit locations runs counter to official ideologies. Even there, however, such economic considerations are now beginning to play their part.

Industrial location is a complex subject, but there is order in the complexity. The task of the geographer is to understand this order and apply it to reality. It is through this application that we can acquire a deeper knowledge of the location of industry and discover why countries and regions possess their own particular industrial patterns.

Industrial change

Industrialisation is, by definition, a dynamic phenomenon, altering its character and position in response to the changes in the environment. In the recent past, and in the immediate future, specific types of change can be identified, especially in the production and structure of industries.

Changes in industrial production
Since the 1960s, the world – and the developed countries in particular – has been experiencing a technological revolution. This has been as profoundly significant as the Industrial Revolution of the 18th

131

and 19th centuries. New inventions – the computer, the silicon microchip, advanced automation, high-frequency telecommunications – have completely transformed the manufacturing process. Increasingly, production is being undertaken by robots, releasing vast labour supplies from manual drudgery. In the short term this leads to unemployment; in the long term it might lead to a movement of working populations into service activities and to an increase in those employed in such fields as education, health care and the diffusion of information. High technology might also lead to greater leisure, with shorter working weeks, longer annual holidays and earlier retirement.

Other changes in industrial production include a movement away from traditional raw materials and fuels (iron ore, coal, oil) and towards newly acquired resources (atmospheric elements, marine life, nuclear fuels) and the introduction of recently discovered commodities (man-made fibres, petrochemical goods, high-technology computer hardware).

Changes in industrial structure
Alterations in the size, ownership and employment characteristics of industries are the result partly of economic necessity and partly of political ideology. One very significant development during the past 30 years has been the growth of multinational conglomerate companies. These are enormous industrial units, which have worldwide functional linkages and, in certain instances, some degree of social, cultural and even political power. Such companies include BP, Esso (Exxon) and Shell – all oil-based conglomerates; ICI, the chemical giant; and Coca Cola, the soft drinks company. The last named owns bottling plants in all but 65 countries in the world – an economic empire to rival any political one the world has ever known. Such multinationals are so powerfully international that they can relocate their plants between continents for reasons of labour cost savings. Fiat, for example, has moved much of its car production to South America. The growth in company size can also be seen within countries; mergers, take-overs and growing monopolies allowing economic savings to be made.

Another change evident is the growing trend towards government ownership of industry. This is especially the case in Third World countries and nations of socialist or communist political persuasions, where nationalisation has become a cornerstone of government policy. One need think only of such countries as Zimbabwe, Libya, the countries of Eastern Europe, and France during the early 1980s, to see that such is the case.

One country which seems to be going against the trend towards greater industrial size and increased government ownership is Britain. After 1979, when the Conservative Party came to power, the government began to dismantle large nationalised industries and actively to encourage the propagation of small firms. By a process known as 'privatisation' such companies as British Airways, British Telecom and the British Oil Corporation were denationalised and split up; by financial incentives many new companies were set up.

Finally, there has been an evident change in labour relations within many countries. In some Third World countries (such as India and Zambia) and in a few developed countries (such as Spain and France), worker participation and company co-operative schemes have been introduced. Elsewhere – notably in Japan – the management/worker division is breaking down. In many factories there are no separate facilities (restaurants, rest rooms and so on) for the two sides of industry. Instead, all share common experiences. Such developments in industrial relations are sure to spread to many more countries in the near future.

Summary

1 Industries can be classified into primary, secondary, tertiary and quaternary activities, or else according to economic bias – raw material, power, labour and market orientation. Manufacturing alone can be subdivided into craft, domestic and factory activity.
2 Firms and industries are functionally interlinked. Links vary in distance and strength. Major companies have international links, for the provision of raw materials, capital and even labour supplies.
3 Industrial location is influenced by physical factors (climate, relief, resources, accessibility) and by human factors (capital and labour availability, management, demand, change and politics).
4 Linkages can lead to agglomerations where external economies of scale are achieved. Savings are made through sharing transport, welfare, administrative and training facilities.
5 Locational quotients are used to measure the degree or importance of an agglomeration. They also help to measure the growth rate experienced by an industrial agglomeration.

6 New firms may locate according to optimal locational factors, but firms already in existence tend to remain where they are. This inertia can be attributed to tradition and cost.

7 Theories of industrial location include those of Weber (who stressed minimum costs), Hotelling (who stressed mutual interdependence) and Lösch (who stressed maximum profits). Pred suggested a behavioural matrix – locational decisions being determined by levels of intelligence and knowledge.

8 Industries continue to change in production techniques, products, transport used, size and ownership. Multinational companies have political power and can upset traditional location theories. In some countries, firms are getting larger (in the Third World); elsewhere they are getting smaller (e.g. in Britain, as a result of privatisation).

Data–response exercises

1 Redraw Figure 9.2 to show the real input and output linkages of an actual firm or industry. State whether the linkages are strong or weak, permanent or temporary. How might government policy affect these linkages?

2 Examine the various ways in which industry can have far-reaching consequences for the physical landscape, as suggested by Figure 9.3 (Seaham). In what ways can the results of pollution be minimised?

3 Discuss the various industrial location options in Figure 9.5, diagrams (e) and (f). Which factors might influence such locational decisions?

4 Divide the industrial regions in the world (Fig. 9.7) into those in developed countries and those in less developed countries. Examine the major industries to be found within each region and suggest reasons for their past growth. Why are there so few industrial regions south of the Tropic of Cancer?

5 Points R and M are 150 mm apart and they represent centres of raw materials and market, respectively. Draw concentric rings to portray transport costs around each point: seven around R at 20 mm intervals and nine around M at 15 mm intervals. These isotims (lines of equal cost) represent increases of £1 per unit of production. Draw isodapanes (lines of equal total transport costs) for £8, £9 and £10, these to be drawn between points where isotims intersect. Comment on the resulting pattern and the implications for industrial location.

6 On a sketch map based on OS map B (Yorkshire) show the location of the mills, quarries and factories in relation to relief. Comment on this relationship. What evidence is there on the map to suggest that the area shown was once important for the woollen 'cottage' industry? Where, on the outskirts of Keighley, might a new trading estate be constructed for maximum economic benefit at minimum cost to the environment?

7 Under what circumstances might the most profitable location for a firm (see Fig. 9.13) move away from the point indicated? Why might even successful and fully-informed businessmen not reposition their factories to the new optimal location?

8 Account for the existence in Figure 9.14 of large areas within the USA where the motor industry seems not to have been located. Assess the economic base potential of these large areas.

10 Communications

Introduction

As mentioned in previous chapters, population, resources and economic activity are unevenly distributed around the world. Both within countries and regions, and between continents and land masses, there are positive areas and negative areas: areas with excessive human activity and areas with limited or totally absent human activity. The world also suffers from economic unevenness since maldistribution of wealth is not spatially proportional to human needs. There is a lack of equilibrium: areas where resources are supplied are not necessarily the areas where the same resources are demanded. There is little coincidence of surplus and deficit in the economic sense.

Communications help to redress such imbalances. Only through movement can the disadvantages of maldistribution be lessened or corrected: through the diffusion of commodities and information and through the spread of social, economic and political awareness. Because there are such diverse kinds of movement – and because movement is, by definition, a mobile, dynamic, transient aspect of geography – then the topic of communications is perforce a wide and changeable one.

The questions to be answered in this chapter are:

- What types of communications are there, and how important are they to human activity?
- How have the major modes of transport developed, and where are they found?
- How successfully does each type of movement compete with others, and what determines their eventual use?
- Can different flow and network characteristics be identified and measured?
- What changes in communications can be predicted and which can be planned?

Types of communication

Communications may be defined as the means of transmitting people, resources, goods, the spoken and written word, ideas and information from place to place. As such, and in its widest sense, the term includes all modes of transport (road, rail, water, air and pipelines) together with all kinds of telecommunications (telegraph, teletex, telephone, television, satellite transmission and computer linkage). It might also include, under certain circumstances, such natural means of movement as rivers and winds. However, for the purposes of this chapter, only the more limited scope of the term will be used, with greatest concentration on transport systems.

Roads

Roads developed first and are found in all countries. No specialised machinery or technique is necessary for their use so that all countries, however backward, possess them in some form. In primitive regions they may be simple paths suitable only for foot or hoof traffic, but in advanced regions they are more likely to be well made and suitable for the heaviest and most modern vehicles. Although stone-slab surfaces date back to Persian and Roman times, it was not really until the 18th century that roads proper ceased to be mere dirt tracks, rutted in summer and waterlogged in winter. The first metalled surfaces appeared in Britain (designed by such men as Telford and McAdam) but soon spread throughout the Western world. Vehicles, too, improved and carriages became swifter, smoother and larger. The invention of the internal combustion engine gave the greatest incentive of all to road traffic improvements and since then this particular form of transport has changed beyond all recognition. The development of wider, straighter roads has culminated in the appearance of motorways, and vehicles can now travel at speeds once unimaginable (see Fig. 10.1). Loads have also grown and 'juggernaut' lorries carrying 40 tonnes are commonplace.

Today, Britain has more metalled road surface per square kilometre than any other country in the world. Other developed countries also have very advanced road patterns: West Germany has more kilometres of motorways than anywhere else, and the USA has half of all the motor cars in the world. Outside Europe and North America, good roads are less common and tend to peter out beyond urban environs. Even so, much construction is taking place and many developing countries see road building as the most important aid to economic expansion.

Railways

It is, perhaps, a sobering thought that until the railways emerged in the 1830s, man could travel no faster than a horse could gallop. Railways appeared during Britain's Industrial Revolution and later were constructed throughout the developed world. They developed partly for strategic or political reasons and partly for economic reasons. In many countries they were built especially to penetrate isolated regions and help promote political unity: Russia was crossed by the Trans-Siberian Railway, North America by the Canadian Pacific Railway. Elsewhere they aided the exploitation of mineral deposits, as in Australia and Latin America. In Britain, railways were the most important land transport system throughout the Victorian age. Only fairly recently have they declined in significance, this being the result of an increase in the use of motor vehicles on the one hand and greater air traffic on the other. Since World War 2, and especially since the Beeching Report (1963), widespread rail closures have occurred and the heyday of the railways in Britain can truly be said to be over. Associated with railways, but also linked with roads, are trams. These first appeared at the end of last century and are still fairly important in many European cities.

Water transport

Water transport can be undertaken either along inland rivers, lakes and canals or across the oceans. This distinction is pertinent since the two types have different historical backgrounds and vary in importance. Rivers, if naturally navigable, have always been used for transport, but only during the last 200 years have canals been specially constructed on a large scale (although both Egypt and China do have canals dating back more than 2000 years). Britain pioneered inland water transport but now has little use for it, owing, among other factors, to the narrowness and shortness of her canals (see Fig. 10.1). In Europe, conversely, there is a large and efficient network extending from the Channel coast to Switzerland and Austria. The Rhine is navigable from Rotterdam to Basle (850 km) and numerous other waterways lead from it, such as those to the rivers Marne, Moselle, Ems and Oder. The new canal link-

Figure 10.1 Parallel transport systems in England
The Watford Gap, Northamptonshire, forms a natural break in the Jurassic Limestone hills which stretch from Gloucestershire to Lincolnshire. Communications have exploited this gap: the Grand Union Canal (18th century), the London–Birmingham railway line (19th century) and the M1 motorway (1950s). Also here is a container depot and a motorway service station.

ing the Rhine with the Danube (via Nürnberg) can accommodate barges up to 1500 tonnes in capacity.

Up to the middle of last century, ocean transport was almost entirely dependent upon sailing craft, and journeys were consequently slow and laborious. Ships, too, were unsophisticated and could be divided merely into three groups: warships, fishing craft and merchantmen. Much has changed since then. Coal-powered, and subsequently oil-powered, vessels were introduced and ships became more specialised in function. Apart from liners (for passengers), merchant shipping now comprises cargo liners (including container ships and bulk ore carriers), tramps, coastal craft and tankers. Sizes, too, have increased, especially for oil tankers, which today carry as much as 500 000 tonnes dead weight.

Britain once had the world's largest merchant fleet, but now ranks seventh. Other large merchant navies belong to the USA, the USSR, France, Japan, Norway and Greece. In gross registered tonnage, Liberia has the largest fleet of all, but this is because, owing to lax insurance regulations, it provides a 'flag of convenience' for the ships of other nations. Japan ranks second in gross merchant tonnage, a large proportion of this being in the form of tankers.

All vessels follow set shipping routes and in this way ocean traffic is kept regular and orderly. The main routes cross the North Atlantic, but other important routes include those through the Mediterranean to the Indian Ocean, the Cape Route and those across the north Pacific. Two major ship canals have been constructed to shorten these routes: the Suez Canal (opened 1869) and the Panama Canal (opened 1914). Such is the importance of both of these that plans are afoot to widen and deepen the Suez Canal and to cut a second waterway through Central America.

Since World War 2, water transport has changed considerably. In particular, canal widening, the modernisation of docking and berthing facilities and the introduction of containers have speeded up movements and facilitated cargo handling.

Air transport

Of all transport developments of the 20th century, those in air transport have been the most striking. Who would have thought, when the Wright brothers made their historic flight in 1903, that aircraft would become one of the most important and safest means of passenger transport within just three generations? Improvements have indeed been rapid: jet engines replaced propellers, radar was introduced, the size of aircraft has grown to 'jumbo' proportions, supersonic speeds have been achieved, and vertical take-off is now possible.

Today, across the world, air transport is used extensively for both passengers and freight. Broadly there are two types of services: those operating for particular purposes on an *ad hoc* basis and those operating to regular schedules. Into the former category would come charter flights (for example, those for tourists in summer and for mineral deposits between inaccessible mines and industrial regions), and into the latter category would come those services run by British Caledonian, TWA and the other world airlines. Increasingly, the routes of both types radiate from the developed regions and, especially, from the great capital cities and industrial centres of the world. Wherever possible they mark the shortest distances between places and thus use the 'Great Circle' routes

to economise both on time and fuel. Many cities, including London, New York, Cairo and Bangkok, possess major international airports, and many others are developing their own international facilities. In a few areas, such is the difficult terrain that air transport provides the only communication possible and assumes a correspondingly greater significance. Domestic air services are important within countries where population densities are sparse and distances great, and where topography is dangerous or heterogeneous. In many very large countries, such as Australia, air medical services are of crucial significance.

Pipelines

Originally used only to carry water, pipelines now transport a variety of commodities: oil, natural gas, milk, chemicals and even some solids like coal (though in a liquified form known as 'slurry'). Of all these, oil and natural gas are by far the most important, especially in North America where pipeline development is more advanced than anywhere else. There, 200 000 km of oil trunk line exists and over 450 000 km of natural gas line, both figures excluding great lengths of gathering and local-distribution pipes. The longest single pipeline, however, is in Russia, where the 'Friendship Pipeline' carries oil across 4828 km from the Ural–Volga region to the satellite states of Eastern Europe. Western Europe has been slower to develop pipelines and here a network has existed only since the 1950s. Even so, there are many pipelines taking petroleum inland from the major coastal refineries (Rotterdam, Marseilles, Genoa and Trieste) and natural gas pipelines have been constructed in Northern Italy, Aquitaine, the Netherlands, the North Sea, and from the USSR to Western Europe.

In Switzerland and Austria, short pipelines carry milk from farms to dairies, and in Britain chemicals are piped from Fawley oil refinery to the ICI plant at Severnside. Other products may also be carried through pipelines (powdered solids, for instance) and for these much pipeline development is likely to take place in the future.

Transport competition and modal choice

Natural resources, manufacturing equipment, labour, capital, markets and technological skills are rarely found together. Each must be brought into contact with the others, and only through lines of movement can this contact take place. Communication systems provide these lines of movement and are, in consequence, inextricably linked with economic activity; without them there would be no economic activity. They are both the result and the cause of industrial and agricultural progress: the more advanced a country becomes, the more extensive, efficient and important will be its systems of transport and telecommunication, and the more certain its continued economic expansion.

Each individual method of transmission has its own character and specialised uses, but all share the same basic function: to provide movement. There is, therefore, some competition between them. This is especially true of transport systems. Whenever the movement of goods or passengers is required, customers are faced with a choice: which method should be used or, as in the case of **modal-split** decisions (that is, where more than one transport system must be adopted), which combination of methods should be used?

The problem can be difficult and it involves the careful appraisal of the relative merits of each possibility. The factors to be considered include costs, the operating distances, speed, the particular requirements of the commodities being transported, flexibility of routes and services, destinations, and the quantity and frequency of transport movements. Each mode of transport has its merits and limitations, but these are both inconstant (owing to variations in demand and supply, changes in human needs and desires, and technological advances) and subject to individual value-judgements. The transport system chosen one year by a customer may not be the same as that chosen the following year, neither may it be the same as that chosen by another customer.

Economic distance

As a general rule **economic distance** is the prime determinant of modal choice. This is the extent to which the costs of transport are covered by the value of the commodities being transported. Transport itself increases the cost of a commodity but there will come a point where the costs of transport push total costs and profit margins beyond the selling price of the product, that is, exceed the amount a commodity is worth. At that point, transport becomes uneconomic and will cease. Bearing this in mind, it is no wonder that a £400 item of jewellery would have a greater economic distance than £400 worth of coal and would therefore be transported further.

CONTAINERISATION

The Humber provides a deep, wide and naturally sheltered estuary, which has the added advantage of a deep-water channel that swings from one side (at Immingham) to the other (at Kingston upon Hull). Recent transport improvements on Humberside have transformed a formerly declining fishing centre into a region of major industrial potential (see Fig. 10.2). The motorway link with the national network has brought Humberside nearer the domestic markets, and the new suspension bridge has greatly improved the area's accessibility. Kingston upon Hull is an important port and Immingham has expanded with new railway/coal-handling facilities. Grimsby especially is growing in significance with new container facilities.

Containerisation has been one of the most important developments in cargo transport in recent years. Containers are metal boxes of a standard size (2.4 m × 2.4 m × 3, 6, 9 and 12 m long) in which goods, of the same type or mixed, are packed by the despatcher. They are handled by standardised equipment (cranes and loaders) and can be carried by any form of transport. There are numerous advantages to this system of carriage. Containers are sealed, which minimises breakages and theft, and efficient handling methods facilitate speed, reduce costs, and provide regular and frequent services. By removing the need for dock (stevedore) labour, they reduce the importance of ports as trading centres and hence avoid possible delays and inefficiency incurred during trans-

hipment. Specially designed freightliner trains, lorries, aircraft and ships have been built, and numerous ports have been converted to handle container traffic. Apart from Grimsby, other British ports now able to handle containers include North Shields, Felixstowe, Harwich, Tilbury, Glasgow and Manchester.

The effect of the 'container revolution' has been widespread. It has helped railways compete more successfully with roads and ocean transport to compete more successfully with air over intercontinental routes. It has also affected the location of industry, diminishing the need for manufacturing firms to locate near the coastal ports. Instead, container terminals (which can be inland) are exerting a locational pull.

In consequence, many traditional docklands have undergone fundamental physical and human changes. Firms have closed down or moved; dockers have been made unemployed and buildings have become redundant. In many places – in New York, London and Liverpool, for example – redevelopment schemes have attempted to generate new life in these areas: warehouses have been converted into flats or workshops and modern offices, and entertainment facilities have been introduced. At Kingston upon Hull both the docks and fish market are experiencing such changes – reflecting not only the coming of containerisation but also the general recession in manufacturing and fishing.

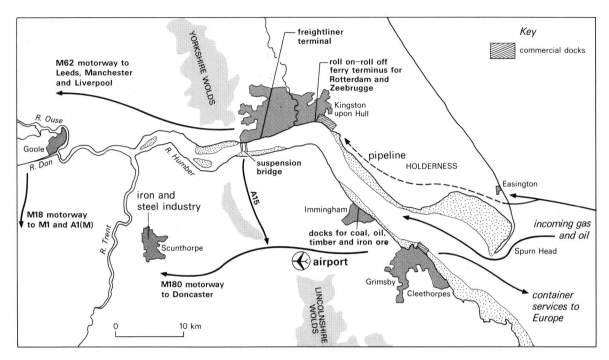

Figure 10.2 Transport improvements on Humberside
Despite the recession of the early 1980s, Humberside has progressed as a major industrial growth pole over the past 10 years. However, the long-term effects (and success) of the Humber Bridge are still to be judged.

Transport costs

But what determines economic distance itself? The answer lies in transport costs rather than in physical distance. These are determined by numerous factors apart from distance; for example, by terrain, type of carrier and fuel used, type of commodity, the origin and destination of the cargo, and the degree of competition from alternative transport systems. Of course, long journeys tend to cost more than short journeys, a bulky cargo tends to cost more to transport than a compact one, and transport over difficult terrain will tend to cost more than transport over flat relief and oceans. In reality, however, the situation is far more complex than this.

Transport costs are made up of three elements: running or line-haul costs, which are incurred in the movement process and are largely composed of fuel costs and wages; overhead costs, incurred in the building of equipment, terminal facilities, repair shops and offices; and transfer costs, which are incurred indirectly through such aspects as insurance cover for cargo. These three exist in varying proportions and for this reason systems of transport are suited to different purposes and for different distances.

In Figure 10.3 the costs of four methods of transport are compared. Ocean transport involves high overhead costs, in needing port facilities, but low line-haul costs. Road transport has low overhead costs but high line-haul costs. Rail transport occupies an intermediate position. With the possible exception of road transport, total costs do not rise proportionally with distance. As can be seen, road is cheapest over short distances (OA), rail over medium distances (AB), ocean transport and pipelines over long distances (beyond B and C respectively). Air transport (not shown) has very high fixed costs and also high running costs – thus is largely used for valuable freight and for passengers.

Another determinant of transport costs is the type of load carried. Non-breakable, non-perishable commodities such as coal and iron ore will travel more cheaply than those needing careful handling, such as foods and precision instruments. Manufactured goods tend to be carried at higher rates than do raw materials or semi-finished goods, since they are usually more fragile and of higher value and can thus

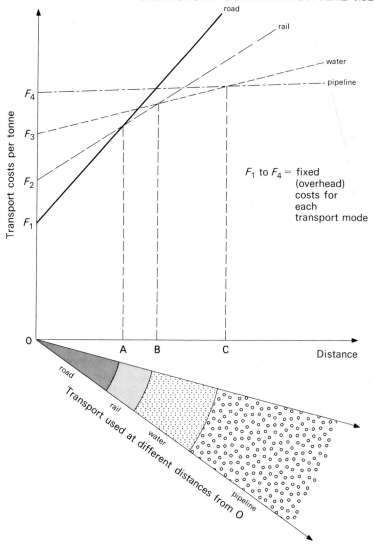

Figure 10.3 Transport costs graph
The lower the running (line-haul) costs per unit-kilometre, the more horizontal the graph line.

bear higher freight charges. Passengers travel most expensively of all, not just because they need more space and special facilities but also because they incur high transfer costs, that is, they need to be insured for large amounts of money.

The nature of transport movement is a further factor to be considered. Journeys that involve transhipment (the transfer of cargo from one transport system to another) will be more costly than those in which the same mode of transport is used throughout. In the same way, large quantities normally travel at lower rates per unit-kilometre than do small quantities, and commodities that are transported regularly are usually given more favourable rates than those that travel irregularly. In passenger transport, the same is true:

season-ticket holders travel less expensively than those who buy tickets separately each day.

If vehicles must travel empty – for example, when returning from a delivery – it might pay a transport authority to offer cheap 'backhaul rates'. In this way, the vehicles are filled and at least some extra revenue is obtained. This is why coal is carried cheaply through the Great Lakes (in the opposite direction to iron ore movements) and why cheap off-peak fares are offered by public transport.

Profits
Notwithstanding all these considerations, it would be misleading to imagine that the total cost of transport is the same as the amount a customer pays. Between

the two is the transport owner's margin of profit and it is this that ultimately determines freight rates.

To a certain extent, the profit anticipated by the provider of transport is dependent upon the degree of competition he faces. If there is little competition, a monopolistic situation may develop whereby an owner can charge almost what he likes and still find customers, especially if demand for his particular mode of transport is inelastic or stable. Where there are many substitutes, conversely, strong competition brings about keen prices, and profit margins are cut to a minimum. Significantly, freight rates charged on Britain's canal system fell drastically when railways were first built and, more recently, rail charges in Canada fell when the St Lawrence Seaway was opened in 1959.

Non-cost factors

It is also at times of strong competition that non-cost factors play a more important role in modal choice. When prices are about the same (and often even when they are not), customers are likely to choose the mode of transport that offers most convenience, reliability and speed.

Indeed, it can be argued that non-cost factors are now becoming relatively even more important in modal choice decisions. This is especially true of passenger transport. With greater knowledge, education and wealth, people have increased their mobility and are more willing both to use and to pay for alternative transport methods. Improved technology has further helped this development since it has provided a greater number of options. One hundred years ago a long-distance land journey almost certainly had to be undertaken by rail, and the English Channel could only be crossed by boat. Today, long-distance journeys over land can be by rail, road or air, and the Channel can be crossed in a boat, aeroplane, hovercraft and, should the Channel tunnel ever be built, in a train as well.

COMPARATIVE ADVANTAGES AND DISADVANTAGES OF TRANSPORT SYSTEMS

Advantages

Disadvantages

Roads
(1) Great flexibility of service since numerous routes and destinations are possible.
(2) Offers directness; door-to-door communication possible.
(3) Great speed and cheapness over short distances; continuous movement possible.
(4) Wide range of goods can be carried; roads are more able than other systems to handle outsize objects.
(5) Offers maximum access along their linesides; maximum scope for intervening opportunity.

(1) Roads and motor vehicles need constant maintenance and this adds greatly to running costs.
(2) Can be very slow, since delays are possible (e.g. due to weather).
(3) Of little use for large quantities of freight since only relatively small amounts can be carried in each vehicle.
(4) Motorways are detrimental to the beauty of the countryside and to urban living; motor vehicles cause noise and air pollution.
(5) Demand regular servicing – including policing, traffic direction, repairs and provision of road furniture.

Rail
(1) Provides a fast and reliable service. Trains, running on their own tracks, can be timed to minimise the chances of congestion and delay.
(2) Heavy and bulky goods can be carried as well as large quantities of any cargo; rail is especially suited to steady flows of traffic between set places (e.g. movements of coal and iron ore between mines and factories).
(3) Particularly suited to passenger transport since it provides speed, cheapness, comfort and safety; this advantage is greatest for distances under 500 km since, above this distance, the competition from air strengthens.

(1) Construction costs, maintenance costs and operating costs are all high; this remains true whether the system is used or not.
(2) Can be expensive to use, especially over short distances or for small amounts of cargo.
(3) Inflexible service since tracks cannot easily be moved and transhipment of cargo is often necessary at termini.
(4) Indirect or circuitous routes since lines are determined by relief (hence a slow and expensive movement of commodities in areas of rough topography).
(5) Traffic flow is variable, especially commuter movement around towns and seasonal flows of farm pro-

(4) Offers reasonably good access along its lineside (although this is dependent upon the number of stations along each route); rail can provide a magnet to industry and stations become centres of new urban complexes (e.g. Crewe, Swindon, Peterborough).

(5) Relatively clean form of transport (little air pollution).

Water

(1) Low running costs make this the cheapest transport system over long distances. Large vessels, especially, run economically since fuel costs can be spread over greater quantities. Distance does not add greatly to total transport costs.

(2) Capacity for heavy and bulky cargoes.

(3) Ocean transport has a natural route network, which is 'free' to use. This allows flexibility of service, frequency of movement and little congestion (except where water channels are narrow, as in the case of the Straits of Dover).

(4) Canals provide good access along their linesides and can encourage the development of industry and commerce. Some towns have grown largely through their connection with canals (e.g. Stourport).

(5) Causes relatively little pollution (although oil discharge from tankers is a problem).

Air

(1) Fast and efficient system which is especially suited to passenger traffic, offering comfort and high quality service; today, long-distance passenger movements are made almost entirely by air.

(2) Suited to high quality, expensive and perishable cargoes for which speed is essential; aircraft may also carry freight too small to interest the providers of other transport systems.

(3) Can often reach areas inaccessible to other modes of transport (e.g. areas of inhospitable environment such as central Brazil and northern Canada.

(4) Offers complete freedom of movement and this provides potentially flexible routes and service (although most air movements are channelled along strict routes and political factors may restrict both landings and flightpaths).

Pipelines

(1) Very efficient, fast service provided with maximum safety and dependability.

(2) Continuous flow can be carried at a constant rate.

(3) Very cheap, especially over long distances, since running costs are low.

(4) Cause no air pollution and, when buried underground, inflict no environmental damage.

duce; at times when traffic is slack, capital and labour are underemployed.

(6) Cannot accommodate awkward loads since cargo must fit both train and route dimensions (about 3 m width).

(7) Lines established in the past may become obsolete and a financial burden.

(8) Interruption of other transport flows (e.g. road traffic at level crossings).

(1) Very slow movement, hence unsuitable for perishable or urgent cargoes. There may also be delays at locks and docks, and navigation may be impeded by poor weather conditions.

(2) Unsuitable for short journeys since transhipment is both costly and time consuming.

(3) Canals are very expensive to build, maintain and dredge, and also follow inflexible and circuitous routes. An adequate supply of water may be difficult to obtain and the limited dimensions of barges may be too small for modern requirements.

(4) As ship size increases, the number of ports capable of receiving ocean-going vessels is declining; this results in less flexible routes and services for the movement of such commodities as oil; supertankers, for example, cannot use the Suez Canal and large ships can no longer enter the Port of London.

(1) Very expensive (though becoming less so) and this disqualifies all heavy, bulky or low-value cargoes.

(2) Aircraft are expensive to build and operate, and require elaborate provisions in the form of airport facilities, controlling systems and maintenance.

(3) Dependent on weather conditions and therefore can provide an unreliable service.

(4) As aircraft become larger, the number of airports capable of being used is declining. This reduces flexibility. Also there is a growing difficulty of finding suitable sites for airport building. Some airports are far away from urban centres and this offsets the advantage of speed and convenience.

(5) Offers no access between termini and therefore minimum potential for intervening opportunity.

(6) Airports use up valuable land and aircraft cause noise and air pollution.

(1) Very inflexible since they operate only from point to point on set routes.

(2) Can carry only limited range of goods.

(3) High installation costs.

(4) May easily be damaged by both natural and human action: frost heaving or earth movements may lead to pipe splitting, and warfare may result in deliberate damage; when pipelines are underground, there is the further problem of locating and repairing damage.

Transport flows

Transport flows can be defined as the movements of goods and services between places, and they exist to even out the maldistribution of world resources. In effect, every flow provides a link (though not necessarily an economic one) between a point of supply and a point of demand or, to put it another way, between a point of surplus and a point of deficiency. Without such interaction, economic development would be impossible.

These flows vary in direction, scale, speed, capacity and content, depending on the methods of transport used. They take place between all regions and countries, and in duration can be anything from seconds to days, months or even years. Their capacity (the amount of traffic possible in a given period) is dependent upon their technological character. Railways, for instance, have a capacity determined by tracks and train movements. Vehicles can only pass on separate lines, so double tracks give over twice the capacity of single tracks. Straight railway lines across flat terrain allow faster traffic than winding, uneven lines, and the highest capacity would be achieved if all trains were run at the same speed, at regular intervals, using the same stopping points. Both road and air transport have potentially higher capacities than rail since neither is restricted by fixed tracks. As already mentioned, the content of flows varies between passengers and all types of goods.

To distinguish between different flow types in these ways is a relatively simple matter; to account for their development and characteristics, however, is not. This is because they are the result of numerous and complex economic, social and even political forces. On the one hand, they are determined by the customers, who decide which routes they will use and what volumes of traffic will flow along them. On the other hand, they are determined by the owners or providers, whose actions make all movements possible.

The Ullman model

One of the first to study transport flows was the American geographer Edward Ullman who, during the 1940s, devised a simple model of interaction. He identified three basic factors that determine flow: complementarity, intervening opportunity and transferability.

Complementarity is the degree to which two regions complement each other. In order for interaction to take place, the demand for a good or service at one place must be matched by the supply of the same good or service at another. Moreover, that same demand must be backed by the ability to obtain (usually the ability to pay for the supply). Developed, mid-latitude countries, buying raw materials from developing tropical countries in exchange for finished goods, may be seen as an example of how complementarity works. Yet complementary regions need not be different, either environmentally or culturally. Two areas may be similar, but there may still be interaction between them. Provided a region is not totally self-sufficient, it is bound to be complementary with at least one other region.

Apart from complementarity there must also be an absence of intervening opportunity. A potential buyer is unlikely to go far afield if he can obtain what he wants close at hand: transport flow will occur between the nearest complementary regions (or the most easily reached). It is more convenient for a Cornish shoe manufacturer to buy his leather from, say, Northamptonshire than from Argentina. Between himself and the English East Midlands there are no other leather suppliers; if there were such an intervening opportunity, he would doubtless use it. Arguably, Japanese cars are sold in British garages because there are no nearer car supplies of similar quality, style and price.

Intervening opportunities continually appear and disappear so that interaction flows are in a constant state of flux. In recent years, the making of synthetic rubber has reduced the interaction between the East Indies and Europe since the demand for natural rubber has declined. Similarly, the manufacture of artificial nitrate fertilisers in Norway has reduced the flow of natural fertiliser from Chile to Western Europe.

Even when there is no intervening opportunity, interaction can only take place with products that are transferable. In short, a product or service must be mobile, not just physically but economically. If a buyer cannot afford a particular product, that product, to all intents and purposes, might just as well be fixed to the spot. In such a situation there will be no flows and the buyer will either look elsewhere for the same commodity at a cheaper price or else go without.

This Ullman model demonstrates a straightforward balance between complementarity, which may encourage flows, and intervening opportunities and transferability, which may discourage them. It is but a short step from here to the measurement of interactions. This involves the use of gravity models.

Gravity models

Newton's Laws of Motion state that the strength of attraction between two universal bodies is directly proportional to the product of their masses and inversely proportional to the square of the distance between them. Since his day, the same principle has been applied to other phenomena, and in geography it has been employed in various aspects of spatial activity. The gravity model has been used for delimiting market areas (as in the case of the *Law of Retail Gravitation*) and we have already seen how it can be related to population movement (Ch. 6). Other possible uses include the study of shopping patterns, the delimitation of urban fields and even the measurement of political influences.

The application of the gravity model to transport flows has shown that interaction has a regularity that can be analysed. Complementary regions are linked by flows, which reflect the relative surpluses and deficiencies of the regions. The greater these surpluses and deficiencies, the greater will be the flow between them. The chance of intervening opportunities occurring increases as distances become greater, leading to a decline in the number and extent of flows. Transferability decreases with economic distance so that, beyond a certain point, commodities will not be bought and sold.

Interaction is, then, determined by the relative importance of the regions involved and the distances separating them. The greater the importance and the shorter the distances, the greater will be the interaction. Taking this a stage further, to its Newtonian conclusion, it should be possible actually to predict flows by multiplying the mass of two regions and dividing the result by the distance between them. However, this is not easy. How, for example, does one measure mass and distance in economic terms?

Population size could be used as an indication of mass, but this would imply that countries with equal numbers of people would have similar flow characteristics, and this is not the case. Purchasing power is, perhaps, a more accurate measure, but this still ignores such factors as culture, education, human desires and standards of living, all of which may affect the nature of interaction.

Distances, of course, can be measured in kilometres but, as already stated, economic distance is of greater significance in our study, and the measurement of this is difficult. Even so, attempts have been made and a set relationship between distance and flows has been established. This is based on the general principle of **distance decay** whereby the amount of inter-

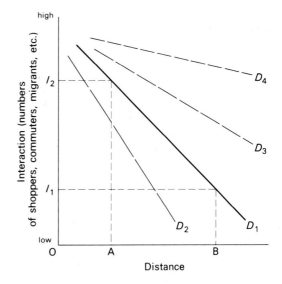

Figure 10.4 Distance decay relationships
These graph lines show an inverse relationship between interaction and distance: as one increases the other decreases. Movement is high between close points (OA) and low between distant points (OB). The extent of interaction change with distance is reflected in the gradient of the line. D_1 shows a proportional relationship: if distance halves, the amount of interaction doubles. D_2 shows an inelastic relationship, D_3 and D_4 elastic relationships.

action between two places decreases as the distance between them increases (Fig. 10.4). This law may seem obvious, but its importance lies in its application to flow studies. The rate of interaction decline varies between commodities so that, for each flow, a different graph must be drawn. If the wrong distance decay rate is chosen for a particular investigation, the conclusions are likely to be wrong and the study will be worthless.

Gravity models, despite the difficulties inherent in their use, provide a simplified explanation of interaction flows, and as such form the foundation of more advanced study of spatial activity.

Transport networks

Transport flows should not be studied only in isolation. They are parts of more comprehensive transport structures and as such should be considered in relation to each other. Overall transport structures, or networks, are integrated patterns in which groups of centres (nodes) are linked by set routes. Each node may be a settlement or junction and each link a line of contact – road, rail, air, waterway or, indeed, any

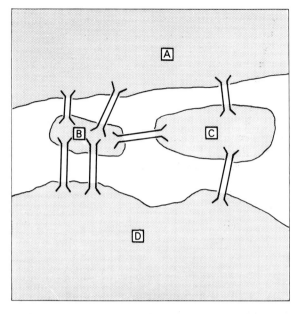

Figure 10.5   The Königsberg network problem
An early network problem, and one which led to the study of transport networks, developed in the 18th century and concerned the Prussian city of Königsberg. Seven bridges connect four land areas. Is it possible to visit all four areas, return to your starting point, and cross every bridge only once?

other form of communication. The study of transport networks is not new (Fig. 10.5), but it has become more important in recent years as geographers have grown aware of the relationship between transport systems and economic development.

Networks differ in concentration, extent and efficiency, and result from various physical, cultural, technological and economic factors. There is an infinite number of types but six principal ones can be identified (Fig. 10.6). These were first recognised by Bunge (*Theoretical geography*, Gleerup, 1966) and are based on the hypothetical assumption of five nodes.

The 'Paul Revere' network is the simplest and exists where a single route connects all nodes (Fig. 10.6a). Its main disadvantage lies in the fact that any return journey (say from E to A) must pass through the intervening nodes, which can be slow and tedious. A solitary railway line linking a port with a mining settlement would be of this type of network – for example, the line from Sept Îles to Schefferville in Labrador. Developing countries also tend to have this type of network, for instance Argentina has the railway line from Bahia Blanca to Zapala.

The 'travelling salesman' network provides the

shortest route around all nodes, but journeys between nodes still involve movement through other nodes (Fig. 10.6b). In this case, travel from B to D would mean passing through C. Such a network may exist in less developed regions, in areas of difficult terrain or in islands. The main road around the Isle of Arran (Scotland) is of this type.

'Centre-orientated' networks tend to result in congestion at certain points since cross-country movement is impossible. In Figure 10.6c, all traffic must pass through D, which will thus be congested. Many country towns are linked by road to surrounding villages in this way so that inter-village movement must involve those towns. On a larger scale, both rail and

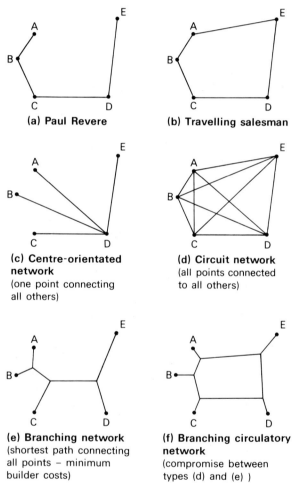

(a) Paul Revere

(b) Travelling salesman

(c) Centre-orientated network
(one point connecting all others)

(d) Circuit network
(all points connected to all others)

(e) Branching network
(shortest path connecting all points – minimum builder costs)

(f) Branching circulatory network
(compromise between types (d) and (e))

Figure 10.6   Transport network types (after Bunge)
These are idealised patterns between hypothetical points. However, most real world networks can be classified into such standardised shapes.

road networks in south-east England centre on London, making that city the route focal point, and the railways of the Prairies (Canada) centre on Edmonton.

The 'circuit' network is the most efficient since all nodes are connected to all others by the shortest route and movement between any two settlements need take in no other settlement (Fig. 10.6d). This pattern thus offers the least cost to the user but has the disadvantage of being the most costly to the builder. Roads, especially those in developed countries, tend to have this type of network.

If circuit networks are most preferred by the customer, 'branching' networks are most preferred by the builder. Such a pattern provides the shortest route connecting all the nodes while, at the same time, allowing all journeys to bypass intervening nodes. Thus, travelling from B to D in Figure 10.6e would not involve A, E or C. Railway networks tend to be of this type.

'Branching circulatory' networks are a compromise between circuit and branching networks. They provide fairly efficient routes at less than maximum costs. The London Underground railway system is of this type.

Often, areas contain not a single network but several in superimposition. This is because transport systems fall into hierarchies. For example, roads can be viewed not as one network but as many, each superimposed on to the others. Below the motorway network is the 'A' class trunk road network and below

that a minor road network. At the lowest level, there is a network of bridleways, footpaths and tracks. Similarly, rail networks can be subdivided between major routes and branch lines, and air networks between international, national and local traffic.

Network efficiency
The efficiency of all networks can be ascertained from a measure of common factors: connectivity, density, extent, fineness, rate of flow, flexibility, technological characteristics and degree of stress.

Connectivity. Connectivity is the relationship between the number of nodes and the number of links in a single network. The most common measure of this is the **beta index**, which is calculated by dividing the total number of links by the total number of nodes. Hence, in Figure 10.6, parts (a) and (c) have a beta index of 0.8, part (b) of 1, and part (d) of 2. An alternative measure, the **alpha index**, is more useful for comparative purposes but involves complicated mathematics. On a smaller scale, the **König number** can be used to find the centrality of any node. This is the maximum number of links from each node to the other nodes in the network. Lower values indicate greater centrality (Fig. 10.7).

These measures not only help comparisons between networks but also give an indication of the level of economic development achieved in any region. It is generally true, for instance, that networks in

Table of shortest routes between pairs of nodes (by number of links)

	Ex	Sw	Btl	Bm	Mcr	Car	Lds	H	R	Lon	Cam	Dvr	Stn	König number	Shimbel number
Exeter	—	2	1	2	3	4	4	5	3	2	3	3	3	5	35
Swansea	2	—	1	2	3	4	4	5	3	2	3	3	3	5	35
Bristol	1	1	—	1	2	3	3	4	2	1	2	2	2	4	24
Birmingham	2	2	1	—	1	2	2	3	1	2	3	3	3	3	25
Manchester	3	3	2	1	—	1	1	2	2	3	4	4	4	4	30
Carlisle	4	4	3	2	1	—	2	3	3	4	5	5	5	5	41
Leeds	4	4	3	2	1	2	—	1	1	2	3	3	3	4	29
Hull	5	5	4	3	2	3	1	—	2	3	4	4	4	5	40
Rugby	3	3	2	1	2	3	1	2	—	1	2	2	2	3	24
London	2	2	1	2	3	4	2	3	1	—	1	1	1	4	23
Cambridge	3	3	2	3	4	5	3	4	2	1	—	2	2	5	34
Dover	3	3	2	3	4	5	3	4	2	1	2	—	2	5	34
Southampton	3	3	2	3	4	5	3	4	2	1	2	2	—	5	34

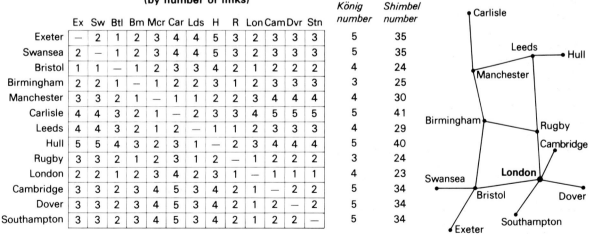

Figure 10.7 Simplified topological map of the motorway network in England and Wales
This can be viewed as an example of a branching circulatory network. The beta index is 14 ÷ 13 = 1.08, a figure indicating a network of an advanced economy. The König number for each node can be calculated from the table: the nodes with the greatest centrality are Birmingham and Rugby. The Shimbel number (the total of each row) is sometimes used to show the most central node of an entire network – in this example, London.

developed countries are of greater connectivity than those in developing countries. A beta index value of 1.0 may be taken as an economic dividing line: values above that level indicating advanced economies, values below indicating more backward economies. For example: the railway beta index in France is 1.42 and 0.76 in Sri Lanka; the road beta index in West Germany is 1.23 and in Hungary 0.86.

Density. The density of a network may be expressed either as the number of links per unit area or as the total network length divided by the area that it covers. Alternatively, the **eta index** may be used, which is obtained by dividing the total length of a network by the number of links that make it up. No matter which method is employed, it is clear that, in Figure 10.6, part (f) has a greater network density than parts (a) and (c), and part (d) has the greatest network density of all.

As with connectivity, network density may indicate economic prosperity: the greater the density (or the lower the eta index), the more advanced is the country. Thus, the eta value of the road network in France is 42 km, in Mexico 75 km, in Algeria 90 km and in Angola 122 km.

Extent. The extent of a network – whether it be dispersed or compact – can be measured by the **diameter index**. In simple terms this is the number of links used in crossing a network from one side to another at its widest point. Again referring to Figure 10.6, to cross from C to E would involve two links in parts (a), (b) and (c), three links in part (e), but only one link in part (d). The lower the index, the more compact the network.

Fineness. Fineness is the degree to which a network's individual links have an effect upon the areas through which they pass. This depends partly upon the accessibility to each flow as it passes between nodes. For instance, road networks have greater fineness than rail networks: along the average trunk road there are many points at which other roads join, whereas along a railway line entry and departure are possible only at stations, and even then only if the trains stop. By the same token, air networks have the least fineness of all, their flows being totally enclosed between nodal points.

Flexibility and rates of flow. Rates of flow and flexibility also vary between networks. Roads can usually accommodate more vehicles than can railways over a given distance and time, and are also capable of allowing the use of a greater diversity of traffic. Railways, after all, can take only vehicles with the correct wheels, gauges and dimensions.

Technological characteristics. Technological characteristics relate largely to speed potentials, whereas stress is a measure of congestion. In both cases, air networks have a distinct advantage over rail networks, which, in turn, have an advantage over roads.

Finally, it should be mentioned that network patterns do not simply indicate the economic character of the regions where they are found, but also reflect their own functions and *raisons d'être*. The British motorway network is different from that of France, but not because of any differences in prosperity between those countries. Britain's network reflects the need to connect the major industrial growth points. France's network reflects the overriding importance of Paris as the industrial, cultural, social and educational centre of the country. The motorway networks of other countries may reflect yet other functions and purposes.

The development of networks

Most transport networks are not planned from scratch but develop gradually over the years. Broadly they result from two motives – political or strategic reasons and economic reasons – and their patterns are determined by relief, the shape and size of the area to be served, the population density, technological levels and various chance decisions.

The only networks to have been planned as a whole from scratch are likely to be those resulting from purely strategic motives. They are often conspicuous on maps since they either cover sparsely populated regions or else seem unrelated to relief and areas of settlement. The villages and towns found in these networks post-date the original routeways, and the lines of communication themselves are usually regular and straight. The road networks built by Wade and Roy in 18th century Scotland are strategic in origin, so too is the rail network in India (largely being constructed after the Indian Mutiny in 1857) and the new Chinese road pattern in Tibet (after the Communist revolution in 1949).

However, networks of strategic value are not common and most networks stem from economic considerations. Indeed, it would be true to say that such motives have always been the most important in network development, even in earliest times.

The Phoenicians, Romans and Vikings all had a great web of sea routes across the then known world and they traded in cloth, jewels, spices and other valuable goods. Later, in the Middle Ages, networks of trading and transport became much more widespread. Europeans reached India by sea in 1498 and China in 1513. Above all, the European discovery of the Americas in 1492 spread world trade, changing the relative position of Western Europe from the edge of the civilised world to its centre, forming a bridge between east and west. In this period, too, began the notorious slave triangle: manufactured goods from Europe to West Africa, slaves from there to the West Indies whence sugar, rum, cotton and tobacco returned to Europe.

Networks were further extended as a result of the Industrial Revolution. They grew more widespread, both within and between countries, and many of today's major road, rail and canal patterns date from this period. Where railways were built specifically to open up sparsely settled interiors, networks frequently developed in fan shapes whereby 'export lines' branch out from common centres. Such networks provide the most efficient method of tapping the widest possible territory and can be seen in the Pampas (Argentina), the North American spring wheat belt and the Murray–Darling Basin (Australia).

Network prediction

Since the nature of networks – their connectivity, density, extent, fineness, flexibility and technological characteristics – is determined by many known geographical factors, methods of predicting communication patterns cannot be too difficult to formulate. Once the effects of the six determining variables (a region's topography, shape, size, population density, level of economic development and such extraneous factors as historical, social and political phenomena) are fully understood, the network that a given region is likely to develop can be worked out. All that is required is a study of cause-and-effect relationships: if A, B and C regional factors are known, X network must result.

Such predictive analysis can be divided into two: forecasting whole networks, their evolution and design, and predicting individual flows, their alteration and importance. Both require some degree of environmental and behavioural understanding, and mathematical skill.

Network prediction is greatly simplified if it is based on a premise of isotropacy – uniform land surfaces and homogeneous population characteristics. On such landscapes geographers have identified three kinds of transport networks that are likely to result (see Fig. 10.8). The hexagonal pattern might result where population density is low, where capital availability is limited, or where the need for communication is restricted. All three conditions might exist within Third World countries. The rectangular pattern represents the next stage up in economic development, possibly to be found where capital is available yet not abundant or where population density might increase. Such networks are common in areas of pioneer advancement – in the North

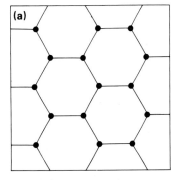 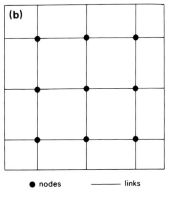 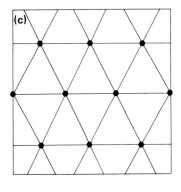

● nodes ───── links

Figure 10.8 Optimum network designs
These diagrams show idealised transport patterns that might be predicted over uniform surfaces. Hexagonal networks, in (a), assume three links per node; rectangular networks, in (b), assume four links per node; triangular networks, in (c), assume six links per node. The last is the most efficient, the first the least efficient.

147

American Mid-West, on the Dutch polders and in the Australian outback. The triangular pattern might be found in areas of abundant capital, high population density, and considerable economic mobility. Such networks would be found in established regions of the developed world, where many transport links are essential to sustain a high standard of living.

Predicting what network should be found on a given region is relatively easy; predicting how that network is likely to change is much more difficult. This is partly because networks do not alter in a predetermined sequence, and partly because future variables are unknown.

Hexagonal networks rarely evolve into rectangular networks, or rectangular into triangular networks, for reasons which should be apparent from the diagrams. Thus, it is common for a network not to be modified but to be overlain, with an additional network superimposed. Britain's motorway network can be viewed separately from the trunk road network, the one overlying the other.

Any modifications made to a network are likely to be piecemeal and as such are difficult to forecast accurately. If a single town expands, it will probably require greater network centrality, that is, have more links with other towns. This will lead to more links being constructed in that part of the network. Other parts of the same network may or may not be affected. A country advancing economically will probably require greater overall network connectivity (efficiency); a country experiencing population growth, greater network density (more numerous links). But whether such network modifications alter the extent, fineness or flexibility of the network is open to doubt.

On a very local scale, predictions of individual flow changes can be a relatively straightforward matter and many geographers have attempted it. Zipf and Stouffer studied migration flows (see Ch. 6) and the Ullman model can easily be adapted to allow for predictive analysis. Such analysis can be based on the gravity model (see Fig. 10.4) or else on the following equation:

movement between towns A and B =

$$\frac{(\text{population A}) \times (\text{population B})}{(\text{distance A–B})^2}$$

By the use of such methods, geographers can attempt to forecast future changes in flow characteristics (frequency, speed and so on) and, through that, future additions to network links.

Models of network development

Generally, the longer the period over which a network has developed, the more likely it is to be dense, highly connective and multimodal. In the most developed regions, the separate systems of transport – road, rail and canal – will form not their own individual networks, but overall and combined networks, in which complementarity exists as well as competition. The ways in which such networks develop are, however, diverse and complex. For this reason, simplified models have been proposed, the most famous of which are that of Taaffe, Morrill and Gould (*Geographical Review* **53**, 1963, pp. 503–29) and that of Lachene (*Papers of the Regional Science Association* **14**, 1964, pp. 183–96).

Figure 10.9 is based on the development of transport in Nigeria and Ghana, and contains six phases. Stage 1 shows a scatter of small coastal ports and trading posts, each with a limited hinterland. Stage 2 occurs when two of these grow (P_1 P_2) and develop links with two interior settlements (S_1 S_2), perhaps for political or administrative reasons or to exploit natural resources. In stage 3 the two major ports enlarge their hinterlands at the expense of the smaller ports, feeder development continues and small nodes grow up along the main lines of penetration. Stage 4 is reached when intervening nodes develop their own hinterlands (N_1 N_2) and some of the large feeders begin to link up. Stage 5 results when links develop between all the major settlements. From this point, economic activity is at its peak and national trunk routes may be built (linking S_2, P_1 and P_2). If these become fully developed, stage 6 is reached and the development of the network is complete.

Figure 10.10 represents a flat uniform area upon which population is, at first, evenly spread, and the communication network consists of a regular pattern of paths and tracks. Gradually, a few settlements grow more than others, perhaps through chance or greater potential for economic prosperity; these are sited at the intersections of the tracks. After a time, railways are built linking these settlements, but only a limited number since their construction requires high capital investment. Once complete, these railways encourage further growth in the towns they connect and these develop into pre-eminence. At a later stage, motorways are built to link the major settlements, and economic activity is at its maximum. The final stage may be induced by government policy. A region that has been bypassed by network development might be declared a depressed area and a new road might be constructed into its heart to assist economic growth.

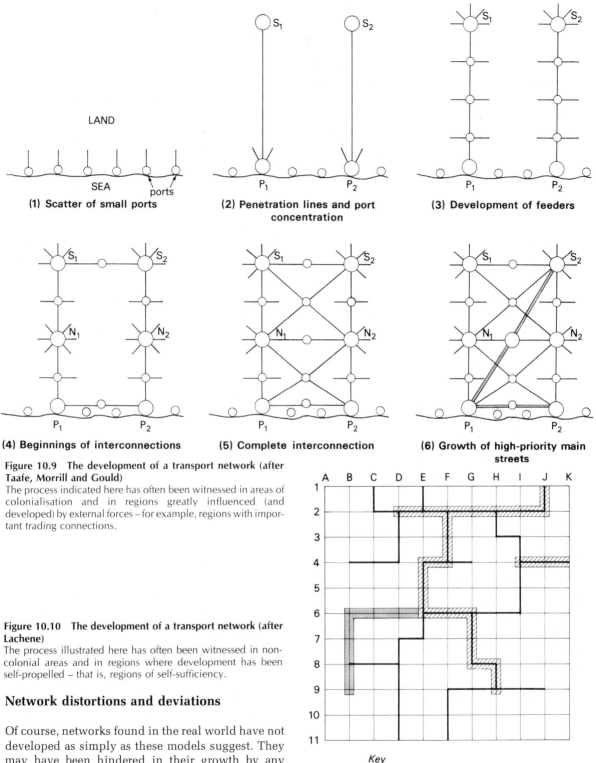

Figure 10.9 The development of a transport network (after Taafe, Morrill and Gould)
The process indicated here has often been witnessed in areas of colonialisation and in regions greatly influenced (and developed) by external forces – for example, regions with important trading connections.

Figure 10.10 The development of a transport network (after Lachene)
The process illustrated here has often been witnessed in non-colonial areas and in regions where development has been self-propelled – that is, regions of self-sufficiency.

Network distortions and deviations

Of course, networks found in the real world have not developed as simply as these models suggest. They may have been hindered in their growth by any number of economic, geographical or political factors, and may change in shape over time. Indeed, even completed networks may possess distortions. The shortest distance between two points is a straight

Key

railway lines

motorways and railway lines

road into a depressed area

underlying grid = original network of tracks across uniform area

149

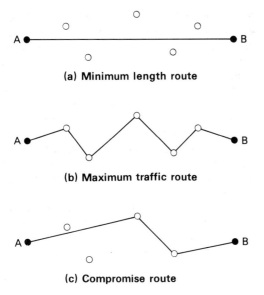

(a) Minimum length route

(b) Maximum traffic route

(c) Compromise route

Figure 10.11 Positive route deviations
Such apparently circuitous routes are made deliberately and by choice. They are intended for definite economic or social reasons – to increase revenue for example or to serve a community.

line, but rarely do links demonstrate this. More often they deviate and run between nodes by apparently strange and circuitous routes.

Deviations in routes and networks may be positive or negative: positive as a response to extra traffic and negative where they avoid geographical features. Figure 10.11 shows how positive deviations might develop. To maximise profit, a builder or user of transport must minimise costs and maximise revenues. Part (a) shows the least-cost route, but this brings in limited traffic. The intervening nodes are not served and revenues are consequently low. Part (b) shows a maximum traffic route, but the cost of building it (or the cost of use) would probably be prohibitive. The 'best' route economically might be a compromise something like that shown in part (c). Examples of positive deviations are almost too numerous to mention, since nearly all routes include them. Every long-distance coach service, for instance, contains them, as do most rail routes. The railway line across East Anglia from Chelmsford to Norwich does not go direct but via Ipswich and Stowmarket.

Figure 10.12 shows how negative deviations might develop. The avoidance of obstacles (human or physical) is often necessary to reduce the costs of route construction and use. If land and water transport cost

the same per unit of cargo, movement between A and B would be cheapest in a straight line and ports would be built at P_1. If, on the other hand, land transport was much more expensive than water transport, the carrier would wish to minimise the former. Ports would therefore be built at P_2. Negative deviations like these are everywhere apparent and we need only look at the roads, railways and canals of any country to see this to be so. In south-west England, for instance, roads and railways tend to encircle the heights of Dartmoor and Bodmin Moor. Even political, as well as physical, divisions may produce negative deviations: there are many instances of transport routes meandering, or even stopping, at a national frontier. On a more local scale, deviations are often related to land ownership. In 1846 the main London–York railway line was taken through the small town of Peterborough, instead of through the much more important town of Stamford, because the Marquess of Exeter refused to allow the track to be laid in his estate of Burghley.

Networks at climax

Developments in communication networks can be viewed in much the same way as ecological plant succession. There is a progression of events, at each stage of which certain environmental conditions hold sway. In a lithosere and hydrosere there is, at first, a botanical desert, being bare rock and water respectively. Then, by a series of steps, plant colonisation

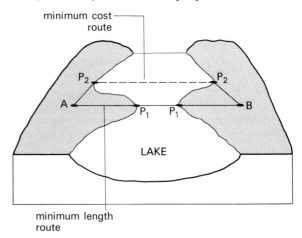

Figure 10.12 Negative route deviations
A non-direct route may have to be taken because of obstacles and barriers. Economic as well as physical and political restrictions may create such a route.

takes place and communities evolve into higher and stronger forms, forest being the final result. Likewise with transport routes. First a blank landscape exists; then develop the first simple lines of communications between a few points (footpaths between villages, for instance); then a greater number of links and nodes stretching further afield; then a degree of route infilling with the evolution of cross routes. Eventually, the whole area is covered by a dense mat of routeways.

Just as plant succession is said to reach a **climax**, so too does network development. With economic progress, networks enlarge and become more complex. Many deviations occur and highly integrated flows evolve, both resulting in the appearance of complicated route-patterns. At such a stage, the point of maximum efficiency may be passed: links become duplicated, capital expenditure becomes wasteful, flows become congested, nodes become overstressed.

Climax networks can be found in most developed countries, but nowhere are they exemplified so well as in west and south Yorkshire. Here, during the 19th century, were all the ingredients for the over-development of transport: a coalfield, heavy industry and textile manufacture, abundant labour supplies and amassed capital. Town councils and companies vied with each other for bigger, better and longer transport routes, and large amounts of money helped realise their ambitions. The result was more canals, railway lines and roads than Victorian England could possibly need, and chaos.

Transport policies and planning

Since communication networks, if allowed to develop naturally, may reach climax proportions and become inefficient, and since also they are dynamic features (altering in response to changes in the human environment) it has long been agreed among geographers and politicians that some degree of control should be exerted. Route flows and route patterns, if they are to serve the public for whom they are constructed, must be planned and designed.

Transport, in particular, requires controlled development. This means that individual flows and entire networks should be modified, planned and positioned in order that they evolve in the most efficient way and for the greatest benefit. Such policies should be based on satisfactory prediction, on the correct interpretation of physical restraints and on a clear understanding of future needs.

Elsewhere in this book, comments are made about the regulation and redesign of transport networks. In regions where economic development needs to be given a boost, entirely new routes and connections are built – for example in central Wales, the Mezzogiorno (Italy), the Amazon Basin (Brazil) and northern Nigeria. In regions where climax congestion already exists, networks are reduced and flows are cut – in the British rail network for instance. Even on a small scale, within urban areas, transport planning has become common: leading to the increased use of one-way systems, road class segregation, pedestrian precincts, bypasses and so on.

Transport policies can conveniently be subdivided into two groups: those intent on changing flow characteristics and those intent on changing network form. Into the first category would come such planning controls as the standardisation of freight rates; limitations concerning the size, shape and weight of vehicles; restrictions on the length of time drivers spend at their controls; laws to curb the use of particular transport modes for carrying certain goods; the imposition of differential fare structures; and the use of subsidies and grants for particular commodity routes.

Into the second category would come those planning controls aimed either at expanding or contracting the total number of transport links and nodes. Such controls are not easy to design: it is not simply a case of adding to or subtracting from networks at random. For example, planners intending to enlarge a network must decide what kind of links to build, where to put them and how best to connect them to an existing network. If capital is limited, they must also decide which links should be built first and which last. Such decisions can only be taken as a result of extensive study, research and discussion (see Fig. 10.13).

First, planners must establish the existing accessibility of each node (town) – to find how central each one is. These nodes can then be placed on a rank hierarchy. Secondly, they must decide which nodes need to have a higher centrality index – which towns would benefit most from extra links. Thirdly, they must work out which new links would have the greatest effect in improving the overall efficiency of a network (preferably at least cost). Fourthly, they must decide which new links would be most feasible, both economically and constructionally; a new link over mountains or marshes, however badly needed, is unlikely to be built first! Such decisions would certainly have been made when it was decided to extend

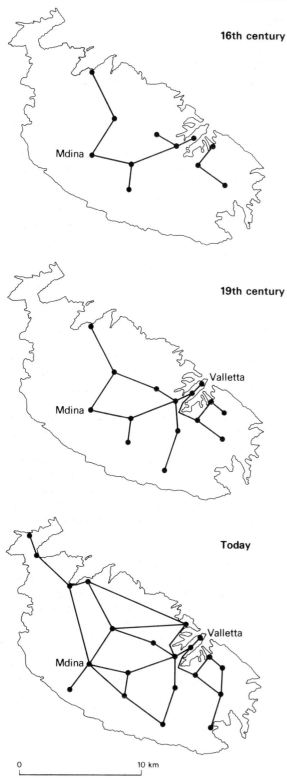

the London underground railway network. The Jubilee Line is the newest addition, but why the planners decided to construct the section from Baker Street to Charing Cross before the section from Charing Cross to the East End is open to argument.

Few countries today allow the development of transport networks to continue unchecked. Most governments have policies that aim to rationalise the various systems of transport into a comprehensive and effective service. In many countries, transport companies have been nationalised and route services integrated. Such policies allow communication networks not only to be more economic but also to be developed to satisfy social requirements. Not a few routes are run at a loss and maintained at government expense or at the cost of more profitable routes. In this way, transport networks have widened their functions and have become even more significant in our daily lives.

Societal impact of communication development

Changes in communication systems – their flows and networks – must necessarily have profound results on human activity. Such results can be short term and long term; can be beneficial and disadvantageous; can be direct and indirect.

Throughout this book the impact of transport development is frequently suggested. Improvements in communications increase migration, help to advance agricultural and industrial output, expand trade relationships, and affect both the growth and structure of urban areas. They also – and more unfortunately – cause noise and air pollution, accelerate the spoliation of the countryside and result in a greater number of deaths and serious injuries. In

Figure 10.13 Development of a main road network in Malta
Until the end of the 16th century, Mdina was the capital; thereafter Valletta became the capital and the development of Malta's road network shows the change. The network characteristics on each map can be measured. The present road pattern is not perfect and many new links could be constructed. Which new links will be built first depends on government planning policies (themselves based on various physical and economic feasibility factors).

152

Britain alone there are over 7000 road deaths per year and over 80 000 bad accidents. Deteriorations in communications, on the other hand, have other types of impact. The closure of railway lines and rural bus services reduces mobility and limits personal choice with regard to jobs, creates settlement blight and village depopulation, and could lead to social, cultural and even political isolation.

It is true to say that communications have played a decisive role historically in the making of the human environment. The Rothschild banking family fortune was originally acquired with the aid of carrier pigeons, these bringing the news of Wellington's defeat of Napoleon at Waterloo to Britain faster than official messengers, thus allowing Rothschild to buy stocks and shares at low prices in advance of the subsequent boom. In 19th-century North America, the building of transcontinental railways not only allowed the Mid-West and Pacific coast to be developed but also led directly to the near extermination of the native indian tribes. In all countries, the invention of the internal combustion engine has had all manner of repercussions – on economic progress, national power and personal wealth. Without his motor factory profits, William Morris (Lord Nuffield) might not have been such a generous philanthropist.

Even the way in which transport development is planned has an impact on people's lives. The use of subsidies as an incentive to the expansion of flows, for example, can have indirect results. In Belgium, early morning fares for workmen are kept artificially low, giving manual workers cheaper travel than skilled white-collar workers. Thus, low income groups can commute over larger distances than can higher income groups. This results in town-based firms finding it easier to recruit low wage workers from far afield than high wage workers from close at hand, government subsidy having the effect of allowing employers to maintain cheap labour. In Britain, the withdrawal of subsidies for commuter traffic has led to a steep rise in commuter fares. In consequence, people may be less willing to live in the country while working in the town, preferring to live near their work. Thus, house prices around urban peripheries have stabilised and those close to city centres have soared. In London, this can be seen in the rejuvenation of such formerly poor areas as Islington and Camden – which are now highly fashionable and expensive.

In short, all communication developments, and the policies that are introduced to regulate them, have diverse and extensive effects on human life.

Summary

1 Communications (movements of goods, services and ideas) help to balance the unevenness of human activity. There have been two recent periods of rapid communication development: 1750–1830 (in roads, canals and railways) and the 20th century (in airways, motor transport and telecommunications).

2 Progress in information technology – through computers, cable television and wave bands – will be crucial in future economic development. A new generation of industry and a new employment structure are likely to emerge.

3 Modal choice is determined by relative advantages and disadvantages. User considerations include cost, convenience, flexibility of routes, speed and reliability.

4 Transport costs involve fixed and running costs. Water traffic has the highest fixed and lowest running costs (hence used for long distances); road traffic has low fixed and high running costs (hence used for short distances).

5 Flows (their direction, scale, speed, capacity) result from complementarity, the degree of intervening opportunity and transferability – according to Ullman.

6 The gravity (distance decay) model suggests that flows and distances are inversely related: the greater the one, the smaller the other.

7 Networks have set patterns (according to Bunge) and their efficiency can be measured by the beta index, the König number and the alpha index.

8 Network development can take place through a sequence of stages – densities, fineness and connectivity increasing by degrees. The limit of network efficiency is reached at the climax.

9 Transport flow and pattern changes can be predicted through an interpretation of known cause-and-effect phenomena. Positive deviations arise out of economic advantage, negative deviations out of physical necessity.

10 Most countries now have transport planning policies. These can be comprehensive or piecemeal. All policies should take into account the social impact of communication change: the removal of a rail service can bring economic disaster to an entire community.

Data–response exercises

1 Compare the impact on the environment suggested by the three modes of communication illustrated in Figure 10.1. In what ways can the pollution caused by these three be minimised?

2 For Figure 10.3 construct the likely cost curve for air transport. What would be the consequences upon the other cost curves of (a) a drastic fall in the price of fuel; (b) a substantial increase in the costs of labour?

3 Outline the conditions that might lead to an inelastic distance-decay graph line (see Fig. 10.4) and those that might lead to an elastic one. In which countries are inelastic distance-decay relationships more likely to be common?

4 From a topological map of the minor (C grade) roads south of the A357 in OS map A (Dorset), calculate the connectivity and density of the network, using more than one method in each case. Account for the efficiency indicated by your findings and comment on those factors that appear to influence this network.

5 With the aid of a sketch map, discuss the relationship between communications and relief in OS map B (Yorkshire). Suggest and account for a possible route for a new A class road to be built from Bingley to Denholme via Wilsden.

6 Calculate the beta index of each of the three networks in Figure 10.13 (Malta), and in each case find the most central node. In each case suggest how the efficiency of the network might be improved. Which kinds of networks do these diagrams most closely resemble?

11 Trade and commerce

Introduction

In Chapter 10, we considered movements – the different types, their development, characteristics and spatial patterns. The reasons behind movements were not considered in any detail; these are discussed elsewhere in the book. Movements of people, goods, services and ideas take place for various political, social and economic reasons: migration may be the outcome of persecution or of recreational need, the transport of commodities takes place for reasons of supply and demand, the dissemination of knowledge may result from cultural necessity. Movements with an economic motive are the links that allow trade and commerce to take place.

In this context, the present chapter can be viewed as an extension of the previous one – economically inspired movements being a specialised form of communication. Although normally used synonymously, trade and commerce have slightly different meanings: the former can be defined as the *spatial* interchange of custom – the buying and selling of goods and services between regions and countries – whereas the latter can be defined as the *physical* interchange of custom – the buying and selling of goods and services at the points of contact. This distinction is pertinent: trade includes world trading patterns and routes, trading restrictions and trading blocs; commerce includes retailing, financial services, money market institutions and fiscal planning (the determination of taxation policies, budget conditions and so on).

Both trade and commerce are part of economic life and they arise out of the fact that no two areas are exactly alike. Every region in the world is unique – having its own climate, relief, products, culture, technology, transport facilities and needs – and each is dependent to a greater or lesser extent on other regions. The most fortunate areas cannot be entirely self-sufficient; the most primitive societies exchange their own commodities for those they require. A rising standard of living and a growing economic sophistication tend to broaden the range of goods and services demanded by a community so that, the more

advanced an area becomes, the more it is likely to look elsewhere to satisfy its needs.

This chapter will concentrate largely (though not wholly) on trade, since this aspect of economic movement is of most concern to the geographer. The questions to be answered by this chapter include the following:

- What kinds of trade occur, and how have these developed?
- Which goods and services take part in world trade, and what is their relative importance?
- What relationships exist between trading countries, and how significant are they?
- How do trading patterns change, and why is world trade restricted?
- What are the world's main trading blocs, and how do they operate?

Types of trade

Trade can be classified in a number of ways (see Fig. 11.1). Different classifications can be used for different purposes, although it is normal in geography for the criterion of distance to be the one most commonly utilised. All classifications allow the establishment of hierarchies whereby types of trade can be ranked according to scale and importance. Unfortunately, there is no room here to make detailed hierarchical analysis of either trade or trade routes.

Trade takes place at different scales and can be observed at local, interregional and international levels. Local trade was the earliest to develop, a simple form beginning even among the most primitive peoples. It involves relatively short distances and small quantities of goods. The point of contact may be a small market place and the commodity producers themselves usually do the buying and selling. Exchange of this kind might take place between adjacent localities: for example, between mountain and valley areas, arable and pasture lands, or coastlands and interiors.

Interregional trade takes place across greater dis-

TRADE AND COMMERCE

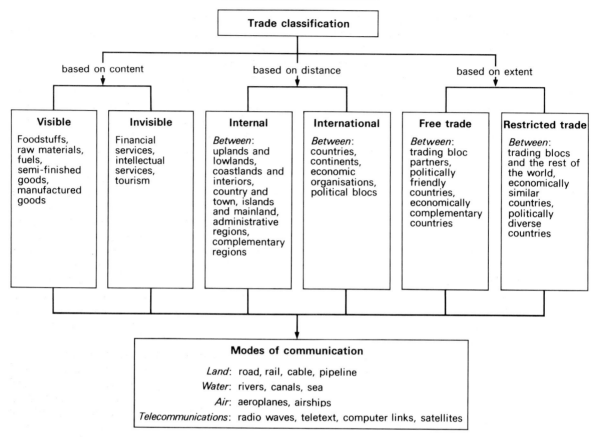

Figure 11.1 Types of trade
Trade takes place in different ways and for different reasons. Trading links change in response to social and political as well as economic forces.

tances but still within the confines of a single country's boundaries. Traders or merchants appear at this level, responsible for buying from producers and selling to consumers and for transport between the two. In Britain, such trade has taken place at least since the Iron Age, when Celtic routes crossed the country from coast to coast. In places, these trackways still survive: the Cotswold Way (the Humber to the Severn), the Ridgeway (Devon to Norfolk) and the Pilgrim's Way (Dorset to Kent). Later, in Saxon times, this trade expanded further, and drove roads developed along which cattle and sheep were driven to distant markets.

Today the volume of internal trade varies widely from country to country. It is determined by the size of the country, the spatial distribution, the variety and extent of its resources, the size and wealth of its population, political associations and agreements, and the degree to which transport and marketing

facilities are developed. Advanced countries tend to have much interregional trade and less-developed countries have little. In Britain, about 75% of all commodity movements is inter-regional. Farm produce is taken from countryside to towns, manufactured goods from town to country and from town to town. China clay is transported from Cornwall to Staffordshire; fruit from the Vale of Evesham to the Birmingham and London markets; hops from Kent to breweries elsewhere. The transport of Worcester sauce from Worcester to our dinner tables must alone account for thousands of pounds' worth of trade each year!

International trade covers the greatest distances and takes place between countries and continents. Like other types of trade, this also has a long history. In the ancient world, extensive caravan routes ran through the Middle East and China, and the discovery of sea routes further increased the importance of Asia as a trading centre. More recently, the growth of European culture and industrialisation spread trade worldwide. Emphasis moved from small-scale shipments of high-value goods to bulk movements of crude or low-value goods. At the same time technological and scientific progress revealed uses for some commodities formerly neglected – metallic ores, vegetable oils, rubber, nitrates and so on. As the economy of Europe expanded, so the search for more raw materials grew. This led, at least in part, to imperialism and it is certainly a fact that the development of the colonies did much to foster and encourage international trade.

Up to 1914, world trade was still dominated by colonial movements. Since then, however, much has altered. In particular, the numbers of countries and commodities involved have grown. The reasons for this are manifold but include the decline of the British Empire, the economic and political growth of the USA and USSR, and the development of formerly backward countries. Today, the extent to which countries depend on international trade varies. Some, like Britain and Japan, depend heavily on it; others, like Russia and China, do not. There are various environmental, economic, social and political reasons for this.

Composition and volume of trade

Trade is essentially a two-way process, since every region is involved in both the export and import of goods and services. Generally – and especially in the past – areas export those commodities in which they have a surplus, or which they produce efficiently or cheaply, and import those commodities in which they have a deficit, or which they can only produce inefficiently or at great cost. There are some exchanges between countries of similar goods but these are often related to such factors as design differences and fashion. Ideally, total exports and total imports should balance. If the value of all exports exceeds the value of all imports, the balance of payments is said to be favourable; if the value of all exports is smaller than the value of all imports, the balance of payments is said to be unfavourable.

These total values take into account invisible as well as visible trade. Invisible movements are those concerned with services and most commonly include such activities as insurance, banking and money spent by tourists. Visible movements are composed of goods, and these can be categorised as foodstuffs, industrial raw materials (either agricultural products or minerals), fuels and manufactured goods. This chapter is largely concerned with these visible movements.

Cereals, meat, dairy produce, beverages and fruit are the most important foodstuffs entering trade. These originate either in areas where the population is insufficient in number to consume all the agricultural products or where physical factors make the growing of particular crops especially profitable.

The most important industrial raw materials are mineral ores, textile fibres, timber, wood pulp and vegetable oils. These tend to come from areas that are environmentally or physically fortunate enough to possess such primary products but lack either the population or technical know-how to utilise them.

Fuels have always been important in international trade, but the types and their significance have varied with time. Once coal was dominant, but today crude oil far outstrips all other sources of power. In some places electricity is traded, for example from Sweden to Denmark via undersea cable, but this is of minor importance on a world scale.

Manufactured goods include machinery, textiles, chemical products and petroleum by-products and originate from highly industrialised, developed and populated regions or else from newly developing countries such as Korea and Brazil. Semi-finished goods are also traded since the manufacturing process often takes place in two or more different areas, a product being half made in one region and completed in another.

For well over a century, world commodity flows have been dominated by two types of trade. On the one hand, there is a movement of primary products from tropical regions and 'new' lands of the southern hemisphere to the industrialised countries of the northern hemisphere and a return movement of manufactured goods. On the other hand, and in addition to this north–south flow, there is an east–west traffic in finished products (mostly machinery) between Europe and North America, which is largely the outcome of the historical, ethnic and cultural links between those two regions.

Notwithstanding these characteristics, many changes have occurred in recent years. In particular, both the volume and variety of trade have increased, and no longer can only wealthy countries afford the resources of other lands. Since World War 2, world trade has risen five-fold in terms of value (even taking inflation into account), but this increase has not been uniform throughout the commodities involved.

There has been a fundamental change in the mix of products in terms of both bulk and value. Petroleum now dwarfs all other goods and accounts for more than half of the tonnage of world shipments. Indeed, such is the unique character of the oil trade that it may be considered separately from other types of movement. It takes place between specialised ports and refineries and in purpose-built tankers or pipelines. Also, since two-thirds of this traffic originates in the Middle East, its flow runs counter to the north–south, east–west movements mentioned earlier.

Among thg other commodities, manufactured goods (especially plastics and electronics) have tended to become increasingly important at the expense of primary products in terms of value. This is caused by all manner of factors: for example, greater specialisation, higher standards of living, the development of formerly backward countries and increased advertising. Also, over the years, advanced countries have increased their dominance of world trade (now accounting for about 70% of total value), the Third World has experienced a fall in its share of world trade (now about 20% of total value) and the contribution of the Communist world has remained fairly constant (about 10% of total value). In the future these trends are likely to continue. Another trend in recent years has been the entry into world trade of rapidly industrialising countries such as Taiwan, Hong Kong and Singapore, which can undercut developed countries in the sale of manufactured textiles, electrical equipment and steel.

A country's participation in world trade grows as it develops economically, and rich nations import and export at the expense of poor nations. Indeed, the situation may be further exacerbated by two other factors. The first is that developed countries are now producing and exporting truly global products (like Coca Cola or BP oil) against which small, new companies in developing countries may find it hard to compete. The second is that some developing countries themselves are failing to expand their foreign trade even to the level of the world average. The problem is even more serious if such developing countries have economies very dependent upon the exports of single commodities, as do Malaysia (rubber) and Ghana (cacao).

National trading links

It follows from what has been said earlier that a country's dependence on trade is related to its economic

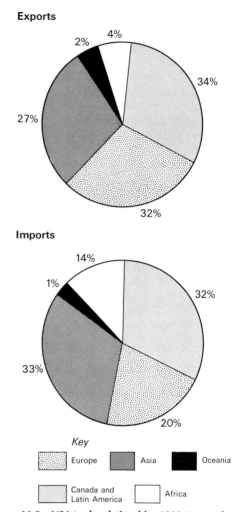

Exports

4%
2%
34%
27%
32%

Imports

14%
1%
32%
33%
20%

Key

Europe
Asia
Oceania
Canada and Latin America
Africa

Figure 11.2 USA trade relationships 1982 (proportion of total trade with major world regions)
US trade with all other countries has risen by 60% over the last five years. However, this increase has not been uniformly spread throughout all countries, for political and economic reasons. Trade with Singapore and Algeria has doubled in the past five years; exports to China have increased five times and imports from China three times; imports from Norway, Kuwait, Saudi Arabia, Egypt and Nigeria have multiplied two, nine, three, five and three times, respectively. Some of these increases can be attributed to the US demand for crude oil. All trade with Iran has decreased almost to nothing – doubtless as a result of the political tensions between these two countries.

attributes and attitudes. A nation with surplus capital, raw materials and labour would tend to be less reliant on imports than one with a deficit of such ingredients and perhaps more reliant on exports. A country with a high standard of living would generally need more trading links with the rest of the world in order to maintain its economy than would one with

SINGAPORE – ENTREPÔT OF THE EAST

The island of Singapore (measuring 42 km by 23 km) lies at the southern tip of the Malay Peninsula in the East Indies. It became an independent republic in 1965, is a member of the Commonwealth, and has a population of 2.5 million (75% of which is Chinese, 15% Malayan and 10% Indian and European). Over 80% of the population lives in the city of Singapore, situated on the south of the island.

Though small and overcrowded, Singapore is one of the richest countries (on a per capita basis) in Asia and its people have a standard of living equal to many in the developed world. The wealth and economic success are founded not on raw materials, for the island has no mineral resources, but on trade. Indeed, Singapore City is the fourth largest port in the world and its petroleum refining capacity is the third largest in the world.

Singapore's most important natural advantage is position, and this it has made full use of in its development as a trading centre. It lies between the Pacific and Indian Oceans and at the hub of eastern shipping routes (see Fig. 11.3). At such a point, development as an **entrepôt** was almost inevitable: a port to which goods in transit are brought for temporary storage before being re-exported. In this way Singapore has become internationally important over the past hundred years, as a freight handling and storage centre for transhipment. It now boasts vast warehouse facilities, extensive dock areas, highly automated loading and unloading methods and modernised container equipment.

To complement its entrepôt function, Singapore has also developed its own industries (including tin smelting, rubber processing, petrochemicals and the manufacture of steel, textiles and electrical goods), and its own highly sophisticated international financial services. It is, in fact, now one of the major commercial centres of the world, having wide-ranging banking, insurance and broking sec-

tors and attracting foreign investment from major international companies and national governments. It is also a designated freeport, so that all commodities landed, handled, manufactured and reshipped are exempt from customs duties and tariffs. This not only speeds up transhipment but further encourages the development of foreign-owned manufacturing industries.

Today, then, Singapore is the market place for South-East Asia. It imports the produce of neighbouring countries (rubber and tin from Malaysia, rice from Burma and Thailand) stores them, and perhaps processes them too, and then re-exports them to the developed world. It imports finished goods from the developed world and redistributes these to its neighbours. Its three most important trading partners are Japan, the USA and Malaysia, each accounting for about 15% of total trade.

After a considerable boom during the Vietnam War of the 1960s and 1970s, Singapore's entrepôt functions have gone into a slight decline, made worse by the fact that many neighbouring countries are beginning to develop their own port facilities and processing industries. However, this decline is relative. With its advantageous position, its modern technical facilities, its political stability and the commercial acumen of its people, Singapore will remain extremely important to world trade.

Figure 11.3 Singapore as a trading centre
Location has caused Singapore to become a trading hub and to grow as one of the richest ports in the world.

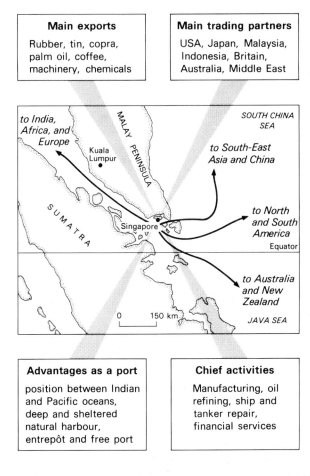

Main exports
Rubber, tin, copra, palm oil, coffee, machinery, chemicals

Main trading partners
USA, Japan, Malaysia, Indonesia, Britain, Australia, Middle East

to India, Africa, and Europe

Kuala Lumpur

MALAY PENINSULA

SOUTH CHINA SEA

to South-East Asia and China

SUMATRA

Singapore

to North and South America

Equator

0   150 km

to Australia and New Zealand

JAVA SEA

Advantages as a port
position between Indian and Pacific oceans, deep and sheltered natural harbour, entrepôt and free port

Chief activities
Manufacturing, oil refining, ship and tanker repair, financial services

a low standard of living. However, the paradox of trade is that participation can be inversely related to dependence. As a country advances economically, it may take a greater part in world trade yet become less and less dependent upon it, since technological development sustains a higher degree of self-sufficiency. An extremely primitive country may be unable to participate in the very trade on which it is dependent for survival, it being too poor to buy the foreign goods it needs.

The pattern of world trading routes, and the trading links each country has with other countries, are not just a reflection of economic complementarity. It is true that a nation buys from countries goods and services that it cannot itself produce efficiently, and sells to countries goods and services that the recipients require, and which it can produce effectively, yet this is not the whole story. There are, in addition, various social, cultural and political dimensions in trade.

The exchange of similar goods often takes place between two countries for no better reason than that they are political allies: high technology, for example, has a two-way trade movement between Britain and the USA; motor vehicles are traded in both directions between the USSR and East Germany. Conversely, essential trade (from an economic point of view) may not occur between countries for reasons of political hostility. During the 1970s, much-needed supplies of copper were not being imported by Britain from southern Africa owing to the political tensions (and trade sanctions) that existed between Britain and what was then Rhodesia (now Zimbabwe). The USA, in particular, has trading links which are very biased politically (see Fig. 11.2). Other factors that may upset the rationale of world trade include the existence of subsidies, monopolistic dumping and ghost protection (artificial free trade). Only occasionally do trading relationships cut diametrically across political associations and friendships – and normally only when it is economically unavoidable. Few countries in the world (least of all, many black African nations) like to be seen trading with South Africa, but do so because that particular country is not only very advanced technologically but also contains the largest mineral reserves in the world of gold, vanadium, chromium ore and diamonds. The USSR frequently buys large quantities of grain from the USA and Argentina to supplement its own shortages, despite the capitalistic tendencies of those two countries.

Finally, it should be remembered that trade can be viewed as a barometer of political as well as economic fortunes. A nation experiencing an increase in trade might not only be passing through a period of economic growth but also be developing a more stable domestic political system (as in the case of Venezuela), a more extrovert diplomatic role in world affairs (as in the case of China) or a more powerful military presence (as in the case of Israel and Cuba). Conversely, a country's trade slump might indicate not so much economic misfortune as a decline in political determination and confidence – which would reduce the value of a country's currency and limit borrowing capabilities.

Free trade and protection

Some world trade takes place completely free of restrictions; some is subject to control. In either case there are arguments for and against.

Advantages of free trade
(1) It allows countries to specialise in the production of those goods and services to which they are best suited. This increases efficiency and reduces costs.
(2) It enables countries to obtain either goods and services more cheaply than they can produce themselves, or those they do not possess (for example, Iceland has no coal, Sweden no oil, and both countries must import fuel supplies).
(3) It permits some goods, which otherwise are available only in season, to be obtainable all year round (like fruit in Britain).
(4) It gives the consumer a greater choice of products and a wider range of designs and styles (for example in furniture, in clothing fashions and in machinery).
(5) By expanding the global market, it enables the benefits of large-scale production to be achieved, which in turn lowers costs. Switzerland and Denmark, especially, benefit in this way in respect of specialised intricate equipment (e.g. watches) and dairy produce, respectively.
(6) It increases competition and thereby promotes efficiency in production and a reduction of financial waste. Without trade, a monopolist may gain control of a home market.
(7) It encourages cultural and political links between countries.

Together these advantages produce higher living standards, promote economic and cultural development and allow for greater political unity. They are at their maximum when trade is free and are limited when protection controls operate. Even so, controls do exist and can be instigated in various ways.

Trade controls

(1) **Customs duties or tariffs** may be charged on imports and are usually levied at the point of entry into a country.

(2) **Financial subsidies** to home producers may enable them to compete more successfully with foreign producers. This may increase exports and decrease imports.

(3) **Quotas** may be adapted to fix the maximum physical amount of a commodity that can be imported during a particular period.

(4) **Exchange controls** can be used to restrict the movements of foreign currency. By limiting the amount of money spent on foreign goods, governments can determine the quantity of imports.

(5) **Physical controls**. Occasionally, a complete ban or embargo may be imposed on commodity movements. This may happen in wartime or for particularly dangerous goods like narcotics.

(6) **'Unofficial controls'**. Obstructions caused by bureaucratic 'small print' and tradition frequently limit trade. For example, it is difficult for EEC members to export to Japan.

In addition to these controls, all of which may be the outcome of governmental policy, there are other, natural, restrictions to world trade. The lack of mobility of the factors of production (land, labour, capital, enterprise) and the existence of different national currencies and banking systems are two such examples.

Reasons for protection

It can be argued that trade controls exist because countries think and act nationally rather than internationally (see Fig. 11.4). This may be so, but protection policies can still be justified on the following grounds:

(1) To improve the terms of trade or to correct a temporary balance-of-payments deficit.

(2) To protect 'infant' industries against the competition of larger, established foreign industries.

(3) To enable an industry to decline gradually or

restructure by cushioning the effects of a falling home demand. The British cotton industry has been helped in this way.

(4) To prevent the 'dumping' of cheap foreign goods on the home market, a practice which gives foreign firms an unfair competitive advantage.

(5) To maintain home employment and protect the standard of living. This is especially common in times of economic depression.

(6) To help a country achieve self-sufficiency (as in many developing countries).

(7) To encourage the production of a commodity of strategic importance (as with armaments in most countries).

(8) To foster closer political ties (as in trading blocs).

(9) To aid political bargaining (for example, the USA prohibits trade with Cuba for ideological reasons, and a great many countries have sanctions against South Africa).

(10) To promote social policies (for example, Britain limits the import of cheap coal in order to safeguard the future of her own mining regions) or to avoid government–trade union confrontation and anti-government voting at elections.

Figure 11.4 Demands for protection
People demand protective measures usually for very personal reasons.

Arguments against protection

Notwithstanding the above reasons for protection, trading controls can still be criticised as running counter to the advantages inherent in free trade. In particular, protection policies can be faulted on five counts:

(1) They prevent countries specialising in their most efficient production and can perpetuate inefficiency (e.g. agriculture in France, owing to EEC farm policy).

(2) They can restrict the volume of trade and thereby cause lower living standards and higher prices.

(3) They tend to be self-perpetuating. Once controls have been imposed, they are rarely removed.

(4) They may lead to reprisals by other countries. Exporting countries may retaliate with their own import controls and this could create political tensions.

(5) They increase the prices paid by consumers for goods and so have inflationary consequences.

The General Agreement on Tariffs and Trade

Before the 19th century, protection was the norm and free trade was practically unknown. Barriers were set up either simply to raise revenue or to protect home producers, and few people realised the potential advantages of uninterrupted commodity movements. Only at the beginning of last century did free trade begin to develop.

Britain was the first major country to remove restrictions. This was partly because British goods dominated world trade and would probably benefit most from freedom of movement, and partly because many British statesmen saw free trade as a socially moral policy to pursue. Thus, during the Victorian Age, barriers were continually removed and by the end of the 19th century much world trade was free.

Since then, however, protection has been revived. Serious economic depressions, the development of various political unions and ideologies and, especially, the two World Wars have caused nations once again to seek refuge behind trade barriers. It was to counteract this revival that the General Agreement on Tariffs and Trade (GATT) was formed. GATT was set up at Geneva in 1947 by 23 world nations. Its aim was to encourage the gradual removal of trading barriers, and this it has since done through a series of 'rounds' or meetings. The Kennedy Round of 1964–67 (instigated in 1962 by President Kennedy of the USA), in particular, saw a leap forward in the spread of free trade.

Today GATT incorporates over 75 member countries and represents almost the whole of the trade in the free world. Even so, it is doubtful if world trade will ever again be as free as it was when the British Empire dominated the world economy. Although each GATT member is committed to the principle of free trade, it also reserves the right to use protection under special circumstances. These circumstances are those listed earlier under 'Reasons for protection', and in reality always exist.

Trading blocs

Although completely free trade may no longer be possible on a world scale, it is possible on a regional or continental scale. This is because of the existence of trading blocs or customs unions.

Such economic groupings are not new. In medieval times the Hapsburg empire enjoyed free trading among its member states; Germany had a trading union (the 'Zollverein') long before it became united politically (1871); and even the American Constitution (1789) laid down that no State could restrict trade without Congressional consent. None the less, only since 1945 have customs unions grown to be a major force in world trade. Nowhere have they developed more successfully than in Europe.

In 1948 Belgium, the Netherlands and Luxembourg formed the economic union of 'Benelux', and three years later these three combined with France, West Germany and Italy to form the European Coal and Steel Community. At first this had only limited aims, but it was important since it laid the foundation for the European Economic Community (EEC). Better known as the Common Market, this came into being at the Treaty of Rome (1957) and was planned to work towards complete economic unity (and eventually towards complete political unity as well). By the end of its first 10 years, economic success was almost complete: trade between the member states was mostly unrestricted and had grown by over 320%.

During the same period, another customs union developed. This involved Britain, Norway, Sweden, Denmark, Switzerland, Austria and Portugal, and became known as the European Free Trade Association (EFTA). Less comprehensive and cohesive than the EEC, this can be viewed as a more cautious attempt at economic union. Nevertheless, it has been a moderate success and certainly has helped the development of its member countries.

During the 1960s, various attempts were made by Britain and other EFTA members to join the EEC.

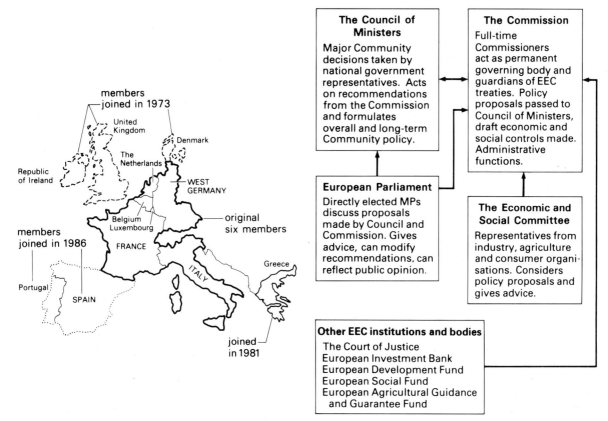

Figure 11.5   The European Economic Community
The Common Market represents 12 countries and over 300 million people. Its aims are diverse in both scope and effect, having economic, political and social aspects and wide ranging repercussions. For these reasons the Community is not universally popular. Many criticise the EEC's aims as too ambitious and too comprehensive; its organisation as too bureaucratic, unwieldy and unrepresentative; its policies as unfair. Those member states that have large and inefficient farming economies (France, Greece, Spain) tend to benefit most; those with heavy industrial economies (West Germany and the UK) tend to benefit least. The general aims of the Community can be summarised thus: to advance free trade and free movements of labour and capital; to stabilise markets and encourage self-sufficiency; to revitalise industry and depressed areas; to extend political bonds through common laws and foreign policies; to extend cultural standardisation through common controls, civil rights, health levels and safety requirements.

However, these failed and it was not until 1972 that negotiations resulted in the expansion of the Common Market from six members to nine (to include Britain, the Republic of Ireland and Denmark). Since then, further expansion has taken place: Greece became a member in 1981 and another two countries, Spain and Portugal, joined in 1986. Whether the Community continues to be as beneficial for the 12 as it was for the original six remains to be seen. (See Fig. 11.5.)

The evident success of trading blocs in Europe has encouraged the formation of others elsewhere. Mexico and all the South American countries, except the Guianas, now belong to the Latin American Integration Association (LAIA), and many of the small states on the American isthmus are part of the Central American Republic Trading Bloc. The Communist countries of Europe have combined into 'Comecon', in order to promote free commodity movements, and many of the African countries are now developing concessional trade agreements.

It is generally true that the larger the trading bloc, the more advantageous it will be for its member countries. However, all countries do not necessarily benefit equally. There is a tendency for those countries or regions furthest from the location of the bloc's central authority to benefit least, and those areas closest to the central authority to benefit most. In the EEC, for example, it is recognised that Belgium, northern France and northern West Germany derive greater benefit than southern Italy and Scotland (the central authority being located at Brussels). It is partly for

163

this reason that considerable amounts of money are spent annually on regional development policies, helping to develop the less prosperous areas.

The existence of trading blocs has a marked effect upon the composition, volume and direction of world trade. Overall they may reduce long-distance flows and promote short-distance flows. This is because trade between bloc members is likely to grow at the expense of trade between members and non-members. For example, before Britain joined the Common Market, much of her trade took place with Commonwealth countries. Today, the high tariff wall surrounding the EEC inhibits this trade and Britain is forced to buy 'dear' primary products from within the Community rather than 'cheap' primary products from elsewhere. Thus, British food imports from traditional suppliers like New Zealand have been displaced by products from new suppliers such as France and West Germany. New Zealand and other Commonwealth producers of primary goods, finding their trade with Britain reduced, must find new markets for their commodities in countries like Japan, which do not belong to a strong customs union.

The trade trap

It has already been stated that many Third World countries depend upon the export of foodstuffs or raw materials for economic survival. They produce primary commodities for the developed countries and use the income earned to finance industrialisation or agricultural improvement, and to import manufactured goods and technology from those same developed countries. Such a trading relationship is based on demand/supply complementarity and should be mutually beneficial to all participants. (Sadly, much of the money earned by Third World countries is used – together with further borrowed finance – to buy arms.)

However, it is often the case that mutual benefit does not result. In many instances, trade is to the advantage only of the developed nations, and Third World countries are doomed to suffer a poverty circle known as the trade trap. In essence this trap consists of what Americans would call a 'no-win situation', or a 'Catch-22' position. It can take many forms. For example, if a Third World country exports non-essential commodities to the developed world (such as coffee, tea or fruit), then it is faced with a volatile and elastic demand. If price goes up, the developed countries would merely do without those goods or switch to alternatives. If a Third World country exports essential commodities (such as cotton, rubber or metals), then it is faced with the danger that developed countries – not wishing to be dependent on the less developed world – might develop their own substitutes (such as man-made fibres, plastics and alloys). In either case, the Third World country cannot be certain of a consistent income from its exports.

Money earned from exports can be utilised in a Third World country's development programme. However, industrialisation would mean that such a country can process more of its own raw materials and manufacture more of its required finished goods. This would reduce the size of its raw material exports, thus reducing its income from trade and hence leading to a shortage of money with which to finance industrial development. Nor would the export of manufactured goods from its new factories help a Third World country to offset lost earnings from raw material exports. Such goods would be cheap on the world markets (because of the use of cheap labour) and would undercut similar goods produced by developed countries. Faced by so-called unfair competition, developed countries, through tariffs and customs restrictions, would soon reduce trade relations and protect their own industries. Third World countries might thus be left with surplus stocks of finished goods, which their own populations cannot afford to buy.

Indeed, even by specialising totally in the production of cash crops or raw materials for export (to the detriment of domestic living standards), some Third World countries still cannot earn enough through foreign exchange to finance essential imports – capital goods, fuels, food supplies and so on. Furthermore, such countries fail to increase exports because they lack investment capacity and cannot divert economic activity to domestic requirements since this would reduce exports and diminish further their already inadequate income of foreign currency. To bridge the financial gap, many countries in this position are forced to raise loans to pay for much-needed imports. From this point the trade trap deepens, as a country must export raw materials merely to repay interest charges on foreign debts.

An answer to the vicious circle of trade-inspired poverty might appear to be 'aid through trade' agreements between developed and less developed countries. By these, a developed nation could agree to purchase fixed quantities of raw materials from a Third World country at artificially high prices. This would reduce the latter's precarious dependence on the variability of world demand and price levels. However, even such agreements are economically dangerous and could well backfire. Guaranteed high prices for agreed quantities of material exports could remove any incentives for a Third World country to become more efficient, more advanced and more competitive. Economic stagnation would result.

Of course, the seriousness of the trade trap varies according to a Third World country's economic balance. The countries that suffer least are those with a wide range of export goods and a rapidly expanding domestic market for manufactured goods. Those that suffer most have a severely limited range of exports – Honduras (bananas), Burundi (coffee), Mauritius (sugar) and Chad (cotton), for example. For such countries, slight changes in world demand, in trading agreements or in domestic economic development, could be just as disastrous as a failed crop harvest.

Summary

1 Trade can be internal or international, visible (dealing with goods) or invisible (dealing with services). Free trade has no barriers; protection results from quotas, levies and exchange controls.

2 In world trade, raw materials move from less developed to advanced countries, finished goods in the opposite direction. Oil is the most important commodity in world trade in terms of tonnage. The international price for oil is no longer determined solely by OPEC due partly to the importance of Britain's North Sea reserves.

3 Increasingly, similar goods (e.g. cars, machinery) are being exchanged between developed countries, and less developed countries are exporting cheap manufactured goods (e.g. textiles, steel, plastics). The latter development is causing structural recession in developed countries.

4 A nation's trading links with other countries are determined by politics as well as by economics. Little trade takes place between Eastern and Western Europe or between China and the USSR.

5 Free trade is hypothetically advantageous to all countries but is unrealistic when nationalistic countries compete in an unequal world. Protection helps to shelter infant industries and to reduce the effects of recession. It also enables a government to court political popularity.

6 GATT (the General Agreement on Tariffs and Trade) was set up to promote free trade but has had only limited success.

7 Trading blocs encourage free trade on an intra-continental scale. However, they are not equally beneficial to all member countries: in the EEC France benefits more than Britain from the trading policies.

8 Many Third World countries, which rely on raw-material or food exports, enter a circular trade trap. Dependence on trade creates poverty, which exacerbates dependence on trade.

Data–response exercises

1 What are the possible changes likely to occur over the next 20 years in the US trading relationships with the rest of the world (see Fig. 11.2), bearing in mind the USA's role in world political affairs and the effects of the economic depression of the 1980s?

2 Critically examine the logic behind the demands for protection in the cartoon (Fig. 11.4). Discuss the possible results, short term and long term, if a country such as Britain were to impose such protective measures.

3 Examine the argument that the Common Market (Fig. 11.5) is too bureaucratic, unwieldy and unrepresentative. To what extent are the member countries complementary to each other in political and economic conditions?

4 Draw annotated sketch maps, similar in style to that of Singapore (Fig. 11.3), to show the position and trading links of Hong Kong, Cape Town and Rotterdam.

5 India: 48% of exports = primary goods
  UK: 82% of exports = secondary goods
  Denmark: 37% of exports = primary goods
  Account for the differences in these trading figures and suggest which particular goods might be involved in each case. What changes are likely to occur over the next 20 years?

6 Construct a flow diagram of Western Europe to show the tourist trade between countries. Outline the ways in which governments can attract foreign tourists.

12 Economic development

Introduction

From a discussion about trade, trading relationships and commercial movements between and within the developed world and the Third World, it is but a short step to a discussion about economic development – the subject of this chapter.

If trade is viewed as an economic response to world inequalities, then economic development may be seen as a natural phenomenon, which both causes and is the result of those same inequalities. If, on the other hand, trade is viewed as a means by which some countries can become richer at the expense of others, then economic development may be seen as the process by which the wealth gap is widened. Trade and economic development are, therefore, linked. It is only through commodity movements and economic expansion – the growth of industrialisation, agricultural technology, service activities and financial expertise – that commercial, social and political inequalities can be created and corrected.

The questions we must ask ourselves in this chapter are as follows:

- What kinds of economic and social differences exist in the world, and why do they occur?
- Where are rich and poor areas found, on both a world and a local scale, and are they spatially related?
- Why do some regions remain poor while others grow rich?
- What problems do underdeveloped regions face, and how hopeful are their prospects?
- How can less developed areas become better off, and by what means can economic development be achieved?
- What is meant by 'development', and is it possible (or even advisable) for Third World countries to reach developed-world living standards within the limits of finite resources and fixed culture patterns?

The imbalance of wealth

Wealth, like most other things, is not distributed evenly throughout the world. There are 'haves' and 'have-nots'. Some areas and peoples are economically and technologically advanced whereas other areas and peoples are not. Such differences can be seen at every scale. They exist between continents, between countries, and between regions within countries. They can even exist within a single town, village or street.

This imbalance is normally related to the degree of economic development. On very local scales, wealthy regions can be referred to as 'affluent', poor regions as 'deprived' (as in the case of differences within towns, see Ch. 16). On an international scale it is more usual to speak of wealthy regions as 'developed' and poor regions as 'developing'. Indeed, today the world is commonly divided into three economic groupings: 'developed countries', 'less developed countries' (LDCs) and 'least developed countries' (LLDCs) – see Table 12.1.

All this terminology, however, is vague, unsatisfactory and, therefore, open to misconception. The terms are both subjective and perceived: subjective since, being based largely on the bases of Western standards and values, they tend to ignore cultural traditions and historical attitudes; and perceived since they can be easily defined but not so easily measured. No reliable index of economic prosperity has yet been found and different geographers use different objective yardsticks. One measure uses income levels; another is based on health, diet and medical facilities; yet another involves employment figures. A fourth uses an index based on infant mortality rates; the higher the rate, the less developed the country. Sweden (16 per thousand) and Tanzania (150 per thousand) fit fairly well into this measure, but the same cannot be said of many other countries: Taiwan, at 34, scores surprisingly low, and Yugoslavia, at 105, surprisingly high.

A more accurate measure of prosperity, used by the United Nations, is an index of living standards. This combines many different aspects: health, diet, educa-

Table 12.1 The least developed countries.

LLDCs	% Adult literacy rate	% Average annual population growth	Life expectancy at birth	% Urban population
Afghanistan	15	2.5	49	18
Bangladesh	29	2.9	49	15
Benin	14	2.7	48	17
Bhutan	26	1.9	46	8
Botswana	35	1.9	58	35
Burundi	26	2.0	45	5
Cape Verde	39	1.8	59	25
Central African Republic	10	2.1	46	45
Chad	18	1.9	43	22
Comoros	61	2.2	49	15
Ethiopia	19	2.0	41	20
Guinea	24	2.8	46	22
Guinea-Bissau	9	1.4	43	28
Haiti	28	1.5	54	30
Laos	31	1.3	44	18
Lesotho	56	2.1	54	9
Malawi	28	2.7	49	14
Maldives	72	2.4	49	14
Mali	13	2.5	45	25
Nepal	22	2.1	48	10
Niger	11	2.7	46	18
Rwanda	19	2.7	49	10
Somalia	64	2.1	47	35
Sudan	24	2.5	49	30
Tanzania	68	3.3	55	19
Uganda	29	2.8	58	18
Upper Volta	8	1.5	46	12
Western Samoa	91	0.9	66	25
Yemen Arab Republic	19	1.7	45	15
Yemen People's Democratic Republic	31	2.1	48	40

tion, employment, working conditions, transport, consumption and savings, housing, clothing, recreation, social security and human freedom. Even so, this method has drawbacks. Data may not always be obtainable, nor accurate when obtained. Moreover, the concept of living standards ignores differing human perceptions, values and ideals. People with a high living standard can be less contented than others with a lower living standard.

In reality there is a broad spectrum ranging from abject poverty to considerable wealth, between which are various intermediate levels of economic prosperity. 'Undeveloped', 'underdeveloped' and 'developing' have slightly different shades of meaning within this context. Such terms may not be definable, or even measurable, but they are recognisable.

A further feature of economic development is that of dynamism. Most regions are richer now than they were, say, at the beginning of this century. Even the poorest areas are probably less poor (in spite of rapid population growth). Thus, what concerns the geographer is not just the spatial pattern of economic advancement but also the way economic development is progressing. Are rich countries growing richer at a faster rate than poor countries? Are the contrasts in wealth between regions increasing or lessening? Are any areas actually growing poorer?

Exact data are not available, but on present evidence, two processes seem to be taking place. First, the gap between rich and poor is narrowing within developed countries and widening within less developed countries. This may be caused by govern-

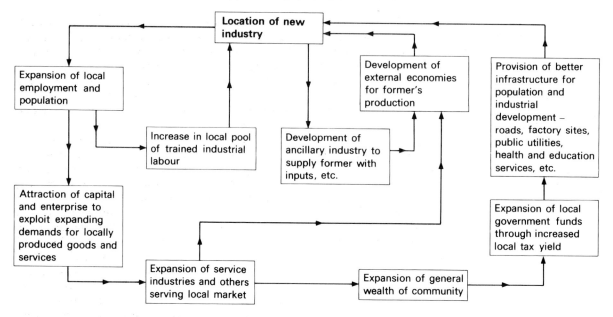

Figure 12.1 Myrdal's model of cumulative causation
The box marked 'location of new industry' can be seen as the birth of industrialisation in a particular area. In time, more industries will locate there to produce a growth pole. Occasionally, cumulative causation may work in reverse. A factory may close and create an overall regional depression since other factories dependent on it close also. (This diagram is adapted from Models of economic development by D. Keeble in *Models in geography*, edited by R. J. Chorley and P. Haggett (1967); London: Methuen.)

ment regional policies and social welfare schemes in the former, and the maintenance of minority rule or inadequate economic planning in the latter. Secondly, the gap between developed and less developed countries is broadening as the former are growing more wealthy at a faster rate than the latter.

The factors that determine the degree of development and the nature of its progression are diverse and interrelated: physical, economic, demographic, social and political. Developed countries are usually found in temperate locations and less developed countries in tropical locations. There also appears to be a correlation between advancement and areas settled by white or European peoples and between underdevelopment and areas not settled by those people. There might also be a connection between underdevelopment and a recent colonial past.

The Myrdal model of cumulative causation

To recognise and map regional inequalities of wealth are relatively simple tasks. To account for them is more difficult. This is because they develop gradually over long periods and, as already mentioned, arise from the interplay of complex physical and human

factors. Nevertheless, attempts have been made to explain such spatial patterns and various theories and models have been proposed.

The most famous of these is that first formulated by the Swedish economist Myrdal in 1956 (Fig. 12.1). He argued that regional differences are the natural outcome of economic development and the inevitable result of market forces. No one region can prosper, he said, without adversely affecting the prosperity of another. Economic growth takes place initially where there are such natural advantages as a source of fuel or a supply of raw materials. Once in existence, this region of economic development sets in motion the process of cumulative causation. In effect, centripetal forces begin to operate whereby capital and labour are attracted into the expanding area, which further stimulates its prosperity at the expense of the surrounding regions. At the same time, by the **multiplier effect**, growing industries produce other, secondary, industries, which are dependent on the original ones, together with improved transport facilities and social services. This chain reaction produces self-sustaining economic growth.

Myrdal called the movement of wealth from the poorer regions to the central rich region the **backwash effect**. It takes place because of the better facilities and opportunities offered by the growing region. In many cases it can be exemplified as a 'brain drain', with doctors and other professional people moving from poorer to richer regions and as a 'brawn drain', with manual workers in poor countries taking up menial jobs in rich countries. To aggravate the differences further, a rich area may flood the markets of the poorer areas with cheap products, thereby preventing the latter from developing their own industries. The result is an industrially expanding region on the one hand, and stagnating, or even declining, regions on the other.

Eventually, the increased wealth in the initially developed area would percolate downwards to the less developed areas. This, Myrdal christened the **spread effect**. An expanding economy may increase the demand for the raw materials and agricultural products derived from poorer regions, and will create surplus capital, which can be invested in newly developing areas. Advanced technology might also be diffused over an ever wider area. In these ways, the economies of the poor regions may be stimulated and the process of cumulative causation thereby triggered off in those parts.

There are, therefore, three stages of regional differentiation: a pre-industrial stage, where there are few regional inequalities; a stage when cumulative causation is at its maximum, a single region is advancing faster than other regions and, hence, the imbalance of wealth is at its greatest; and a third stage when the spread effect begins to reduce spatial differences.

The Myrdal model has been criticised for being too qualitative in nature and too unreal in assuming a free market economy. None the less, it has the advantage of being simple and practical. Its basic principle can, moreover, be applied on almost any scale. Within countries, cumulative causation can be seen to have created regional variations. In Britain, for example, such places as South Wales, West Yorkshire and Tyneside developed as growth poles after the Industrial Revolution, and London has so developed since the beginning of this century. The backwash effect can now be identified as the so-called 'drift to the South'. The spread effect is being assisted by government regional policies. In Brazil the same sort of process can be seen to have taken place (see Fig. 12.2).

On a continental scale, cumulative causation nor-

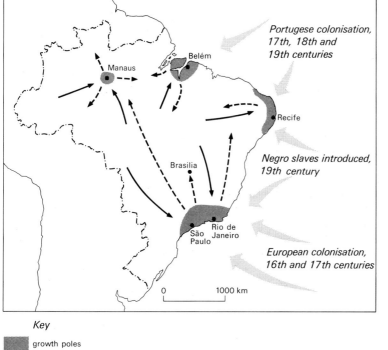

Portugese colonisation, 17th, 18th and 19th centuries

Belém

Manaus

Recife

Negro slaves introduced, 19th century

Brasilia

Rio de Janeiro
São Paulo

European colonisation, 16th and 17th centuries

0   1000 km

Figure 12.2   The Myrdal model applied to Brazil
Before colonisation, this whole area was inhabited by indian tribes, fairly evenly scattered and living through hunting, gathering and subsistence farming. European settlement led to the appearance of growth poles: the South-East (because of coffee and gold), the north-east coast (because of sugar cane), Belem and Manaus (because of rubber). These regions became advanced to the detriment of elsewhere, drawing labour and capital from the interior. Since World War 2, however, successive Brazilian governments have encouraged decentralisation and the dispersal of economic activity: Brasilia was built (1956) and became the new capital (1960); the Amazon Basin is being developed (through new roads and oil exploration); the north-east interior is being turned into a major farming region (through irrigation schemes). Finance for such decentralisation projects comes partly from central government and partly from regional authorities (and through foreign loans and investment).

Key

growth poles

movements of labour, showing backwash effect (until 20th century)

movements of capital, showing spread effect (since 1945)

mally takes place in and around major urban–industrial complexes. In Europe, the growth pole can be mapped as the Ruhr–northern France–Belgium–south-east England belt. On a world scale, Myrdal's model does much to explain the division between developed and developing nations. In this instance, the spread effect is typified by the aid provided by the advanced countries to Third World countries in such fields as medicine, education and technology.

Other models have been devised more specifically to explain inequalities just within developed countries. One of these emphasises a region's 'export base' and suggests that the greater the exporting potential an area has, the higher will be the rate of its economic growth and the wider will be the gap between itself and areas less able to export goods and services. Another concentrates on income levels. In either case, as with Myrdal, the generally accepted view is that spatial differences in wealth usually emerge during economic development.

Friedmann's centre–periphery model

Whereas Myrdal investigated the variations in economic growth between regions, other theorists have concentrated more on spatial characteristics. One of these is Friedmann, who attempted to explain not the ways in which development can take place, but the nature of the relative locations of rich and poor areas. In his model, the world can be divided into dynamic, rapidly growing central regions, and slower growing or stagnating peripheral regions. Within this pattern four distinct zones can be identified:

(1) *Core regions.* Urban–industrial concentrations with high levels of technology, large amounts of capital and labour, complex economic infrastructures and high growth rates.
(2) *Upward-transition regions.* Peripheral to core regions and greatly influenced by them. Characterised by the intense use of resources, immigration and constant economic growth.
(3) *Resource-frontier regions.* Existing outside upward-transition regions, these are typified by new settlement and development of virgin territory or the exploitation of newly discovered mineral deposits.
(4) *Downward-transition regions.* Most peripheral of all, these zones are characterised by stagnant or declining rural economies with low agricul-

tural productivity. They may also be areas where primary resources have been exhausted or where industrial complexes have become inoperative or derelict.

Outside these four zones are a few regions with special features. Areas along political boundaries or coastlines fall into this category.

As with Myrdal's model, this centre–periphery pattern can be applied on any scale from global to local. On a world scale, developed countries fall into the first and second regional types, less developed countries into the third and fourth. The North Atlantic Seaboard (eastern North America and Western Europe) can thus be viewed as the core region for the Western world. On a national level, core regions are normally conurbations, like Greater London and Rotterdam. South-east England typifies an upward-transition region; northern Scotland, Italy's Mezzogiorno and northern Greece may be considered downward-transition regions. The American Mid-West could once have been described as a resource-frontier region, and today, Siberia, the Australian interior and even Alaska fall into this category. On a local scale, city centres may exemplify core regions and, at the other extreme, blighted and ghetto urban areas may represent downward-transition zones.

Theories of underdevelopment

Myrdal devised a model to explain why some regions become richer while others become poorer; Friedmann's model suggested a spatial relationship between rich and poor areas. Other geographers and economists have attempted to explain why poor regions remain poor: why, that is, more undeveloped areas and countries do not experience economic growth but, instead, stay undeveloped. Theories of this nature can be divided into three: classical, poverty-cycle and dualistic economy.

Classical theories
Classical theories first originated with early economic theory and through the work of such well known economists as Adam Smith, Ricardo, Malthus, Mill and Keynes. Briefly, these theories link economic development with labour supplies, market size, capital availability and the relationship between demand and supply. For example, a country which has a small labour supply is less able to introduce the

RELATIVE CHARACTERISTICS OF DEVELOPMENT

Low levels of development

(1) Per capita incomes are low (below $500) and capital is scarce.
(2) Uneven distribution of wealth within individual countries (e.g. in Colombia 2.6% of the population owns 40% of the national wealth and in Gabon 1% owns 56% of total wealth).
(3) Primary industries (farming, forestry, quarrying, mining, fishing) dominate national economies.
(4) High proportion (over 70%) of population engaged in agriculture (e.g. Colombia 72%, Guinea 95%).
(5) Farming (apart from plantation agriculture) is mostly at the subsistence level and is characterised by inefficient methods and underemployment. Farm holdings are small, mechanisation is limited and crop yields are low.
(6) Populations are predominantly rural, with over 80% living in the countryside.
(7) Birth and death rates are high and the expectation of life low. Population structure tends to be progressive with a high proportion of children.
(8) Inadequate or unbalanced diets resulting from a relatively low output of protein foods. Hunger and malnutrition common.
(9) Balance of payments deficits and international debts. Importers of capital and high technology.
(10) High incidence of diseases and poor medical services. Very poor social conditions with overcrowding, poor housing, few public services and bad sanitation. Poorly developed infrastructure.
(11) Poor educational facilities and high levels of illiteracy, which hinder scientific and technological advancement. (In parts of Africa as much as 80% of population is illiterate.)
(12) Women held in inferior position in society, but respect for elders. Fairly strong extended family ties.

High levels of development

(1) Per capita incomes are high (above $4000) and capital readily available.
(2) Comparatively even distribution of wealth within individual countries (e.g. in the USA 10% of the population owns 27% of national wealth).
(3) Manufacturing and service industries dominate national economies.
(4) Very small proportion (under 10%) of population engaged in agriculture (e.g. Britain 3%, West Germany 8%).
(5) Farming is mostly commercial, efficient and highly mechanised. Farm holdings are generally large and crop yields high.
(6) Populations are predominantly urban, with over 70% living in towns.
(7) Birth and death rates are low and expectation of life high. Population structure is stationary or regressive and often there is a high proportion of people over 60 years of age.
(8) Generally adequate supplies of food, balanced diets. In fact, overeating is sometimes a problem.
(9) Surplus wealth with investment in poorer countries. Exporters of capital and high technology.
(10) Low incidence of diseases and good medical services. Generally good social conditions with adequate housing space and a high level of public health facilities and sanitation. Highly developed infrastructure.
(11) Highly developed educational facilities and low levels of illiteracy.
(12) Women increasingly treated on equal terms with men, and children with adults. Weakening ties within extended families.

division of labour and thus lacks the essential ingredient for economic growth – since only specialisation can lead to increased productivity, rising national income and higher investment. Similarly, a small or limited market size restricts the expansion of firms, which, in consequence, continue to make low profits. This limits investment and holds back economic development. However, such classical theories fail to take into account political, social, cultural and behavioural factors, and fail to appreciate factors of location. Both Switzerland and Luxembourg are tiny countries with limited labour supplies and markets, yet both have experienced considerable economic growth.

Poverty cycle theories

Poverty cycles have variously been explained and described. Most theories, however, agree that underdevelopment is self-fulfilling as shown in simplified form in Figure 12.3. The crux of the poverty cycle is the assumption of cause-and-effect linkages: lack of finance leads to low productivity, which, in turn, leads to low investment, low demand and low incomes. Poverty thus spirals downwards. However, there is one major fallacy of such cyclical theories and that is the supposition that low savings are the inevitable result of low incomes and lack of capital. Historical evidence tells us that this simply is not true: countries are never so poor that they cannot save or

171

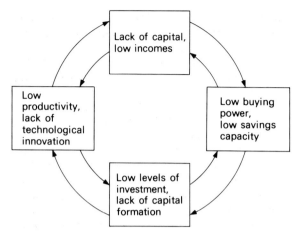

Figure 12.3 The poverty cycle
This can be read in either direction. There is, in addition, a social welfare cycle whereby ill health, poor diets and bad medical care lead to reduced work capacity, which leads to low productivity, low incomes, low capital investment and a general lack of money with which to finance welfare improvements.

invest. There is always spare money, even in the poorest of countries. Few countries have not been able to fight a war when necessity demanded, even in the most uneconomic of times. Even relatively poor societies have spent surplus money producing national monuments: the Egyptian pyramids, the Greek acropoli, the Inca and Aztec temples, the cathedrals of medieval Europe. The fact is, countries can always divert some funds into national schemes and away from industrial and agricultural development, even when capital is supposedly in short supply. There must be other reasons (perhaps non-economic ones) to account for the fact that surplus money in underdeveloped countries is not diverted into economic investment.

Dualistic economy theories
The theories of dualistic economy go some way to explaining why capital in poor regions is not diverted into profitable investment. The cornerstone of these theories is the assumption that backwardness is the result of cultural inferiority and that economic development is linked directly to social motivation. Whereas some peoples are energetic and experimental, others are conservative and apathetic. If a country contains both groups, dual economies may result: a small, modernised, efficiently organised sector run by progressive traders and entrepreneurs (often foreigners or colonialists); and a large, traditional, inefficiently organised sector in the hands of disinterested labourers and peasants (often the native

peoples). Economic development thus takes place at two levels. Wealth fails to percolate downwards because of political corruption, social barriers and foreign exploitation. Such theories may appear to be accurate in many parts of the world but equally seem to be disproved by history. Some tropical countries, which today are backward, were once highly developed (such as Peru and Ethiopia), whereas others, now advanced, and located in temperate regions, were once uncivilised (such as Germany and Denmark).

The Third World and its problems

Those countries that can variously be labelled as undeveloped, underdeveloped and developing are often grouped under the general heading of the 'Third World' (the Western and Communist being the First and Second Worlds, respectively). As such this includes most of the countries of Africa, southern and South-East Asia and Latin America. These regions together account for over 65% of the world's total population but only 10% of its total energy consumption and 7% by value of its total manufactured goods. Their average per capita income is just $210, compared with an average of $2690 in developed countries.

Of course, there are wide variations of wealth within the Third World and it would be wrong to assume that the same standards of living exist everywhere. Some countries, like Bangladesh and Somalia, are extremely poor and are progressing very slowly; others such as Brazil and Taiwan are experiencing rapid economic development. Even so, it remains true that many problems are common to them all. These are summarised below.

Environmental problems
Most tropical climates hinder both human and economic activity. On the one hand, their heat and humidity can cause lethargy, reduce work capacities and nurture diseases. On the other hand, they can restrict capital utilisation: poorly constructed roads may be washed out or baked into furrows (depending on season), and dust and torrential ran can lead to the breakdown of machinery. Floods and droughts are common and in some regions, such as the West Indies, hurricanes can cause tremendous damage. Agriculture, in particular, is made difficult under these environmental conditions. Soils are naturally

poor, easily leached and soon exhausted, and numerous farming pests and diseases thrive. The tsetse fly prevents efficient cattle-raising over large areas of Africa and the sigatoka disease can destroy banana plantations in the Caribbean. Locusts can still cause mass destruction wherever they go uncontrolled.

Another environmental problem is that Third World countries may lack those raw materials and power supplies upon which developed areas have become prosperous. Known reserves of coal, oil and metallic minerals are absent in many parts of the Tropics and even where new deposits are found, physical conditions make their exploitation difficult. The use of hydroelectric power is a potential aid to development, but it is limited by the inaccessibility of areas suitable for its generation (mountainous terrain or large rivers). Thus, many Third World countries lack even the resource base for economic progress.

Economic problems
The economies of most Third World countries are unbalanced and inefficient. Agriculture is dominant and tends to be poorly organised with primitive techniques and insufficient (or no) machinery. Subsistence farming is prevalent in many parts, but this often means 'self-insufficiency' as farmers may fail to produce enough food even for their own families. Pakistan has over 70% of its population employed in farming, yet must still import food, and this is by no means unique.

In areas where commercial farming is practised, the problem is more one of commodity dominance, whereby exports are based on a single agricultural product: Ghana (cacao), Gambia (groundnuts), Malaysia (rubber) and Sri Lanka (tea). Such an imbalance makes these countries vulnerable to natural disasters, to changes in world prices, to demand fluctuations and competition.

Economic problems such as these are further exacerbated by lack of economic infrastructure: most Third World nations do not have the essential framework for development. Efficient transport services and networks, marketing, industrial and commercial facilities and skilled labour are all missing. Inadequate education and training leads to a shortage of technologists and technicians. Moreover, native workers have in some areas been found to be transitory, moving from place to place and from job to job. In consequence, some countries' factories in the Third World possess no permanent workforce.

In developed countries, an economic infrastructure has grown up over the centuries, but in developing countries it must be created fairly quickly. This, however, is expensive and is greatly hindered by the fact that most Third World nations lack capital. It has been estimated that a country needs to invest 12–15% of its net national income in order to diversify and develop with self-sustaining growth. In the USA, about 20% is invested, whereas most developing countries invest only 5–6% annually.

The shortage of indigenous capital is worsened by the inability of much of the Third World to attract capital investment from outside. Foreign investors prefer to sink their money into the rich economies of developed countries rather than into poor developing countries where risks are greater and returns more uncertain. The scarcity of capital also makes investment rates very high, so that countries that borrow may frequently find difficulty in reducing, or even maintaining, the debt. The economies of many Third World countries are also characterised by high rates of inflation and this further discourages capital investment and economic growth.

Finally, it can be argued that, since many Third World nations were once colonies, they are still living under the detrimental influence of their former mother countries, and that some remain in the shadow of exploitation and of deliberate policies not to develop indigenous skills. Certainly it is true that much economic control is exercised from outside. However, it should be remembered that this foreign influence, though possibly a result of an imperial past, is also a consequence of the present. The natural lack of resources, technology and capital means that most developing countries must either obtain help from external sources or else stagnate. Without British, German and Russian money, for example, India might not now have an iron and steel industry, and without Russian finance and technical aid Egypt could not have built the Aswan High Dam.

Social problems
The social problems being faced by the Third World are perhaps the greatest and most insuperable problems of all. Other difficulties – serious as they are – can be solved from outside; these can only be solved from within. People must have the will or desire to improve their conditions if development is to take place. In most developing countries, society is complex and traditions are entrenched. Customs, laws, religious beliefs, taboos, social behaviour and cultural traits, together, act towards a maintenance of the existing order of life. It is these very aspects that are difficult to break down.

We have already learned about the population growth experienced in Third World countries (Ch. 5). Every year, millions more people must be fed, clothed, housed and found employment. A high incidence of disease, poor diets and illiteracy are matched by low standards of medical care and poor education. Above all, the need for economic progress is balked by an inherent and strict social order.

Agricultural improvements, especially, are hindered. Land tenure systems maintain small farm holdings and powerful landowners who may levy high rents and offer tenants only poor security of tenure. Many African herders measure wealth in numbers of animals and therefore become more concerned with quantity and less with quality. In the same way, the Hindu religion leads to unproductive cattle grazing in India.

In more general terms, family, caste and class groupings can act against a country's economic health. The closeness and cohesion of the extended family unit, though possibly beneficial from a sociological viewpoint, can retard labour mobility. In such families a few elders wield considerable power and may forbid their younger relations from moving away. The caste system has a similar effect, assigning specific roles to specific groups. Class divisions in the Third World are often much stronger than their counterparts in developed regions. There is a vast difference between rich and peasant populations, and an individual born into the lowest stratum of society – regardless of his abilities, intelligence and character – will often find social advancement almost impossible.

The most extreme example of how economic progress can be hindered by beliefs is perhaps found in the Islamic world. There, strict and orthodox Muslims have traditionally been forbidden from employment in such activities as mining and money lending, both normally essential for development. In north Africa, Pakistan and South-East Asia this fact has certainly limited the potential for economic growth. In the Arab countries the influence of Islam has been lessened by the relaxation of religious ideology and the separation of church and state affairs, but still economic progress can be slow.

Political problems
The various problems outlined above are frequently accompanied by political instability. This may be due, at least in part, to the inability of Third World governments to cope with the difficulties facing them.

At its mildest, this instability may be exemplified by the existence of numerous and diverse political parties, frequent elections, short-lived governments, administrative incompetence and corruption. At its worst, it may result in government repression, rioting, guerilla warfare and civil war. Often political reaction sets in to produce dictatorial regimes and military juntas. Under these conditions economic and social progress is naturally inhibited.

The Third World and its prospects

The prospects for the Third World vary from place to place, depending on the exact nature and extent of the problems being faced. Some countries, like Ethiopia and Mali, have little chance of economic progress in the foreseeable future; others, like Brazil and Nigeria, are already making rapid advances.

Yet how may development take place and what must a government do if it is intent upon a course of economic expansion? These questions are difficult. First, a country must decide exactly how it wishes to progress, and secondly it must find the best methods suited to its own unique circumstances. The improvements taking place in one area may not be those necessary – or even desirable – elsewhere. There is, moreover, the political aspect to be considered. Different ideologies favour different courses of action, and economic planning in a democratic country is likely to differ from that enforced under totalitarian or communist regimes.

A further and more fundamental problem arises when a country has to decide upon the form development is to take. 'Development' does not necessarily mean 'economic growth', and governments must weigh up the relative merits of the alternative courses of action. Growth is not always the most beneficial policy to pursue. In the past it was mistakenly assumed that growth was good and that the mere introduction of foreign money, technology and know-how would automatically generate an economic miracle in the Third World. Today we are more realistic. Each country must determine its own form of economic development and must tackle its own problems in its own way.

Development policies
A few nations (Haiti, for example) seem entirely uninterested in economic growth; some (such as Thailand) seem to want to develop slowly, paying due regard to their technological and resource limita-

tions; some (such as China) appear determined to grow quickly. The vast majority of Third World countries, however, seem to be developing at a constant and moderate rate, and within the confines set by their physical and human environment.

Less developed countries may progress economically through agricultural improvements or through industrialisation (or both together). But before either of these can take place, the necessary infrastructure must be provided. Communications, power supplies and various service facilities must be improved and expanded. Only upon these can further aspects of development proceed.

Much is already being done and in many countries agricultural improvements are under way. These include: better seed strains and animal breeds, greater use of fertilisers, insecticides and machinery; the reform of land tenure systems; the introduction of co-operation (as in Egypt); the extension of farming into formerly uncultivated regions (as in Sri Lanka and Brazil); and the establishment of agricultural schools and colleges. Also, many one-commodity economies are being diversified. In Brazil, for instance, coffee is now grown with cotton, citrus fruits and sugar cane.

Much industrialisation is also taking place and, in fact, this particular development is seen in many countries as the most likely to bring about general prosperity. Industries, it is imagined, improve living standards, enable a country to raise per capita incomes, absorb excess population by providing extra employment, help solve balance of payment problems, reduce the economic dominance of agriculture, and even help to increase political power. Whether this is true of course, is debatable. Even so, many developing countries now have new power stations, expanding manufacturing complexes and growing quaternary facilities.

Yet the process of industrialisation is not easy. It involves the use of mineral resources, labour supplies, capital and technological know-how and can take generations to reach completion. For this reason, many countries have introduced **intermediate technology** as the first step along the industrial path. This is where small-scale or labour-intensive industries are set up to utilise the local skills and tools available and serve local needs. Such a policy may be especially successful in areas where labour is plentiful and capital scarce. In China intermediate technology has resulted in a great number of 'cottage industries', which employ traditional craftsmen. Larger scale industrial development is often economically

impracticable: the domestic market may be too small to absorb mass production and the world market may already be dominated by companies of the developed world. Only a relatively few developing countries such as Korea and Taiwan have successfully established large-scale manufacturing industries.

Types of growth
Although both agricultural improvements and industrialisation help the development process, they can be undertaken in varying proportions. Sometimes a country will encourage only one, sometimes both. This is because economists differ in their views of the relative importance and economic effectiveness of development policies. Some propose policies of **balanced growth**, others of **unbalanced growth**.

Balanced growth is where agriculture and industry advance side by side and with mutual benefit. Improved farming supplies extra food and raw materials, creates a large rural market for manufactured goods and releases labour to work in industry. Industrial expansion, in turn, provides farm machinery, fertilisers and a market for agricultural products. In this way a spiral of growth is set in motion and development progresses on a broad front.

Unbalanced growth occurs when either agriculture or industry is developed alone. Such a policy can be supported by the argument that the development of a growth pole – even when it is dominated by a single economic activity – will have a spread effect on other regions and activities. One development naturally gives rise to others and, through the multiplier effect, produces an overall economic expansion.

Which policy is the better depends largely on circumstances and resource availability. In many communist countries, unbalanced growth policies have been adopted partly for political or strategic reasons. There, concentration has been on heavy manufacturing at the expense of agricultural improvements. In Commonwealth countries, balanced growth policies are more common because both agricultural and industrial aid are being provided from outside. (See Ch. 18.)

In either case, careful planning is essential. On a national scale, governments may need to instigate harsh and unpopular measures (more easily done under dictatorships than under democracies). On a world scale, the developed countries must provide the right kind of aid. The development of less developed countries is for all our benefits, and it is important for future generations that success is achieved with a minimum of further delay. In short, the prospects for the Third World are inextricably linked with the policies of the developed world. These links are discussed in greater detail in Chapter 17.

Theories of economic growth

None of the theories mentioned so far has attempted to explain how economic development can actually take place. They have been more concerned with aspects of economic diversity: why differences of wealth occur, how these differences can be mapped and why they are growing more extreme. In this section, theories that try to clarify the actual process of economic growth will be considered: how exactly a region can pass through a sequence of stages from a level of undevelopment to a level of high advancement, that is, from poor to rich.

There have been many such theories. Some stress the importance of resource development and exploitation; others, like that of Adam Smith, stress labour organisation. Karl Marx saw a one-way evolution from primitive culture, through feudalism and capitalism, to socialism and communism. Some theories, like that involving the model of spatial diffusion, examine the physical spread of economic development; others, like that of Rostow, examine the role of technical innovation.

A model of spatial diffusion
Many geographers have noted that human activity tends to spread outwards from core points to peripheries, rather as ripples spread out across a pond from a dropped stone. Spatially, economic growth does the same – diffusing over an area, like the spread of a disease, from a given growth point. In effect, advanced economic activity would eventually spread throughout a given country. This process is shown in Figure 12.4 and it has obvious links with the Taaffe, Morrill & Gould model of transport network development (see Ch. 10).

Four distinct stages can be identified. In stage 1, there is a totally undeveloped area where traditional livelihoods and primitive agricultural methods exist.

Figure 12.4 Economic development by spatial diffusion
Economic growth spreads through an idealised sequence of stages. This hypothetical island gradually becomes covered by urbanisation, industrialisation, agricultural improvement and an advanced cultural society.

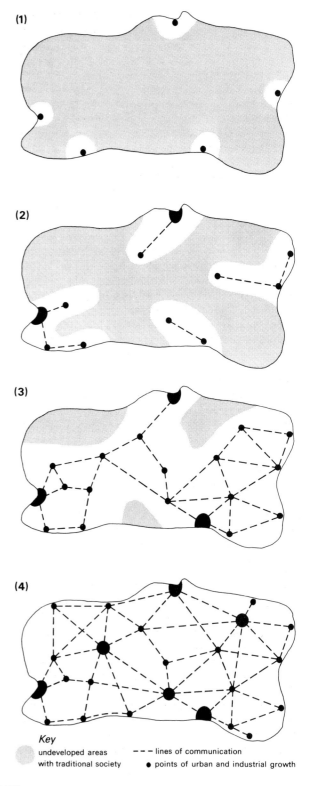

Key

undeveloped areas with traditional society

- - - lines of communication

● points of urban and industrial growth

Around this area are a small number of trading posts or ports, representing potential growth points. In stage 2, sometimes called the 'spurt' phase, certain of the trading posts become more important and extend their influence inland. Small pockets of the land area are thus developed. In stage 3, further growth occurs as the trading posts develop into industrialised centres and extend their spheres of influence. These newly civilised and economically advanced zones begin to join up, thus isolating the backward regions. In stage 4, economic growth is complete and the whole area has successfully been covered by industrialisation, urbanisation, high agricultural technology, leisure facilities and an advanced standard of living.

The USA can be seen to have experienced growth in this way, the original growth points being the colonial centres of New England and the Gulf of Mexico, and economic diffusion taking place across the Mid-West during the second half of the 19th century. This diffusion was accompanied by a continual increase in the number of states belonging to the Union. The same sort of spread is also occurring in Nigeria, where diffusion is northwards.

Rostow's theory

Walter Rostow first proposed his theory in 1955. Unlike the model just outlined, he was more concerned with the successive economic changes that are likely to take place on the same area of land. Thus, his theory is not so much spatial as temporal.

Rostow identified five stages of economic development (Fig. 12.5). The traditional society is characterised by the dominance of agriculture, which is largely at the subsistence level, and the non-realisation of potential resources. In the second stage, economic growth begins to speed up. There is an expansion of trade, perhaps an increase in external influences, and an introduction of modern methods of production, which are used alongside the more traditional techniques. The take-off stage occurs when old traditions are finally overcome and modern industrialised society is born. Investment rates rise from 5% of national income to 10%, one or more major manufacturers emerges, political and social institutions are transformed, and growth becomes self-sustaining. The fourth stage sees the steady consolidation of the new industrialised society: investment continues to grow, some industries fade as others expand, large urban regions develop, and transport facilities become more complex. This progression reaches its zenith in the fifth stage, which is

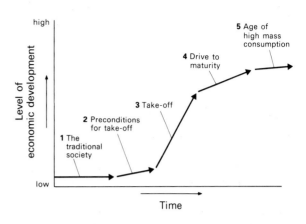

Figure 12.5 Rostow's model of economic development
These stages can be equated figuratively with an aeroplane: stage 1 a stationary plane (stagnant economic backwardness), stage 2 the movement along the runway (infrastructure improvement gaining momentum), stage 3 take-off (industrialisation transforming economic life), stage 4 the ascent through the clouds (self-propelled growth gaining speed), stage 5 the high-level flight (confident progress and increased social well-being). Many geographers see a possible sixth stage: the plane returning to earth (slowly or quickly) signifying an economic depression or crash and a return to lower level technology and traditional values.

characterised by mass production, the growth of quaternary occupations, an increase in materialism and the allocation of resources to social welfare.

This theory has been criticised for placing too much emphasis on capital formation and for lacking a mechanism to link the five stages. Even so, it is clear, simple, and moreover can be seen to have worked in the advanced countries of the world. Europe is thought to have been in the first stage until sometime in the Middle Ages, and in the second stage from then until the 18th century. In Britain take-off occurred at the Industrial Revolution. This was inspired by agricultural improvements generally and by coal mining and the invention of new machinery for textile manufacture in particular. From then on, growth became a natural state of affairs, passing through the fourth stage during the Victorian Age and reaching the fifth stage during the present century.

Whether the same progression takes place in developing countries remains to be seen. Certainly, at present, the Third World contains examples of countries passing through each of the first three stages: Chad, Nigeria and Brazil respectively. The effect of external aid is, perhaps, merely to speed up the pro-

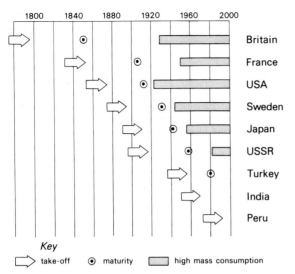

Key

take-off ⊙ maturity ▨ high mass consumption

Figure 12.6 The Rostow model applied to selected countries
The time gap between take-off and high mass-consumption
varies from country to country for diverse political, economic
and social reasons.

cess. By definition, countries that pass the point of
take-off will no longer require help. (See Fig. 12.6.)

Summary

1 Inequalities of wealth can be measured through
   incomes, health, infant mortality rates and general living standards. However, the very concept
   of wealth and the terms of development levels are
   subjective and based on Western perception and
   value-judgements.
2 World inequalities appear to be widening. But are
   rich areas necessarily getting happier and poor
   areas unhappier? Development can lead to dis-
   contentment.
3 Myrdal's model of cumulative causation states
   that spatial economic differences are the natural
   result of the multiplier effect. Growth poles are
   magnets that draw wealth inwards.
4 Friedmann suggested that wealth patterns are
   concentric, the richest (core) regions being central, the poorest (downward-transition) regions
   most peripheral.
5 Underdevelopment may be explained through
   classical economic theory (e.g. Malthus, Keynes),
   poverty cycle theory (e.g. downward poverty
   spiral) or through dualistic economy theory (e.g.
   colonialism).

6 Given the enormous physical, economic, social
   and political problems faced by the Third World,
   it is unlikely to develop quickly or successfully.
   Inflation, indebtedness and political instability
   are the greatest hindrances to growth.
7 Economic growth can be balanced or unbalanced, according to the resources available and
   the ideologies of the rulers of less developed
   countries. Intermediate technology (halfway
   development) is the most likely policy to succeed
   according to many geographers and politicians.
8 Rostow's theory of economic growth suggests that
   all countries go through five stages: 1 stagnation, 2
   infrastructure development, 3 sudden industrialisation, 4 widespread progress and 5 a leisure-
   based consumer society. There is perhaps a sixth
   stage – a period of decline and a return to craft
   industry.

Data–response exercises

1 Redraw Figure 12.1 to show the multiplier effect
   resulting from the location of an actual new industry in an area that you know. Fill in each box
   according to real events.
2 Discuss the correlation between the economic
   growth of regions of Brazil (see Fig. 12.2) and the
   physical environment. How successful has the
   spread effect been in Brazil?
3 Examine the external factors that might affect the
   poverty cycle (Fig. 12.3) and the ways in which
   the cycle might be broken.
4 On a sketch map, attempt to divide Africa into the
   four zones of economic development suggested
   by Friedmann. Comment on the pattern you draw.
5 Account for the different time lags between take-
   off and the stage of high mass-consumption in
   Rostow's model of economic development (see
   Fig. 12.6). What can be done to minimise the
   length of this time lag?
6 Draw annotated sketch maps to show the geographical factors that have led the Netherlands to
   be 'developed' and Bolivia to be 'less developed'.
   In each country, discuss the extent to which the
   physical environment can influence social and
   political conditions.

Project work

1 Various models and theories can be tested against reality through fieldwork. Von Thünen's and Sinclair's theories of farmland location, Thomson's hierarchies of industrial complexes, Weber's locational triangles and material index formula, Lösch's hexagonal market areas, can all be proved or disproved in the study of actual examples. In each case, two areas might be compared: one that approaches an isotropic surface and one that contains great topographical variations. Find out whether the theories apply more readily to the former or the latter.

2 Environmental relationships and hypotheses of a cause-and-effect nature can be tested. For example, distance decay graph lines can be drawn using specific towns and the flows of public transport between them. More statistical studies could be made using the Spearman rank correlation coefficient (R_s) – for example to test the relationship between relief and agriculture. Rank farms or parishes (a) in order of the extent of a particular land use (e.g. pasture), and (b) in order of the proportion covered by a topographical index (e.g. land over or under a certain height). Apply the formula

$$R_s = 1 - \frac{6\Sigma d^2}{N^3 - N}$$

in which d^2 is the square of differences in rank of each item and N is the number of items being studied. R_s values vary between $+1$ and -1. Positive R_s values show a positive relationship and negative R_s values an inverse relationship. The greater the value, the closer the relationship. (Note: the same formula may be used for the study of any relationship, e.g. mortality rates and gross domestic product, population size and extent of foreign trade, the nature of topography and the number of factories.)

Further reading

Bale, J. 1981. *The location of manufacturing industry* 2nd edn. Edinburgh: Oliver & Boyd. A well planned and comprehensive introduction to industrial geography, with case studies. The use of humorous drawings, newspaper extracts and reproduced advertisements adds to the clarity of the text.

Boyce, R. R. and A. F. William 1979. *The bases of economic geography*. London: Holt, Rinehart & Winston. The British edition of an American book. Well written, well illustrated and comprehensive, though rather racy in style.

Cox, K. R. 1972. *Man, location and behaviour*. New York: Wiley. Economic activities studied through concepts, theories and case studies. Heavy going and technical, so recommended to students wishing to specialise in quantitative techniques. The summary at the end of each chapter is useful for quick reference.

Dawson, J. and D. Thomas 1975. *Man and his world*. London: Nelson. Straightforward, readable book for general use. It is technical without being turgid. Recommended as a useful reader.

Estall, R. C. and R. O. Buchanan 1980. *Industrial activity and economic geography* 4th edn. London: Hutchinson. A readable, concise study of the forces that influence the location of industry. The increasing importance of government policy is covered and some good case studies are included.

Hoskins, W. G. 1955. *The making of the English landscape*. London: Hodder & Stoughton (and Penguin). A fascinating, readable and illuminating introduction to historical geography in which the evolution of the rural and urban landscape is treated in a literary and enthusiastic style. By the same author are *English landscapes* (1973) and *One man's England* (1976) – both BBC publications – which further add to our knowledge. All three books are richly illustrated and highly recommended.

Huggett, R. and I. Meyer 1979–1982. *Geography: theory in practice*. London: Harper & Row. Series of books dealing with individual topic areas – agriculture, industry, communications, settlements. Each volume gives a comprehensive grounding in all of the modern aspects of human geography and a digest of the principal ideas now prevailing in the subject. A readable series in which the texts are well illustrated and subdivided into numerous sections. Case studies, exercises, carefully composed questions, project work suggestions and booklists are all liberally provided.

Newbury, P. A. R. 1980. *A geography of agriculture*. Plymouth: Macdonald & Evans. Well composed and illustrated study, comprehensive in scope, which uses the author's own fieldwork together with contributions by farmers and agricultural authorities. A lot of help is also given to students undertaking their own field studies.

Paterson, J. H. 1976. *Land, work and resources*. London: Edward Arnold. A study of industrial geography from an economic standpoint: through resources, division of labour, transport, exchange and trade, and incomes. Well written and useful for background reading.

Simmons, I. G. 1981. *The ecology of natural resources* 2nd edn. London: Edward Arnold. A good reference book for those concerned with the use and misuse of our natural resources. Some of the points made are alarming, others give food for thought.

Tarrant, J. R. 1974. *Agricultural geography*. Newton Abbot: David & Charles. A detailed, exhaustive coverage of the subject. Provides ample information but does little to guide or encourage further study by students.

Part IV

SETTLEMENT

Oh! it really is a very pretty garden
And soap-works from the rooftops could be seen;
If I had a rope and pulley
I'd enjoy the breeze more fully
If it wasn't for the houses in between.
Edgar Bateman, Music Hall song

As one who, long in populous city pent,
Where houses thick and sewers annoy the air
Forth issuing on a summer's morn, to breathe
Among the pleasant villages and farms.
John Milton, *Paradise Lost*

INTERNAL STRUCTURE OF TOWNS AND CITIES

Land-use theories – bid-rent analysis – commuter movement – CBD – transition zones – inner-city problems – segregation – industries in towns – urban villages – shopping hierarchies – rural–urban fringe

---

RURAL SETTLEMENT

Village society – settlement sites – forms and morphologies – architecture – planned settlements – refugee camps – distribution and pattern – nearest neighbour analysis

---

URBAN SETTLEMENT

Definitions of towns – urban growth – bastides – specialist towns – urban zones – pre-industrial cities – market areas – urbanisation – fields of influence – break-point theory

---

SETTLEMENT CLASSIFICATION AND HIERARCHIES

Urban and rural settlements – size, form and function – rank-size rule – primate cities – central places – Christaller and Lösch – city-rich and city-poor sectors

13 Settlement classification and hierarchies

Introduction

In many respects, settlements are central to all human geography since it is only through their development that man can adapt the environment to suit his own ends. They are the most visible sign that human culture has been imposed on to the natural world. For this reason, geographers have long been fascinated by settlements – their forms, sites and locations, patterns and distributions, and their tendency towards change. These aspects can be studied in a world, regional or local context and are linked to other facets of geography: to relief, geology and soils, to climate and weather, to social interactions, to economic conditions, and to political or defensive factors.

In essence, settlement geography – the subject of the next four chapters – involves three approaches: the study of settlement units as separate entities, the study of settlement groups as composite parts of overall physical environments, and the study of settlement societies as socio-economic phenomena. The first of these approaches includes such topics as settlement sizes, locations, functions and morphologies; the second includes settlement hierarchies, spacing and fields of influence; the third includes settlement histories, populations and social cohesions. The thread of all these approaches runs through the ensuing chapters.

Yet before any of these aspects can be fully studied, settlements must first be described and classified, compared and categorised. Thus, the questions to be answered in this chapter include the following:

● What particular kinds of settlements exist, and how can they be classified?
● What aspects distinguish different types of settlement, and can these be objectively measured?
● Do settlements fall into official categories and, if so, can these categories be ranked into hierarchies?
● Are settlements distributed according to identifiable and regular hierarchic patterns?
● How relevant are theories of settlement spacing to the real world?

Types of settlement

Though each one is unique, settlements fall naturally into groups. They can be classified by size, function, form, site and situation, age, building materials and cultural characteristics. Such classifications are, of course, man-made; they are divisions that man has identified and are useful only for the purposes for which they are devised. The fact that there are various classifications shows that geographers study settlements for different reasons.

There are temporary and permanent settlements. The former may be occupied for only a matter of days (as in the case of nomad tent groupings), for a few months (when farming moves from place to place with the seasons), or for a limited number of years (as in the case of the primitive hut complexes of shifting cultivators). Permanent settlements (with which this and subsequent chapters are concerned) are usually those which, having been sited and constructed, remain indefinitely.

Most commonly, settlements are divided into 'rural' and 'urban' categories. These terms lack precision but are useful since they attempt to recognise and distinguish both the physical and human characteristics of man-made structures. However, there are different types of both rural and urban settlement. Rural settlements can be subdivided into farmhouses, hamlets and villages; urban settlements may be grouped into towns, cities and conurbations. Both categories can be classified according to size, function and form; both can be defined by subjective and objective analysis.

However, throughout the following discussion, certain points regarding settlement classification should be remembered. The first is that definitions are valid only within the context of their own utility: to describe a settlement through its functions is pertinent only when functions are relevant to the aims of study. The functional criterion for definition or description would be of limited value when aspects of settlement shape or size are being considered. The second point is that classifications are never perma-

THE CHANGING NATURE OF AN ENGLISH SETTLEMENT

The problems of settlement classification, and the dynamism of settlements themselves, are best exemplified through the study of a particular place. Rothwell in Northamptonshire – within that part of Midland England known as 'the Shires' – can be taken to demonstrate this point.

Rothwell (see Fig. 13.1) first appeared as a tiny, Celtic-built hamlet some time during the Roman occupation of England in the first three centuries AD. It is thought to have been situated near to where the fish pond can now be found, close to a well which (under the Saxons) was to give the settlement its present name ('red well', so called because of the ironstone in this vicinity). The population, in these early days, was probably no more than 60 and the settlement itself only a cluster of farm cottages.

Through the Dark Ages, Rothwell grew but slowly so that, by the Norman Conquest, its population was less than 300. Thereafter, however, both its importance and its functions were to change. Under the Norman barons, a church was built, an annual charter fair was begun (1204) and the market square was laid out. As a trading centre for the surrounding countryside it grew as a major service settlement: by the 16th century a market house, Jesus Hospital and a number of grand merchants' dwellings had been constructed and the population had risen to about 1000. By the 18th century, Rothwell had also become an important centre for horseracing and foxhunting.

Further change came with the Industrial Revolution. Local iron-ore deposits gave rise to the building of engineering works, and the local cattle-grazing economy enabled the growth of the leather and shoemaking industries. Rows of Victorian artisans' terraces were built (many with backyard workshops); factories, warehouses and metalled road surfaces appeared, and Rothwell assumed all the characteristics of an industrial town.

Between 1801 and 1911 its population rose from 1409 to 4416.

Today, Rothwell is truly a small town in size, functions and form. It has a population of around 6000, four churches plus a Salvation Army Citadel, three schools (infants, junior and comprehensive), a large health centre, a fire station, council offices (within the old manor house) and a wide selection of retail outlets (including two supermarkets and a specialist home-furnishing shop).

However, it is debatable whether it can still realistically be called an 'industrial town'. Many of the factories and workshops have closed down. More than 70% of the working population either travel out to employment in Northampton, Kettering, Market Harborough and Corby or else work in local service activities – retailing, for example, hotel work, financial and insurance occupations and teaching.

Perhaps, then, Rothwell has now become a commuter or service town. Perhaps it is even becoming a tourist town: an antique shop has started up, three of the local stately homes have been opened to the public, and some of the town's old cottages are being purchased by London and Birmingham people as second homes or weekend retreats. Even the annual Rothwell Fair has been reconstituted and has become an important tourist attraction each June.

Rothwell, like many other English settlements, continues to change in both size and function. It is growing in area and population and is taking on new service activities. There are many such settlements, just as there are also many settlements that are getting smaller in size and losing former activities, tertiary and quaternary. The problem of settlement classification is compounded by such changes, and the faster those changes are the more difficult becomes that classification.

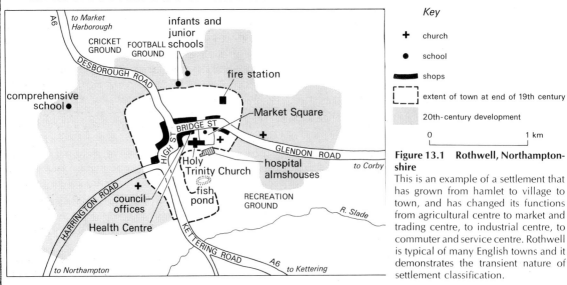

Figure 13.1 Rothwell, Northamptonshire

This is an example of a settlement that has grown from hamlet to village to town, and has changed its functions from agricultural centre to market and trading centre, to industrial centre, to commuter and service centre. Rothwell is typical of many English towns and it demonstrates the transient nature of settlement classification.

nently valid: settlement characteristics are constantly evolving; the ideas of geographers are forever altering; and the relationship between the physical and human environment is always changing. Definitions used today may not have been used years ago, or indeed may have been wrong years ago. Some new classifications might develop in years to come. The third point is that settlement classification is, as yet, an incomplete science and as such incorporates many vague and debatable terms. Such words as 'rural', 'urban', 'industrial', 'nucleated', 'dispersed' and 'planned' can mean different things to different people.

Settlements are essentially dynamic structures: they change with time and in response to the changing characteristics of the environment. This is especially the case with the larger settlements, since change is accompanied by growth. As a settlement becomes larger, it can fundamentally change its character – its size, shape, plan, building styles, functions and importance. Thus, whereas an isolated dwelling or hamlet may remain the same for years as a 'static organism', a town or city will alter constantly: it will expand upwards and outwards, develop new functions and lose old ones, undergo redevelopment and experience social or economic transformation.

Finally, it should be borne in mind that all settlements have their own peculiar identities. Physical sites, roles and functions, history, architecture and street plans all render every settlement unique. As Alnwick once wrote: 'there are newborn baby towns, doddering old-man towns, towns in a hectic whirl of youth, poor guttersnipe towns, fat millionaire towns, quiet studious towns . . . towns are very human'.

Classification by size

This is a very simple, straightforward method of settlement classification using population statistics:

Settlement	Population
isolated dwelling	1–10
hamlet	11–100
small village	101–500
large village	501–2000
small town	2001–10 000
large town	10 001–100 000
city	100 001–1 000 000
conurbation	1 000 001–10 000 000
megalopolis	over 10 000 000

In Britain this classification may seem to work fairly well. Thus, Finchingfield in Essex, with about 1500 people, may be termed a large village and Launceston in Cornwall, with 5000 people, a small town. Kendal (Cumbria) has a population of 25 000 and is a large town; so too is Taunton (Somerset) with 40 000 people. York (110 000) is classified as a city and Glasgow (1 728 000) as a conurbation. However, difficulties arise with numerous exceptions. Many settlements may be villages by size yet resemble towns in character and, of course, vice versa. Similarly, in other countries, definitions may vary. What Australians call a town might be no more than a village in England.

Such difficulties highlight the drawbacks inherent in classifying settlements simply by size. Nevertheless, the resulting order, as listed here, forms a useful foundation for more detailed analysis.

Classification by function

Traditionally, classification by function has always been susceptible to vague terminology; using purely qualitative techniques, no more than a general guide to settlement type can normally be given. Adjectives such as 'industrial', 'administrative', 'commercial', 'residential' and 'cultural' are often ascribed to settlements without any real basis in statistics. These labels describe merely the general character or apparently dominant functions of settlements and as such are frequently misleading. Oxford, for instance, is still sometimes called a 'university city' as if the vast car industry there did not exist.

Another vague classification attempts to differentiate settlements according to the types of industry found in each. Thus, it has been generally recognised that small settlements up to and including large villages tend to be dependent upon primary production (usually agriculture but sometimes fishing, mining or quarrying), whereas larger settlements (from small towns upwards) tend to be dependent upon secondary, tertiary or quaternary industries. It is further suggested – although this applies mainly to Western industrialised countries – that as settlements grow larger their dependence upon service industries becomes greater.

Such links between settlement types and industrial characteristics are, of course, open to criticism. There are, for example, many small villages dependent on

Figure 13.2 Rural settlements in Wales
The uplands of Dyfed are scattered with isolated dwellings, hamlets and small villages. The nearest town to these settlements is Carmarthen, over 15 km distant.

manufacturing and many large towns dependent on agriculture. It is because of such drawbacks that the functional approach to settlement classification has moved towards more scientific and quantitative techniques. These are discussed later in this chapter.

Classification by form

This method is based on settlement structure – that is, the buildings and services found in each place – and has arisen out of subjective considerations. It applies especially to countries in the developed world.

Isolated dwelling

This is usually just a farm or manor house lying by itself in the midst of countryside (see Fig. 13.2). It can be fairly self-sufficient and has generally resulted from economic need rather than social preference. In Britain isolated dwellings tend to be more common to the north and west than in the lowland zone. The wheat farms in the Canadian Prairies and the *estancias* in the Argentinian Pampas are examples elsewhere. Sometimes an inn or hostelry is found in isolation, situated on an important trade route. For example, there are some lonely inns high up in the English Pennines alongside once-busy drove roads. Similar stopping places are found across the Gobi Desert.

Hamlet

This is a small group of houses, perhaps half a dozen or so, with possibly a small church or other religious meeting place and inn but nothing else. Often hamlets have grown up around farms or manor houses (see Fig. 13.2).

Small village

At this level of settlement a number of social features begin to appear, together with service centres. There is usually a religious centre, an inn, a small post office, which also acts as a general store, and often a bank, a village hall and possibly a small primary school.

Large village

Large villages exhibit a greater variety of social and economic functions. Churches of various denominations are found, as are several inns and a group of specialist shops – a butcher, grocer, baker, ironmonger and so on. More than one bank and school are commonly found. There might also be a small cottage hospital, although hospitals and clinics more often appear in the next settlement grade up.

Town

Apart from the existence of factories, there is now greater competition between similar functions. Thus, there are probably several churches of the same denomination and several shops specialising in the same goods. Towns are also likely to have large chain stores such as, in Britain, F. W. Woolworth and Marks & Spencer. Many levels of educational institutions might be found, from infants' schools upwards, often to colleges or universities. Towns may also differ from smaller settlements in having railway and bus stations, and places of amusement like cinemas, bingo halls and theatres.

Of course, the bigger the town, the greater will be the number and size of all these establishments. Some geographers have identified a further characteristic of towns: economic specialisation. They argue that towns do not simply have industries, but invariably specialise in a particular type of manufacture. Certainly there are many examples that seem to bear this out. Doncaster and Bradford are centres in Yorkshire for engineering and woollen textiles respectively, and traditionally we associate Nottingham with lace and Luton with hats.

City

In earlier times, the definition of a city was simply a town with a cathedral; in other words, a town at the centre of a diocese. This, however, takes no account of size or importance, and as such can be misleading. For instance, St Davids (Dyfed, Wales) has a cathedral, but with only 2000 inhabitants could scarcely be classed a city in terms of size. In Britain, a more specific meaning of a city is now used, namely, a settlement which has been granted that title by royal authority, usually through the granting of a charter of incorporation. Birmingham became a city in this way in 1889.

Perhaps a more universal definition of a city is a settlement where there is a considerable 'diversity of function': that is, where all types of occupations, industries and services are represented. Cities are much larger than towns and have a greater number of economic functions. They tend to have transport termini, major financial institutions and regional administrative offices.

Conurbation

This term was first used by the urban geographer Patrick Geddes in 1915 and is applied to a large area of urban development which has resulted from the merging of originally separate towns or cities. Within each conurbation there is normally a common industrial or business interest and a common shopping and entertainment centre. Examples of such agglomerations in Britain include Greater London, Manchester and Merseyside, and abroad Chicago, Tokyo and the Ruhr coalfield (West Germany).

Megalopolis

This is a fairly recent term and describes an area in which large towns and even conurbations have merged together into a vast urban zone. The largest and best known example is in north-east USA, where a band of urban land use stretches for 1000 km from Boston to Washington.

Theories of classification

The above methods of settlement classification have largely resulted from practical observation; they rely on generalisations rather than on hard and fast rules. This has led many geographers to attempt a more precise approach.

One of the earliest methods, in this respect, was devised by Harris (*Geographical Review* **33**, 1943, pp. 86–99). His classification was based on employment statistics so that the most important single function in each settlement could be distinguished from other, less important functions. A 'manufacturing town' could be so defined if at least 45% of its total working population was employed in some form of manufacturing. A 'mining town' was where at least 15% worked in mining; a 'transport town' where at least 11% were employed in the transport industry and a 'university town' where 25% worked in higher education. There were other, similar, definitions for 'retail towns', 'wholesale towns' and 'resort and retirement towns'.

There are of course, certain drawbacks to this method of approach. One is that it does not allow for the recognition of all types of urban functions since all study is dependent on the limited statistics available at any one time. Another problem is that the use of labels can sometimes hide the importance of functions rather than reveal them. For instance, a town may be defined as a 'wholesaling town' in terms of employment and yet receive most of its wealth from, say, retailing. Even in Harris's own work this fault is apparent. Of all the towns he studied in the USA 80% were classified as 'diversified towns' yet many of these turned out to be among the country's major manufacturing centres. Conversely, those classed as 'manufacturing towns' were also major educational or transport centres.

Since Harris's time there have been further attempts to classify settlements. Many have tried to overcome the various pitfalls of earlier methods by taking into account a greater number of functional factors and using more quantitative techniques. Pownall's method, for example, was based largely on averages found in occupational patterns (*Annals of the Association of American Geographers* **43**, 1953, pp. 332–50), whereas Nelson preferred the more complicated 'arithmetic mean' as a foundation for study (*Economic Geography* **31**, 1955, pp. 189–210).

A far more comprehensive method was that expounded by Moser and Scott (*British towns: a statistical study of their social and economic differences*. Edinburgh: Oliver & Boyd, 1961). This took into account not just demographic and economic features, but also social aspects. For their investigation Moser and Scott considered 157 towns in England and Wales, each with a population of more than 50 000 (in the 1951 census). For these towns 57 different variables of statistical information were gathered, including such items as social class, population changes in age and sex structure, household composition and overcrowding. To this was applied the technique of **component analysis**, whereby the 57 variables were simplified down into four main components. Each town was then assessed according to these four components and grouped so that those in each group were more similar to each other than to those in other groups. By this method 14 main groups emerged, examples of these being 'seaside resorts', 'large ports', 'commercial centres' and 'newer industrial suburbs'.

Settlement hierarchies

The study of settlement classification – and especially of the different sizes of settlements – has led inevitably to the study of hierarchies. Many geographers believe that settlements have grown, not at random, but in a logical order so that their sizes, and even their functions, relate to an overall regularity.

Auerbach first noticed this relationship in 1913, but it was not until 1949 that his ideas were expressed in precise mathematical terms. This was due to the work of Zipf who proposed the **rank-size rule**. This theory states that 'if all the urban settlements in an area are ranked in descending order of population, the population of the nth town will be 1/nth that of the largest'. In other words, the second most important town in a given area or country will have half the population of the largest, the third most important town would have one-third the population of the largest, and so on downwards. For example, if the largest city in a country has a population of 5 million, then the town which ranks tenth in size will have one tenth the population – half a million.

At the time of Zipf's investigation, the towns in the USA fitted fairly well into this theory. New York, the largest city, had a population of about 8 million, compared with Chicago (the second largest), which had nearly 4 million. The third ranking city, Los Angeles, had about a third of New York's population (about 2.6 million) and Philadelphia (ranking fourth) had 2 million.

Of course, it is true that settlements at the upper end of the hierarchy are less numerous than settlements at the lower end. In a given area there would be relatively few, if any, conurbations, a greater number of towns, even more villages, and perhaps thousands of hamlets. There is, in addition, a tendency for many settlements in the same country to be similar in size. These facts, naturally, modify Zipf's original rank-size rule. Instead of the regularly decreasing hierarchy he suggested, there is more likely to be a **stepped order**, in which not one but a number of settlements may be found at every level, each place

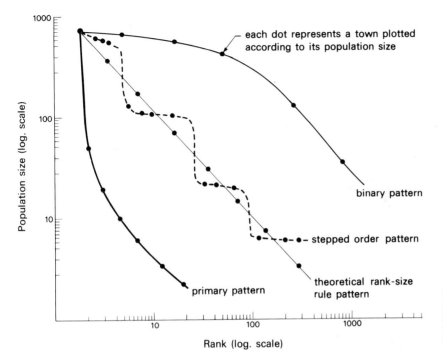

each dot represents a town plotted according to its population size

Population size (log. scale)

binary pattern

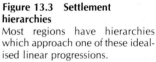

stepped order pattern

theoretical rank-size rule pattern

primary pattern

Rank (log. scale)

Figure 13.3 Settlement hierarchies
Most regions have hierarchies which approach one of these idealised linear progressions.

resembling the others in size and function (see Fig. 13.3).

Another modification that is sometimes apparent is called the **binary pattern**. This is found where a number of settlements of similar size dominate only the upper end of the hierarchy. In the USA, where Zipf's theory once applied, this particular pattern is becoming increasingly clear.

However, the rank-size rule, even in its modified forms, does not always match reality. In many countries, although the lower ranking settlements may fit well enough into Zipf's theory, the largest city might be much larger than twice the size of the second city. In some instances it is as much as three or four times larger than the next city down, or in the case of some (such as Montevideo) even greater still. This tendency has led to the **Law of the Primate City**, first proposed by Jefferson in 1939 (*Geographical Review* **29**, pp. 226–32). Jefferson suggested that it is natural for one particular town to develop into by far the most important settlement in a given area as a result of various social, economic and political factors. Once a city outgrows the size of its neighbours, for whatever reasons, it is given an impetus to grow further away from them in both size and functions. Such a place is called a **primate city** and in it can be found specific and unique characteristics. Here, wrote Jefferson,

would be the finest goods, the rarest articles, the greatest talents and the most skilled workers. In short, a primate city would attract a far larger proportion of the population, economic activity and social functions than any other centre, and in time would acquire an unusually high concentration of wealth and, often, political power.

Some geographers, such as Linsky, think that primacy is typical of developing countries (where there is a short history of urbanisation), and that commercial and industrial expansion leads to a situation more akin to the rank-size rule. Certainly the developing world has many countries with primate cities: Iran, Colombia, Uruguay, Peru, Venezuela, Nigeria and Algeria, to name but a few. But to generalise in this way is dangerous. There are primate cities in many highly industrialised countries: London, Paris, Stockholm, Copenhagen and Tokyo.

Finally it may be interesting to consider the case of Italy. In that country there are several cities below the size of Rome, which are similar in size: Venice, Milan, Naples, Turin, Florence. At first this may seem to follow the stepped order or binary pattern hierarchies, yet in fact it tends to confirm the primacy law. Up to 1870 Italy was divided into separate and independent states. Each of the towns just mentioned was originally the primate city for its respective state.

Theories of settlement hierarchies are not limited to those based on population size. These are useful in providing empirical evidence of the presence or absence of settlement ranking, but alone they do not aid the understanding of the processes involved in settlement spacing. In particular, they do not suggest exact functional hierarchies of settlements. These are discussed below.

Hierarchic distributions of settlements

Functional hierarchies are, essentially, based on the extent to which settlements have an economic impact on their surrounding areas. Unlike the size hierarchies mentioned previously – which rank the largest settlement first – hierarchies based on function rank first the settlement with the largest market area – by having the largest shops for example, the most specialised services or the most dominant financial organisations. Such hierarchies may bear some correlation with size hierarchies, but the two need not be totally parallel. A village is likely to have a smaller market area than a town, but two towns of equal size may not have similar sized market areas. In terms of rank, one town might outstrip another in functional importance, irrespective of the fact that they have the same populations.

It is but a short step from the study of functional hierarchies to the study of settlement distributions based on those hierarchies. In this context, two theories have been expounded. Each of these suggests not only that there is a definite link between settlement functions and their spatial location but also that regular patterns may be found in distributions, which can be both measured and accounted for. These theories are those of Walter Christaller and August Lösch.

Christaller's central place theory
In arriving at his theory Christaller made assumptions not dissimilar to those of Von Thünen (Ch. 7). These included an isotropic or homogeneous surface on which topography, soils, climate, resources and population are evenly distributed, with equal ease and opportunity of movement in all directions. Consumers would have identical needs and tastes (that is, the same demands) and would aim to minimise the distances they travelled to obtain goods and services. Producers would aim to maximise their profits.

Christaller also assumed hexagonal market areas.

these being the most efficient way of covering a plain with no overlaps and no gaps (Fig. 13.4). The same principle was applied to industrial location, as discussed in Chapter 9.

The cornerstone of Christaller's theory was that settlements serve as 'central places' for goods and services and that different goods and services have market areas of different sizes. Low-order goods such as groceries and hardware would have relatively small market areas, and high-order goods such as furniture and jewellery would have relatively large market areas. The larger the settlement, the more goods and services it will provide. Thus, large towns might be 'high-order centres' and act as central places for large market areas; small villages might be 'low-order centres' and act as central places for small market areas. For example, a farmer's wife is likely to use her local village shop to buy bread, but would need to travel to the nearest town for clothes or household goods. For very specialised goods and services, a dining-room suite or hospital treatment, for instance, she may have to go to the nearest city. Thus, the village grocery store would serve a small area of surrounding farmland, the town would serve a large area and attract custom from further afield, and the city may be used by people in the whole region.

The result of this would be a hierarchy of settlements and a mesh of hexagonal market areas (Fig. 13.5). All settlements of equal size would have the same functions, would serve hinterlands of the same size and would therefore be equally spaced. By reducing the numerous hinterlands of all goods and services to a smaller number of common ones, Christaller identified seven orders of settlement. Over a given region there will be few large settlements in

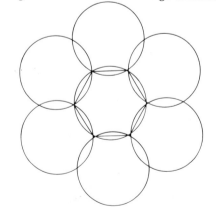

Figure 13.4   Development of hexagonal market areas
The hexagon allows for the perfect tessellation of a two-dimensional surface.

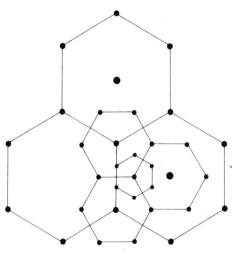

Figure 13.5 **Hierarchy of settlements and market areas (after Christaller)**
A mesh of units in descending order covering a uniform surface.

relation to smaller settlements because people need high-order goods and services less often than low-order goods and services. Each settlement would provide all the facilities of lower order settlements together with some of its own specialised ones. The largest settlement in a region would provide the largest number and greatest variety of goods and services of all, the smallest settlement the least number and most limited variety.

Through this settlement hierarchy Christaller found a regular progression, a relationship he called K = 3. Each settlement is surrounded by six other settlements of the next grade down (situated at the

corners of the hexagonal market areas) and on average would serve one-third of the population of each, since each of the smaller settlements is equidistant from three of the next grade up. Thus, each settlement would serve the equivalent of three centres. This can be seen in Figure 13.6.

Continuing the progression through the hierarchy it can be stated that each settlement would serve three times the trading area of the next settlement down and have three times the population. For every one of the largest settlements there would be three of the second grade, nine of the third grade, 27 of the fourth grade and so on. Assuming the smallest settlements are 7 km apart, the second smallest would be 12 km apart ($\sqrt{3} \times 7$) and the next smallest 21 km apart. The resulting progressive hierarchy can be shown diagrammatically and numerically (Fig. 13.7).

Since the above information applies to the buying and selling of goods and services, Christaller called it the **market principle**. He also devised a **traffic principle** (K = 4) and an **administrative principle** (K = 7), and these show different hierarchic patterns.

The traffic principle could be applied to regions where transport costs are particularly important. Here the number of settlements serving as central places at decreasing grades would run 1, 4, 16, 64 and so on, and the hexagonal hinterlands would be so arranged as to maximise the number of settlements along straight lines, thereby facilitating movement (Fig. 13.8).

The administrative principle could be applied to regions where advanced systems of central administration have developed. Here the numerical progression would be 1, 7, 49, 343 and so on, and the

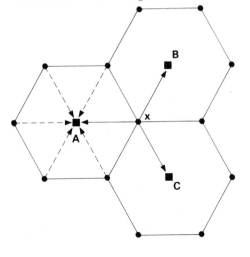

A, B and C are settlements of equal size.

x is one of the settlements of the next grade down.

A serves six smaller settlements each of which has a choice of using three larger settlements. Thus, on average 1/3 of each smaller settlement uses each large settlement.

A would serve 1/3 of six settlements plus its own small low-order market area, equivalent to 3 small settlements.

Figure 13.6 **K = 3 market principle (after Christaller)**
It is assumed that smaller settlements are located at the angles of the hexagon market areas of larger settlements.

market areas would be drawn so that the number of settlements dependent upon any one central place is maximised. This eliminates any shared allegiances where one small settlement is administered by more than one larger settlement (Fig. 13.9).

The Lösch theory

In 1954 Lösch modified and refined Christaller's earlier hypotheses. He too used hexagonal hinterlands, but did not assume an even spread of population.

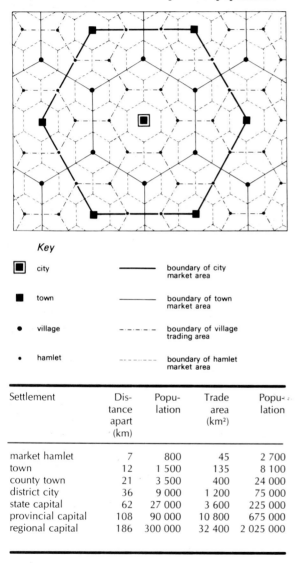

Key

◼	city	————	boundary of city market area
■	town	————	boundary of town market area
●	village	–·–·–·	boundary of village trading area
•	hamlet	-------	boundary of hamlet market area

Settlement	Distance apart (km)	Population	Trade area (km²)	Population
market hamlet	7	800	45	2 700
town	12	1 500	135	8 100
county town	21	3 500	400	24 000
district city	36	9 000	1 200	75 000
state capital	62	27 000	3 600	225 000
provincial capital	108	90 000	10 800	675 000
regional capital	186	300 000	32 400	2 025 000

Figure 13.7 Christaller's settlement hierarchic mesh (K = 3)
This is a totally regular distribution of dispersed settlement, all central places of equal size being equally spaced.

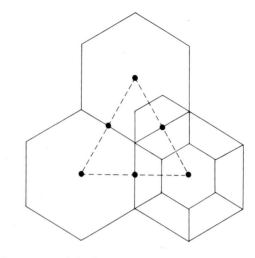

Figure 13.8 Christaller's traffic principle (K = 4)
Here settlements are located in linear distributions to allow for easy communication links.

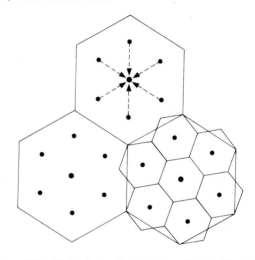

Figure 13.9 Christaller's administrative principle (K = 7)
Small market areas are set within larger market areas so that local authority boundaries fit into regional authority boundaries.

Assuming different goods have market areas of different sizes – and therefore different K values – Lösch was able to superimpose a number of hinterlands around fixed central places (Fig. 13.10a). Apart from Christaller's 3, 4 and 7, he added K values of 9, 12, 13, 19 and many more (up to 150 different goods were considered in all). Lösch then rotated these hinterlands around each major settlement and brought them to rest where the greatest number of lowest order towns existed in the minimum of space (Fig. 13.10b). At this point also there was the greatest even

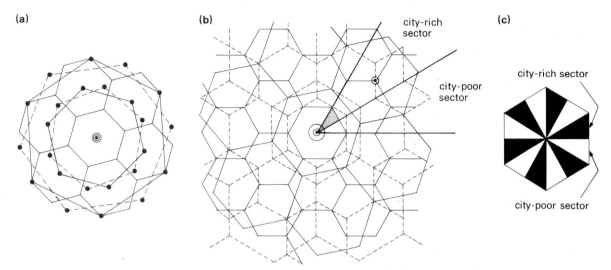

Figure 13.10 The Lösch theory of distribution
This interlocking mesh is the result of careful alignment so that settlements are positioned in spatial bands or wedges.

spread of similarly sized towns with the minimum total distance between them.

From this pattern there merged six sectors in which many settlements existed and many services were offered, and six sectors where settlements and services were sparse (Fig. 13.10c). Between these city-rich and city-poor sectors Lösch located the main transport routes and these radiate outwards from the metropolis at the centre. Such an arrangement is called the 'Löschian economic landscape', and provides not a rigid hierarchy of settlement size but a continuum along which all central places can be positioned.

Theories and reality

Both Christaller and Lösch have been criticised for proposing settlement patterns which are palpably unrealistic. Homogeneous regions do not exist, market areas are never hexagonal (due to physical geography and transport networks) and man does not always act rationally. Producers may not aim for maximum profits and customers may not always shop at their nearest store. Towns of equal size rarely share the same functions. Some, like tourist resorts, are overendowed with functions, given their population size, and others, like mining towns, are underendowed. Even the organisation of retailing is changing so that the appearance of such multiple stores as Tesco, Boots and Marks & Spencer has distorted market areas. On the one hand, such stores might support

the running of a few outlets which function at a loss (at least on a temporary basis); on the other hand, they might dominate disproportionately large hinterlands. Government policies and planning may further distort settlement patterns, stopping urban spread in one place while encouraging it elsewhere.

Notwithstanding these drawbacks it would be wrong to discount central place theory altogether. Christaller himself noticed a regularity of settlement spacing in his own part of southern Germany, and later geographers have successfully applied his principles to other regions of flat relief: the American Mid-West, the Argentinian Pampas, the Chinese lowlands and, in England, East Anglia.

Similarly, the Löschian landscape should not be discounted merely because of its complexity or its assumed absence of the irrationality of human behaviour patterns. Many geographers have tested the Lösch model and have indeed discovered the existence of settlement-rich and settlement-poor sectors around central places – for example, around Exeter, Norwich and other county towns in England, and around certain Japanese towns and in central USSR. Even around London there is some evidence to support the validity of the Lösch theory (see Fig. 13.11), despite the fact that the findings here can be accounted for through purely physical factors.

The value of the Christaller and Lösch theories is that they provide idealised patterns from which deviations in the real world can be measured. The former is suited to retailing and as such is more relevant to settlement patterns in rural areas and those in

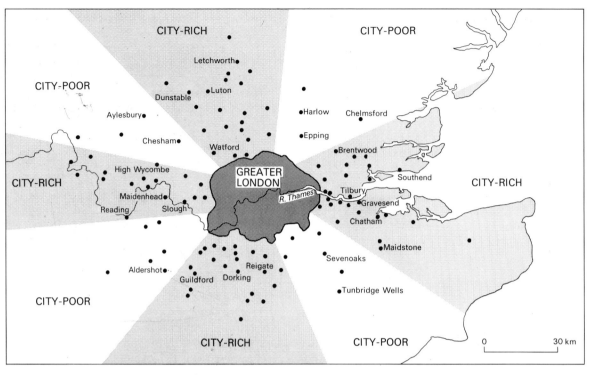

Figure 13.11 The Lösch landscape in south-east England
The city-rich and city-poor sectors around Greater London – four of each – can partly be explained by physical geography: the sectors up stream and down stream along the Thames have numerous settlements, the hilly areas of Epping Forest, Chilterns, Hampshire Downs and Kent Downs have few settlements. Even so, modified Löschian distribution seems apparent and even accentuated by lines of communication – the M1, M4 and M2 all run through city-rich sectors.

developing countries where towns have relatively few functions. The latter is suited to manufacturing industry and is more relevant to industrialised areas and to developed countries. They have stimulated further study in other human activities (especially in retailing and consumer behaviour) and have helped planners and market researchers to formulate development policies.

Summary

1   All settlements are unique in form and character, so definitions are necessarily subjective. Even so, classification is possible through the recognition of common features.

2   Traditional classifications are based on population size (e.g. in ascending order from isolated dwelling to megalopolis), function (e.g. employment statistics, as suggested by Harris), and on form (e.g. types of shops, number of churches and schools, architectural styles).

3   Settlement hierarchies can be primate (one dominant city), rank-size (regular descendancy according to proportioned relationships) or binary (several, equally large, dominant cities). Respectively, these tend to be found in less developed, developed and highly developed countries, since they may be linked to levels of economic and social development.

4   Hierarchic distribution theories suggest that settlements are regularly spaced according to functional extent. Christaller's central place theory states that all settlements of equal size are equally spaced and have the same-sized hexagonal market areas. Lösch modified this theory to produce segments of high and low urban density.

5   All settlement-hierarchy theories provide idealised patterns against which reality can be measured. They help to explain the complexities of human behaviour but should not be viewed as physical truths.

Data–response exercises

1 From OS map A (Dorset) draw a sketch map to show the location of hamlets and villages, distinguishing clearly between these two types of settlement. Using examples from this map discuss the reasons why rural settlements are difficult to classify.

2 Discuss and account for the criteria you would adopt in distinguishing the settlements shown in OS map B (Yorkshire) between rural and urban. Could any of these settlements justifiably be classed as both rural and urban?

3 From statistics obtained either from regional textbooks or from census returns, plot on log-scale graph paper the town populations of selected countries. Suggest which hierarchies your resulting graphs must resemble, and comment on your conclusions.

4 For the Christaller settlement mesh (Fig. 13.7) examine the possible patterns of communications that might develop between the larger market centres. How would the existence of a major physical barrier (e.g. an estuary or mountain ridge) affect the settlement mesh?

5 Suggest possible examples where Christaller's traffic principle (Fig. 13.8) and administrative principle (Fig. 13.9) patterns might be found in the real world. Account for your conclusions.

6 Where might the Löschian sector landscape (Fig. 13.11) be found to exist other than around London? What changes might affect the continued existence of this landscape? (Atlases and regional textbooks should be used.)

14 Rural settlement

Introduction

The geographical use of the term 'rural settlement' is variable. Some use it simply to describe any place set in the midst of countryside (or more vaguely as a 'non-urban' place); others see it as a settlement whose inhabitants depend on agriculture for their livelihood. Both definitions have drawbacks. The former is too wide and might include, not just farming communities, but also those based on mining, quarrying, forestry, and sometimes manufacturing and even tourism. The latter is too limited. Today, and especially in advanced countries, a settlement that appears to be agricultural in nature may in fact consist of people unconnected with the soil: those working in service industries (e.g. shops), those working in nearby towns and those who have retired.

Whatever the definition used, however, there is no doubt that rural settlements form an essential part of the human landscape and, as such, deserve special study. Ranging in size from isolated dwellings to villages, they are found everywhere and accommodate well over half the world's population. They are especially numerous in developing countries: in India, for example, there are over 600 000 villages and these, together with hamlets and farmsteads, account for 80% of the total population. Even in developed countries, up to 20% of the population live in rural surroundings.

Such is the scope and importance of this chapter that the questions it will attempt to answer are necessarily wide ranging and diverse:

- In what ways have rural settlements developed and changed over the years?
- What determines the nature of rural society and how does that society differ from urban society?
- Which factors must be considered in rural settlement location analysis?
- What are the morphological characteristics of rural settlements – their shape, size and appearance – and how do they differ?
- How are rural settlements distributed over the landscape and can their distribution patterns be formulated into theories?

- What kinds of investigation and fieldwork can be undertaken to increase our understanding of rural settlements?

Historical development

Agricultural settlements were the first stable communities to appear in the world and their development can be viewed as the inevitable result of economic and social progress. Once man passes from the hunting stage to sedentary farming, he looks naturally towards a permanent system of communal living, for reasons of friendship, mutual help and protection from enemies. In some cases his gregarious nature leads to extreme clustering: the Tukano Indians of Colombia live in houses built for twenty people or more, the Dayaks of Borneo often have whole tribes – perhaps 600 people – under a single roof. More usually, however, settlements consist of separate dwellings built in groups to varying degrees of compactness.

The earliest villages appeared in Egypt, Mesopotamia and the lower Indus Valley during the Neolithic Age (6000–5000 BC). From there village life spread westwards into Crete, Greece and Phoenicia and eastwards into China (during the Bronze Age) and later still into Africa (and indeed, in that continent some villages are still appearing for the first time).

In Britain the history of rural settlement goes back well over 4000 years. The first major group to live in stable communities were probably the Celts who, armed with primitive implements, cultivated the light soils of the uplands: of the chalk and limestone downs, of south-west England, Wales and Scotland. Their villages have not survived, being deserted in later times in favour of more sheltered spots, but enough remains to show what they were like: the earliest being simple groups of hut circles (as found on Dartmoor), the later ones being more complex stone structures (like Chysauster in west Cornwall).

The colonisation of the English lowlands, which were naturally marshy and densely forested, took place mainly during the Dark Ages, first by the

Saxons and later by the Danes and Norsemen. Such was the multiplication of villages during these centuries that, by the Norman Conquest (1066), most of the settlements we know today were in existence. One feature of this growth of settlement was the setting up of 'daughter villages' by communities that had become overcrowded. These often retained their original name but with some qualifying addition: for example, on the Chiltern Hills there is Great Missenden and Little Missenden, Much Hadham and Little Hadham.

Medieval England saw the consolidation of village life and a general increase of settlement size. Some new villages did appear (connected with castles or monasteries), but many more disappeared. The Black Death (1348–50) not only killed about one-third of the country's population, but led to over 1300 settlements being deserted, only to be seen today as faint ridges in the ground or derelict churches standing in the middle of nowhere. Rural communities of types other than those of agricultural origin developed during the Industrial Revolution, usually for mining or

REFUGEE CAMPS

A refugee camp is a unique type of rural settlement. Since it is a temporary, unplanned agglomeration of living units inhabited by displaced persons seeking refuge. Such a place would be 'rural' in the sense that it is residential in character – having no industry or commercial base – and is often located in the midst of countryside.

Refugee camps vary enormously in character, origin and organisation. However, they normally consist of tents, rudely built shacks of wood, corrugated iron sheeting and other waste material, improvised vehicles and, sometimes, caravans and mobile homes provided by relief organisations. Standards of sanitation, health care and food provision are usually low, and both educational and administrative services are minimal. Some camps are extremely temporary – existing only a matter of weeks – others survive for so long – perhaps many years – that they become permanent.

Reasons for refugee camps

(1) *Natural disasters.* Floods, earthquakes, droughts and volcanoes are examples of natural disasters, which can cause homelessness and destitution. Many refugee camps appeared, for instance, in southern Italy in 1980 and in Central America in 1979 after earthquakes, and in the Karamoja district of Sudan in 1981 after a prolonged period of drought.

(2) *Man-made disasters.* Fires, excessive pollution and soil contamination may all cause human evacuation. For example, there has been the Three-Mile Island radioactivity leak in the USA (1978), the industrial chemical explosion at Seveso in Italy (1979), and various anthrax scares in the Scottish islands (1982). Each of these led to the establishment of temporary refuge settlements.

(3) *Political upheaval.* The partition of India and Pakistan in 1947 and the designation of the new country of Israel in the same year both created millions of stateless people who were forced to search for new settlements away from the places of their birth. In the latter case Palestinian camps have survived to the present day in various Arab States. The division of Cyprus has similarly created refugee camps.

(4) *Non-integrated minorities.* In many countries there

are cultural or racial groups that have never been fully incorporated into the states where they live and are, thus, destined to a separate and often migratory settlement existence: the Kurds within Iran, the Basques in France and Spain, the Palisarios in Morocco, and even the Romany gypsies in several European countries.

(5) *Wars and invasions.* In Pakistan many Afghan refugee camps appeared after the invasion by the USSR of Afghanistan in 1979; throughout the 1960s and 1970s many refugee camps appeared in South-East Asia as a result of the Vietnam War and its aftermath, especially in Kampuchia and Thailand.

Organisation of refugee camps

(1) *'Autogestion'.* Many refugee camps are self-administered, whereby the refugees build their own shelters and administer their own affairs. Sometimes national governments may give some limited financial aid.

(2) *International secular administration.* Such voluntary organisations as Oxfam, War on Want and the Red Cross work relentlessly to provide refugee camps with basic facilities – water, shelter and medical services.

(3) *International religious administration.* The Quakers, the World Council of Churches, the Catholic Fund for Overseas Development and the British Council of Churches (especially the first named) run their own refugee camps, financed entirely from voluntary subscriptions.

(4) *National governmental control.* In a few instances a state government will take responsibility for the care of the homeless or expelled foreign populations by building makeshift houses and distributing rations. However, it is often the case that this undertaking is inefficiently practised and relief programmes are marked by corruption and inept administration.

(5) *International control.* The United Nations (through such subsidiary groups as its Children's Fund (UNICEF) and the Relief and Rehabilitation Administration (UNRRA) plays a major role in the administration of refugee camps that have arisen out of political turmoil. This administration is frequently accompanied by UN peacekeeping forces.

quarrying, and some have appeared this century, but by and large the character of English villages had already been formed.

The study of rural settlements involves an investigation into their many aspects – place names, sites, forms, sizes, architectural styles and distribution. All these result from the complex interplay of both physical and human factors. The evidence supplied by any one village, obtained either from fieldwork or from maps, is able to tell us not just its present functions but also its origins and historical development. Place names are a good example of this. The growth of villages in Britain, as outlined earlier, can be traced through their names since most place names incorporate both a meaning and a cultural origin. Thus, prefixes like 'Tre-' (house), 'Pol-' (pool) and 'Pen-' (headland) are Celtic and are commonly found in Cornwall and Wales. Suffixes like '-ing' (people), '-ham' (enclosure), '-ton' (village) and '-holt' (wood) are Anglo-Saxon and are common in lowland England. Suffixes like '-by' (village), '-garth' (enclosure) and '-thwaite' (clearing) date from the Scandinavian invasions and are most common in northern and north-west England.

Rural society

Rural settlements have a much longer history of development than urban settlements and so their human characteristics have a much deeper foundation. These characteristics – demography, way of life, intellectual outlook, environmental perception, aspects of behaviour and sociological interaction – are the direct result of man's long and involved relationship with his surroundings and they represent the most natural of human conditions.

Unlike urban, industrial and scientific societies, rural society is the one aspect of modern human existence that maintains a link with earliest history. Modern urbanised and industrial societies stem from the industrial revolutions of the past (in ancient Egypt, Greece and Rome, for example, and in 18th-century Europe); modern technological and consumer societies stem from human advances within the last hundred years. Only rural society has origins in prehistory since it, alone, is solely based on primary activity.

For these reasons, rural society is essentially different from any other form of society. This is true all over

WHY AREN'T THEY ALL WEARING SMOCKS – AND WHERE'S THE VILLAGE IDIOT?

Figure 14.1 An English village
An image of English village life: the butcher bowls a leg-break to the squire at the crease; the church bells ring out for evensong; yokels gossip in the public bar. Such scenes certainly exist in English literature – and here and there in reality, too – but not to the extent some people might imagine.

the world, in both developed and less developed areas, and it can be seen in any comparative study of behavioural patterns in town and country. In general the essential characteristics of the rural way of life are marked by conservatism, stability, introversion and phlegmatism.

Compared with other societies, rural society tends to be slower, calmer, quieter and less stressful. Such characteristics can be seen in many economic, sociological and geographical aspects. In country districts, people tend to be healthier and to live longer. They are less mobile (occupationally and spatially), more superstitious and traditional, more introvert and suspicious of strangers, and more wary of change and progress. They tend to have closer horizons and a narrower view of world affairs.

All these aspects, generalisations though they may be, are relevant to the work of the human geographer, since the character of society determines human activity – agricultural, transport and occupational patterns, settlement characteristics, political behaviour and demographic structure. Some of these activities, in the forms found in rural areas, are mentioned elsewhere in this book. In the context of rural settlement, the nature of rustic society undoubtedly makes isolated dwellings, hamlets and villages undynamic – that is, makes them stable in terms of forms, patterns and distributions. It also makes them unique in character. We all have mental pictures of what rural settlements are like, and although these images vary between countries, they have common elements. An English village (see Fig. 14.1) is essentially different from a French or German one, and these are different again from villages in Bolivia, Nigeria or India, but all can be pictured as traditional human constructions in which man lives close to his environment. The only real difference between Third World and developed world rural society is the *extent* of its characteristics, that is, whether these are extreme or not. The rural characteristics mentioned above are more accentuated, exaggerated and pronounced in countries of the Third World than in countries of the developed world where urbanisation and tourism are, together, altering the character of country life.

Settlement location

Rarely, if ever, were settlement locations chosen at random. Early man lived by the soil and was much closer to nature than we are today. He knew how best to utilise the resources around him, and chose wisely the locations for his dwellings, whether these be farms, hamlets or villages. Essentially he looked for natural advantages. On the one hand he selected suitable sites – actual plots of land where a settlement could be built. On the other hand he selected suitable situations – areas or districts which offered the greatest potential for settlement growth.

The major considerations for settlement location are summarised below, but two points should be stressed beforehand. First, most locations offer more than one advantage and the early settlers chose those positions which provided the best combination of advantages. Secondly, most villages were built under economic and social conditions totally different from those of today. In some cases this led to villages being abandoned as sites were found to be unsuitable for later economic or social conditions. More often, however, settlements have not become deserted. The reasons for their original location may no longer apply, but through inertia they remain indefinitely; many settlements in the Nile Valley stand on the same sites that were occupied 6000 years ago.

Water supply

Water has always been the most important requirement for life and early man looked for a regular supply of fresh water perhaps more than any other factor. This he needed both for his own consumption and for economic activities (milling corn, using the water wheel, cleaning wool, and so forth). Thus, his settlements were sited where water supplies were available: at oases and water holes in arid or semi-arid regions; elsewhere along rivers or at pools, lakes, springs and wells.

In many places, spring-line settlements are found, sited along the base of chalk, sandstone or limestone hills where water emerges from the permeable rock. In England such settlements exist along the edges of the North and South Downs, Chilterns and Cotswolds.

Dry land

Where land is liable to be marshy or damp, or suffer seasonal flooding, settlements may be 'dry-seeking', in which case upstanding or prominent features are favoured: hill tops or knolls, patches of dry land and gravel terraces. Often a line of hamlets and villages may be found, not along valley floors, but along valley sides at some height above the flood plain. Examples of dry-point villages abound. In the Tigris–Euphrates

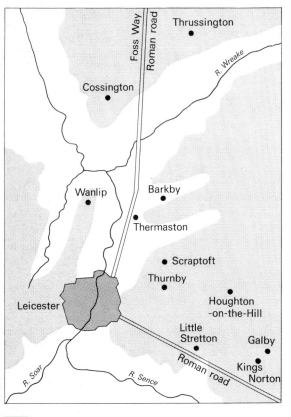

land over 70 m

Figure 14.2 Settlement sites in Leicestershire
Much of Leicestershire is floored with boulder clay and was once densely forested. Here and there, however, islands of glacial sands and gravels are exposed, which gave rise to areas that were more lightly wooded and therefore more easily cleared. The Saxons chose these sites for their first villages, and those to the east of Leicester are examples of such settlements. Along the river valleys (the Soar and Wreake valleys especially) gravel terraces provided early dry sites above the alluvium, and here strings of villages were located. The same is true along many other river valleys in England, notably along the Great Ouse and Yorkshire Derwent. The siting of Saxon villages was not notably linked with the line of Roman roads. In many cases the Saxons feared 'Roman spirits' and deliberately located their settlements away from Roman ways.

Valley (Iraq), ancient settlements still survive on slightly raised platforms; along the Rhine and Elbe, there are villages along the valley terraces; and in the Low Countries, mounds or *terpen* have been used to enable settlements to rise above the polders (e.g. Antwerp). In England, dry-point villages are found in all low-lying regions: Haddenham in the Fens, Wedmore in the Somerset Levels, and Minster-in-Thanet in Kent. Along river valleys, villages may be found on

dry sites above flood levels (see Fig. 14.2). Along the Thames Valley the Saxons once had to choose dry islands ('eys') for their villages: Bermondsey, Chelsea, Battersea, Hackney.

In areas that have been artificially drained, as in Bengal, the Netherlands and Lincolnshire, settlements are often sited on man-made dry points such as banks and dykes.

Defence

In early times, and especially in areas of political instability where fighting was common, a safe refuge was often an essential requirement of a settlement site. Locations were chosen which could be easily defended: hill tops, rocky outcrops, peninsulas, river loops or confluences, and islands. Defensive settlements are found in numerous areas, for example, in Portugal, central Spain, the Apennines (Italy) and southern France (Fig. 14.3). In New Mexico, the Hopi Indians chose the top of *mesas* for their villages, such was the danger of attack.

Defensive sites in England have been chosen since Celtic times when hill forts were constructed on high eminences. These are now deserted but many others of later date still survive. It has been estimated that well over a thousand hill villages exist in England alone, with a further 200 in Wales. They are most common where tribal wars were once frequent, as in the case of the Welsh Marches and Scottish Borderlands.

Shelter and aspect

Shelter from bad weather and outlook to sunshine are further siting considerations. Where possible, exposed spots are avoided and valleys, rain-shadow areas and the lee side of ridges are preferred. In many regions – as can be seen in the Alps and in Norway – the sunnier south-facing slopes are more densely populated than the colder north-facing slopes, and valley sides are preferred to frost hollows in valley bottoms. In England there are numerous examples of settlements tucked snugly in hollows or little valleys out of the cold blasts of the northerly and easterly winds.

Agricultural land

Since early man lived almost solely by farming, he needed to find situations for his settlements which offered opportunities for agriculture. This meant he looked not just for suitable sites of the kind mentioned above, but also for areas of fertile soils or rich pastures. Those places with the most varied land

Figure 14.3 A strategic settlement site: Cordes, south-west France
The end of a moorland ridge provides a defensive position for a small town. The surrounding lowlands are well cultivated and contain farmsteads of more recent date than the hilltop houses.

were especially prized since these allowed mixed farming: water meadows for cattle, friable clays for arable cultivation, rough pastures for sheep, and woodlands for pigs and horses.

The importance of good farmland can be judged from the fact that fertile areas tend to have a far greater density of villages than infertile areas. In England, East Anglia and the Midland Plain have more settlements per square kilometre than the Chiltern Hills and the Pennines, and in Europe, the Paris Basin and North German Plain have more than Armorica and the Black Forest.

Trade

A great many rural settlements have grown up purely as trading centres and their location has consequently been determined by routeways rather than by any direct physical factors. Sometimes they may be placed at junctions (bridges, fords or crossroads); sometimes they may be strung along a major line of communication such as a trunk road, canal or railway line. Along a river, the lowest bridging point is particularly favoured for settlement, this being where three different means of transport can be served: road, river and ocean.

There are many trading villages in England. Some stand on the old Celtic ways, others on old Roman roads, the latter often being identified by place names that incorporate 'street' or 'stret'. Examples of trade settlements include Corbridge (Northumberland), Farningham (Kent) and Tebay (Cumbria). Those of Roman origin include Chester-le-Street (Durham) and Stretton on Foss (Warwickshire).

Service opportunities

Service opportunities

Some rural settlements have been established for no other purpose than to serve another community. The best examples in Europe are those situated adjacent to the castles, cathedrals and monasteries that were built during the Middle Ages. They supplied the nearby strangers, be they soldiers or monks, with food and equipment, and in return received a degree of protection and economic stability. In Britain, Ludlow (Shropshire), Castle Bolton (North Yorkshire), Abbeytown (Cumbria) and St Davids (Dyfed) were originally founded for this reason. Durban, Amiens and Chartres are examples of similar settlements in France.

Other villages have developed around large mansions or at the gates to the grounds of stately homes. These, also, are service settlements and grew partly to provide the local squire with his daily provisions and partly to accommodate the numerous servants employed by him. In England, Hatfield, Penshurst and Harewood are examples of such villages.

Village forms

Most of the rural settlements now in existence appeared spontaneously and developed over time in response to various geographical factors. Each is distinctive in its site and situation and each possesses its own individual characteristics.

Notwithstanding this uniqueness, these settlements – and especially villages – can be classified into groups within which similarities are apparent. In particular, they can be classed according to their forms: the degree of compactness of their dwellings, and their overall shape. The most common forms are illustrated in Figure 14.4.

The ways in which any village has grown have been determined by a combination of four factors. These are topographical (the physical nature of the site and situation); economic (the system of farming or the type of trade being undertaken when the settlement was founded); historical (the necessity for defence or the opportunities for serving other communities); and cultural (the village forms adopted by different racial or tribal groups).

Differences in settlement compactness may exemplify this. Some villages are very compact and have dwellings positioned cheek-by-jowl, resulting in high densities. Other villages are extensive and have dwellings well spaced out. The former could be the result of a scarcity of land (as on a hill top or along a

valley), the need for protection, a central water supply or a cultural tradition. The latter could be the result of plentiful land (as on a flat lowland area), a peaceful existence, or a lack of close community ties.

The study of village forms involves certain problems. Two villages may share the same plan yet not the same reasons for it. Conversely, two villages may be found in close proximity, and apparently within the same physical and human environment, yet possess totally different forms. Also we must ask whether the forms of villages, as seen today, are the *original* forms, as built by the first inhabitants, or the outcome of successive changes and modifications.

Loose-knit (fragmented) villages

Loose-knit (fragmented) villages

In these settlements, dwellings are scattered irregularly over a fairly large area, too close to be considered isolated yet far enough apart to suggest no evident interrelationship and no obvious nucleus. Such loosely framed villages are probably the result of the gradual clearance of woodland and the individual squatting of settlers who built their homes wherever a space appeared. There would have been no community spirit, no tribal leader and hence no concerted plan of development. The only reason why the cottages were not built further apart was perhaps because their inhabitants shared the same facilities: using the same fertile soils, water supply, road, shelter and so on. Often a centre of village life – a church, public house or smithy – would appear later and be built somewhere within the conglomeration.

In England such villages are found everywhere; Middle Barton (Oxfordshire) and Heddington (Wiltshire) are good examples. Similar settlements exist elsewhere, notably in Germany where *Drubbel* villages have been built on the infertile geestlands. These are usually extremely small, consisting of, perhaps, no more than ten dwellings.

Clustered (nucleated) villages

Clustered (nucleated) villages

These occur where dwellings are in close juxtaposition and there is a fairly well defined division between settlement and countryside. They most often focus upon route centres and their shapes are normally determined by the pattern of communication, at road junctions for example, in which case their form would be Y-shaped, T-shaped, cruciform (at a cross roads) or star-shaped (at multiple junctions).

This clustered form may result either from the need for trading links or from the necessity of defence. In Europe, nucleated villages are also usually associated

VILLAGE FORMS

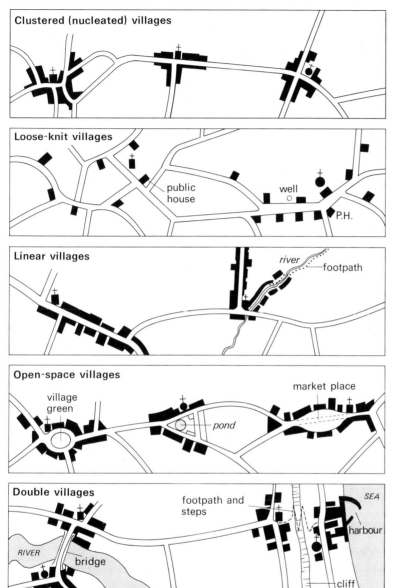

Clustered (nucleated) villages

Loose-knit villages

public house

well

P.H.

Linear villages

river
footpath

Open-space villages

village green

market place

pond

Double villages

footpath and steps

SEA

harbour

RIVER
bridge

cliff

Figure 14.4 Village forms
Some villages are formless, but many show the idealised shapes illustrated here. Any Ordnance Survey map would give examples of these.

with the old open-field system of agriculture in which a concerted farming effort of a tribal group or community was required. In England, they appeared largely under the Saxons and examples include Stow-on-the-Wold (Gloucestershire), Bowes (Durham) and Southam (Warwickshire). In Central Europe they are known as *Haufendorfs* (literally 'heaped-up villages') and exist most commonly in Germany, Poland, Hungary and the Ukraine. In some cases they are still to be found in the middle of farmland under strip cultivation.

Linear villages
These elongated, or 'shoe-string', settlements may have developed either for reasons of trade, in which case they would be aligned along a road, river or canal, or for reasons of physical limitations, as with settlements lying along narrow valley floors or along narrow ridges. They can be several kilometres in length but as little as a single line of dwellings in width.

Like clustered villages there is also an apparent correlation between linear patterns and strip farming.

In England, for instance, many such villages developed during medieval times when strip fields were cultivated at right angles to the line of dwellings, thereby providing each cottage with its own 'back field'. In modern times, linear settlements have also appeared as a result of tourism – where lines of holiday homes develop along coastlines.

British examples of linear settlements abound: Long Melford (Suffolk), Boughton Street (Kent), Combe Martin (Devon), and Henley-in-Arden (Warwickshire). In South Wales and the Pennines many villages are sited along the floors of steep-sided narrow valleys, and in the Fens they are situated along drainage dykes.

In Central Europe these villages are known either as *Waldhufendors* or as *Strassendorfs* and are found in areas that were once heavily forested – the Black Forest, for instance, and along the Elbe Valley. They are also to be found in eastern Canada where the early colonists built their homes along river banks and cultivated the land in long narrow strips running up the valley sides.

Open-space villages

These are nucleated settlements set around a central open space, normally a green but commonly also a market place, pond or church compound. The open spaces themselves can be of any shape (although commonly rectangular, round or triangular) and of any size, being anything from a tiny plot to the equivalent of half the total area covered by the village. The buildings around these open spaces usually face inwards so that those on opposite sides look towards each other.

The origins of these open-space villages are still not fully understood, but evidence suggests that many could have begun as defensive sites. Their central areas would thus have acted as enclosures (into which animals and farmers from surrounding regions could retreat in times of war) and the buildings around as artificial barriers. Many African settlements still exhibit these fortified characteristics. The Zulu *kraal* type of village, for instance, is grouped around the perimeter of a circular pound and between the huts are narrow openings, which are closed at night by thorn fences. The pound acts as a night pasture for animals, which are thus safeguarded from marauders. Similar villages are to be found in Uganda (Fig. 14.5).

In Britain open-space villages generally date back to Saxon times and most commonly contain greens. It has been estimated that over 1475 village greens exist in England alone and so numerous are they that the village green has almost become the hallmark of English rural life. This does not mean, however, that they are found to the same extent everywhere. More exist in lowland than in upland areas, and more exist in eastern than in western districts. Examples include Therfield (Hertfordshire), Finchingfield (Essex), Arncliffe (North Yorkshire), Dufton (Cumbria), Nun Monkton (North Yorkshire, see Fig. 14.6) and Wall (Northumberland).

It is fairly safe to assume that many of these English open-space villages do have origins related to defence. Some are sited on hill tops and others are to be found situated adjacent to castles (like Bamburgh, Northumberland). In many cases, also, greens possess wells, water pumps or ponds and this may again indicate their former use as defensive enclosures. Where problems of origin arise is where open-space villages are so situated that defence must always have been difficult. It can only be assumed in these instances that open spaces were used to serve other purposes; to provide ground for sports, games and fairs, for example, or to allow for the periodic holding of markets. Whether market places grew out of original greens or were initially part of village structure is not known for sure.

The varying shape of open space is equally problematical. Triangular greens occur everywhere, but not so other shapes. Square greens are characteristic of northern England and round greens of south-east England. In some areas 'lens' or oval greens are found, these being in the centre of cigar-shaped villages where space is created by the widening of the main street. Cultural differences must certainly be a contributory factor causing these various shapes, but may not be the only reason for them.

In Europe the same varieties of open-space villages can be found. The *Rundling*, for instance, is common in Eastern Europe and is characterised by closely built cottages situated within a circular fence and about a round green. The *Angerdorf* is the elliptical or lens-shaped type of village and is common in Germany and Poland.

In both Britain and Europe it is probable that far more open-space settlements existed once than are found today. This is because, in many places, population growth and later building construction have caused original greens and squares to be obliterated. In some villages the space has been covered with tarmac for modern purposes, usually for car parks.

Figure 14.5   Karamojong villages in Uganda
Here the native tribes rear cattle on the natural savanna grasslands. Protection is still important and huts are enclosed within compounds. The central open space is used for night pasturage and can be viewed as the forerunner of the European village green.

Double villages
These settlements, although clustered, can be distinguished by the fact that they are normally in two halves. Most often they exist on either side of a bridge or ford, but they can also occur at the top and bottom of a steep slope or cliff, in which case the two parts might be linked by a precipitous flight of steps. Sometimes the two parts grew independently, sometimes together as a single community.

A double village may have a single name; a single name but with some additional, qualifying adjective (e.g. 'upper' and 'lower' or 'east' and 'west'); or two

different names entirely. Examples of such villages in England include Bourton-on-the-Water in the Cotswolds, Glenthan (Lincolnshire), East and West Looe (Cornwall), Lynmouth and Lynton (Devon) and Staithes (Cleveland).

Morphological characteristics of rural settlements

Apart from sites, situations and forms, rural settlements vary in other ways: in size, facilities, building plans, architectural features, constructional tech-

Figure 14.6 An English open-space village: Nun Monkton, North Yorkshire
This large village green is surrounded by inward-facing cottages. The central pond may indicate an early defensive function and the maypole shows that the green may still be used for local festivities.

niques and building materials. These differences occur both between countries of different environments and between regions and localities within countries, and are the result of complex physical and human factors. There is insufficient space here to cover all aspects of these differences, but a few generalisations and examples may suffice to demonstrate their variety and determinant factors.

Settlement size is often a reflection of prosperity. Villages are larger where resources are plentiful (as on flat, fertile land) than they are where resources are poor or scarce (as in mountains or on infertile land).

Thus, in Africa only *Bourbis* (small settlements consisting of less than 10 huts) exist on the desert borders, and large villages (over 100 huts) are to be found in the Hottentot regions. In Britain, villages tend to be larger in the eastern lowlands than they are in the uplands of the north and west. In the same way, intensive farming gives rise to generally larger settlements than extensive farming. Thus Egypt, India and China have generally bigger villages than Australia, Argentina and the USSR.

Differences in settlement appearances are perhaps best exemplified in Britain, where there are possibly greater variations in relief, climate, economic prosperity and culture – in relation to land area – than anywhere else in the world. Nearly all villages in this country have a parish church, but this may vary in architectural design. Styles change with age: Saxon, Norman, Early English (1200–1300), Decorated (1300–1400), Perpendicular (1400–1500), Classical (17th and 18th centuries) and Victorian Gothic (19th century). The oldest churches have towers, sometimes tall and slender with pinnacles (as in Somerset), sometimes short and squat (as in Cornwall and the Pennines). Spires first appeared in the 13th century and became especially characteristic in a broad belt of country running across England from the Humber to the Severn.

Until the 18th century, rural cottages and houses were invariably constructed of local materials, and a geological map can still provide evidence of settlement appearance. Local stone was used where available: granite and slate in Cornwall, Wales and Scotland, limestone in the Pennines and Cotswolds (the latter characterised by mellow, honey-coloured villages of Jurassic Limestone), and flint in chalk downlands (in Wiltshire and Sussex). In lowland regions, where the rock is clay, building materials were brick, timber or wattle-and-daub. In some areas the latter two often gave rise to black and white 'magpie' cottages in Tudor and Stuart times (as seen in East Anglia, southern England and the West Midlands).

The shape, design and orientation of houses also vary regionally. Some buildings are tall, have steeply pitched, hipped roofs, perhaps with dormer windows; others are small and have gently pitched or flat roofs, perhaps with pediments, balustrades and ornamental tilework. In East Anglia, old cottages have 'pargeting', carved patterns in the exterior stucco, and down the length of eastern England, 'Dutch gables' are common features as a result of influences from across the North Sea. In some places, cottages face the adjoining road; elsewhere they are end-on. For many centuries after the Black Death, few rural buildings were constructed facing south because of the superstition that the plague had been brought to England on the south wind.

Paradoxically, settlement characteristics are not only distinctive between regions within the same environment but can be similar between widely different environments. This is mostly the result of human migration, since settlers into a new land often try to re-create the features of their homelands. Thus, the appearance of many villages in New England owes much to British rural traditions, and in parts of the American Mid-West, houses resemble those in Scandinavia, whence came the first immigrants.

Planned rural settlements

So far it has been assumed that hamlets and villages have developed gradually and naturally with population growth and economic progress. Their locations were carefully chosen but, thereafter, their forms and characteristics evolved over the centuries. However, this is not true of *all* rural settlements. Many have been planned as single units and were built as whole entities from scratch.

The *raison d'être* of these planned settlements varies. Some were constructed for a particular economic purpose; some were built for social reasons and conform to particular standards, architectural styles and shapes; and some were built by whim for no special reason at all.

All these types of planned rural settlements are to be found in Britain. The Romans built them to help open up new farmlands, and later, in the Middle Ages, they were constructed as commercial centres in order to help foster trade and produce wealth for their founders. Many owed their existence to far-sighted kings, ambitious ecclesiastics and rich landowners. In the 13th century, for example, New Winchelsea (Sussex) was built with royal permission, granted by Edward I, and Salisbury developed when Bishop Poore vacated his Cathedral seat at Old Sarum in favour of a more sheltered spot next to the River Avon. In Scotland and Ireland, new villages were constructed when farming was being extended, and these largely reflect the traditions of their English founders: Inveraray (Strathclyde) (Fig. 14.7), for example, and Castlewellan (County Down, Northern Ireland).

During the 18th century, many planned villages resulted from the spread of landscaped parklands and the demands of landowners. In 1764 Sir Gilbert Heathcote created an estate at Normanton (Rutland, now part of Leicestershire) and in so doing demolished an entire village to rebuild it outside his park. The same happened at Wimpole (Cambridgeshire) and at Milton Abbas (Dorset). The latter was built on the linear pattern and has since become a famous tourist attraction (Fig. 14.8).

In more recent times rural settlements were planned to house factory employees. In the 19th century many of these appeared as 'model villages' and were financed by humanitarian industrialists: New

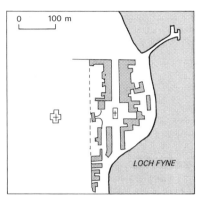

Figure 14.7 A Scottish planned rural settlement: Inveraray, Strathclyde
An 18th century village built by the local laird for commercial reasons.

Figure 14.8 An English planned linear village: Milton Abbas, Dorset
The dry valley provides shelter for this 18th century settlement. The foreground shows part of the landscaped Milton Abbey estate. The Earl of Dorchester removed the old village from beside the abbey and constructed this 'model village' further afield where it could not be seen from the mansion. The cottages have formal classical lines and thatched roofs.

Lanark (near Glasgow) by Robert Owen, Saltaire (near Bradford) by Titus Salt, Port Sunlight (Merseyside) by W. H. Lever and Bournville (near Birmingham) by the Cadbury family.

Perhaps the best example of a village built purely by whim is Portmeirion in Gwynedd, Wales. This was begun in 1926 and was the brainchild of Sir Clough Williams-Ellis, an eccentric architect. It is an entire, mock-Italian village, complete with domes, campanile, lighthouse and cloisters, making, today, a curious tourist attraction.

Outside Britain, planned rural settlements are commonly the product of government policies and have been designed with particular agricultural, not to say political, systems in mind. Into this category would come the *kilkhozy* type of village in the USSR, the canal colony villages of the Indian Punjab, and the *ujamaa* settlements of Tanzania. In Israel there are two kinds of planned village: the co-operative settlement and the collective settlement or kibbutz (Fig. 14.9). The former is circular and focuses on central

communal functions, the latter is totally self-sufficient, in which people live, eat and farm together, have no private possessions, and share the total income equally among themselves.

Distribution and pattern of rural settlements

Rural settlements can be studied not just individually but also in relation to each other. In particular, their locational characteristics can be analysed, explained and even measured. Within this spatial context are two elements: distribution and pattern.

Strictly speaking, distribution concerns the nature of the spread of settlements of any size across the countryside – where they are located and where they are not. Pattern, on the other hand, concerns the character of the settlements themselves – whether they are nucleated (as villages) or dispersed (as isolated dwellings). The distinction is pertinent since, whereas distribution is normally the outcome of physical factors, pattern tends to result more from economic, historical and cultural factors.

Settlement distributions vary in character, from very sparse to very dense, and can be clustered, random, regular or clustered linear (Fig. 14.10). With each of these, generalisations can be made. First, settlements are usually more numerous on fertile soils and on areas of gentle relief than where natural disadvantages make farming difficult. Secondly, clustered or random distributions are common in regions of uneven topography – especially where water supplies are limited or where sudden changes in soil fertility occur – as settlements congregate in the better locations. Thirdly, regular distributions tend to be found in areas of uniform or flat relief and on lands recently drained or otherwise brought under cultivation. Fourthly, clustered linear distributions occur along human or natural bands – routeways, valleys and coastlines, for instance. For these reasons, settlement densities are generally high in rich farmlands (e.g. the Paris Basin and the English West Midlands) and low in mountainous districts (e.g. the Pyrenees and Wales). Irregular distributions are to be seen in nearly all hilly regions, whereas regular distributions exist in such places as the Ganges Plain, the Canadian Prairies, the Dutch polders, East Anglia and the English Fens. Clustered linear distributions are found along Alpine valleys, the Mediterranean coast and on both sides of the English Channel.

Generalisations such as these are not as simple to make with regard to settlement patterns. This is because, on the one hand, patterns result from various and complex social, historical and political factors (which are difficult to measure) and, on the other hand, they are liable to change over time as farming techniques develop and populations alter in character or expand in number. Further difficulties of analysis arise from the fact that patterns are frequently blurred. Sometimes a clear nucleation may occur, sometimes a clear dispersal, but most often an intermediate pattern exists in which both nucleated and dispersed settlements are found (Fig. 14.11).

Many theories have been put forward in an attempt to account for different settlement patterns. Some link them with agricultural systems, some with the need for protection, some with population size and some with culture. The truth is probably a combination of all four.

There is little doubt that nucleated patterns arise in systems of communal agriculture, as practised under the open field system, whereas dispersed patterns can result from individual cultivation and piecemeal extension of farmland. In Britain, the Saxons demonstrated the validity of the former and the Celts of the latter so that, even today, nucleation is a feature of England and dispersal a feature of Wales and Scotland. There is also doubtless a link between nucleated villages and arable farming, and between dispersed, isolated dwellings and pastoral farming. Animals usually need more attention than crops and therefore require farmers to be closer at hand. In the same way, intensive agriculture probably leads to compact vil-

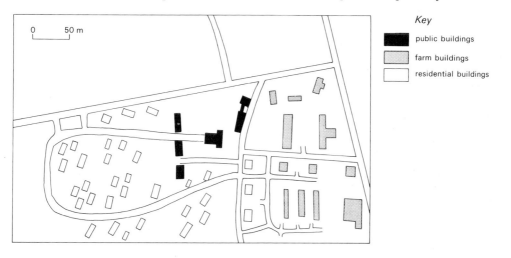

Figure 14.9 An Israeli planned rural settlement: a kibbutz
Here distinct land-use zoning allows for the separate growth of different parts of the village. Such a settlement is common in areas of pioneer advance and agricultural development.

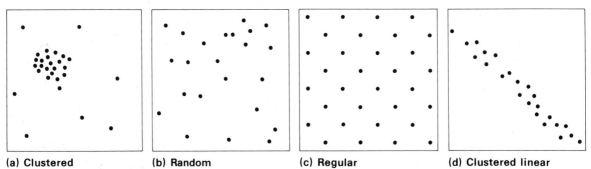

(a) Clustered **(b) Random** **(c) Regular** **(d) Clustered linear**

Figure 14.10 Distributions of rural settlement
Set distributions arise out of distinct physical characteristics and human needs. However, they are not necessarily permanent, but could change with time. Different distribution types may be found in fairly close proximity.

lage communities and extensive agriculture to widespread hamlets and farmsteads. Hilly or mountainous terrain tends to produce more dispersal than does low or flat topography, and the New World generally more dispersal than the Old World. In the Canadian Prairies, isolated farms can be many kilometres apart, a degree of spacing unimaginable in, say, Belgium.

Since villages provide greater protection than isolated dwellings, nucleation is often a reflection of social or political instability. Thus, the Dark Ages in England saw the growth of nucleated settlements, as did 18th century India, the 1950s in Kenya (during the Mau Mau uprising) and, at about the same time, Malaysia during the communist guerilla activity. For the same reason, pioneer regions developed nucleation: the American Mid-West and New England, for instance, both of which suffered from Red Indian warfare.

The greater the population density in a region, the

greater is the likelihood of nucleation, sometimes for no other reason than lack of living space. Where severe overcrowding occurs, this nucleation reaches extremes. In the valleys of Hadhramaut (southern Arabia) dwellings may be in blocks six to eight storeys high – like miniature skyscrapers – and in China some villages are so compact that half their inhabitants are housed under a single roof.

Some cultures are more naturally inclined towards nucleated settlements than others and this fact may occasionally lead to different patterns occurring, even between regions of similar environments and historical backgrounds. Communities with strong family, clannish or tribal ties, for example, are more likely to produce nucleation than communities where such ties are weak. In the North American Mid-West the native Indian reservations have noticeably more nucleated settlement patterns than areas of European colonisation. However, whether this

Nucleated **Dispersed**

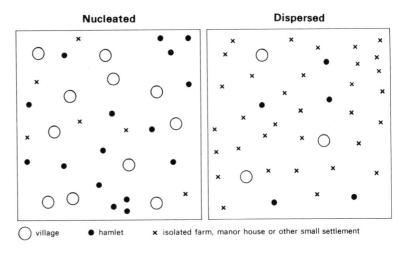

Figure 14.11 Patterns of rural settlement
These patterns evolve through complex interactions between man and his environment. Essentially, patterns reflect the way man lives and makes a living. Even a relatively small area may contain both pattern types.

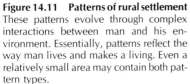
○ village   ● hamlet   × isolated farm, manor house or other small settlement

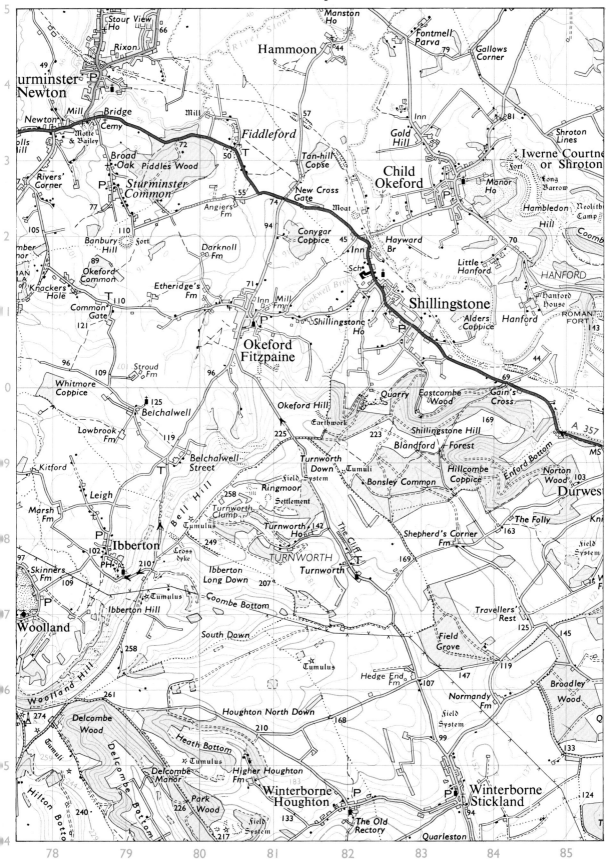

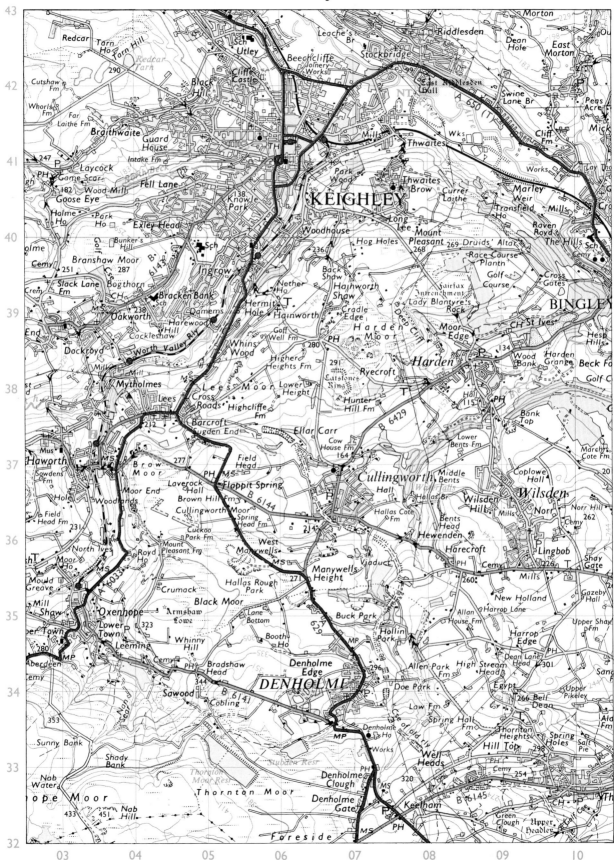

nucleation is related entirely to cultural bonds or to other reasons (economic necessity, strategic motives and so on) is not known.

The above influences help to explain why different settlement patterns might occur, but do not really explain how or why such patterns might change over time. Does dispersal sometimes result from the break-up of original nucleation, or does it pre-date nucleation? In Europe the former seems to have been the case. As civilisation progressed, the need for protection and co-operation (which foster village life) declined and people tended to move out from villages to live on their own lands. This move towards dispersal was further encouraged by the disintegration of feudalism: as peasants became free they tended to move away from the estates of their former landlords. In Germany and Scandinavia this process coincided with upsurges of radical feeling. In France it took place after the Revolution (1789) when the expansion of large estates was banned and lands were divided up among the proletariat. In England, dispersal occurred at the time of parliamentary enclosures when farmers left the villages to live in the midst of their own fields.

In other parts of the world a similar development has taken place. Under the British Empire, for instance, such was the colonial stability created by the *Pax Britannica* that protection became unnecessary and dispersal accordingly resulted. However, the same is not true everywhere. In Russia, Israel and areas of political unrest or declining agriculture, nucleation is growing as farmers leave their homes to seek safety or employment in villages.

In short, both processes may be observed. In regions of nucleation, the loosening of community bonds, the changes in agricultural systems and the decline for the need for protection may encourage dispersal. In regions of dispersal, the need to provide and obtain service facilities may encourage nucleation. Overall, nucleated settlements can be seen as a symbol of constraint – physical or human – and dispersed settlements as a symbol of freedom.

Nearest neighbour analysis

Settlement distribution can be measured mathematically, and in this way it is possible to compare the characteristics of different areas. The method adopted is **nearest neighbour analysis**, using the formula

$$R_n = 2\bar{d} \sqrt{\frac{n}{A}}$$

A is the size of the area concerned; $\bar{d}$ is the mean distance between settlements (taken as an average of the distances between them) and n is the number of villages. R_n represents the nearest neighbour index.

In theory, indices can range from zero (when there is no distribution at all) to 2.15 (when settlements have the maximum spacing and are regularly distributed). A purely random distribution would have an index value of 1.0. Values above 1 indicate a tendency towards spacing and those below 1.0 indicate clustering.

Summary

1 Rural settlements represent the oldest human communities. They developed through agriculture and have remained functionally close to the land.

2 Rural society is more traditional, conservative and stable than urban society, and perhaps has fewer economic or social prejudices. Where industrialisation occurs, the country way of life is breaking down and villages are suffering from the influx of tourists, commuters and retired people.

3 Settlements have developed at particular locations – for water supply, dry land, defence, shelter and aspect, agricultural or trade potential and service opportunities. Military settlements have always existed. Some rural settlements disappear (e.g. after the Black Death), others relocate.

4 There are five distinctive village forms: loose-knit, clustered, linear, open-space and double. These have developed for special reasons: loose-knit for largely cultural reasons, clustered and open-space often for defensive purposes, linear and double for trading reasons.

5 Some villages have been planned from scratch: to replace earlier ones that have disappeared, at a whim of a landowner, to help colonise newly won lands or to provide tourist facilities. Model villages were sometimes built by companies to house a workforce.

6 The pattern of settlements (nucleated or dispersed) concerns the character of settlements – their shape and form. Distribution (clustered,

random, regular or clustered linear) concerns the spatial spread of the settlements – their proximity to each other. The latter can be measured mathematically through nearest neighbour analysis.

Data–response exercises

1 With the aid of sketch maps compare the sites, situations and forms of the following villages on OS map A (Dorset): Sturminster Common, Okeford Fitzpaine, Ibberton, Winterborne Houghton.

2 Using sketch views compare Cordes (Fig. 14.3) and Nun Monkton (Fig. 14.6) with respect to morphology and architectural characteristics. In each case discuss the relationships between village form, topography and agriculture.

3 Describe, discuss and illustrate the distribution and pattern of the rural settlements shown in OS map A (Dorset).

4 What evidence is there to suggest that the pattern of old settlements in OS map B (Yorkshire) is more dispersed than the pattern of newer settlements? Why should the new settlements in this area be more nucleated?

5 Apply nearest neighbour analysis to the area covered by OS map A:

(a) Measure the distance from each village and hamlet containing a church with either a tower or spire to the nearest other similar settlement.

(b) Add up all these distances and divide the total by the number of links. This will give the observed mean.

(c) Determine the density of points (settlements) in the area by using the formula

$$\text{density} = \frac{\text{number of points used in study}}{\text{area of study site}}$$

(d) Calculate the expected mean in a random distribution using the formula

$$\frac{1}{2\sqrt{\text{density}}}$$

(e) Determine the random scale value (nearest neighbour index) by the formula

$$R_n = \frac{\text{observed mean}}{\text{expected mean of random distribution}}$$

(f) Discuss the significance of your answer.

Note: The index number found may not be entirely accurate since nearest neighbour villages, in some cases, may lie just off the map extract.

15 Urban settlement

Introduction

Urban settlements are larger than rural settlements and are, therefore, of greater importance in the human landscape. They are also more dynamic, constantly changing their appearance and character in response to the demands of progress and the variable requirements of man's activities.

This chapter aims to summarise the major aspects of urban settlements as separate entities – their individual features as opposed to their collective interactions. The questions it will attempt to answer are as follows:

- What is meant by the term 'urban settlement', and how do definitions vary?
- How have urban settlements developed over the ages, and what are the forms they have acquired?
- Which factors cause towns to grow and populations to become more urbanised?
- Which functional and physical characteristics distinguish towns, and what factors determine their appearance?
- How are urban settlements distributed, and what patterns can be found in their distribution?
- What influence does each town have over its surrounding area and does such influence change over time?

Definition of urban settlement

Everyone knows what a town looks like and most of us know what it is like to live in or visit one. But how can a town actually be defined and when does a rural area become urban?

The problem is difficult for two reasons. The first is that towns differ widely in size, appearance, form and functions. There are small towns of only local importance and large towns of world importance; there are old towns rooted in an agricultural past and modern towns founded for 20th century industrial purposes; there are towns providing different economic and social services – commercial towns, mining towns, seaside resorts, university towns and so on. The second difficulty arises out of the fact that the countryside is rapidly assuming many of the characteristics formerly thought of as being 'urban'. No longer are rural areas divorced from urban areas, nor do they support only populations that depend upon agriculture. No longer is the dividing line between countryside and town easy to draw.

The distinction between rural and urban areas has become so vague that many geographers now believe no effort at all should be made to differentiate between the two. The United Nations itself has even suggested that settlements should be graded only according to size and thereby placed on a continuum ranging from isolated dwellings in remote countryside to overcrowded inner city districts.

Nevertheless, it remains true that urban areas possess many characteristics that distinguish them from rural areas. These characteristics are physical, economic and sociological. Most towns, for instance, can be identified by their closely packed buildings and streets, high population densities and non-agricultural functions. They are also distinctive in terms of their human aspects: numerous and diverse groups of people living in close proximity, sharing the same social facilities yet lacking strong social contacts. Individual anonymity is often a feature of such areas, together with human mobility (occupational and geographical), social instability, complex class structures, wide variations in human wealth and heterogeneous ways of life.

For census purposes and other statistical records, however, more precise urban definitions must be adopted. This is where confusion may occur, for no universal method exists and individual countries have developed their own classification systems. Some use function as a criterion, some population size, some the form of administration. Israel and Italy define a town as a settlement in which a high proportion of the working population is non-agricultural. In Denmark, Sweden and Finland, it is simply a settlement with at least 250 people. Canada and Venezuela take a population of 1000 as the minimum, Argentina and Portugal take 2000, the USA 2500 and India 5000. In most Central American republics, and in Brazil and Bolivia, almost any administrative centre is labelled a town. In Africa a town is normally a term used only for a European settlement.

Clearly, classifications and definitions of urban settlements vary from place to place and alter according to their use. The distinction between towns and villages is pertinent only for those involved in specialised study, and will be made depending upon the purpose for which the distinction is needed.

History of urban growth

It is not known for sure why the first towns appeared in the world or when they were built. Some probably grew out of villages, as is demonstrated by the fact that they developed in the heart of fertile agricultural areas; others probably originated as commercial centres, and developed in places where farming was difficult but where trade or industry was possible.

The first truly urban settlements were made feasible during the Neolithic Age when agricultural improvements (such as the introduction of the wheeled cart and ox-drawn plough) together with technological progress (including the development of sailing boats, canal systems, irrigation and metallurgical skills) permitted some groups of people to leave farming. Only when agriculture is efficient enough to produce a surplus will populations diversify their occupations – to include hand-manufacture, trade and community organisation – and begin to live in towns.

The earliest urban settlements appeared in Mesopotamia some time between 5000 BC and 3000 BC. They grew up around temples or palaces, and developed commercial functions under the auspices of the priests. The southern part of the Tigris and Euphrates basin in particular had a dense population at that time and its chief city, Babylon, grew to have over 80 000 inhabitants.

In time, trade expanded and more towns appeared elsewhere – in Egypt, the Indus Valley, China and South-East Asia. By 1500 BC, urban life was common around the eastern Mediterranean, and such places as Knossos (Crete), Troy and Mycenae had already come into existence. These benefited from their maritime locations and were able to extend commercial links further afield than had formerly been possible. Copper and bronze were fashioned, paper was made and wealth filtered throughout the then known world.

The growth of Greek civilisation (8th and 7th centuries BC) further spread the idea of urban life as city states like Athens set up daughter settlements around the Mediterranean – towns such as Cumae, Syracuse, Massilia (Marseilles), Cyrene, Neapolis (Naples) and Alexandria. New technological advances took place: improved ships, implements and weapons, and the introduction of coinage, which alone did much to encourage trade and urban growth.

The rise of the Roman empire extended economic progress and new administrative systems over a wider area, and it was not long before towns appeared all over north-west Europe (e.g. Bordeaux, Cologne, Lyons and Paris). London was founded during this period, together with York, Lincoln, Colchester, Exeter, Winchester and other '-chester' towns in Britain. Rome itself grew to have as many as 250 000 inhabitants, but even the colonial centres (those built for strategic and commercial reasons) often attained populations of 100 000. It was from its towns that the Roman empire spread its culture, law and language across the map.

Only limited town growth took place after the collapse of Rome. It is true that some urban settlements expanded, but many others stagnated and a great number disappeared altogether. This was partly because the tribes that now dominated Europe – Saxons, Huns, Goths and Vandals – were agriculturalists by nature and preferred to live in small village communities rather than in large towns. Not until the Middle Ages was the idea of urban life revived and towns once more expanded.

From the 11th century onwards, trade spread, new industries and crafts developed, and population grew. Some old Roman towns were rebuilt and enlarged, but many new towns were founded from scratch. Some appeared around cathedrals, castles or markets, some at the coast as ports, and some at the junctions of major trading routes. The great cities of Amsterdam and Venice emerged at this time and capital cities like Paris and London mushroomed, the latter accommodating over 200 000 people by 1600. Meanwhile, German knights and traders carried the concept of town life into Eastern Europe, and the

Moors founded new cities in Spain, such as Granada and Cordoba.

It was also during the Middle Ages that towns first appeared in the New World. In the Andes and Central America, the Inca and Aztec civilisations built cities; elsewhere urban development came as a result of European exploration and colonisation. The earliest of these were no more than small coastal trading posts, but these soon developed their own hinterlands and expanded accordingly as commercial centres. Williamsburg (Virginia), Montreal, Boston, New Amsterdam (later renamed New York), Rio de Janeiro, Melbourne and Sydney were among the first.

The greatest extension and expansion of urban settlement the world had ever known came during the 18th and 19th centuries. Improvements in agriculture, increased trade and more efficient communications all had the most profound influence on towns, increasing their size, speeding their growth, and transforming their characteristics. The use of new raw materials, fuel supplies and machinery (collectively the outcome of the Industrial Revolution) resulted in the appearance of the first real industrial towns. Some of these were grafted on to existing settlements and others, such as Birmingham, Bradford and Middlesbrough, grew almost from nothing (often on or near coalfields). In either case they were distinctive: congested working-class housing grew up around factories and mills, with a minimum of open space. Such towns originated in Britain but later appeared elsewhere – in Western Europe, the USA, Russia, Japan and, during this century, in China, Africa and South America.

Since then only the intervention and use of the internal combustion engine has had such a marked influence on urban settlement.

Planned urban settlements

Almost every age has seen the appearance of some planned urban settlements: towns and cities that did not develop gradually but were built from scratch to preconceived designs. The Ancient Greeks planned towns, so did the Romans, both choosing to adopt the regular grid layout for their streets and building plots. Later, during the early Middle Ages, more planned towns were constructed, many being **bastides** or military towns built by kings or local barons to protect their rural possessions and populations from

attack. These are common in the French Aquitaine (such as Montauban), in Wales (Flint, Conway and Caernarfon) and in northern England (Carlisle and Berwick). Only later did they become commercial centres and lose their military function.

During the Renaissance (c. 15th–18th centuries) towns and cities were planned not so much for economic or military reasons as for pure ostentation. The emergence of powerful rulers, the increase in wealth and, above all, the flowering of 'good taste' led to the building of settlements whose magnificence and splendour may never be surpassed. Often surrounding great palaces, these towns were usually formal in layout (in squares or crescents) and Baroque in style (an architecture combining, in bizarre fashion, Classical and Byzantine). In Europe these marvellous places include Versailles, Karlsruhe, Nancy, Potsdam and Mannheim. In Britain the designs were slightly more restrained, but no less spectacular, resulting in the Classical Georgian spa towns of Bath, Buxton, Harrogate, Leamington and Tunbridge Wells.

Other planned cities have been constructed for administrative purposes and, in many cases, as capitals. One of the first of these was St Petersburg (now Leningrad), founded in 1703 by Czar Peter the Great. Later examples include Washington (founded by the American revolutionaries), Ottawa (rebuilt during the middle of last century), New Delhi (designed by Lutyens at the beginning of this century) and Canberra (founded in 1908). These have features in common: all are regular in plan, tend to centre on government buildings and attempt to combine beauty with functional efficiency. Each was intended as an urban showplace in order to enhance the prestige and reputation of its respective country in the eyes of foreigners.

Two recent examples of planned capital cities are Brasilia and Islamabad, both founded in the 1950s but neither yet fully complete. The former was sited in the heart of the Brazilian interior with the intention of counteracting the natural movement of population to the coast and, especially, to the South-East. It is a 'futuristic' city whose daring architecture has attracted both admiration and criticism. Islamabad is situated near the old town of Rawalpindi and is Pakistan's attempt to develop not just a new administrative city but a major industrial centre as well. It is planned to accommodate over 2 million inhabitants when finished. Built on the linear pattern, its architecture combines modern functionalism with traditional Muslim designs.

Figure 15.1 Caernarfon from above
This vertical air view shows the compactness of the town, and its varied morphology.

CAERNARFON – A WELSH BASTIDE TOWN

Caernarfon dates back to the 13th century when, during the reign of Edward I, it was founded as one of the many 'English boroughs', which were built to encircle the newly subjected kingdom of Wales. Its site was chosen for its defensive properties: being at the mouth of the River Seiont and on a peninsula overlooking the Menai Strait it is surrounded on three sides by water. Such a defensive situation was strengthened by the construction of 3 m thick town walls (see Figs 15.1 & 2).

The castle and original town were laid out as a planned whole, the castle itself being positioned at the river end of a rectangular enclosure within which a grid road pattern was established. A central market place was also designed, thus facilitating the settlement's later growth as a commercial centre for the surrounding countryside.

Today, the town walls are almost totally intact and the castle is one of the most complete in Britain. The narrow streets of the old town still end at impressive gateways and many of the buildings date from the late Middle Ages.

Not until the 19th century did Caernarfon expand out-wards from its original confines and develop new func-tions. The railway line and, later, the metalled roads brought industry and suburban growth; the rise in leisure activities and public interest in historic buildings brought holiday-makers. The town's original defensive and mar-ket functions have given way to tourism – with new shopping facilities within the old town and hotel accom-modation in the inner suburbs. Because of the sheltered nature of the Menai Strait – once so important for Caernar-fon's ocean trade – the town has also become a yachting haven.

With a population now approaching 12 000, Caernar-fon ranks as a minor regional centre – the lowest category in the urban hierarchy of Wales. In the next category upwards comes Colwyn Bay (40 km distant), a major regional centre with a population of around 50 000. Further upwards still comes Wrexham (80 km distant), a provincial capital with a population of around 110 000. At the top of the hierarchy, of course, is Cardiff, the national capital, with a population of 300 000.

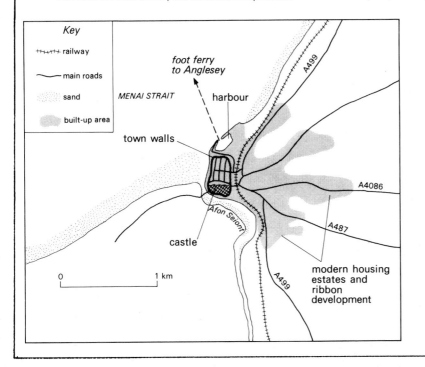

Figure 15.2 The position of Caernarfon
Centred at a river mouth, the town has expanded in wedges inland towards the Snowdonia mountains.

Urbanisation

As urban settlements continue to grow in both size and number, so the proportion of the world's popula-tion living in towns and cities is rising (see Fig. 15.3). It is the increase in this proportion that is called urbanisation, and it has become not only one of the main features of life over the last 200 years, but also one of the major causes of modern economic and social problems. In 1900 only about 10% of the world's population could be called urban. Today about 30% live in towns, and by 1990 this figure is likely to be over 50%.

The reasons for urbanisation are numerous and complex, but the main factors are summarised below:

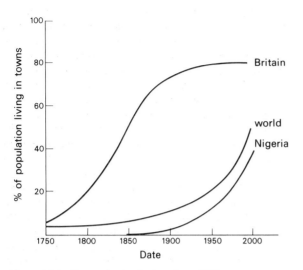

Figure 15.3 Rates of urbanisation since 1750
In developed countries urbanisation has slowed up, but at a high level; in less developed countries urbanisation is beginning to accelerate. Such graph lines can be linked to economic and social conditions.

(1) *Agricultural improvements*. Farm mechanisation releases farm labour for work in industry, and increased food supplies sustain a larger non-agricultural percentage of the population. In Europe this movement away from farming was further encouraged by the opening up of the grain lands of North America last century.

(2) *Industrialisation*. Dependence of manufacturing on raw materials and power supplies (e.g. coal) leads to the clustering of factories in relatively few locations. The resulting agglomerations create external economies of scale and industries grow and multiply accordingly. Large-scale output requires large amounts of labour and, as output rises, the demand for labour rises also.

(3) *Market potential*. The development of light industry leads to an increase in the importance of market-orientated locations. Towns provide large, ready-made markets for consumer goods, and therefore attract new industry. These new industries bring with them new labour supplies which, in turn, increase the size of the potential market, the snowball effect being set in motion and urban growth becoming self-sustaining. Industrial links lead to communication development so that towns become route centres, which further attract assembly industries.

(4) *Increased service activities*. Tertiary and quaternary industries grow because of increased trade, higher standards of living and the need for greater economic and social organisation. Many services, by their very nature, tend to be centralised in towns: retailing, entertainment, catering and administration.

(5) *Transport improvements*. Better communications not only encourage the expansion of towns along major routes, and make more easily available the necessary volumes of food for urban people, but also increase population mobility. People are able to move from countryside to towns more quickly and easily than before, so that net immigration into urban areas goes up. In Victorian England the railways were an important factor in urbanisation; many towns grew after the building of a station (e.g. Peterborough and York) and some even appeared from nothing as railway industry towns (e.g. Swindon and Crewe, both of which grew up at major railway junctions). In London, the rail termini (Euston, King's Cross, Paddington, etc.) were originally built on the capital's periphery. They have since been engulfed by later development. In the present century the motor car has extended urbanisation further, causing the dispersal of towns, the spread of suburbs and the transformation of villages into dormitory settlements.

(6) *Social and cultural attraction*. Towns – especially if they are large, old or cultural – may act as magnets to their surrounding populations because of their social facilities: cinemas, theatres, art galleries and so on. Many people simply enjoy being near the centre of urban life. Towns also provide better utility services (gas, electricity, piped water) than country areas and this too attracts population.

(7) *Increased education*. As people become more knowledgeable, their ambitions grow. Towns are seen as centres where opportunities abound and success is more attainable. The mass media have helped distribute knowledge over a wide area and may have made some people more aware of the inadequacies or limitations of their lives. Years ago ignorance of towns would have preserved much personal contentment in the countryside.

(8) *Natural population growth*. Towns expand largely through immigration, but some growth is naturally self-sustained. Birth rates are often higher in urban areas, partly because the immi-

grants are usually of fertile age and partly because the greater wealth of towns makes large families more viable.

(9) *Perception*. Often people move to towns because they think life there will be better than in the countryside – because they imagine the 'streets are paved with gold'. Once settled in an urban area, they may find they were wrong but cannot afford to move back whence they came.

Characteristics of urbanisation
Urbanisation does not always take the same form, nor does it progress at the same rate everywhere. In older countries, such as those in Europe, it is generally dispersed, the growth in the urban population taking place through the expansion of numerous towns. In newer countries, such as those in Africa and South America, urbanisation is more concentrated and only a few very large cities are emerging.

The rate of urbanisation varies from country to country because the factors leading to it (those listed above) vary in their effectiveness. In the past, what is now termed the developed world experienced the highest urban growth rate and the greatest rural depopulation, so that now most advanced countries have over 70% of their inhabitants living in towns. In the developing world, urbanisation was very slow or non-existent until fairly recently. Today the situation is reversed. In countries like Britain, West Germany and the USA the urban proportion of population is about constant as the migration into towns is balanced by the migration into the countryside of people escaping from the drawbacks of urban life. In developing countries, on the other hand, a fast rate of urbanisation – seen as a means to development – is leading to rapid urban growth.

At this point, two tendencies should be borne in mind. The first is that, in developed countries, town growth still continues physically if not in terms of population. The same number of people may live in urban areas, but at lower densities. In England and Wales, for example, the total urban area doubled between 1900 and 1960 whereas the percentage living in towns rose only from 77% to 80%. The second point to remember is that, in developing countries, the rate of urbanisation is not as fast as town growth might imply. Rural as well as urban populations continue to expand rapidly and it is likely to be many years before the percentage living in towns rises above 25%. The countryside is becoming more densely peopled but no less agricultural in nature.

Urbanisation brings in its wake both advantages and disadvantages. On the one hand it leads to material and economic progress, higher living standards, more efficient and specialised services and the development of new technologies and skills. Through the accumulation of wealth, also, cultural activities thrive: art, literature, music, philosophy. On the other hand it threatens the world's most fertile agricultural areas, exacerbates water-supply and waste-disposal problems, produces serious traffic congestion (which can hold back industrial expansion), creates noise-, air- and water pollution, and causes personal frustration and stress.

At its worst, urbanisation – especially when accompanied by rapid town growth – can result in slum housing and poverty. In 19th century Britain, the desire of landowners or building contractors to house as many people on as little land as possible led to the notorious 'back-to-back' terraces (found commonly in Yorkshire) and tenement blocks (found commonly in north-east England and Glasgow). Certainly these closely packed buildings helped solve the housing shortage problem, and probably also provided better living conditions than were common in rural districts at that time, but still their conditions were meagre in the extreme. In present-day Africa, South America and Asia the **shanty town** is a normal addition to many a city. The suburbs of urban settlements in these areas are often unable to cope with the floods of people moving into them (from the countryside and inner-city areas), having insufficient jobs, houses or social facilities. The result is that the new immigrants squat on the edge of city areas and build themselves temporary homes: usually rudely constructed shacks of scrap metal, wood, tar-paper and hessian. Agglomerations of these shacks form settlements of a unique character which, although exhibiting some positive characteristics, lack schools, metalled roads, piped water, sewerage, power supplies and health facilities. Fire risks are extremely high and diseases are rampant. Only slowly are such places being replaced by permanent dwellings, but these are frequently in the form of tower blocks of flats (as in Rio de Janeiro and Hong Kong), which are themselves likely to deteriorate into slums.

Pre-industrial cities

Many towns and cities have grown into major urban centres yet have never experienced the changes brought about by an industrial revolution. These have

Figure 15.4   A pre-industrial city: Venice, Italy
The skyline of jumbled roofs is broken only by church domes and campaniles. The city grew rich in medieval times on trade with the Orient and is constructed on numerous islands in the lagoon (wood piles acting as foundations). Most of the buildings date from the Renaissance. This photograph shows the north-west view towards the Italian mainland to which Venice is joined by a causeway. On the left horizon is part of the Mestre industrial complex, which is partly responsible (through pollution) for the present sinking of Venice.

been called **pre-industrial cities** and were first studied by Gideon Sjoberg (*The pre-industrial city: past and present*, Free Press, 1960).

These urban settlements tend to have particular characteristics. Generally they are small – rarely having populations above 100 000 – and are compactly situated within defensive walls. They lack any plan or form: houses are closely packed together and streets are narrow and irregular. Unsophisticated technological skills limit the heights of buildings so that the general low uniformity of the skyline is broken only by the occasional palace, castle or religious centre, which therefore dominates the townscape.

Pre-industrial cities have two main functions: to serve as markets for local agricultural goods and to accommodate craft industries. These, together with poor transport facilities, are reflected in their land-use patterns. All social, administrative and religious buildings are situated at the centre and these are surrounded by the opulent homes of the wealthy inhabitants. Wealth and social class decrease away from the urban core so that the poorest people live around the town's periphery. Also around the periphery would be those who work in agriculture or in noxious pursuits considered intolerable nearer the town centre (such as those causing excess noise, fumes or smells). In some cases a **faubourg** may be found outside the defensive walls, a settlement on its own exclusively for foreigners.

There is, in addition, often a cell-like structure in which occupational, cultural, ethnic or family groups reside in separate compounds or 'quarters'. So crowded and clustered are the buildings in these quarters that land-use types may be superimposed, one plot of land serving more than one function. A temple or church, for instance, might also act as a school or even a market place and within a single dwelling a man might live, produce his wares, store them and sell them to the public.

Of course, not all towns unaffected by industrialisation will exhibit all the above characteristics. Even so, many pre-industrial cities can be identified, especially in the Third World, for example the old cities of Delhi (India), Lahore (Pakistan) and Ibadan (Nigeria). In Europe many towns were once pre-industrial in form (during the Middle Ages) and some of these still survive almost intact. In England they include Shrewsbury, Norwich, Salisbury and Winchester, and across the Channel Venice (Fig. 15.4), Amsterdam, Bruges, Ghent and Heidelberg. Often considerable modern commercial and industrial development

has taken place beyond the old medieval sections of these towns, but their pre-industrial hearts have remained – largely because of planning restrictions and positive conservation policies.

The distinction between pre-industrial and industrial cities is not all-embracing. Many urban areas do not fit neatly into either category: tourist resorts, dormitory towns and military camp settlements, for example. Nevertheless, the identification of the two kinds of urban settlement is pertinent since it is through the comparison of the two that we can measure the impact of industrialisation.

Urban regions

'Million cities'
The many cities now in existence with populations exceeding one million are a fairly recent phenomenon. In 1800 there was only one 'million city': London. Paris became the second in 1850 and New York the third in about 1870. By the turn of the century there were eleven, by 1940 fifty-one, and by 1970 there were 129. Today 'million cities' number over 180 (see Fig. 15.5). There are now thirty cities with over 3 million people and fourteen with over 5 million people.

Of today's million cities, nearly a third are political capitals, over a third are great commercial ports, and most are multifunctional cities especially noted for their high levels of industrial output and internal commerce. A few were once capitals and still retain much of their former prestige and character: Leningrad, Rio de Janeiro and Karachi. All are easily accessible: most are sited at the coast, on navigable rivers or lakes and, except for a few ports, nearly all are situated in industrialised or rich agriculture regions. Some are primate cities containing high proportions of the total populations of their respective countries: Buenos Aires, Santiago, Copenhagen, Paris, Vienna and Tokyo.

Conurbations
In many areas, continued town expansion has led to the appearance and spread of conurbations: gigantic urban sprawls containing, normally, over a million people and sometimes as many as 5 million or more. They are usually based on heavy manufacturing or commerce and are sited either on major coalfields or around natural harbours (coastal conurbations such as the Christchurch–Poole belt are the exception and tend to be relatively small).

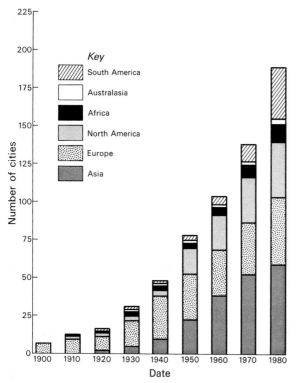

Figure 15.5 Growth of million cities in the 20th century
Over 10% of the world's population lives in million cities, most of which are situated in the Temperate Zone. However, in recent years many new million cities have started to appear within the Tropics.

Most conurbations are without form or plan and, although they are served by a close network of communications, through-movement (that is, travel across them from one side to the other) can be difficult owing to congestion and the lack of direct routes. Closely packed working-class housing and factories are common features of their central parts, and monotonously uniform suburban districts characterise their outer areas.

Two types of conurbation may be identified: **polycentric** (or polynuclear), which have resulted from the fusion of a number of distinct towns and cities, and **monocentric** (or uninuclear), which have resulted from the expansion of a single major city. Examples of the former include the Pittsburgh district, the western side of Lake Erie, the Lille–Roubaix–Tourcoing triangle in north-east France, the Ruhr coalfield (West Germany) and Upper Silesia in Poland (around Katowice). Examples of the latter type include London, Paris, Buenos Aires, Sydney and Chicago. In general, polycentric conurbations are

characteristic of 'old' countries (like those in Europe) and monocentric conurbations are characteristic of 'new' countries (such as those in the Americas, Africa and Australasia).

In Britain, conurbations were first officially recognised in the 1951 census, and today seven major and numerous minor ones exist, the latter including relatively small urban agglomerations such as Sheffield–Rotherham, Greater Bristol, Teesside and the Potteries. The eight large conurbations in England now account for about 40% of the total population of the country, the one conurbation in Scotland (Clydeside) accounting for about 30% of the total population of that country. (See Table 15.1.)

Of the conurbations in Europe, that around the Ruhr coalfield in West Germany is the largest. This covers an area of 2500 km² and extends across more than 50 km from Duisburg in the west to Dortmund in the east. At its northern edge lies Recklinghausen, at its southern edge Solingen, and to the west it is bounded by the Rhine. In total more than 10 million people live in the area, working mostly in heavy industry (especially iron and steel), chemicals and textiles.

Megalopoli

In some parts of the world, even larger urban areas are now developing (Fig. 15.6). These vast urban zones or megalopoli are supermetropolitan regions, which extend across many kilometres and link formerly separate conurbations. Some of these zones have evolved naturally – such as those on the Atlantic Seaboard of the USA and in Japan – and some have appeared by design or by planning – such as that in the Netherlands.

In England two megalopoli may form in the not too distant future. One will be U-shaped around the southern Pennines and stretch from Leeds to Liverpool via Sheffield, Nottingham, Derby and Stoke-on-Trent. The other may result from the merging of London and Birmingham along the line of the M1 motorway and through the New Town of Milton Keynes.

It has been suggested that a colossal urban belt may even emerge eventually from Liverpool to northern Italy. This would run through London, across the Straits of Dover through Randstad, the Ruhr region, along the Rhine Valley to Lorraine and Geneva and then, jumping the Alps, to Milan and Turin. Such a belt would be 1280 km long and accommodate 80 million people.

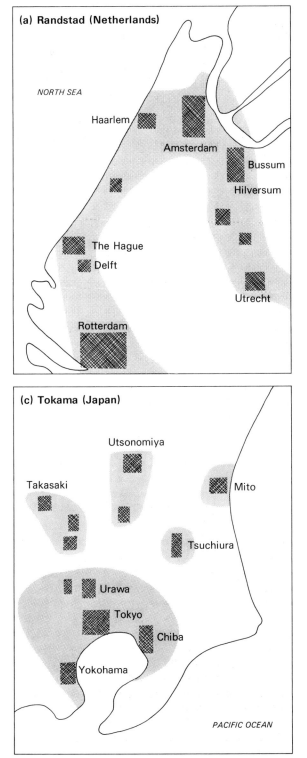

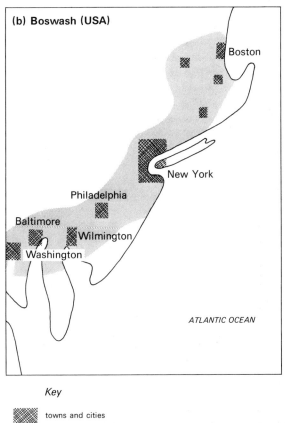

Key

▨ towns and cities

░ areas of present and future suburban growth

Figure 15.6 Urban zones

These topological maps show polycentric megalopoli, each growing out of previously separate conurbations. When complete, Randstad will be a ring urban zone, Boswash a linear zone and Tokama a dispersed zone. Randstad forms a comprehensive and economically balanced urban unit in which the old towns have functional specialisation: Rotterdam as a trade and heavy industry centre, The Hague as political capital, Amsterdam as a tourist and cultural centre, Hilversum as a light engineering centre. The 'green heart' at the centre will act as a recreational area and source of food. In time, Randstad may grow further and extend corridors of development southwards into Belgium and north-east France and eastwards into the Ruhr conurbation of West Germany. Boswash stretches over 700 km and also contains cities that are functionally complementary: Washington DC being the federal capital, New York the industrial and commercial centre, Boston the educational and artistic centre. Tokama is the largest of all urban zones – and likely to grow even larger in the near future. Tokyo is the administrative and cultural centre, Yokohama the main trading port.

Table 15.1 Britain's conurbations.

Conurbation	Approx. area (ha in thousands)	Approx. population (thousands)	Approx. density (persons/ha)	Character
Greater London	158	6696	42	monocentric; grew as a major port and as the national administrative capital: centre of commerce and high-level service activities
West Midlands	90	2645	29	polycentric but dominated by Birmingham; grew near a coalfield and based on the iron and steel and engineering industries
Greater Manchester	129	2595	20	polycentric but dominated by Manchester; grew on a coalfield and based on the cotton industry
West Yorkshire	204	2038	10	polycentric including Leeds, Bradford, Halifax, Wakefield; grew on a coalfield and based on the woollen industries
Clydeside	85	1713	20	monocentric around Glasgow but now extending along the Clyde estuary; grew on a coalfield and as a shipbuilding port
Merseyside	65	1513	23	monocentric around Liverpool; developed near a coalfield and as a major trading port
Tyne and Wear	54	1143	21	polycentric but dominated by Newcastle; grew on a coalfield and as a shipbuilding centre
South Yorkshire	156	1302	8	polycentric but dominated by Sheffield; grew on a coalfield and based on the iron and steel industry

SPECIALIST TOWNS

Many towns and cities have gained an international reputation for certain specialist functions – for activities and features that not only bring in many tourists and visitors but also engender considerable wealth through related or subsidiary industries. Such towns may either have become well known gradually over the centuries (and so have little need for publicity) or else may have invited attention by advertising.

Some of the principal specialist town functions are as follows:

Religious towns
These normally form the focal points for particular religions or beliefs. They contain many religious buildings (both for worship and administration) and cater for both tourists and pilgrims. Into this category would come Rome (for the Roman Catholic Church), Mecca (for the Muslim world) and Salt Lake City (for the Mormons).

Education towns
These usually centre on universities and colleges. They frequently have historic foundations and contain student-based functions – book retailing and publishing, entertainment services, high technology activities. Examples of such towns include Oxford and Cambridge (UK), Heidelberg (W. Germany) and Cambridge, Massachusetts (USA).

Festival towns
These may have acquired singular reputations for annual events, often of a musical nature but possibly of theatrical, poetic or social activities. Such places would have to cope with a seasonal influx of tourists who would fill the hotels and provide finance for associated business – the making of souvenirs, catering, local craftwork and currency exchange. Examples of such festival towns are many: Edinburgh (the performing arts), Salzburg (Mozart music and opera), Bayreuth (works of Wagner), Oberammergau (decennial Passion Play), Haarlem (flowers and bulbs).

Conference towns
These are a fairly recent phenomenon. They provide large scale facilities for lectures and conferences, mass hotel accommodation and numerous leisure features such as casinos and night clubs. Occasionally, such places may also cater for major expositions. In Britain, examples include Blackpool, Scarborough and Brighton; in mainland Europe there are Frankfurt, Leipzig and Liège; in North America there are Dallas, Memphis, Toronto and Vancouver.

Distribution and hierarchies of urban settlements

Like all other aspects of human activity, urban settlements are distributed irregularly over the Earth's surface and owe their locations to numerous and diverse factors: relief, climate, mineral deposits, communications, trade patterns, historical evolution and culture. Some towns have special siting requirements, like mining and quarrying towns, tourist resorts, seaports and strategic bases; some were built to preconceived plans; and some appeared almost by chance.

Notwithstanding this, there is still some evidence to suggest that regular distributions do occur among urban settlements and that such distributions do relate to functional hierarchies. Mention has already been made (Chs 9 & 13) of the theories of Christaller and Lösch. These theories apply to all settlements, rural as well as urban, and state that central places of equal size are equally spaced out and that larger settlements are fewer and more widely dispersed than smaller settlements.

Such theories have been successfully tested against real world examples and it is now generally accepted that regularity is an inevitable result of rational human behaviour and uniform topography. The more homogeneous the natural environment, the more regular will be the spatial pattern of towns and cities. Thus, in the Mid-West of the USA, the level nature of the Mississippi Lowlands ensures that the major urban settlements correspond with Christaller's suggested distribution (see Fig. 15.7).

Apart from Christaller and Lösch, other academics have also studied the general nature of the functional hierarchies and have attempted to rank settlements in descending order of political and economic importance. Some geographers have taken administrative and political functions as the major criteria, others have taken retail facilities (the number and floor space of department stores, supermarkets, chemists, ironmongers, and so on). One hierarchy categorises, in descending order, metropolitan capital, provincial capital, major regional capital, minor regional capital – these becoming more numerous down the hierarchy. Thus, such a four fold ranking applied to England might be exemplified respectively by London; then cities such as Manchester, Birmingham, Liverpool and Newcastle upon Tyne, in second place; followed by such county towns as Ipswich, Norwich, York, Exeter and Nottingham; leaving in fourth place a number of such market towns as Kettering, Dun-

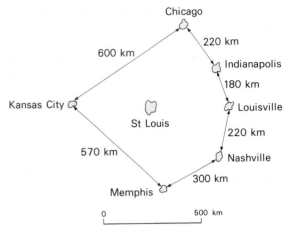

Figure 15.7 Urban distribution in mid-west USA
Each of the above towns, except Chicago which has 3 million people, has a population of around 0.6 million. St Louis is equidistant from its six neighbours (400 km). The resulting distribution shows regularity and has some similarity to that suggested by Christaller.

stable, Beverley, Harrogate, Ludlow and Penzance. Another similar hierarchy numbers regional centre, area centre and local centre – these possessing a different range and a decreasing number of retail outlets.

Urban fields

Urban settlements exist not in isolation but within the functional framework of entire regions. Every town has links with its surrounding area and these can be physical, economic or social. This interaction is of mutual benefit since advantageous movements flow in both directions: that is, movements of people, goods, finance, information and influence from a central town to its surrounding region and from the surrounding region to a central town.

Functional regions of this type have various names: *umlands, spheres of influence, zones of influence, tributary areas,* and *urban fields.* The last named is perhaps the most generally accepted. Sometimes the term 'city regions' is used, but this must be deprecated since it leads to confusion: first, because some geographers use the term to describe particular quarters or zones within towns; secondly because other geographers use the term specifically to mean the cluster of urban settlements sometimes found around large cities. A city region, defined in the latter sense, comprises all those places dominated by a major city, which have expanded rapidly because of their rela-

SOLVING THE HOUSING PROBLEM IN THIRD WORLD CITIES

The great majority of towns and cities in the Third World contain spontaneous or squatter settlements. These are collections of rudely built shacks put up by newly arrived migrants from the country or from other parts of the urban area. They may occupy any waste land, next to railway tracks, beside warehouses and factories, along the edges of major trunk roads. A large area, normally at the periphery of an urban settlement, where masses of shacks are built is most commonly called a **shanty town**. Here, social facilities (such as housing, medical and educational amenities) are at a minimum and human problems (such as overcrowding, diseases and dissatisfaction) are at a maximum. In some parts of the world a shanty town may be considerably larger in area and more populated than the city it adjoins.

Naturally most Third World governments are concerned about the existence of squatter settlements in and around their major cities, and many are attempting to deal with the problem. A summary of schemes aimed at solving this problem follows.

Housing schemes

(1) *Adaptation and rehabilitation*. In some countries – in Bolivia, Mozambique and Pakistan, for instance – governments have attempted to improve shanty-town conditions without removing the inhabitants. The shacks are strengthened and reinforced with concrete, water and electricity supplies are installed, roads are paved and the squatters are given some landowner rights and are encouraged to organise self-help programmes to improve medical and educational services. Such schemes have the advantage of cheapness but often fail radically to correct poor shanty conditions: germs are not destroyed but merely continue to fester behind brick and plaster; metalled road surfaces might actually hinder drainage and runoff – leading to sewage collecting on the surface. Physically and socially, such rehabilitation schemes merely paper over the cracks.

(2) *Site and service programmes*. These are becoming the most commonly undertaken schemes in the Third World and have been introduced most successfully in Malawi, Zambia, Brazil and India. Each programme involves, at government expense, the construction of 'informal housing'. An area of open land is allocated and then divided into small housing plots. Boundaries are pegged out; basic sewage, power and water facilities are provided; and simple concrete buildings are put up, perhaps no more than four walls and a roof. Then, newly arrived migrants are given landownership rights and are installed into the housing plots in order to complete the work for

themselves. It is up to the dwellers themselves to improve, decorate, subdivide and furnish the buildings provided, or if only land plots are given, to construct their entire homes. Such site and service schemes are fairly cheap and have the added advantage of maintaining the social cohesion of immigrant groups.

(3) *Formal development schemes*. These have become less commonly undertaken over the past 20 years but can still be seen in action in such countries as Singapore and Hong Kong. By these programmes, massive public building results in the appearance of formal estates, most often in the form of high-rise blocks. Recent immigrants whose shanties have been bulldozed away are rehoused in these flats and apartments. In Caracas (Venezuela) 85 superblocks (each at least 15 storeys high and containing up to 450 separate apartments) were built between 1954 and 1958; in Singapore today, well over half of the total population lives in dwelling units constructed by the city's Housing and Development Board.

However, formal housing schemes have generally not been a great success. Apart from their expense, which many governments cannot afford to bear, they have resulted in many social problems. In particular, public housing frequently imposes conditions with which the ex-shanty dwellers are unable to comply. They may not be able to pay the demanded rents and are prohibited from earning extra money by subletting or using their homes for trading purposes. Many cannot adjust to clinically clean conditions or to high-rise living in which the keeping of pets or other animals is not allowed and the growing of vegetables is impossible.

The fact is that the 'unofficial' character of shanty towns is more suited to the circumstances of mass immigration into Third World cities than is the 'official' character of formal public housing estates. Shanties do have distinct advantages for squatters: they give families control over their own budgets (how much to spend on housing and how much on food and clothes); they give a sense of security by providing family groups with land plots, cheap shelter and a foothold on urban living; and they allow people to progress at their own speed, altering and improving their surroundings to suit their changing needs and wants. Indeed, it can be argued that shanty towns are the best possible structures to accommodate newly arrived immigrants from the countryside, since they allow for a slow adjustment to urban society. They are cheap, flexible and geared to the requirements of their inhabitants.

tionship with it. These places are related to each other by functions. Some may be commuter towns, some manufacturing centres and some shopping or administrative towns, but all are bound together by social and economic links and usually, also, by a continuous built-up area. Such a city region is often dominated by light industry and may resemble a loose-knit conurbation or even a megalopolis.

An urban field, conversely, includes the whole area – rural as well as urban – that is influenced by a central town and whose character is determined by the nature of that town.

Functional relationships within urban fields

(1) *Agricultural relationships.* The surrounding countryside supplies a town with essential food provisions, especially with fruit, vegetables and dairy produce. In return the town acts as a collecting and marketing centre for agricultural commodities.

(2) *Industrial relationships.* Urban factories may process the raw materials obtained from the surrounding area – lumber mills, textile manufacturers, steel works, canning industries, and so forth. The local countryside may use products supplied by the town, e.g. farm machinery, artificial fertilisers and transport equipment.

(3) *Trade relationships.* The surrounding region provides a proportion of the retail custom of a town's shops. In return the town supplies specialised services, e.g. professional and health facilities.

(4) *Commuting relationships.* People travel into a town to work, perhaps from dormitory towns some distance away or from small villages. In the reverse direction some town dwellers might travel out from the urban centre to work in small-scale agriculturally based industries in surrounding villages.

(5) *Social relationships.* People travel into a town from the surrounding region to enjoy the entertainments, recreational or cultural facilities offered (theatres, museums and so on). Many town dwellers travel in the opposite direction to the countryside or to the coast for picnics, recreation or sightseeing.

Size and shape of urban fields

Unlike the theoretical market areas of Christaller and Lösch, urban fields are neither regularly shaped nor consistently sized according to the population and functions of their central places. Some urban fields are determined in form by relief and may be elongated along valleys or truncated by mountains, rivers or coastlines; some are shaped around communications, broadening near railway stations or extending along main roads to become star-shaped. Some urban fields are small, others very large; some towns have strong functional links with their surrounding regions, others have weak links.

The factors influencing the size of urban fields are numerous and include the character of the towns themselves, the urban facilities offered, the employment structure, and the population density of the regions. Although large towns generally have large urban fields and small towns small urban fields, towns of equal size do not necessarily serve areas of equal size; neither does it follow that towns of the same size and functions exert equal influence over their respective regions. Many have a weak influence over their hinterlands yet are bigger than others that have a strong influence. Industrial and mining towns may provide fewer shopping facilities than some smaller mixed-function towns and thus have more limited urban fields (being smaller in size or weaker in influence). Other towns may exert a disproportionately large influence over their surrounding areas – the centres of communications, for instance (such as Brecon, Wales), administrative capitals (such as Bodmin, Cornwall), or tourist resorts (such as Oban, Scotland). These tend to have very large urban fields. Such differences can, for example, be seen in the English Midlands (Fig. 15.8).

The employment structure of a town can be viewed as a combination of two elements. On the one hand, there are **basic** or **city-forming** workers whose efforts are towards the production of goods and services for

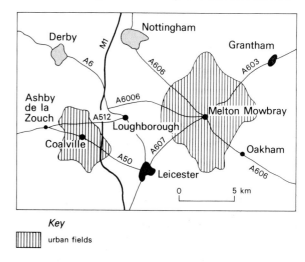

Figure 15.8 Two urban fields in the English East Midlands
Melton Mowbray has about 20 000 inhabitants. It is an old market town with strong ties with its surrounding rural area and has a fairly large urban field. Coalville is larger (population 30 000), but has grown only as a coalmining town over the past 200 years. Consequently it has a fairly small urban field. The shapes of these two urban fields are also influenced by the proximity of nearby towns and the nature of transport facilities.

'export', that is, for helping to earn money from the surrounding region. On the other hand, there are **non-basic** or **city-serving** workers whose efforts are to serve only the needs of the urban population itself. The latter, it can be argued, depend on the revenue earned by the former for their existence. It can also be argued that the ratio of basic to non-basic workers in any town can determine the size of its urban field. A town with a high proportion of basic workers will normally have a larger sphere of influence than will a town with a low proportion of basic workers. Tourist resorts generally have a very high proportion of basic workers and therefore have large urban fields to match.

Areas where population density is fairly low, or where towns are widely spaced, tend to produce large urban fields, whereas areas of fairly high population density, or where towns are close together, tend to produce small urban fields. Towns within a conurbation, for example, would have limited spheres of influence since they must compete with all other towns within the same conurbation. Towns in the heart of farmland, conversely, may have influence over very large agricultural areas. Halifax (population 100 000) and Norwich (population 120 000) are towns of similar size but their urban fields are vastly different in extent. The former only caters for people close by, since other people use other parts of the West Yorkshire conurbation (Leeds, Bradford, Huddersfield and so on). The latter serves much of Norfolk since it is the only town of significance between Cambridge and Yarmouth. Whereas Halifax's urban field measures less than 20 km across, that of Norwich measures over 70 km across.

Both the shapes and sizes of urban fields, then, vary from settlement to settlement. It should further be borne in mind, however, that both are dynamic and change continually in response to economic, technological and social conditions. Adjustments may result from developments in transport, urban facilities and human behaviour. Improved public transport or the greater use of the motor car will widen urban fields, whereas deteriorating public transport will have the opposite effect. Similarly, the opening of a new stretch of motorway or a new bridge will extend a town's influence. A newly built shopping precinct will probably encourage people to travel into a town from further afield than before; the closing of a popular department store may severely restrict the area from which the town's custom is drawn.

In short, the shapes and sizes of urban fields differ in time as well as in space, and each one is unique at any moment.

The delimitation of urban fields

All towns have more than one urban field. This is because they offer a wide variety of goods and services, some of which are of low order, therefore having relatively small market areas; others of which are of high order, having relatively large market areas. The area served by a tobacconist will be smaller than that served by a department store, and a university or hospital will have a different sphere of influence from that of a bank, a solicitor or an administrative centre. In other words, around each town there is likely to be a succession of urban fields of different shapes and sizes, each being the zone of influence of a different urban function or facility.

It is also true that a town's total influence over its surrounding region tends to decrease with distance. The functional linkages of a central place are likely to be strong with its immediate environs and weak with far-off districts.

For these reasons, and to simplify the mapping of spheres of influence, settlements are sometimes said to have two grades of urban fields: a primary one in which movements are mainly concerned with low-order goods and services and take place fairly frequently, and a secondary one in which high-order linkages exist and where movement is infrequent. The former covers a fairly small area, the latter a much wider area. London, for instance, has a strong influence over south-east England, its primary urban field, and also a degree of influence (administrative and financial) over the whole of Britain, its secondary urban field. Similarly, Newcastle upon Tyne has a small primary urban field (Tyneside) and also a larger secondary urban field (the North-East).

Since all settlements have their own urban fields, it should be stressed that there is a hierarchy of urban fields just as there is a hierarchy of towns. The fields of the largest settlements encompass the fields of smaller settlements which, in turn, encompass those of yet smaller settlements. It should also be pointed out that urban fields tend to overlap since people near the edge of two or more fields have a choice and may use each town equally.

For many years geographers have known about the existence of urban fields, but only recently has the recognition of their significance made the delimitation of such areas a central part of human geography. They can help to indicate the nature of urbanisation, aid the understanding of interactions between places,

228

and provide a background knowledge to the general study of regional geography. Urban field analysis can also prove essential to administrative reorganisation and planning.

But how may urban field delimitation actually be undertaken? The task is a difficult one and involves not only careful data collection but also the use of exact cartographic techniques. The type of index employed must be chosen so that it reflects the functions of the settlements being studied, and the eventual urban field maps must avoid confusion and complexity.

At the initial stage, delimitation requires field work. This can be approached in two ways. The first is urban orientated and involves gathering information from the town itself – by asking town dwellers about the areas being served by their various activities: by their shops, schools, clinics and so forth. The second is countryside orientated and involves gathering information from a town's surrounding region by asking country dwellers which places they use for various functions.

In either case, greatest accuracy will be achieved by the adoption of as many data indices as possible. However, this is often impossible or impracticable. Geographers have therefore devised a number of short cuts, normally requiring the use of just one index to express a town's links with its surroundings. This index may be one of the following:

(1) local newspapers and their circulation areas
(2) public transport services
(3) retail deliveries and districts served by wholesalers
(4) education catchment areas
(5) commuter range
(6) hospital and clinic catchment areas
(7) entertainment catchment areas or local radio coverage
(8) membership catchment areas of clubs and societies (e.g. women's institutes, boy scouts)
(9) ecclesiastical parishes and church catchment areas

Of these the first two are, perhaps, most commonly used, partly because information is readily available and data collection simple, and partly because each method provides a fairly accurate gauge of a town's influence. Newspapers, in particular, are useful, and evidence can be gleaned from local news articles, the source of the small advertisements or personal-column entries, and from the areas covered by the 'Births, Marriages and Deaths' pages. In addition,

information can be obtained from the publishers regarding the circulation area. Public transport services can usually be ascertained from rail or, better still, from bus timetables. These provide knowledge not only about the furthest points served by transport but also about frequency of services, thereby giving evidence of both the size and strength of a town's influence.

Should more than one index be used for the same town, the boundaries of the resultant urban fields will rarely correspond. Some functions will cater for just a small catchment area (e.g. a primary school) whereas others will cater for much larger areas (e.g. a newspaper). The result will be a succession of urban field boundaries.

In his study of urban fields in Somerset, Bracey simplified the various boundaries to create three zones of influence. These he called *intensive area*, *extensive area* and *fringe area* (Fig. 15.9). Smailes has suggested an alternative to these: a *core area* (mainly the built-up area itself); the *outer area* in which the town is used for high-order infrequent services and

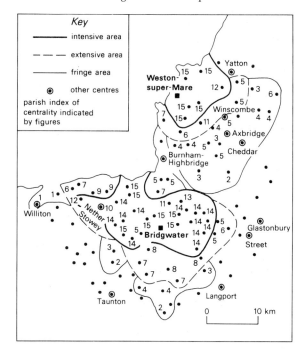

Figure 15.9 Urban fields in Somerset, England
Bracey used the country-oriented approach to delimit urban fields. Using a questionnaire survey he identified urban zones of influence from the data collected from each village, villagers being asked which town they used for selected functions. (After Bracey, H. E. 1953, *Transactions of the Institute of British Geographers* **19**, pp. 95–105.)

low-order frequent services; and the *fringe area* in which the town is used only occasionally for high-order goods and services (*Geography of towns*, Hutchinson, 1966).

Break-point theory

However carefully field work is undertaken for urban field delimitation, and whichever indices are used, various problems arise when spheres of influence are actually mapped. One of these occurs when urban fields between two towns fail to meet, creating a vacuum in which inhabitants are apparently not served by either town. In Figure 15.9, Burnham-Highbridge is in such a vacuum. Another problem arises when two urban fields overlap, so that some people will use two towns equally and those towns will compete for the custom of those people.

It is to solve the latter problem that *break-point theory* has been formulated. This employs a gravity model whereby a single line of demarcation can be established.

The breaking point between two settlements divides those people who will use one town from those who use the other. If the two towns in question are of equal size and importance, the breaking point is, of course, likely to be halfway between them. If they are not of equal size, the larger settlement will probably have a greater attraction than the smaller settlement, and the breaking point will be nearer the latter. To find the exact point of break, the following formula can be applied:

$$\text{distance of break point from A} = \frac{\text{distance between A and B}}{1 + \sqrt{\dfrac{PB}{PA}}}$$

where PA and PB are the populations of the two settlements in question.

If two towns A and B have populations of 25 000 and 9000 respectively, and are 32 km apart, the break point can be calculated thus:

$$\text{distance of break point from A} = \frac{32}{1 + \sqrt{\dfrac{9000}{25\,000}}}$$

$$= \frac{32}{1.6}$$

$$= 20 \text{ km}$$

Alternatively, a similar formula can be used with the number of shops or a centrality index instead of population – although such methods would require more fieldwork.

Summary

1 Urban settlements are places divorced from primary activity; they have high densities of buildings and people, and contain diverse mixture of social functions. However, exact definitions are difficult since all classification is subjective.

2 Towns first appeared after agriculture had become sufficiently productive to support a non-farming population – in ancient Greece and Rome, medieval Europe and in the colonial New World.

3 Although most have evolved naturally, some towns have been planned and built from scratch, often as military or administrative centres. Such urban areas have definite, usually regular, patterns.

4 Urbanisation (the growth of urban populations) has arisen for economic and social reasons. However, the advantages offered by towns are frequently perceived erroneously. Too rapid urbanisation results in slums and shanty towns.

5 Sjoberg recognised distinctive features of pre-industrial cities – low skylines, irregular morphologies, cellular land-use patterns and a fall in social class outwards from city centres.

6 Conurbations occur when towns merge, megalopoli when conurbations join. Such urban zones can be polycentric or monocentric in form, evolutionary or contrived in origin.

7 Urban settlements fall into natural hierarchies, usually based on size and function. Their distribution can be explained by means of central place theory (Christaller), especially in areas of flat relief (e.g. mid-west USA).

8 Urban fields (hinterlands subject to the socio-economic and political influence of central towns) vary in shape and size according to relief, communications and urban function. It is possible to delimit urban fields using statistical information only (by using break-point theory) or by fieldwork (by using commuter, shopping, newspaper or transport data).

Data–response exercises

1 Using Figures 15.1 and 15.2 draw a sketch map to show the form and internal structure of Caernarfon. Analyse the structure you have drawn.

2 Account for the differences in the rates of urbanisation shown in Figure 15.3 and discuss the possible changes likely in the future. Examine the factors that may have led the graph curve for Britain to be S-shaped. Is such a curve typical of a developed country?

3 With the aid of sketch maps, compare the sites, situations and forms of Keighley and Denholme in OS map B (Yorkshire).

4 Discuss the factors that have led to the growth of million cities (Fig. 15.5). Why has the growth rate of million cities in the Third World (especially South America) far exceeded that in the developed world (especially Europe) during the 20th century?

5 Calculate the break points between selected towns in an individual region (e.g. East Anglia) using an atlas to obtain the distances between them, and official statistics to find the size of the urban populations. On a sketch map, plot the fields of influence to be expected from your calculations. What local characteristics (e.g. relief, quality of communications) are likely to modify this theoretical model? (A similar exercise could be undertaken using the number of services offered in a town instead of population figures.)

6 Account for the sizes and shapes of the urban fields of Somerset shown in Figure 15.9. To what extent is topography a determining factor?

16 Internal structure of towns and cities

Introduction

In all countries the combined effects of population increase, urbanisation and improved technology have caused urban settlements to grow and become more complex. It is therefore not surprising that, over recent years, much interest has been generated in the internal characteristics of towns and cities.

Urban areas are heterogeneous structurally and demographically: their buildings vary in size, shape, height, arrangement, age and function; their populations vary in density, occupation structure, social status and often, too, in ethnic or cultural origin. This chapter is largely concerned with this heterogeneity of character. However, before proceeding to further detail, two points should be stressed. The first is that urban characteristics are the result of numerous factors – topography, history, economic motive, human culture and chance – all of which make every town unique. The second is that urban characteristics are never static but are subject to constant change in both time and space. Nevertheless, certain general patterns and processes of internal urban characteristics can be identified. Regular features do occur, and these can be accounted for and mapped. These common elements of towns and cities will be discussed in the ensuing pages.

The questions to be addressed in this chapter are as follows:

- To what extent do the land-use differences within towns exhibit fixed spatial patterns and, if such patterns exist, are they found in all towns to the same extent?
- What factors determine the internal structure of urban settlements, and how important are those factors?
- How do city centres differ from other urban areas, and what affects the commercial and industrial character of these city centres?
- What are the special characteristics of suburbs, and how are shopping districts distributed within them?

- What are the social and political features of urban areas, and how do these change?

Theories of urban structure

A town might appear at first to be an amorphous mass but, on closer inspection, it may in fact conform to a particular shape and be similar to many other towns. It might be square, rectangular, round, semicircular or, most commonly, stellate, stretching out in a star-shape along major communication routes.

In the same way, the internal structure of a town may not be entirely haphazard. It is usually possible, for example, to distinguish a degree of order in certain urban land-use groupings: buildings of different sizes, shapes and functions being so spaced as to produce distinctive 'urban regions' or zones, each one having its own material and human character, which makes it different from adjacent areas.

Even a glance at a map or a stroll through the streets will reveal some of these zones. Main shopping districts, office premises, administrative buildings and entertainments usually occupy central positions; working-class housing may be found close to factories (which themselves may align with railways, roads or canals), and high-class housing may be found on the urban periphery.

Sociologists and urban geographers have made a special study of these land-use zones and have attempted to explain their origin, development and spatial distribution. In particular, three main theories of urban structure have been proposed: the Concentric, Sector and Multiple-Nuclei theories. These are examined below and with reference to Figure 16.1.

The Concentric theory
This was first suggested by Burgess after a study he made of the structure of Chicago in the 1920s (R. E. Park & E. W. Burgess, *The city*, University of Chicago Press, 1925). He put forward the idea that towns expand outwards evenly from an original core so that each zone grows by gradual colonisation into the next

THEORIES OF URBAN STRUCTURE

Concentric model
(after Burgess)

Sector model
(after Hoyt)

Multiple-nuclei model
(after Harris and Ullman)

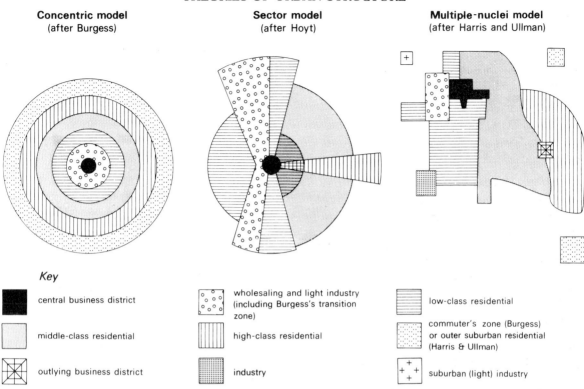

Key

■ central business district

▨ middle-class residential

⊠ outlying business district

wholesaling and light industry (including Burgess's transition zone)

high-class residential

industry

low-class residential

commuter's zone (Burgess) or outer suburban residential (Harris & Ullman)

suburban (light) industry

Figure 16.1 Models of urban structure
Such idealised land-use zones are the result of both physical and human factors. In the Hoyt model a prevailing easterly wind is assumed, causing the low-class housing to be on the western edge of a city.

outer zone. At any one time a number of more or less concentric zones can be identified, giving inland cities an annular or ring-like structure and cities along waterfronts a semi-annular structure.

Figure 16.2 shows the land-use pattern of Chicago as seen through Burgess's theory. At the centre is the **central business district** (CBD), in Chicago called the Loop, which is the focus of commercial, social and civic life. Encircling this is the **transition zone**, an area of industrial premises interspersed with old private houses, many of which are either being adapted for offices and warehouses or are being subdivided into smaller dwelling units. This is the zone often characterised by slum property, immigrant ghettoes, unstable and low social groups, vice and crime. Around its periphery lies a zone of working-class housing, partly occupied by families (including immigrant groups) that have migrated out from the transition zone, and partly occupied by residents who have lived in the same buildings all their lives, many having been born there. In this zone people still need to live in close proximity to their places of work,

lacking the means to commute long distances. The fourth zone is one of middle-class housing, being spacious, usually single-family dwellings intermingled with some exclusive residences and high-class apartment buildings. The outermost zone is called the **commuter zone** and may lie beyond the continuous built-up area of the town. Sometimes within open countryside there are large, detached houses, and villages which have taken on dormitory functions.

It should be remembered that the concentric theory is an 'ideal' model applicable only to Western or developed regions and in the absence of what Burgess called 'opposing factors' — local topographical features, important communication routes and so on. In reality, concentric zones are unlikely to be seen so clearly.

The Sector theory
The idea that urban growth is a process based on sectors rather than on rings first developed during the 1930s and was mostly due to the work of Hoyt who,

233

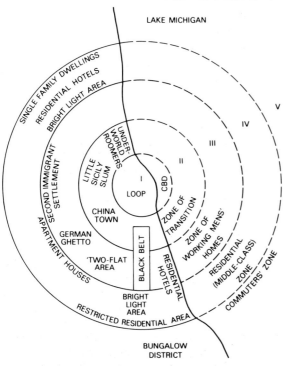

Figure 16.2 The urban zones of Chicago (after Burgess)
Chicago has been built on flat land at the edge of one of the Great Lakes. Landwards there are no physical obstacles to urban expansion.

incidentally, also studied Chicago as Burgess had done. Although he continued to accept the character of the CBD at the city centre, Hoyt argued that land-use groupings spread out in wedges. Once contrasts between material and population regions have developed – for whatever reasons – their continued existence is assured.

Thus, the establishment of a high-class housing area will lead to the most expensive sites for new houses being situated on the periphery of that area. Similarly, new working-class housing is likely to be built next to existing working-class housing and new industries adjacent to old industries. In this way differences in land use are perpetuated as a city expands.

Why this should be so is the result partly of human nature and partly of basic economics. It may also be the result of physical geography and transport routes. A valley floor provides flat land and is normally utilised for road, rail or canal construction. It is therefore also likely to attract industry, which would thus form a linear industrial district. A ridge of high ground, conversely, may create an elongated residential district.

Hoyt supported his model by examining the spatial variations of rents charged in large cities (that is, the extent to which rents altered from area to area). He found that the land rents changed by sectors rather than concentrically. Nevertheless, it would be wrong to see this theory as a radical departure from Burgess's Concentric theory. Rather, it is a modification of it. There is, for instance, often an annular zoning identifiable within individual sectors. Inside a residential sector, old houses may be found in the inner portion and new houses in the outer portion. In a wedge-shaped industrial sector, the factories towards the urban centre may be declining or changing their function; those at the outer edge may be expanding. Mann has actually combined the two theories into a compromise model for British towns (Fig. 16.3).

The Multiple-Nuclei theory
This theory was first proposed in 1945 by Harris and Ullman (in H. M. Mayer & C. F. Kohn (eds), *Readings in urban geography*, University of Chicago Press, 1959). They claimed that, although concentric and sector patterns may exist, reality is far more complex than those two theories imply. In particular, they argued that city growth from a central core is complicated by the existence of several subsidiary centres, each one acting as a growth pole to development. Around such nuclei, land uses that are related or functionally linked will cluster. This creates an overall cellular urban structure.

The types of places that may act as nuclei include airports, industrial complexes, waterfronts, ports or railway stations, university campuses and the hearts of originally independent villages or towns (which may become service centres). Land-use functions cluster in this way because of common siting requirements or mutual economic benefits. Industries may seek locations near transport termini; residential areas may cluster around shopping districts. On a smaller scale, services may seek prestigious postal addresses or be found in competitive groupings: doctors in London's Harley Street, the jewellery quarter in Birmingham and, in almost every town, estate agents and solicitors' offices along particular roads.

The multiple nuclei theory is not as simple in its proposed urban pattern as the two theories already mentioned, but it is probably more accurate. It also has the added advantage of flexibility since it can be applied to most large cities in the world (in both developed and developing regions). The zoning suggested in Figure 16.1 provides merely an example. In

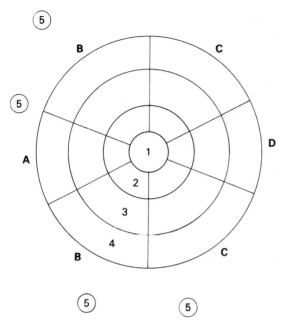

Key

A   middle-class sector

B   lower middle-class sector

C   working-class sector (including council estates)

D   industry and lowest working-class sector

1   CBD

2   transition zone

3   zone of small terraced houses in sectors **C** and **D**; larger by-law housing in sector **B**; large old houses in sector **A**

4   post-1918 residential areas, with post-1945 housing on the periphery

5   dormitory towns within commuting distance

Figure 16.3 The British compromise model of urban land use (after Mann)
An interesting attempt to combine the concentric and sector models was made by P. Mann (in *An approach to urban sociology* 1965, London: Routledge). He devised the above model of internal structure of a hypothetical British city. Assuming a prevailing west wind, he placed industry on the eastern edge of the city and high-class housing on the western edge, so that fumes from the former would not waft over the latter.

reality the character of land-use distributions around growth poles is determined by the unique factors of site and history of any individual city.

Structure theories and their application

Although the theories outlined above do not fit any real towns exactly, they do serve as useful guidelines towards an understanding of land-use patterns within urban areas generally. By studying particular towns and applying structure models to them, evidence can be obtained both for reasons why a regular pattern exists and for reasons why irregularities might occur.

Towns embody the main elements of these theories to varying degrees and in various combinations. Generally speaking, small towns (especially very old-established towns on flat topography) exhibit concentric zones, medium-sized industrial towns have sectors, and large towns have multi-nuclei patterns. It is also generally true that the larger the town

the greater will be the tendency for it to show aspects of all three models.

Many urban geographers have successfully applied Burgess's theory to old British towns. It has been found that many contain four distinct ring zones. The central zone is normally the oldest part (often of medieval origin) now transformed largely to business uses – offices, hotels and shops. The second zone is one of decaying Victorian property with mixed land uses and heterogeneous population. The third zone is a suburban area, mostly built between the two World Wars. The fourth zone consists of fairly open country containing dormitory settlements and a commuter belt. Many English county towns exhibit this type of pattern, their cathedrals forming the centre of their respective CBDs; Salisbury, Canterbury and Lincoln (Fig. 16.4) can be taken as typical examples. Elsewhere the Sector theory may be seen to be more relevant. Abroad it has been applied to Calgary (Canada) and in Britain to many small industrial towns, for example those in the Scottish central Lowlands, South Wales and on either side of the English Pennines. Perhaps most common of all are those settlements that show both concentric and sector patterns. Such settlements can be found all over the world and tend to be those places that have experienced a long and diverse history of urban growth. Indeed, almost every town of over 300 000 inhabitants is likely to show a mixed land-use zonation: such a pattern is evident in British towns such as Sunderland (Fig. 16.5), Sheffield, Nottingham, Huddersfield and York; in West German towns such as Frankfurt, Hanover and Stuttgart, and in Indian towns such as Nagpur, Lucknow and Patna.

However, one interesting point to note is that those settlements that reflect both concentric and sector models in the developed world are essentially differ-

Figure 16.4 Lincoln: an English cathedral city
Once a Roman *colonia* (military settlement), Lincoln grew rapidly during the Middle Ages, becoming wealthy on the wool trade. The castle and cathedral both date back to the 11th century. After the Industrial Revolution, further growth took place (based partly on local iron ore deposits) and port facilities expanded on the River Witham. This view is north-eastwards; in the distance is the line of a Roman road. Today Lincoln is both a tourist centre and an important heavy engineering centre. The CBD — or CCC (central commercial core) as it is often called in the case of fairly small towns and cities, where its features are less distinctive — can be seen in front of the cathedral.

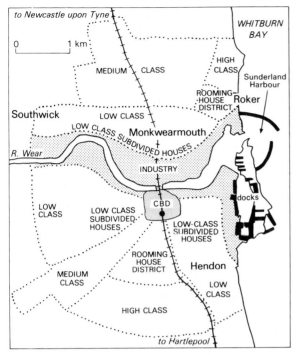

Figure 16.5 Internal structure of Sunderland, England
This pattern seems to suggest a combination of concentric and sector models. The CBD is centred on the railway station and shopping district (now a pedestrian precinct). The industrial belt aligns with the river and sea front. It is interesting to note that, to the north, industry repels all but low-class housing whereas, to the south, the existence of the CBD allows one area of middle-class housing to be located centrally. (After Robson, B. T. 1969. *Urban analysis.* Cambridge: Cambridge University Press.)

ent from those in the less developed world that indicate both models. This is related to all manner of social, cultural and historic factors (see Fig. 16.6).

Mendoza (Argentina) was a colonial town which has subsequently grown with improvements in local agriculture and the development of domestic industry. The CBD moved away from the old colonial centre after the building of the railway line and the construction of modern factories. Shanty towns have recently appeared on the town's periphery.

Bradford was a small village which expanded rapidly during the Industrial Revolution. The original settlement became, in time, the CBD, consisting of three distinct sectors: the wool warehousing and office area, the banking and shopping area and the educational and entertainment area. Around this centre is a ring of Victorian and Edwardian terraced housing, which enveloped such nearby villages as Manningham and Little Horton and, even by the 1930s, had become semi-slum property. Here small

industrial units and, after 1950, large numbers of black and Asian immigrants, moved in to give the area many of the typical features of a transition zone. Beyond this region are council estates and private housing blocks built earlier this century and, beyond these, outlying villages such as Allerton, Cottingley, Eccleshill, Woodhall and Wibsey have now developed commuting functions. Across these ring zones are industrial sectors extending along the streams towards Frizinghall, Thornton, Clayton and Bowling. (The structure of Bradford has been studied in detail by Richardson in *Geography of Bradford,* published by the University of Bradford, 1976.)

The Multiple-Nuclei theory is most applicable to conurbations where minor towns have been engulfed by major ones but continue to function as secondary foci within the resulting agglomerations. It can also be seen to work in many colonial cities in Asia and Africa which have separate European and native centres, each one generating its own growth. Los Angeles has a definite multiple-nuclei pattern and in England special studies of Bristol and Hull have shown that these cities also possess separate growth points. In Bristol there are two shopping centres: Broadmead, where the old market once stood, and another near the university. In Hull the two nuclei are the medieval port and the Victorian railway station.

In the world's largest cities all three model patterns may be observed in superimposition. Sydney (Australia) is such a place: concentric rings of residential development, together with sectors of industries, to the south of the harbour and, within these, 'district zones', which are self-contained social entities.

Perhaps the best example in Britain of a city that combines all three models is the London conurbation. Here the overall pattern is concentric: the CBD being within the original medieval capital (between the Tower, Westminster and Oxford Street); the transition zone existing around this, to include such areas of Victorian development as Holloway, Camden, Notting Hill, Kennington and Elephant and Castle; residential areas further out (working-class housing in areas like Tottenham, Wembley, Sudbury and Clapham, middle-class housing in Enfield, Finchley, Harrow, Wimbledon); and finally the commuter zone within and beyond the Green Belt (including the New Town ring). In addition, sectors of land use extend outwards from the centre: zones of heavy industry and working-class housing along the Thames estuary, the Lee Valley and Wandle Valley, and zones of high-class housing from Regent's Park to Totteridge

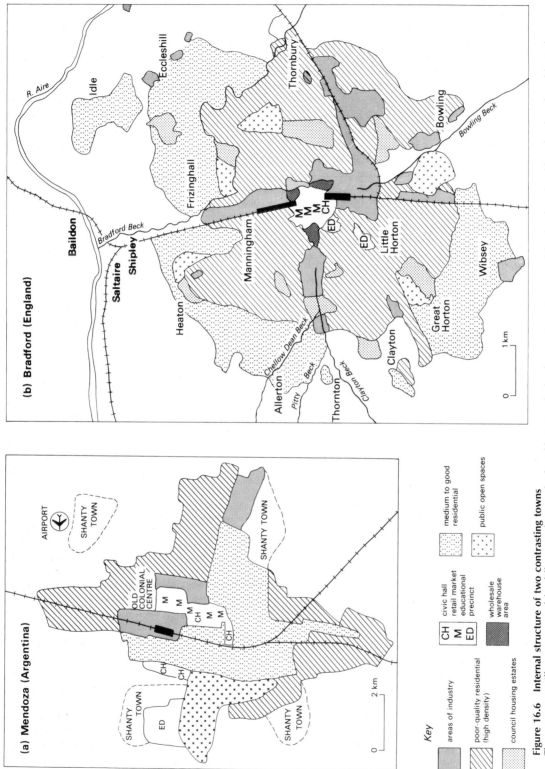

Figure 16.6 Internal structure of two contrasting towns

These two maps illustrate some of the differences that may be found between the land-use patterns in towns of the developed and less developed worlds. Each town has a centrally located CBD and an overall concentric sector structure. However, whereas Mendoza shows the quality of housing decreasing away from the centre (with shanty towns on the periphery), Bradford shows the quality of housing increasing away from the centre (with modern suburbs on the outskirts). Mendoza can be viewed as a Third World pre-industrial city, Bradford as a First World industrial city.

and from Kensington to Richmond. The separate nuclei that can also be identified include the City (business), Westminster (administration) and the West End (shopping and entertainment), the centres of originally independent towns, the railway stations and Heathrow Airport.

Although different land-use patterns may coexist, it has been suggested that they develop individually during different periods in a town's growth. Early growth may be around a central area and other nuclei; later growth would be conditioned by transport routes which create a sector pattern; and finally, adjustments of land use in response to land value changes would reflect a concentric element. Whether this is always true is, of course, open to question.

In any case the study of land-use patterns within towns and cities is difficult, the more so since, today, the process of natural sorting may be distorted by artificial factors. Local authority and central government planning might lead to the deliberate creation of new housing estates, industrial complexes and shopping centres, none of whose locations may correspond to set structures.

URBAN VILLAGES

Within many a town and city there are often to be found traditionally distinct enclaves or quarters which – in human terms if not in physical terms – stand apart from the rest of a built-up area. These enclaves have a social cohesion – a community spirit – more normally associated with rural settlements: intense feelings of kinship among the inhabitants, high levels of social and cultural contact, a well developed sense of neighbourliness, and a possessive, introvert, conservative desire to remain separately identified.

Such areas are known as urban villages and are most common within conurbations where the need for personal identity is perhaps greatest: people tending to feel threatened in crowds. Inside smaller urban settlements, there is usually less necessity for certain residential groups to establish themselves as distinct, the feeling of minority status being lessened. Inside large zones, people tend to react against the potential loss of individuality caused by urban expansion.

The distribution of urban villages within urban regions is random. They frequently grew around an old-established shopping centre or a historic focal point – castle ruins, a medieval guildhall, an old village green and so on. They also may have some aesthetic attractiveness and physical distinctiveness – on a hill-top site, within a river meander, or else along a valley floor, for example. In size they vary from very small – perhaps a handful of streets and less than a couple of thousand population – to a fairly large urban sector – many square kilometres and a population above 10 000.

Examples of urban villages abound. In London there are Chelsea, Barnes, Highgate and Hampstead. In New York's Manhattan there are Greenwich Village and Harlem. Paris has such distinctive sectors as Montmartre, Buttes de Chaumont and Gobelins; Athens has Plaka and Kifissia; Rome has Trastevere and the Ghetto.

Bid-rent analysis

Although urban land-use patterns are the result of all manner of physical and human factors, it can be argued that they are essentially the outcome of economic motives. Recognition of this fact has led to the development of **bid-rent** analysis.

There is competition for all urban sites. The final occupation of each site is achieved by the land use which can derive the greatest utility or profit from that site and which is able to pay most for it. Competition is keenest at the centre of a city partly because this provides the most accessible locations and partly because land here is most scarce. For this reason, land is most expensive at the city centre and the rents charged for it are at their highest. As demand for land decreases away from the centre, and as land becomes more plentiful, bid-rents fall. In other words, the rents people are prepared to pay per square metre of land decrease with distance from a city centre.

Figure 16.7 shows a simplified example of the types of land use that may compete for urban sites and the bid-rents offered by each. At the centre, retailing can outbid other potential uses because it relies on accessibility more than others and, being most profitable, can afford higher rents. Further away from the centre, shops offer progressively lower rents since their profitability decreases with less accessible sites. Between distances A and B from the city centre, offices can bid higher rents than can retail uses (since they are less dependent upon accessibility) and residential uses (since they are more able and willing to pay for the relatively high cost of land). At the outer margin, competition diminishes and the price offered for land by housing is higher than that offered by either retail or office uses. The resulting pattern is similar to that envisaged by Burgess.

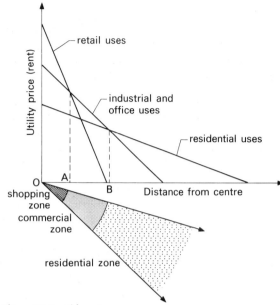

Figure 16.7 Bid-rent curves
These show the relationships between the value of land (the rents that can be achieved) and the use of land. The more valuable the land, the more intensive and profitable will be the land use.

However, a simple pattern like this is likely to be modified in the real world. On the premise that accessibility determines land values, it is to be expected that bid-rents will be greater along major lines of communication (especially roads) than away from such routes, and to be particularly high at junctions. Therefore, a more accurate representation of changes in land rents is likely to be that shown in Figure 16.8. In addition there may be yet more determinants of land values: distance from the nearest regional shopping centre, proximity to a railway station, population density, and the prestige status of an address.

It is interesting to note that a correlation often exists between bid-rent curves and building heights. Where land values are high, buildings also tend to be high so that the greatest possible use is made of the land. As land values decline, building heights decline as the need for intensive land use diminishes. Thus, in physical profile, towns may not be dissimilar to the shape shown in the rent cone diagram (Fig. 16.8); that is, the tallest blocks (usually of offices) being at the city centre, along major routeways and at road intersections, many reaching skyscraper proportions. New York is a prime example of a city where this shape occurs. (Only where planning restrictions prevent the rebuilding of historic inner city areas is it found that high-rise development occurs towards an urban periphery – as in the case of Paris.)

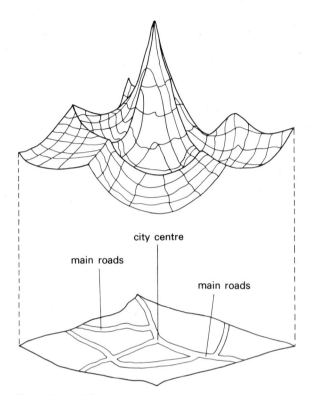

Figure 16.8 Bid-rent cone
The more expensive the land, the more intensive will be the land use, and the higher will be the average building height. High buildings tend to use land more efficiently and profitably than low buildings.

Peripheral pressures

The processes of urban expansion and changing land-use structures are largely the result of centrifugal and centripetal forces. The former encourage the outward movement of people and businesses, thereby causing the dispersal of human activity and the relocation of urban sectors and zones. The latter encourage the inward movement of people and businesses, causing a concentration of human activity.

The main reasons for these forces are listed below.

Centrifugal forces
(1) Traffic congestion, noise and pollution at city centres make living and working there unpleasant, as do high crime rates and vandalism.
(2) Open land towards an urban periphery allows for low-density development, easy vehicular movement and car parking, all of which are necessary for modern industry.

(3) Land values and rates decrease away from city centres.

(4) High building densities towards city centres may make industrial expansion costly or impossible.

(5) Houses in inner urban areas are generally small, cramped and often obsolete; houses in outer urban areas are generally larger, more spaced out and modern.

(6) Some people seem to have a natural desire to live near the countryside.

Centripetal forces

(1) Site attractions like a port or route junctions may encourage industrial growth at city centres.

(2) Accessibility, which is necessary for many businesses, is increased by rail and bus termini.

(3) Functional magnetism and linkages create land-use groupings in which activities benefit from close proximity: lawyers, bankers, clothing retailers, for example, tend to cluster.

(4) Locational prestige results in certain locations becoming particularly attractive to certain land uses: Kings Road (London) for fashion and clothing establishments, Pigalle (Paris) for entertainments, Fifth Avenue (New York) for high-class shops.

(5) Large blocks of flats and offices in or near city centres help offset the cost pressure of high land values.

(6) Entertainments and cultural facilities attract people, especially during leisure hours.

(7) Human nature causes some people to want to live or work 'at the centre of things' and other people to cling to sites no longer suitable for residence or business.

The central business district

A city centre is the hub of business and civic life and it exhibits distinct physical and human features which distinguish it from all surrounding areas. For example, there is normally a concentration of shops and offices, a large number of public buildings, hotels and places of entertainment. These features draw people from the whole urban area (and beyond), from different ethnic groups and from all social classes, and serve the entire community of a region. Such a concentration of buildings and population leads usually to vehicular and pedestrian traffic congestion.

This innermost section of a city can normally be distinguished from the surrounding areas because, beyond the CBD, urban characteristics change: land becomes less intensively used, car dealers, garages, warehouses and workshops begin to appear in greater profusion; old houses (once homes of the wealthy) are converted for professional and other commercial functions or are subdivided into flats and bed-sitting rooms; and extensive features like railway stations and university campuses appear. Those shops and offices located outside the central urban area are fewer and more scattered than those inside and serve smaller sections of the population.

The high land values within the CBD result in buildings that are not only tall but also multifunctional. Ground floors are normally occupied by shops that can attract passers-by with their window displays; higher floors (for which slightly lower rents are charged) are usually rented by professional and office workers or by people not concerned with central services – accountants, solicitors, literary agents, hairdressers, printers, book-binders and high-class clothing manufacturers.

The small residential population within the CBD gives rise to a transitory character whereby streets and buildings are congested during the working day but are deserted at night and at weekends. Only the 'bright light' districts around places of entertainment are busy at leisure times.

CBD characteristics do not necessarily produce a mixed or complex pattern of land use. Indeed, the contrary is often true since an ordered arrangement may be identifiable. In particular, two types of zoning may be found: concentric and quartered.

The fact that land values decline outwards from a city centre can produce a CBD zoning not dissimilar (though in miniature) to Burgess's pattern for cities as a whole. Only land uses with a large turnover and high profits can afford the very central locations – department stores, major chain stores and supermarkets. Land uses with a slightly smaller financial turnover and lower profits would exist further out – smaller shops and financial or commercial premises for example, and the least profitable CBD enterprises would be found at the periphery.

Quarters of segregated land use might be superimposed on to these concentric rings, especially within CBDs of large cities. These districts often result from functional interdependence: for instance, a financial and legal area may exist (with banks, estate agents and insurance companies) and a public service area (with hotels, restaurants and cafés). In London there are newspaper offices in Fleet Street, banks in

Lombard Street and bookshops in Charing Cross Road. In New York, Manhattan has a financial quarter in the south and an entertainment quarter (Broadway) in the centre. Paris has a distinct government area, a local administrative area, a commercial area and a cultural complex.

The final characteristics of CBD areas is one of dynamism. Most are continually changing, both in morphology (structure, size and shape) and in social patterns to meet changing economic conditions. Urban renewal, perhaps made necessary by war damage or slum clearance, especially causes change: new

buildings, new roads, new populations. Old shops may be replaced by new office blocks, old theatres by new department stores.

The locational shift of a CBD can be seen through the identification of **zones of assimilation** and **zones of discard**. The former are areas into which a CBD is growing and are characterised by extensive redevelopment and rising land values. The latter are areas from which a CBD has moved and are characterised by low-grade shops, much vacant property and falling land values.

Over recent years a further feature of CBD dynam-

URBAN POPULATIONS

Not only is it true that urban populations are distinct from rural populations in density, composition, mobility, growth rates and occupations, but also it is a fact that demographic characteristics vary from town to town. In other words, urban populations, although sharing the same overall characteristics, are unique in each urban area.

Population density is of course higher in towns than in the countryside, but differences also occur between towns. For example, it tends to be higher in old towns than in new towns and higher in towns of developing countries than in those of developed countries. The highest urban density in the world is Hong Kong (above 50 000 per km^2); Calcutta has about 35 000 per km^2. Of Western cities, Paris has one of the highest densities: 25 000 per km^2. Within Britain, medieval towns and industrial towns built during the 19th century have densities up to 30 000 per km^2, and New Towns have about 12 000 per km^2. Dormitory and resort towns also tend to have fairly low densities.

Inside cities densities vary spatially. In Western cities they decrease outwards from the city centre, as poor people tend to live in more central locations than do the rich. In non-Western cities the opposite may be true: rich people living near the centre at low densities whereas poor people live at the periphery at high densities (for example, in shanty towns).

Urban populations are also heterogeneous in composition (compared with rural populations, which are more homogeneous). They work in various occupations and come from diverse social, ethnic, linguistic, religious and cultural groups. These variations may enrich artistic life but pose serious problems of adaptation, integration and assimilation. It is partly owing to this demographic mixture that large towns are often marked by high levels of violence, crime and general discontent.

These problems may be exacerbated by the natural segregation of different social and racial groups. Most European cities have Jewish quarters, often dating back many hundreds of years, and these might be seen as one of the earliest examples of spatial divisions within society. Today, greater mobility has resulted in far more ghettos coming into existence. The most conspicuous – and

therefore most emotive – ones are distinguished by colour, such as the 'black' areas in British and North American cities.

The age and sex compositions of populations lead to further differences between urban and rural regions and between individual towns. With the exception of certain places such as spa towns and tourist resorts, urban areas in developed regions have generally higher proportions of young adults than do rural areas. This is because migration from country to town mostly involves people between the ages of 15 and 35, these being the people with greatest energy and ambition. In the same way, military towns, naval bases, mining towns and areas dominated by heavy industry have a preponderance of males; service towns (e.g. market and holiday centres) and areas dominated by light industry have a preponderance of females. In Worthing, on the English South Coast, women outnumber men by three to two, partly because it is a retirement resort and hence accommodates a high proportion of elderly people (females living longer than males on average) and partly because it is a holiday and light industry town.

These age and sex proportions also vary spatially within cities. Near the centre, where many houses are divided into flats or bed-sits, there is a high percentage of young single adults, especially women, and towards the urban periphery the percentage of older, married couples increases. As people grow older, marry and have children, they move progressively outwards from a city centre. As an outcome of these age–sex spatial differences, there are also differences in population growth rates between urban districts. Some areas have rapid increase, other areas have rapid decline. The former may have a high proportion of young adults, the latter of elderly people.

Finally, different growth rates may sometimes be identified between urban and rural populations. In general, fertility rates are lower and mortality rates higher in urban areas. Compared with the countryside, towns have smaller average house sizes, more social diversions and a higher degree of education (and hence birth control), but they also have greater overcrowding and often worse sanitary conditions.

ism has been witnessed: the continued growth around the periphery but a decline at the centre. This expansion results in a CBD being ring-shaped. The heavy congestion, high costs and atmospheric pollution at the city centre will in time adversely affect land values, and progress in telecommunications will make accessibility a less important factor to many businesses. The result is an outward movement of retailing and office premises and the emergence of a 'dead heart'. Many American cities already possess such dead hearts in their CBDs and some British cities (including London) are now showing signs of the same feature appearing. Indeed, such are the detrimental effects of these dead hearts on the social and economic life of towns that politicians and planners now recognise the problem and are seeking to attract populations back into inner city areas. In the City of London, for example, the Barbican has been built to regenerate the area, providing expensive residential flats and a multipurpose arts complex. Elsewhere, similar schemes are helping to revitalise CBDs: old warehouses and tenement blocks are being converted into up-market homes; shopping areas are being turned into pedestrian precincts (often covered); and fashionable boutiques are replacing supermarkets.

Industries in towns of the developed world

All urban settlements possess industries to a greater or lesser extent. Some towns have grown up as manufacturing centres and are therefore dominated by large, often old, factories; other towns have developed manufacturing functions relatively recently and have only a scatter of new, and often small, factories. In either case, the location of industries throughout an urban area may fall into a set pattern.

Generally, industries are dependent not on central locations but on communication networks. Therefore, they may be found away from a town's CBD and adjacent to roads, railways, canals or coastlines. They can also be found in clusters, because they may derive mutual economic benefits, have the same siting requirements, and be kept, deliberately, away from residential or retail areas. Because of this, industries in towns are normally to be found in distinct zones.

There are exceptions, of course, and sometimes scattered industries can be observed both within and outside the CBD. This scattering consists mostly of small-scale workshop undertakings, which require only small amounts of power and raw materials.

Some may be old-established, specialised units that have survived through inertia; others might be linked to retail outlets and therefore require central locations; yet others could be the temporary result of urban blight. The latter are sometimes found in buildings not specifically constructed for their use (being, perhaps, former warehouses or dwellings) and in 'twilight zones' where imminent redevelopment has led to a fall in land values and a high degree of vacancy. Although production in scattered manufacturing units is varied, typical examples include precision engineering, fashion clothing and various 'craft' industries – toy-making, pottery, ornaments, jewellery and so on.

Of all industries, those in the 'heavy' category are most likely to be sited in clusters. Those that rely on large amounts of raw materials, or produce bulky goods, are usually in need of cheap transport and are therefore commonly located next to harbours, canals, railways and major roads. Such industries include iron and steel manufacture and oil refining. Some industries, like motor manufacture, require extensive sites, which are available only outside towns, and others, like electricity generation and chemical manufacture, need large quantities of water for processing, cooling or effluent disposal. Many heavy industries also create a nuisance in the form of either air or noise pollution, and these too will normally be located outside urban areas. Examples of these include those making paint, varnish or grease. Most large towns have heavy industrial complexes away from their built-up areas for the above reasons: London has them along the Thames estuary (Fig. 16.9), New York on the New Jersey marshes, and Chicago on the Calumet waterfront.

Light industries are more likely to be located nearer to residential areas since they have less demanding site requirements and are less destructive to the social and aesthetic environment. Textile, food-processing and furniture factories, for example, are often found interspersed with housing. Light-engineering factories in particular are clean and quiet, and those built this century have largely appeared within suburbs where more space is available and land is cheaper than nearer the city centre. Over the last 50 years, increased use of electricity has allowed a greater flexibility of site choice, and increased use of motor vehicles has added to the importance of roadside locations. Thus, many light-manufacturing complexes are not only situated in suburbs but also tend to be aligned along arterial roads. Around London, for instance, the Great Cambridge Road, Great West Road

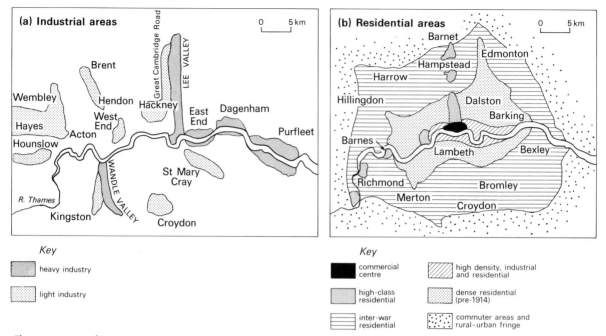

Figure 16.9 Land-use zones in Greater London
Both the concentric and sector patterns are represented here. Industrial zones reflect physical geography, residential zones reflect both topography and the historical development of the conurbation.

and the North Circular Road all support linear factory development.

In addition, modern light industry can be characterised by formal, open layouts with single-storey, purpose-built factories and ample machinery and storage space. In some places, firms with functional links convene into industrial or trading estates where some attempts are made at landscaping. These industrial estates are frequently found on the outskirts of urban areas (at Park Royal, for example, in West London, and along the Team Valley south of Newcastle upon Tyne) or else near motorways. Today, most small towns have their own small industrial estates on their peripheries.

Industries in towns of the Third World

In addition to the locational characteristics of manufacturing already outlined – which are also to be found in urban settlements of less developed countries – Third World towns and cities also have their own particular industrial features.

Whereas settlements in the developed world have industries and occupations that are largely 'formal' in nature – officially registered employment in controlled factories, workshops, offices and retail outlets – Third World settlements are more likely to have 'informal' activities. Indeed, in many South American, African and Asian cities the 'informal' sector is equally important, perhaps more, with the 'formal' sector accounting for less than half the total employment of an urban area.

This informal industrial sector is heterogeneous, mobile and irregularly dispersed throughout an urban area. It is largely composed of small-scale enterprises (one person or family), which operate with outdated equipment (or no equipment at all) at irregular hours and, often, outside the law. Examples might include small-time traders and market stall-holders, pavement retailers, taxi drivers and rick-shaw men, car washers, self-employed mechanics and hot-food sellers, newspaper vendors, scribes and street typists, barbers, shoeshiners, money-lenders and prostitutes.

Such activities are found everywhere, but some are more widespread than others. Whereas some operators are widely dispersed, with each searching for a local monopoly and control over a particular area, others tend to cluster in particular zones. Thus, there might be one shoeshiner in each street and one newspaper vendor in each urban district, but there might be a group of fifty stallholders at a temporary market place and dozens of prostitutes walking the few streets of a 'red light district'.

As the wage-employment opportunities being offered by the formal sector are diminishing in relation to the numbers of new urban immigrants seeking work, so the importance of the informal sector in Third World cities is growing. Increasingly, the working population in these urban settlements is being occupied in informal pursuits. In Accra (Ghana) as much as 60% of the total employment is in the informal sector; among the female-only working population, the informal sector accounts for as much as 80%. Elsewhere, similar figures may be found: in Lima (Peru), for example, in Calcutta (India) and in Rangoon (Burma), in each case the informal sector accounting for 65% of total employment and 78% of female employment.

Suburbs

Around the central core of a town there are areas in which various residential land uses exist. Collectively these are called suburbs. They are a feature of Western cities in particular, and have largely grown up during the present century. In developing countries they are generally less extensive and less distinctive in character.

Reasons for suburban growth

(1) *Improved urban transport.* The introduction of railways, bus services and underground trains first allowed people to live further away from their place of work, but it has been the motor car which has really caused the 'suburban explosion' of modern times. Before this century, housing was still confined to narrow belts of land along major routes; today development has spread between road and railway routes and has thus infilled the previous wedges of countryside.

(2) *Population growth.* Suburbs expand outwards partly as a result of migration from more central areas and partly as a result of immigration from rural districts.

(3) *Higher standards of living.* Greater personal wealth enables people to acquire better housing and causes them to seek more spacious living conditions. A reduction of the average family size is similarly creating lower population densities and urban sprawl.

(4) *The building society movement.* In Britain the influence of building societies should not be underestimated since they have made funds available for house purchase. Most private houses in this country are bought through building society mortgages.

(5) *Human nature.* Suburbs have been called a 'collective attempt at private living', but this seems to be true only in certain countries. In particular, suburbs are most common in Britain, North America and other regions where the British influence has been felt. This is perhaps because Anglo-Saxons, more than other peoples, seem to have a natural desire to live in low density housing and be surrounded by gardens. In many European countries the suburban way of life is less developed and people tend to live in large apartment blocks (e.g. France and Austria).

The character of suburbs

Like the CBD and towns generally, suburbs possess distinctive zones, each with its own material and demographic features. In many instances these zones are the result of the tendency of housing to decrease in age and density with distance from the city centre.

Towards the CBD there are normally old, small terraced houses, or blocks of flats created by recent redevelopment. Here live the poorer people who cannot afford to commute to work or to occupy too much land since bid-rents are high. In some cases overcrowding exists and multifamily dwellings are common. Further away from the city centre are areas of well spaced, semi-detached housing, wide roads, spacious gardens and numerous garages – the whole typifying the term 'suburbia'. Here, middle-class people can afford to occupy relatively large plots of land (bid-rents being low) and single-family dwellings are common.

Segregation is also a characteristic of suburbs. This may occur on two levels: on a broad scale whereby entire sectors are dominated by distinct social or ethnic classes, and on a local scale whereby small individual housing estates, or merely streets, are dominated by different income groups. This segregation relates to such factors as topography, the constraints of costs, the policies of builders or local authorities, human nature and chance. In some urban areas, segregation reaches extremes, for example in those of southern Africa, the Middle East and North-

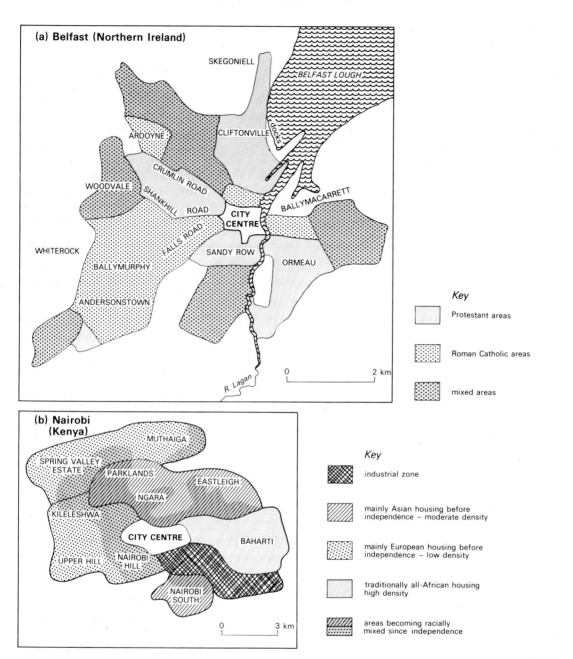

Figure 16.10 Urban segregation

Demographic, social, racial and religious divisions in urban populations are frequently reflected in urban structure. In Belfast, religious segregation of housing does much to irritate the already serious socio-economic and political problems of the United Kingdom province. Despite efforts to mix the two sects over the past 10 years, this strong spatial division persists. In Nairobi, racial and social segregation is the result of a colonial past. Before Kenya's independence in 1963, there were three distinct residential zones: the European zone (mainly high class), the Asian zone (mainly middle class), the African zone (mainly lower class). Since then – and since the departure of many thousands of Kenyan Asians in the 1970s – Africans have begun to spread throughout the urban area, thus diminishing its segregated pattern. However, differences in architecture and housing facilities can still be seen in distinct groupings.

ern Ireland (Fig. 16.10), where strict social, racial or religious divisions exist.

Hilly areas, where the air is clean and scenic views are possible, tend to be characterised by high-quality, expensive housing, whereas valleys and low-lying regions have generally poor quality, inexpensive housing. Occasionally two zones of complete social contrast lie in close juxtaposition: in London, for example, very rich and very poor areas can be found side by side: Hampstead and Kilburn, Chelsea and Fulham, Kensington and Notting Hill. Over the last 50 years in Britain, many council estates have sprung up within suburbs, creating further segregation and possessing, on average, higher housing densities and a higher proportion of working-class families than the surrounding areas of private housing.

Changing socio-economic conditions cause suburbs to change their spatial and demographic character continuously. Sometimes redevelopment or housing rehabilitation can transform a run-down zone into a wealthy, much sought-after zone; elsewhere the reverse might occur. Large, old, formerly pleasant houses may lose their social lustre because of the inhabitants' inability to afford the high cost of upkeep. These houses may be acquired by lower income groups or by new immigrants who proceed to subdivide and sublet the property. 'Social leapfrogging' may result, whereby high-class areas can be reduced in status as they are occupied by successively lower social groups. Even if just a single house loses its high-class character, a 'domino effect' could set in to change an entire suburban zone.

Shopping centre hierarchies

Just as people living in different parts of a large region use different towns for different reasons – local small towns for low-order goods and services and distant large towns for high-order goods and services – so people living within an urban area spend different proportions of their incomes on different goods and services at different shops and at varying degrees of frequency. They would use some shops often to buy everyday commodities and others less often for more specialised commodities.

This fact has led to the recognition of shopping centre hierarchies. Many have been proposed, but the following is probably the most comprehensive for Western towns and cities:

(1) *Individual retail outlets.* These are scattered throughout residential areas and are typified by the traditional 'corner shops' common in old, working-class districts. They sell mostly convenience goods (relying on daily custom) and consumer essentials and often open for long hours.

(2) *Isolated retail clusters.* These are small groups of shops supplying their immediate localities with the necessities of life: food and general household goods. Again, mostly convenience goods are sold, together with some shoppers' and durable goods, that is, goods like shoes and hardware, which are purchased at infrequent intervals.

(3) *Neighbourhood business streets.* Here a full selection of convenience and comparison goods is sold and a full range of services is available; competition exists between similar shops, and there are usually small supermarkets. Street markets may also be grouped under this category although they sometimes only operate periodically, perhaps once a week.

(4) *Principal business thoroughfares.* These attract custom from several kilometres distant and possess major chain stores and department stores. Car parking facilities are often provided nearby. In these centres, and in larger ones, an increasing area is devoted to shoppers' and durable goods at the expense of convenience goods.

(5) *Regional business districts.* These cater for people throughout a whole urban region within a city and usually contain a full selection of major stores. Sometimes these centres are specially built and possess large integral car parks.

(6) *The CBD.* This is the central shopping area for the entire city.

With greater individual mobility (mostly because of increased car ownership), there has been a tendency for individual shops and small retail clusters to decline in importance and for large shopping centres to grow in importance. There is also a tendency for people to prefer outlying urban shopping areas to the CBD, where congestion makes shopping unpleasant.

The spatial distribution of shopping centres is determined partly by land values and accessibility and partly by local authority planning policies. The larger shopping centres are often located at important route junctions: Brent Cross shopping centre in North London is located where the North Circular Road crosses the Edgware Road, and is also close to the M1 intersection.

A recent development in many countries has been the appearance of hypermarkets – gigantic, carefully planned, out-of-town shopping centres catering for car-owning customers and covering 50 ha or more. They usually have large car parks and provide not only a wide range of goods but also such services as restaurants, cafés and, possibly also, theatres, hotels and office buildings. Although hypermarkets first appeared in Europe (in France, Germany and Sweden), they have become especially common in North America; there are examples near Boston, Seattle, Detroit and Washington. They have now appeared in Britain (for example at Huntington, York), although here they tend to take the form of 'superstores' owned entirely by single companies such as Tesco and Sainsbury's.

There are arguments both for and against the building of hypermarkets. On the one hand they can relieve city-centre congestion and make shopping more pleasant and less expensive. On the other hand, they are of little use to the poor, elderly or to those without cars or deep freezers; they can consume vast areas of valuable agricultural land; they disfigure the rural environment; and they can encourage further urban growth. In addition they may have adverse repercussions on more conventional shopping centres. By encouraging people to make bulk purchases at infrequent intervals (say, monthly) rather than to shop on a weekly or daily basis, they could cause the smaller shopping districts to decline in significance, a process which might also change the entire character of urban population movement and community spirit. Indeed, in some towns, hypermarkets (together with out-of-town discount warehouses and mail order businesses) have caused the closure of even large shops, supermarkets and department stores at urban centres. Such closures not only pose a threat to the survival of other town retailers but also can greatly reduce the rate income of urban local authorities.

URBAN TRANSPORT

The problems

(1) Commuter traffic is mostly in public transport (e.g. 90% of London workers travel to work by bus, tube or train).

(2) Congestion causes frustration and delays. Average travel speeds in some towns are down to only 15 km/h.

(3) Many old towns have narrow streets and ancient buildings; traffic flow is hence restricted.

(4) Heavy traffic produces air and noise pollution, which is often exacerbated by tall buildings which hinder the dispersal of fumes and reverberate sound.

(5) Rush hours create problems for transport authorities, which must maintain large amounts of capital equipment that is unused or underused for the rest of the day.

(6) Small rush hours occur in mid-afternoon (the shopping peak) and evening (the entertainment peak).

(7) Urban motorways and car parks use up valuable land, and underground railway systems are expensive and difficult to build.

(8) Prohibited parking in streets and one-way systems hinder shop deliveries; conversely shop deliveries hinder traffic flow.

(9) Urban transport does not mix well with pedestrians; traffic accidents are common; the cost of policing is high.

(10) Present forms of fuel are running out but demand is rising rapidly.

The remedies

(1) The introduction of staggered working hours may ease rush hours.

(2) Modifications in road systems: one-way streets, bus lanes, traffic lights, parking meters, yellow junction boxes.

(3) Building new roads: urban motorways and ring roads. (These, however, involve the demolition of houses and old buildings, generate more traffic and increase congestion and pollution.)

(4) Improved public transport: the restriction of private cars and more reliable services. Some towns have introduced 'park and ride' schemes, commuters parking their cars at the CBD edge and completing their journeys in small, low-cost, express coaches.

(5) New transport systems: electrically driven motor cars, monorail, helicopters. (These, however, have high capital costs and a limited technical life.)

(6) Traffic/pedestrian segregation: pedestrian precincts, subways, high-level footways.

(7) Restriction of car parking provision and increases in parking meter charges to discourage motorists.

(8) Encouragement to industrial, commercial and retailing firms to move away from city centres.

(9) Road safety education and road-sense advertising; drink-driving laws.

(10) Research into alternative fuels and more efficient engines.

Figure 16.11   The urban fringe
Here, at Hillingdon, London suburbia peters out towards the Buckinghamshire countryside. Interspersed with the semi-detached houses, villas and bungalows are segments of Green Belt where the rural–urban fringe is characterised by allotments, playing fields, open-plan schools and patches of recreational woodland.

The rural–urban fringe

Unless a town has an enclosing wall, there is not usually a clear line to show where urban land use ends and rural land use begins. Most towns merge gradually into the surrounding countryside, over a considerable distance, and land use changes only slowly from one to the other. The belt of land over which this intermingling takes place is called the **rural–urban fringe** and is most clearly developed around British towns (Fig. 16.11).

Within this region, land use is in transition both in space and time, and social organisation is in a state of flux. Urban uses stand next to rural uses, and areas open today may, in future, be built over. Different social groups live side by side, some working in town, some in the countryside. In short, there is a general and haphazard mixture: new shopping centres, dormitory towns, modern factories, scattered houses, sewage works, reservoirs, playing fields, golf courses, airports, hospitals, cemeteries, junk yards and small areas of farmland on which market gardening or dairying may be undertaken (often in a half-hearted way).

In time, with natural urban growth and improved transport, these rural–urban fringes become ever wider and, in the absence of planning controls, ever more untidy and ugly. Land values rise as building speculators buy farmland for future urban use, but this only adds to the mixed and changing nature of the landscape. No sooner has one land use been set up than, with increased rents, that use becomes unprofitable. In this way land is brought under successively different uses.

INTERNAL STRUCTURE OF TOWNS AND CITIES

Summary

1 Distinct land-use zones within towns can be understood through the Concentric, Sector and Multiple-Nuclei theories. Small urban areas tend to show signs of the first two, conurbations of all three.

2 Topography and weather influence land-use patterns: upper-class housing being located on hills and on the lee side of prevailing winds, industry on valley floors and facing winds.

3 City centres (central business districts) are characterised by high land values, multilevel commercial land use, functional segregation and tall buildings. The larger the town the more distinct is its CBD. Zones of assimilation and discord occur when a CBD shifts its location, the former being areas which acquire CBD features, the latter areas which lose them.

4 Many CBDs and transition zones are undergoing change: 'gentrification' turns low-class areas into fashionable districts, 'pedestrianisation' removes motor vehicles from shopping precincts.

5 Traditional industries (e.g. workshops) tend to locate towards city centres, heavy industries along transport arteries, modern light industries in out-of-town trading estates. Industries also tend to cluster into specialist groups.

6 In Third World towns 'informal' employment (small-scale, unlicensed activities) can be more important than 'formal' (recognised shops and factories). Informal workers may cluster together in street markets, at railway stations, or in 'red light districts'.

7 Suburbs exhibit distinctive residential segregation – based on class, race or religion – and they can contain ghettos. Many people commute towards city centres but, as firms are now moving to urban peripheries, some commuting also takes place outwards.

8 Shopping centres form hierarchies, from scattered shops to centrally located CBD retail agglomerations. The smallest survive for reasons of convenience: opening long hours and selling low-order goods.

9 Hypermarkets – out-of-town shopping emporia – are undermining town-centre stores and supermarkets. They also destroy the countryside and cater only for customers with cars, money enough to buy in bulk, and home storage facilities.

10 At a city's edge, town merges gradually with countryside across the rural–urban fringe. Here, there are rubbish dumps, open-plan schools and hospitals, leisure facilities and cemeteries.

Data–response exercises

1 From OS map B (Yorkshire) draw an annotated sketch map to show the land-use zones of Keighley. Which theory of internal structure does your map most resemble? To what extent is the structure related to the natural environment?

2 Draw annotated sketch views or sketch maps to show the internal structures of Caernarfon (Figs 15.1 & 2) and Lincoln (Fig. 16.4). Comment on your findings.

3 Account for the differences between the internal structure of Mendoza and that of Bradford (Fig. 16.6). Are such structures typical of the less developed and developed world, respectively?

4 Outline the factors that might alter bid-rent curves as shown in Figure 16.7. Why do some towns not have an urban or architectural outline similar in shape to the bid-rent cone (Fig. 16.8)?

5 Suggest reasons for the land-use zones of Greater London (Fig. 16.9) and discuss how these zones are now changing in response to urban planning policies.

6 Identify suitable sites for (a) a new light engineering factory, (b) a hypermarket in the rural–urban fringe depicted around Hillingdon (Fig. 16.11). What problems would the planners and developers face if such developments were actually to be built in this area?

Project work

1 By observation fieldwork, various aspects of the internal structure of towns can be mapped and studied. For any one specific urban area, the CBD can be identified and its main characteristics (heights of buildings, multifunctional premises, rent, propensity to change spatially) can be noted. Zones of assimilation and discord can also be studied. Alternatively, the overall land-use zones of different towns can be compared and linked to the accepted theories of structure. Across residential areas and suburbs, different architectural and historic zones can be mapped: medieval, classical

(18th century), Victorian, Edwardian, interwar and modern (post-1945).

2 Settlement relationships may be studied through the Spearman rank correlation coefficient and by the construction of diagrams and scatter graphs. For example, the link between population size and retail functions can be studied by comparing different towns or villages and their shopping facilities. Alternatively, the links between rents and land use or topography and residential standards can be studied.

3 Settlement fields of influence can be studied and mapped by using one of the methods of delimitation suggested in Chapter 15. The factors determining the size and shape of these fields can be gauged from maps and local transport information. The theoretical urban fields as determined by the break-point formula can be compared using an atlas and relevant statistical information.

Further reading

Carter, H. 1976. *The study of urban geography* 3rd edn. London: Hutchinson. Well illustrated guide with an emphasis on Western Europe and North America. Interesting Chapter 15 on urban perception.

Chisholm, M. 1979. *Rural settlement and land use* 3rd edn. London: Hutchinson. Slim volume which investigates the influence of such aspects as soils, slope, climate and distance on agricultural patterns. Developed and developing countries considered, past and present conditions. Numerous examples help add interest to a straightforward and readable text.

Clark, David 1982. *Urban geography*. London: Croom Helm. This assesses the contribution of modern geographers to the understanding of urban society. It gives a wide range of examples and detailed references for further study. Concise and very readable despite the preponderance of 'loaded' statements.

Everson, J. A. and B. P. Fitzgerald 1969. *Settlement patterns*. London: Longman. Slim volume with a plethora of statistics and formulae, worked examples, case studies and a useful pull-out map of settlement patterns in East Anglia. Suitable for students wishing to specialise.

Everson, J. A. and B. P. Fitzgerald 1972. *Inside the city*. London: Longman. Companion to the above volume. More comprehensive than the title suggests. Scientific methods of approach handled without jargon and useful suggestions given for fieldwork, surveys and hypothesis testing.

Herbert, D. 1972. *Urban geography: a social perspective*. Newton Abbot: David & Charles. Review of the contribution that social aspects have made to urban structures. Well illustrated and well written. Theories are related to reality and a good overall study is given. In parts the book verges on sociology.

Herbert, D. and C. J. Thomas 1982. *Urban geography, a first approach*. Chichester: Wiley. Heavy tome with an exhaustive and detailed coverage both of all quantitative techniques and of modern societal aspects of the subject. Wide selection of world examples. Can usefully be dipped into.

Hudson, F. S. 1976. *Geography of settlement*. Plymouth: Macdonald & Evans. Very good general book covering all aspects of settlements. Recommended both for complete reading and for 'dipping into'. The understanding of any section is not dependent upon the information in previous chapters.

Johnson, J. H. 1972. *Urban geography* 2nd edn. Oxford: Pergamon Press. Well written, readable text which gives a comprehensive study with factual conciseness. Excellent basic reference book. By the same author is *Urbanisation* (1980, London: Macmillan) a very good, concise, recommended volume for general interest.

Lawless, P. 1981. *Britain's inner cities, problems and policies*. London: Harper & Row. A worrying picture is provided of the plight of urban populations and their further suffering at the hands of planning policies. Latest research findings and future consequences of urban blight are also considered.

Loewenstein, L. K. (ed.) 1977. *Urban studies, an introductory reader*. New York: The Free Press. A collection of 20 essays mostly written in an easy-going, journalese style. Deceptively academic and useful to the student wishing to specialise.

Lowry, J. H. 1975. *World city growth*. London: Edward Arnold. Clearly written account of all aspects of urban geography; well illustrated. Pitched at sixth-form level; a very useful book.

Needham, B. 1977. *How cities work*. Oxford: Pergamon. Concise, comprehensive study of the human dimension of urban areas. Digestible even to the non-geographer. Recommended.

Roberts, B. 1978. *Cities of peasants*. London: Edward Arnold. One of the *Explorations in urban analysis* series of books. An excellent coverage of the various problems faced in Third World towns and cities. Also recommended are the other books in the same series: *The inner city*; *The Soviet city*; *Cities and social change*; *Urbanization and class consciousness*; *Planning for urban happiness*.

Part V

GEOGRAPHY AND PLANNING

But with poetry dead the Government said
That they needed more space for their planes;
They ignored other sites and all citizens' rights
And destroyed these fair meadows and lanes.

Oh who has the power to sever a flower
Or cut down a tall English tree?
But they ruined the land at this spot where we stand
And they put here the mess that we see.
> Margery Roberts, *A New Airport*

The best laid schemes o' mice an' men
Gang aft a-gley.
> Robert Burns, *To a Field-mouse*

PLANNING FOR THE WORLD

International aid – United Nations and Commonwealth – private organisations – arms trafficking – the Cold War – disaster relief – poverty circle – political subjugation

---

REGIONAL PLANNING IN THE THIRD WORLD

Regional inequalities – environmental hazards – regional policy options – financial aid – infrastructure improvement – tourism – relocation of capital cities – resource development

---

PLANNING IN BRITAIN

Barlow report – planning acts – Green Belts – New Towns – Garden Cities – key villages – hedgerow removal – leisure activities – national parks – Countryside Commission – 'honeypots' – public awareness

---

REGIONAL POLICY IN BRITAIN

Development Areas – political expediency – carrot and stick approach – grants and loans – social upheaval – enterprise zones – inflation – trade union intervention

17 Planning for the world

Introduction

In previous chapters in this book we have seen that world inequalities exist in wealth, technology and education, and that some countries are developed whereas others are not. Such economic and social divisions create problems, which require remedies. This chapter is largely concerned with the ways in which these remedies can be instigated and, in particular, the ways in which the advanced countries can help the less developed Third World to advance economically.

There are essentially two links between the developed world and the less developed world. One is trade: the buying and selling of goods and services between countries. This topic was covered in Chapter 11. The other – and that which is mostly associated with planning – is aid: the transfer of goods, finance and services from advantaged countries to disadvantaged countries. This is the topic to be discussed in this chapter – through the consideration of the following questions:

- What forms of international aid exist and how have they developed over the years?
- Which organisations operate aid programmes, and with what degree of advanced planning?
- Have international aid schemes been successful in achieving their ends, and can 'success' be measured or defined?
- Is international aid necessarily the most effective way of reducing inequalities in the world?
- What are the political, strategic and social dimensions of aid?

Forms of international aid

International or foreign aid can be defined as the provision, by some countries to others, of the essential supplies necessary to combat underdevelopment. It can take many forms – financial aid, food and raw material supply, re-equipment and the provision of technical know-how – and may be implemented in many ways. It can take place directly and bilaterally (from one government to another), directly and multilaterally (from many governments to official international aid bodies, which administer aid schemes), indirectly and commercially (by governments and companies through trade and business agreements) or indirectly and socially (by individuals through charity and voluntary work organisations). Some international aid programmes are geared to specific tasks and operate for specified lengths of time – to relieve suffering in areas of natural disasters, for example – whereas others are more general and continuous in character.

For all those planning and administering international aid programmes, the same set of problems and decisions must be faced. What exact form should aid take; which schemes are most urgent; how best can aid be transferred; whence is the finance to come; when should a particular programme cease? For example, financial aid could take the form of commercial low-interest loans, foreign government investment, non-returnable grants or merely fiscal advice. Agricultural help could take the form of fertiliser and seed supply, the sending of farm machinery or simply recommendations concerning land-use techniques and rotations. Decisions regarding the urgency of aid schemes, their intensity and length of operation must be made in the context of optional possibilities. All aid programmes are limited by their own terms of reference, their financial backing and by the intelligence and expertise of their organisers. The most urgent scheme is frequently the one that can be afforded first; the most intense or longest scheme is often the one that is administered by those people with greatest influence and political power. Indeed, urgency itself is a subjective term: to those in need of help, their own problem is the most urgent. Starvation is neither more nor less in need of cure from international aid than, say, fatal disease. There is no internationally agreed hierarchy of world problems. Those who administer aid schemes must decide on the forms of aid to use within the confines of their own perception of problems and the scarcity of their funds.

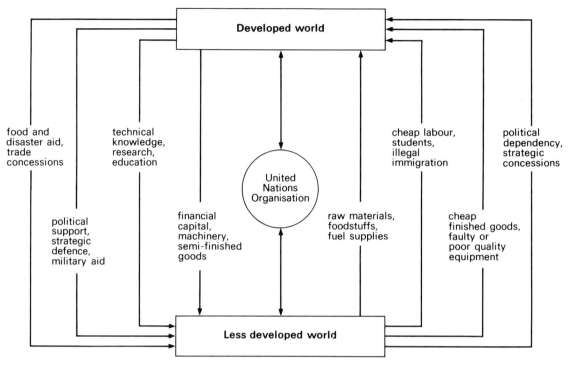

food and
disaster aid,
trade
concessions

technical
knowledge,
research,
education

cheap labour,
students,
illegal
immigration

political
dependency,
strategic
concessions

United
Nations
Organisation

political
support,
strategic
defence,
military aid

financial
capital,
machinery,
semi-finished
goods

raw materials,
foodstuffs,
fuel supplies

cheap
finished goods,
faulty or
poor quality
equipment

Figure 17.1 The give and take of international aid
Very little international aid takes place for purely altruistic reasons: most developed countries that provide such aid usually expect –
and receive – something in return. It is questionable whether the Third World always benefits.

Nevertheless, it is still true to say that international aid – in whichever form it operates – is the result not just of one but of many motives. Of course, a moral conviction, among the countries of the developed world, that poverty, hunger, disease and illiteracy are denying millions of people their basic rights, is a prime reason why international aid exists. Yet it is not the only reason. There is the practical consideration that vast amounts of raw materials and labour supplies in the Third World await exploitation and could provide the developed world with much-needed resources. There is the commercial consideration that increased standards of living in poor countries would increase international trade, thus helping the economies of the developed countries. There is the political consideration that aid can bring strategic or diplomatic advantages to developed countries eager to maintain or expand their global influence. There is the social consideration that certain diseases, if left unchecked, could spread across the world, becoming globally endemic.

The fact is that international aid is a two-way process (see Fig. 17.1) and, as we shall see, it is not

always the recipients of aid – the poor countries – that benefit most.

The development of international aid

Although international aid on a large and worldwide scale has developed only since World War 2, the idea that rich countries should help poor countries is not new. Much aid took place many years ago under imperialism. When European states conquered foreign lands in Africa, Asia and the New World, the primary aim was probably to exploit the labour and mineral wealth of those areas. However, many benefits were provided in return: directly in the form of new roads, railways, towns and medical supplies, and indirectly through the growth of trade, which allowed for the inward flow of capital. In southern Africa, for example, British colonialism through such people as Cecil Rhodes, created a rail network, a system of schooling and efficient administration. Such aid was incidental, took place on a piecemeal basis and occurred only in association with colonialism. Yet it was no less real for all that and should not be underestimated. The Roman Empire did indeed provide financial, agricultural and military aid to its impoverished outposts – England, for example – and the Spanish Empire of the Middle Ages gave a veneer of economic development to South America.

In more recent history, international aid has become more consciously planned and more skilfully organised. It has also become the official *raison d'être* of designated organisations.

The British Empire and Commonwealth

Colonies and protectorates of the British Empire, certainly achieved much economic progress. Conditions in India, for example, were considerably improved through the British Raj. Under successive imperial/colonial administrations, all manner of improvements were instigated: flourishing trade under the East India Company brought in wealth, an efficient civil service was set up, education was extended, diseases were controlled and tribal warring, crime, human sacrifice and 'thuggee' gang murders were reduced. Agriculture was improved through vast irrigation schemes and the establishment of farmer co-operatives, and through the breaking down of some of the social restrictions imposed by the rigid Indian caste system, which had formerly led many landowners to exploit the peasants under them. In addition, an effective financial system provided greater investment, a postal service and telegraph system were introduced, and India acquired new roads, harbours and a complete railway network.

The British Empire is no more, but international aid continues to take place in its wake through the auspices of the Commonwealth. This is a unique world organisation: a combination of nations with different races, cultures and religions, held together by a common bond of friendship, respect and common elements of history. Member states maintain links with Britain, to varying degrees, through defence, trade, language, law, education and an allegiance to the monarchy. The annual Commonwealth Prime Ministers' Conference is an outward expression of this union, but less publicised are the numerous mutual benefits that ensue. Via the Commonwealth Development Corporation there is a constant interchange of knowledge and technological skills, and a steady flow of capital investment continues between the better-off countries (Britain, Canada, Australia, New Zealand) and the less well-off (those in Africa and Asia). Indeed, such is the strength of the Commonwealth that 60% of all Britain's foreign aid goes to Commonwealth countries.

The United Nations

Of greater importance still in the operation of international aid is the United Nations. This was formed after World War 2 (reviving the old League of Nations) with the primary aim of ensuring world peace and the secondary aims of encouraging international co-operation and the equalisation of the world's wealth. Aid provided by the United Nations is initiated under the Economic and Social Council, which is empowered to make studies of international conditions and recommend policies to the General Assembly. This council operates largely through specialised commissions of experts on such themes as economics, transport, education, health and human rights, and co-ordinates the work of intergovernmental agencies. These include Unesco (United Nations Educational, Scientific and Cultural Organisation) which aims to combat such problems as illiteracy, low living standards and agricultural and industrial inefficiency; the ILO (International Labour Organisation) which aims to standardise labour and social conditions; the FAO (Food and Agriculture Organisation) which helps countries improve food production and distribution, to raise their nutritional levels; the IAEO (International Atomic Energy Organisation) which aids the development of the peaceful use of atomic energy; and the WHO (World Health Organisation) which helps prevent the spread of such diseases as malaria and tuberculosis. In addition the United Nations supports a children's fund (UNICEF), a refugee organisation and a special fund for less developed countries.

Purely financial aid is provided through the World Bank Group, the IMF (International Monetary Fund), IBRD (International Bank for Reconstruction and Development), IDA (International Development Association) and IFC (International Finance Corporation). Between them these organisations help make available financial investment for such projects as building dams, harbours, roads and factories, and also for helping rural development and the extension of education.

Concern for the plight of the Third World has intensified in recent years and the United Nations has stepped up its aid programmes. The period 1960–70 was designated the Development Decade and, in addition, the first half of that time saw the setting up of the 'Freedom from Hunger' campaign. In 1969 the

UNFAO approved an 'Indicative World Plan for Agriculture', which projected food needs and food production potentials until 1985, and in 1974 the United Nations instigated 'World Population Year' with the dual purpose of making people in the developed regions more aware of the world population problem and of helping the less developed regions cope more effectively with their increasing numbers.

Other international organisations

Other multilateral organisations include the European Economic Community, which has its own aid machinery; the OECD (Organisation for Economic Co-operation and Development), which is the primary agency through which Western donors co-ordinate their programmes; and the Colombo Plan. The last named originally began as a group of South and South-East Asian countries operating within the Commonwealth, aiming to assist all the poorer countries to develop their resources. It has since expanded to include other nations such as Britain, Canada, the USA and Japan, and has widened its scope to cover all aspects of international aid.

Apart from all the above government-sponsored aid organisations, various voluntary bodies exist. Some of these, like the Red Cross and Church World Service, are truly international; others are more nationally based. In Britain, for instance, there is Oxfam, Christian Aid, War on Want, the Save the Children Fund, and Help the Aged. Even individuals are able to help distribute aid by living and working in developing countries – Britons through VSO (Voluntary Service Overseas) and Americans through the Peace Corps. Although small in total, the aid provided by voluntary groups can often be very significant, especially in times of emergencies (floods, earthquakes, famines and so forth) when their help can be mobilised swiftly, efficiently and without the 'red tape' of more official bodies. Such aid – because it is given at grass-roots level – helps those people most in need, unlike aid provided by governments, which often only goes towards prestige projects.

Arguments against international aid

Despite the fact that international aid has usually resulted in improved social conditions and economic progress throughout the developing world, its usefulness has been questioned. Indeed, some people go so far as to say that the whole idea is ill-conceived and questionable on political, social and economic grounds (see Fig. 17.2).

Politically it can be argued that international aid makes the less developed world overdependent on the developed world and that this may create tensions both between and within countries. The less developed nation might be in conflict with the donor nation over the amount and kind of aid, and the government of the less developed country could face criticism from its own opposition for allowing foreign intervention.

Socially, international aid might interfere with religious, cultural or ethnic traditions which would be best left alone. It is assumed by many advanced countries that their own way of life, based on material wealth, is the desire of everyone. In reality this may not be so and native peoples of the Third World are often made unhappy by the changes in lifestyle that Western-style progress inevitably brings.

Economically, the drawbacks of international aid are even greater. The provision of money, machinery and technological skills (through foreign scientists and technicians) does not necessarily help a less developed country to gain self-sufficiency. It can have a stagnating effect by removing all incentive towards self-help. Once a less developed country becomes dependent upon a developed country, its continued backwardness may be assured.

In terms of finance and capital, the problems inherent in international aid are just as serious. Much of the money provided by the advanced countries is taken up either in administrative costs or is used by the less developed countries to repay their past borrowings. Only a relatively small proportion may actually go towards new schemes. Where bilateral aid is 'tied', the difficulties are exacerbated. Some governments offer a loan to a less developed nation for agricultural or industrial development with the condition that all equipment is bought from the donor country. This 'tied capital' helps to sell the products of the rich countries, of course, but many force poor countries to buy more expensive machinery than could be obtained elsewhere.

International aid has been cynically defined as 'poor people in rich countries giving money to rich people in poor countries'. Naturally this is both unfair and inaccurate; nevertheless, there is more than a grain of truth in it. On the one hand the finance for aid is usually provided by general taxation in donor countries. On the other hand the money, capital equipment or food sent to less developed countries

Figure 17.2   Political views of international aid
For widely different reasons, many geographers – from diametrically opposed political standpoints – argue that international aid is not necessarily desirable. It can be ineffective – or even damaging – for Third World countries, and can drastically alter their cultural characteristics. Both sides argue that economic advancement should be an indigenous process and should proceed at a rate suited to each individual country's environment.

frequently falls into the hands of middlemen and administrative officials. Corruption is not uncommon in much of the Third World, and those responsible for the distribution of supplies may, if dishonest, grow rich on illegal interception. Elsewhere, inefficiency may exist. Ineffective government employees, poor transport facilities or inadequate distribution systems, insufficient finance and restrictive social and cultural divisions, may all result in much-needed provisions never reaching their intended destinations.

International aid and politics

Considering the evident pitfalls of international aid in both concept and operation, and bearing in mind the fact that nearly 75% of all aid is bilateral in nature, it would be wrong to suppose that developed countries help less developed countries for entirely selfless reasons. Economic and social progress leads inevitably to political change and, knowing this, most governments supply aid for ulterior motives. In particular, they see aid as a political lever – a means of strengthening their ties with friendly or neutral countries and in so doing promoting their own national security. In some cases international aid can help to achieve even greater political objectives. Receiving nations may be expected to support, or at least not to oppose, the foreign policies of donor countries and sometimes are asked to 'return the favour' at some future date.

Since World War 2, the world has seen the appearance of two political blocs: 'East' and 'West'. The former comprises the Communist world, being the USSR and its East European satellites, held together by the Warsaw Pact; the latter comprises North America and Western Europe, grouped under NATO (North Atlantic Treaty Organisation). Between these two lies an 'Iron Curtain', a barrier of ideology, distrust and fear.

The effect of this division on international aid has been fundamental. At first the Third World countries, although 'free', were little more than bystanders in the conflict, but gradually the situation altered. The aim of the Communist bloc is to extend communism throughout the world; the aim of the 'West' is to maintain politically free democracies and to halt the spread of communism. The result is that less developed countries have been drawn into the fray and are forced to seek allegiance with one side or the other for their own survival.

This may seem an oversimplified definition of the state of world politics, but it does go some way to explain the character and forces behind foreign-aid movements. Countries of the Warsaw Pact see international aid as a means of extending their own ideologies; NATO countries see it as a means of maintaining their interpretation of human rights and freedom. To these ends, the USSR has provided much aid to such countries as Egypt, India, Libya and Mozambique, and the USA and Britain have countered elsewhere.

Often what begins as economic aid develops into military aid in the form of armaments, warfare know-how and ammunition. In some places this results in all-out war – for example, in Korea, the Middle East, Vietnam, Angola and Ethiopia. In other places the political and military motives behind international aid are less obvious but no less real. Many supposed official economic organisations – for instance, some of those in South America – are in fact possibly run by undercover intelligence services such as the CIA (USA) and KGB (USSR).

As well as the East–West conflict, there is now appearing a further world political division, namely one between black and white. This is becoming ever more apparent and is exemplified through such intracontinental groupings as the OAU (Organisation of African Unity). This was founded in 1963, originally as an association of African countries to promote co-operation and help reduce poverty levels, agricultural inefficiency and industrial underproduction throughout the continent. Today it has rather different principal objectives, the main one being to oppose white supremacy in southern Africa. To this end the OAU provides arms, technological assistance and diplomatic support to various guerilla fighters whose activities are causing border disputes and sometimes total war. The same black–white world conflict is also reflected in various motions and policies instigated by the United Nations General Assembly (for example, trade embargoes on South Africa) and also in the possible misuse of funds by the World Council of Churches.

International aid, when so tied to politics, can be to the actual detriment of the poor in less developed countries. Instead of receiving food, clothes, medical supplies and agricultural equipment, they may only experience invasion, occupation, torture and devastation. If they are suppressed already by their own military or dictatorial régimes, aid from other countries might simply bolster up those same régimes. This may occur either accidentally, as unscrupulous governments intercept important supplies, or intentionally, as foreign countries support governments in less developed countries which share their political ideals, however inappropriate, inefficient or cruel they are. In short, within many countries such as Peru, Brazil, Vietnam, Laos, El Salvador, Angola and Ethiopia, it is even possible that the greatest suffering is caused not by underdevelopment itself but by the aid officially intended to conquer it.

Societal impact of international aid

Apart from the more obvious link between international aid and politics on both world and national scales, there is also a link between international aid and the wider aspects of society – ways of life, social balance, behaviour patterns and so on.

Naturally, and almost unquestionably, aid leads to social and economic progress in the Third World: higher incomes and standards of living, improved educational and medical facilities, better housing conditions and increased leisure activity. However, this does not necessarily mean that the less developed countries are relatively better off than they were. If Third World nations are advancing at a slower rate than developed nations – and evidence suggests that many are – then they are in fact getting poorer in comparison with those developed nations. Indeed, even if development were taken in absolute rather than relative terms, there is no reason to think that aid has been a success in terms of social, economic or political wellbeing. One cannot measure happiness, but it is certainly true that some peoples in the world – the Bolivian and Amazonian indians, for example, and the bushmen of the Kalahari Desert – are more discontented after foreign aid than they were before, since their whole way of life has been destroyed.

The destruction of traditional societies and the introduction of new ways of life and political organisation within alien cultures is indeed a characteristic result of international aid. Third World countries are liable to assume the cultural characteristics of their donor countries – fashions, artistic taste, architectural styles, language and other such aspects. All over South America, Africa and Asia, Western-style clothes are worn, Western-style music is played,

Western-style buildings are constructed. English has become a world language not least because much international aid stems from Britain, the Commonwealth and the USA. In countries where much aid specifically comes from the USA – in Japan (especially after 1945), Venezuela and Colombia, for instance – American influence is all embracing. In such countries Levi jeans, Bermuda shorts and baseball hats are worn, Coca Cola is drunk, hamburgers are eaten and the American drawl is spoken as a second tongue.

Many people view such cultural changes as an unfortunate – perhaps even serious – result of international aid. If the removal of traditional society and its replacement by a modernised materialistic society are also accompanied by military interference, strategic dependency and incompatible economic systems, then Third World countries do indeed come off badly from the international aid deal.

In conclusion, then, we see that there is no easy way forward and that no suitable model exists for developing Third World countries. Perhaps no simple and successful method of international aid can exist while competition between nations for finite resources is inevitably to the detriment of poorer countries. These may be unable to compete owing to their lack of capital, technological skills and advanced economic systems. Perhaps, in the end, the developed world has to be prepared to take a reduction in its standard of living; only then may the vicious poverty circle be broken.

Summary

1   International aid takes many forms: direct (provision of money, goods and services), indirect (through trade agreements), bilateral (between two specific countries) and multilateral (through international bodies such as the Commonwealth and the United Nations).

2   Aid instigated by governments is often politically motivated – given in return for economic or strategic advantage. Aid provided by voluntary bodies is more likely to be altruistic.

3   Even aid given selfishly (e.g. through colonial exploitation) can be advantageous to a receiving country – providing an economic infrastructure, education, law and order, and medical improvement.

4   International aid can be criticised in concept – it can hold back development in a Third World country and make it more dependent upon the West. It can also destroy traditional values, traditions and happiness.

5   Aid often involves an increase in arms trafficking. Military build-up, strengthened political alliances, increased strategic tension – all result from aid and make war more likely.

Data–response exercises

1   Redraw Figure 17.1 showing bilateral aid links between two actual countries, filling in the circles accordingly with real examples of mutual benefit. To what extent does the Third World country you have chosen *suffer* from aid?

2   How can the diverse arguments put forward in Figure 17.2 be (a) supported, and (b) opposed, using real world examples? What arguments are put forward by the political middle ground in favour of international aid?

3   (a) Draw a political map of Africa distinguishing clearly between Commonwealth countries and non-Commonwealth countries. Over each country mark the average annual growth rate in its gross domestic product or its per capita product (information obtainable from the *UN statistical yearbook*).

   (b) Suggest any possible correlation between these growth rates and membership of the Commonwealth.

18 Regional planning in the Third World

Introduction

It is not just the reduction of inequalities on a world scale that interests us but also the reduction of inequalities on national scales. Within many countries there are wide regional divisions – of income, wealth, education, medical services, educational facilities – and these divisions must be minimised if such countries are to achieve balanced socio-economic development.

If international aid can be viewed as the principal means by which planning can achieve a decline in international inequalities, so regional policy can be viewed as the principal means by which national inequalities can be reduced. The greater the economic gap between regions, the more radical and fundamental must be the regional policy applied. Inside Third World countries, this gap between rich and poor regions can be extremely wide, and it is the regional planning policies of such countries with which this chapter is concerned.

The following pages will essentially provide a comprehensive summary of many of the points made in previous chapters, bringing together the main aspects of the regional problems and remedies experienced within the less developed countries of the world. The questions to be answered are:

- What type of regions need the application of regional planning?
- How do governments instigate regional policies, and which methods do they adopt?
- How successful has regional planning been within the Third World, and by what criteria can success be gauged?
- What have been the social, economic and political results of regional policy in less developed countries?

Regional problems

Mention has already been made of the reasons for spatial differences in economic development. Populations, wealth and social advancement are unevenly distributed owing to various physical, economic, cultural, intellectual and political factors. Within Third World countries, such inequalities tend to be extreme: very rich and very poor regions can exist in fairly close proximity yet with little physical or human contact between the two. If it is agreed that such divisions should be bridged and minimised, various problems arise: how best can unequal wealth distribution be reduced, how far can individuals be controlled, how drastic can economic policies be in the correction of agricultural or industrial inefficiency?

Poor regions tend to be located where there are extremes in the natural environment or where the human environment is bedevilled by social, cultural or economic problems. In human terms, inactive populations, unequal racial or cultural characteristics, weak, defenceless or militarily harassed communities, administratively unstable societies or those in political turmoil, and superstitious or traditional behaviour patterns – are all phenomena likely to inhibit development. It is also true that chance factors can play a part in creating underdeveloped regions – bad luck or misfortune often being the cause of poverty.

Some Third World countries have just one distinct region that is backward, often located at the furthest point from the capital city, whereas others have a number of poor regions, these being located separately and irregularly. Each underdeveloped region is marked by its own distinct features (see Table 18.1). Sometimes the backward regions together cover the largest portion of a country – comprising, say, 80% of the total land surface – whereas, elsewhere, backward regions cover only a very small part of a country's total area – perhaps as little as 10%. Of course, the

Table 18.1 Problem regions in South America.

Country	Undeveloped regions	Potential for development
Brazil	1 Amazon Basin: equatorial rainforest; subsistence shifting cultivation; sparse native indian population; primitive way of life; high incidence of disease 2 Mato Grosso: savanna grassland (campos); subsistence pastoralism; pioneer settlement on the *sertão* 3 Dry North-East: barren *caatinga* vegetation; long periods of drought; subsistence mixed farming; depopulation	1 Exploitation of oil and iron ore deposits; export of forest products (including rubber); agricultural clearing schemes for cash crops 2 Cattle breeding and ranching; nickel and tin mining; economic growth around new capital Brasilia 3 Plantations of carnauba and babassu palm trees; irrigation for cotton; intensive pastoral farming
Bolivia	1 Yunga Uplands: high and steep infertile ridges; isolated pockets of intensive farming; summer rainfall and extreme temperature variations 2 Eastern Lowlands: *oriente* tropical forests and marshes; subsistence shifting agriculture; very sparse population; locationally isolated	1 Terracing and contour ploughing for sugar, cocoa and coffee; exploitation of gold reserves 2 Forest clearance schemes for pastoral farming; rubber plantations; exploitation of oil reserves
Venezuela	1 Orinoco Plains: *llanos* region of infertile soils and savanna grassland; winter droughts and summer floods; sparse pastoral population 2 Guiana Highlands: infertile peneplain of igneous rocks; mixed forest and grassland vegetation; extreme climatic variations; very sparse population density	1 Irrigation schemes for cattle ranching, dairying and cash crops; HEP development for industries; oil and natural gas exploitation 2 Mineral mining (for iron ore, manganese and diamonds); heavy engineering development; farming improvements resulting from land settlement schemes

greater the extent of a nation's poor zone, the greater tend to be the difficulties of regional policy.

The underdeveloped regions shown in Table 18.1 exemplify others found in Third World countries. Within many African countries, for example, similar problem areas exist: in the Horn of Africa (southern Ethiopia and Somalia) drought conditions persist; in northern Angola and western Zaïre tropical rainforests create natural hazards, such as diseases, swamps and climatic extremes, which hinder development. In India the far north and south are the poorest regions, the former because of the Himalayas, the latter because of excessive monsoon rains.

It must be remembered that it is not solely the underdeveloped regions of a country that require government planning. The rich areas may equally need help. They may be overdeveloped and have such problems as unemployment or overmanning, pollution, overcrowding, social tension or instability, stretched educational and medical facilities, and food shortages. Indeed, as Myrdal pointed out (see Ch. 12), such problem regions are the inevitable result of economic development: some areas becoming richer while others become poorer. The so-called 'backwash effect' is the reason for the widening economic gap between regions. Only an encouragement of the 'spread effect' – which is the aim of regional planning – can help to correct the disadvantages of regional inequalities.

Regional policy options

The instigation of regional policy, and its subsequent operation and management, raise a complex array of difficulties. A government must first identify the regions in need of greatest help and then decide upon the best course of action required to remedy their problems. Discussions between geographers, psychologists, planners, politicians and economists must take place in order that tactics can be agreed and public opinion can be sought so that policy decisions are introduced with maximum popular support. A government must also decide upon the extent of the financial backing that its regional policy will require,

and also the source of that finance – where the money will actually come from to pay for its planning schemes.

For every decision to be made there are a number of possible options. For each aspect of regional policy development, a government must select from a given set of choices – its ultimate decisions being determined by various physical and human factors. Finance, for example, must come from foreign aid and investment, from funds diverted from other uses, or from domestic taxation. The option chosen will be determined by a country's contacts with other countries, by its burden of debts, by the size of its currency reserves, and by the status or level of subjugation of

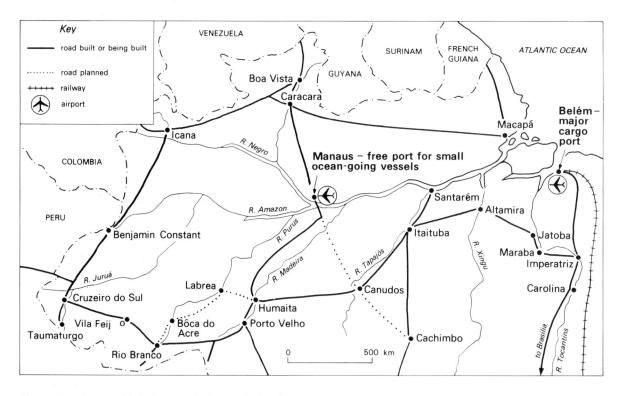

Figure 18.1 Improved infrastructure in Amazonia, Brazil
In order to promote agricultural and industrial progress, the Brazilian government has undertaken a massive programme to improve its country's economic infrastructure: that is, to improve the basic economic facilities that act as a framework upon which development can take place. The Amazon Basin especially is being improved. Road construction is a cornerstone of this programme, with the dual purpose of resettling peasants from the drought-hindered north-east of Brazil and linking Amazonia more effectively with southern Brazil to facilitate the outward movement of forest products and other raw materials and the inward movement of manufactured goods. In addition to road building, other transport improvements are being instigated: Belem now has an international airport, and port facilities are being expanded both there and at Manaus. It is hoped that a band of country 20 km wide will be opened up along the entire length of each road, totalling an area of 60 000 km². Peasant families are being settled in new townships 100 km apart, each with its own schools, clinics, government agencies, credit banks, sawmills, oil-seed processing plants and farm equipment centres. These will form the nuclei of future industrialisation. However, the development of the Amazon Basin has not been without problems: the forcible displacement of the native tribes and the destruction of their way of life have caused great concern, as also has the removal of vast areas of forest, which could upset the world's climate and ecosystem.

its own population. It is also determined by the ideologies, political outlook and dogmatic beliefs of a country's leader.

When a government selects regional development schemes it is presented with a large set of choices. Below is listed this range of options, any number of which may be used to help underdeveloped regions progress socio-economically.

Infrastructure improvements

The improvement of infrastructure is often the first stage in any overall regional policy plans. It involves the construction of those facilities that lay the foundation for further agricultural or industrial development. Thus, there might be the building of new roads, railways and airports; the introduction of efficient telephone links, power supplies and postal services; the modernisation of education and medical facilities; the siting of new warehouses, retail premises and dockside equipment; and the reform of trad-ing, landownership or tax laws. Northern Brazil (see Fig. 18.1), southern India, inland Mozambique and northern Nigeria offer current examples of infrastructure improvement.

Resettlement

Resettlement often takes place in association with the development of a more advanced infrastructure. It involves the building of new villages, towns and cities and the removal of people from the old-established settlements. In Nigeria and Kenya, farm settlement schemes of this nature have proved successful, the newly constructed hamlets and villages bringing people out of the cities to farm previously non-agricultural land. In Tanzania, President Nyerere introduced *ujamaa* settlements in which farming communities live and work by co-operation and collective effort. In some ways such places are not dissimilar to the kibbutzim of Israel, built in order to help the resettlement of newly irrigated desert

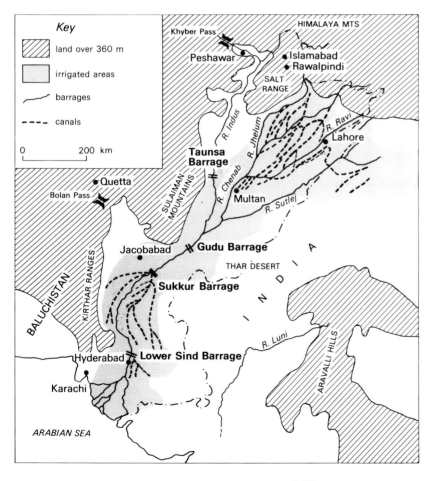

Figure 18.2 Extension of agriculture in Pakistan

Over the past 50 years, Pakistan has attempted to solve its food shortage problem by irrigating the semi-arid lands of the Indus Valley. Today, over 10 million ha are being cultivated, and both tropical and temperate crops are grown: cotton, rice, millet, maize, carrots, oil seeds. In recent years, however, serious problems of soil deterioration have arisen. A higher water table has resulted in the upward leaching of ground moisture, which creates swamps and salt mudflats. About 3 000 000 ha have now been waterlogged in this way and many farmers face disaster. To limit further salination, and to recover lost land, the government has undertaken a massive pumping programme (the pumps being powered by hydroelectricity from the dams). Spray irrigation prevents waterlogging and is now also in progress, but the expense of this method prohibits its widespread use.

265

regions. Occasionally, a government may construct an entirely new capital city within a poor region in order to encourage a more even spread of population and economic activity. In Brazil, Brasilia replaced Rio de Janeiro as capital (1960) and in Nigeria the new city of Abuja aims to replace Lagos (1982 onwards). Each of these two new capitals is significantly located close to the geographical centre of its respective country and within a problem region.

Agriculturalisation

This includes the extension of farming into previously uncultivated areas (by irrigation, drainage, terracing, deforestation and the use of new machinery) and the improvement of farming with higher yields and better produce (by the use of fertilisers, pesticides and new breeding and seeding techniques, by landholding consolidations and by new harvesting technology). The 'Green Revolution' (see Ch. 7) has greatly helped the development of certain poor regions within Third World countries: of inland Peru, western Zambia and northern Sri Lanka, for instance. However, in some instances, agriculturalisation is not without its problems: in Pakistan it has led to soil deterioration (see Fig. 18.2) and in Tanzania it has resulted in discontent, rural depopulation and economic waste.

Industrialisation

The building of new factories and trading estates has, in certain undeveloped regions, provided the impetus for 'cumulative causation' to take place: the multiplier effect operating so that an initial injection of capital and industrial construction leads inevitably to the growth of a manufacturing agglomeration. Footloose industries such as light engineering are most commonly implanted into a problem region, heavy industries being built only where local or imported raw materials are readily available.

Resource development

The development of resources can take many forms and it is normally geared to the specific environmental assets of a given region. Water (rivers and lakes) can be used for drinking, sanitation, transport, agricultural and industrial purposes, fish farming (pisciculture) and tourist facilities (see Fig. 18.3). Minerals can be exploited for their actual or potential usefulness; forests can be utilised for their timber or tree produce (fruit, latex or foliage). Even the climate and landscape of a region can be exploited to further a tourist industry, encouraged by such facilities as hotels, leisure centres and cultural attractions (see Fig. 18.4).

The success of regional planning

It is almost impossible to gauge the success of a regional policy scheme. This is because success is a

---

AGRICULTURAL DEVELOPMENT IN SIERRA LEONE

During the 1970s the government switched to regional policy based on 'development from below' schemes. As part of the 1974–79 Five-year Plan, integrated farming development projects were set up specifically to encourage self-help farming progress. One of these was the Integrated Agricultural Development Project of the Eastern Area (IADPEA).

Apart from financing massive swamp drainage programmes, the IADPEA adopted a strategy whereby the natural and spontaneous improvements that had already begun to take place in the eastern region were encouraged and fostered. Feasibility studies were set up, ecological balances were investigated to assess their capacity for change, and farmers were encouraged to learn new agricultural skills. In particular, the removal of land-owning and trading restrictions by the IADPEA allowed farmers to develop their own methods of development.

The most important factor that helped to produce spontaneous agricultural progress in the eastern region was the increase in diamond mining. This led directly to the growth of towns and population in the area and indirectly to an increase in the demand for food. Local farmers responded to this increase almost entirely under their own initiative; indeed, a multiplier effect developed. Farmers grew more rice, fruit and cassava to feed the increased numbers of local miners, and this brought in more profits to enlarge farms and purchase new machinery. Immigrants introduced new crops (coffee and cocoa), which diversified and further improved agricultural systems. The mining boom also led to the improvement of the local infrastructure (roads and housing facilities), which, in turn, had a beneficial effect on farming. More people flooded into what was becoming a boom region – egged on by the traditional pioneer spirit found in mining boom areas – including merchants, entrepreneurs, money-lenders and other such middlemen. Such people not only helped to develop new agricultural marketing systems but also expanded the credit facilities for farmers – which encouraged further agricultural progress. Throughout this mining-inspired, spontaneous development in farming, the work of the IADPEA was to remove any obstacles that might hinder natural progress.

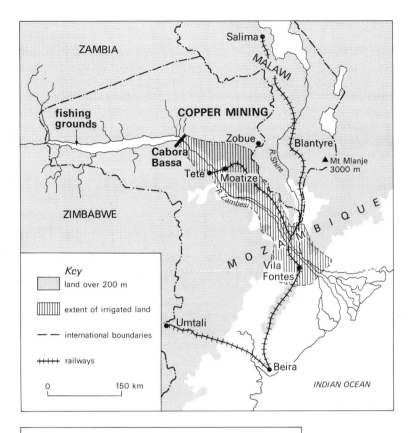

Figure 18.3 Resource development in Mozambique

Mozambique, like most other countries in tropical Africa, has traditionally lacked power supplies and large-scale industry. Today this is changing with the development of hydroelectricity. The Cabora Bassa scheme was started in 1969 in an area that receives 500–1000 mm of rainfall a year (falling mostly in summer) and which, before the scheme, experienced alternating seasons of drought and flood. The dam itself (300 m long at the top, 160 m high) was built where conditions are ideal for HEP plant construction. The Zambezi river flows through the steep-sided, narrow Quebrabasa Gorge composed of hard bedrock. Already, over 1200 MW are being produced and the installation of additional generators is likely to increase this total to over 4000 MW by the late 1980s. This is far more than Mozambique could use and so most of the power will be sold to South Africa, which helped finance the scheme and is the only nearby country sufficiently industrialised to use such vast amounts of energy. Apart from encouraging the development of new industry, the scheme brings Mozambique other benefits. Copper mining can be extended because of the extra power supply and improved communications, and the man-made lake behind the dam (240 km long) provides ideal conditions for a fishing industry – a definite advantage in a country in which the common diet is seriously unbalanced. About 1.5 Mha of irrigated land allows all-year-round cultivation of sugar cane, rice and cotton, and on the plateau, ranching is becoming more important.

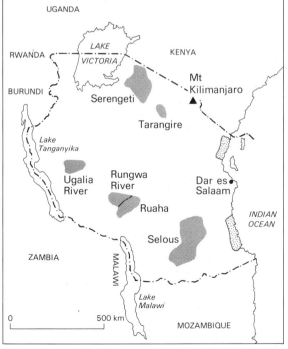

Figure 18.4 Tourism in Tanzania

Since independence the Tanzanian government has attempted to develop its poor regions – those areas furthest inland and at greatest distance from the capital, Dar es Salaam – through tourism. The opening of a new international airport at Arusha, near Kilimanjaro, in 1971 has helped to promote safari holidays in the north of the country; new roads have done the same in the south. The tourist industry now comes under direct government control. Under this control, tourist facilities are built (hotels, swimming pools, golf courses, night-clubs and so on), worldwide advertising is employed and native tribes are encouraged to reconcile themselves to tourist encroachment. The latter has led to the construction of special bush villages where holidaymakers can stay, buy souvenirs and watch specially arranged tribal ceremonies and festivals.

Key

major safari parks and game reserves

new beach resorts

— · — international boundary

subjective term: it can mean different things to different people; it can be measured by different criteria; it can produce both positive and negative results.

If a programme of regional planning produces only some of the consequences that were originally intended, does that programme rank as a success – since some economic development took place and social conditions were ameliorated to a degree – or as a failure – since the total objectives were not realised? Might not the inhabitants of a region subjected to such a programme rate it a success, whereas the government that instigated the programme rate it a failure? Conversely, a regional policy scheme might produce the intended results but at the expense of traditional values and ways of life, or at the cost of physical damage to the local environment. In such an instance, a government would undoubtedly label that scheme a success, but the locals, who have been displaced, 'civilised', 'educated' or in any other ways have had their society destroyed, may well call it a failure. In some cases a scheme may have split effects – some people becoming much better off, others much worse off, depending on how aid funding was organised.

Even in absolute terms, success cannot easily be quantified. It is, for example, unrealistic to compare the socio-economic conditions of a region before and after planning policies have been implemented. Improved conditions are not necessarily the direct consequence of planning. It would be much more realistic – although impossible – to compare a region's level of development after planning with the estimated level that would have been attained without such planning.

By the same token, it is not possible to assess the success of regional policy using only a few yardstick measures. On the positive side, planning might result in higher levels of income, employment and literacy; yet on the negative side, the same planning might result in more social unrest, greater overcrowding and less contentment. The truth is that most planning programmes result in a mixture of plus and minus features and can be ranked as a success or failure at different levels of judgement. Only when the plus side far outweighs the minus side – assuming, of course, that positive and negative factors can be defined – can planning really be called a success.

For these reasons – the difficulties of gauging the degree of planning success – regional policies as operated by many Third World countries have changed over the past decade. There has been a deeper questioning of the meaning of development

and a growing realisation that the economic and social advances made in the developed world are not necessarily suitable for the less developed world. There has, in addition, been a reappraisal of the processes that lead to development – the factors that can either trigger it off or, conversely, can halt it.

Summary

1 Regional inequalities within Third World countries tend to be more extreme than in developed countries – hence they require more ambitious regional policy schemes.

2 Economic backwardness can be explained by environmental hazards, human inefficiency or simply bad luck. In some countries, the poor regions collectively comprise most of the total land surface (e.g. Chad 85%, Peru 60%) since they have a preponderance of difficult conditions.

3 The instigation of regional policy presents a government with many options: which regions to help first, where money should be raised, what development measures to adopt. The most common policies involve infrastructure improvements (in communications, education, public organisation), resettlement, better agriculture and industry, the exploitation of minerals.

4 Levels of success are almost impossible to gauge. The same development programme may be deemed a success by a government (for increasing farm or factory production), but a failure by a local inhabitant (for destroying a traditional way of life).

5 Many regional policy schemes now involve 'development from below' – the encouragement of spontaneous growth on a local scale by native populations.

Data–response exercises

1 To what extent might the backwardness of the regions in Table 18.1 be attributed to the backwash effect, as suggested by Myrdal in his model of cumulative causation? Why did the other regions in these three countries become more advanced economically?

2 Outline the problems that might be faced in the development of the underdeveloped regions shown in Table 18.1. Are these problems typical of development schemes in other Third World countries?

3 Discuss the ways in which the road network being constructed in Amazonia (Fig. 18.1) might be further improved. Examine the drawbacks of infrastructure improvement and suggest other ways in which backward areas might be changed.

4 Investigate further ways in which tourism might be encouraged in Tanzania other than by the methods outlined in Figure 18.4. Would tourist development encourage other forms of economic expansion and, if so, how?

19 Planning in Britain

Introduction

Today the demands placed on Britain's land resources are greater than ever before. Population growth, urban expansion, technological advancement and increased standards of living are, together, exerting such pressure on the landscape that planned control has become imperative. Without control the natural environment is in danger of being misused, mismanaged and, ultimately, destroyed.

This chapter is largely concerned with the mechanisms, ideals and practicalities of general planning policies as operated in Britain since World War 2. Such policies – as opposed to regional policy, which is covered in Chapter 20 – do not have a national scope nor a comprehensively socio-economic dimension. Instead, they tend to be a pragmatic response by central and local government to the small-scale requirements of an ever changing landscape. Within both urban and rural areas, planning policies help to provide improved living, working and leisure conditions.

The questions to be answered in this chapter are as follows:

- What are the problems in planning, and how might they be solved?
- Why is planning necessary, and should it continue in its present form?
- How have planning policies evolved in the past, and how should they develop in the future?
- In what ways can the changes taking place in countryside and towns be controlled?
- How can the environment be improved, and what can be done to help it adjust to modern living and new technology?
- What part can geographers play in planning decisions, and how can they contribute to policy issues?

The difficulties of planning

The problems associated with planning policies are multitudinous. They relate to social, economic and political aspects and are experienced at all levels of the planning process. Also, they are faced not just directly by those actively involved with planning policies but also indirectly by those affected by such policies.

Problems of finance exemplify the diversity of planning difficulties: how much should be spent on a particular scheme, how should the money be raised, how should the cost be recouped, for how long a period should expenditure be estimated? Then, of course, there are the problems of organisation: who should decide on a particular scheme and who should subsequently administer it: planner, local authorities, central government or specially appointed committees? To what extent should laws be changed or introduced in order to aid planning programmes? There are further difficulties regarding planning intentions and implementation.

For both towns and countryside, planning must be geared towards set goals. Economically, it must aim to provide for the 'best locations' for industries and the most balanced spatial distribution of land use; socially, it must help to improve rural and urban environments and reduce differences in wealth. In either case, it should be both effective and efficient in shaping the landscape.

Yet planning is not easy. Besides the difficulties in implementation, its very form is determined by factors that might themselves be transient – the problems being faced at any one time, the ideals of society and the objectives of the planners. What is planned as the best course of action now may not be the best two years hence, neither may it be supported by all members of the public or agreed with by all planners.

In general, planning policies are difficult to instigate for four reasons. First, they require a detailed knowledge not just of geography, but of economics, sociology, politics and psychology. Secondly, they need to combine two approaches: physical planning, concerned with such developments as urban renewal, new town building and rural land use, and economic planning, concerned with spatial aspects of economic progress and resource utilisation. Thirdly, they should be double-edged, involving positive action (allowing for deliberate environmental changes) and negative action (helping the preservation and conservation of what already exists). Fourthly, they must be instigated at all levels, from local (under borough councils) to national (under central government).

The evolution of planning in Britain

Although various economic and social reforms were introduced by successive Victorian governments, it was not really until after World War 2 that the doctrine of *laissez-faire* disappeared. Until then, governments had largely allowed industrial and agricultural changes to take place undisturbed. Only during the past 40 years has the concept of large-scale planning become established.

The first step forward came during World War 2 with the publication of three official reports: the Barlow Report on the distribution of population and industry, the Uthwatt Report on land-use planning, and the Scott Report on the protection of agricultural land. Once peace came, the then Labour government was quick to act, and many of the proposals and recommendations in these reports were incorporated into the 1947 Town and Country Planning Act. This Act can be seen as a turning point. For the first time the government accepted responsibility for most aspects of domestic, agricultural and industrial development, and empowered itself with the means to control human activity. A new government department came into being to administer and formulate planning policy, at first called the Ministry of Town and Country Planning but later renamed the Ministry of Housing and Local Government (today incorporated into the Department of the Environment). In addition, local planning authorities were set up to produce a development plan for each of their individual regions. These development plans were to show proposals for land-use reorganisation over a 20-year period, the intention being to zone industrial, residential, recreational and other land uses into distinct and separate areas. Any landowner (even a householder) wishing to develop a site had to apply for planning permission, obtainable only if his planned development was in accordance with the authority's overall scheme. To aid further the zoning of land use, local authorities were also given the power to acquire properties and sites for redevelop-

ment by compulsory purchase order and to pay compensation to owners for lost rights.

Since the 1947 Act, government planning policies have become stronger, more efficient and more far reaching. Numerous additional planning schemes have been introduced, through Acts specifically concerned with either urban or rural development, and greater effort has been expended on the co-ordination of policies. Today, there is much more contact and co-operation than before between national and local authority planning and between physical and economic planning. Policy co-ordination was particularly encouraged by the establishment of the Department of Economic Affairs in 1964 and by the division of the country into ten Economic Planning Regions.

Later it was realised that the success of planning is often a reflection of the competence of the local authorities implementing it. The improvement of local government efficiency has thus become central to planning policy formulation. To this end the Redcliffe-Maud Commission was appointed in 1966 to investigate ways in which local authorities could be reorganised. The resulting report put forward four proposals: to set up elected provincial councils, replacing the non-elective Economic Planning Councils, to determine regional strategy; to form small 'unitary areas' to replace the larger county, county borough, urban and rural district councils; to set up new 'metropolitan authorities' based on the major conurbations; and to establish a new pattern of small local councils with very limited responsibilities.

Many of these proposals were included under the Local Government Act 1974. By this, some counties disappeared (such as Rutland), some were subdivided (e.g. Glamorgan and Yorkshire) and some entirely new counties were created (e.g. Avon and Humberside). London had already been placed under its own authority (the Greater London Council, established in 1965), but now other metropolitan districts were set up: Tyne and Wear, West Yorkshire, South Yorkshire, Greater Manchester, Merseyside, and West Midlands. However, further changes in the formulation of planning policies came during the 1980s. As a result of political ideology and the alleged inefficiency of many regional authorities in co-ordinating transport and redevelopment plans, much of the responsibility for planning was taken away from local government and given to groups of individuals more likely to reflect public opinion. The Metropolitan Borough Councils, together with the GLC, were abolished, their powers re-allocated to smaller

THE NEED FOR TOWN PLANNING

(1) *Physical growth.* Towns are growing outwards and upwards: The former destroys valuable agricultural land and the latter may be detrimental to urban living (causing local wind eddies, shadows in streets, etc. apart from social problems). Large towns may also create problems of administration, especially when they overlap county or state boundaries.

(2) *Traffic congestion.* This not only causes noise, air pollution and frustration, but also can hinder industrial activity and encourage the depopulation of city centres.

(3) *Food and water supplies.* Town dwellers are often dependent upon distant regions for their food and water. Failures in economic planning, poor harvests, dock and transport strikes, and traffic hold-ups (caused by excessive snow, floods, etc.) can cause food shortages; periods of drought or faults in pipelines can cause water shortages. The problem is exacerbated by the fact that the urban demand for water normally grows at a faster rate than town population growth (because of expanding industries and higher per capita consumption), and fresh water supplies become scarcer (as sources such as wells dry up and other sources become polluted). Political conflict may also arise when towns obtain water from different cultural areas: Birmingham from Wales, Manchester from the Lake District, Glasgow from the Scottish Highlands.

(4) *Building decay.* Industrial and residential buildings in towns are often obsolete and decayed: some because they are old, some because they were poorly built (e.g. Victorian 'jerry-built' terraces and 1960s high-rise flats), some because they were damaged by enemy action during World War 2. Central urban areas are usually the most dilapidated, being characterised by 'twilight zones', that is, zones in which there are numerous slums, poor social services and high crime rates.

(5) *Air and water pollution.* An atmosphere contaminated with grit, dust, noxious factory fumes (e.g. sulphur oxides) and vehicular exhausts (e.g. carbon monoxide) has been a most serious problem in industrial towns. Such places may be covered by permanent clouds and have a high incidence of smogs and fogs. Pollution of this kind is dangerous to health, causing heart diseases, respiratory ailments and lung cancer; it also destroys townscapes, defacing buildings and statues, corroding metal window frames and affecting plant growth. In Britain, the Clean Air Act was passed in 1956 empowering local authorities to designate 'smokeless zones', but still air pollution persists since only relatively few councils have used their given powers. Water pollution is no less serious. Industrial and agricultural effluents together with domestic sewage are sometimes discharged untreated into rivers and seas. This not only produces a dreadful stench but is harmful to human and aquatic life.

(6) *Waste disposal.* Apart from gaseous and liquid effluents there is the added problem of solid waste discharge. Domestic refuse may be piled at local tips, industrial waste (e.g. coal spoil) often forms mountainous heaps. Both are unsightly and both can be dangerous, the former damaging health, the latter causing physical destruction. In 1966, heavy rainfall caused the movement of a coal slag heap at Aberfan (Wales), which resulted in the death of 144 people including 116 children.

In addition, towns are acquiring ever larger car scrapyards and ever more street litter – plastics, bottles, food containers, paper. Some of this rubbish can be burned or recycled but PVC, which is coming into greater use, cannot be destroyed except at enormous cost.

THE NEED FOR COUNTRY PLANNING

(1) *Depopulation.* This is the result partly of improved agricultural technology (reducing the demand for farm workers) and partly of natural decline (as old people, who predominate, die and birth rates fall owing to the out-migration of young adults). Country districts generally offer fewer employment opportunities than do towns, and fewer social, cultural and educational facilities. Depopulation may help agricultural improvements to take place, but it can also lead to social and political difficulties.

(2) *Decline of country occupations.* New technology, changing demands and mass production are causing the disappearance of many rural craftsmen such as blacksmiths, thatchers, wheelwrights and saddlemakers. This not only worsens the employment situation but also leads to the destruction of village life.

(3) *Poor social conditions.* Many parts of the countryside are fairly inaccessible, with poor road and rail networks and inadequate public transport. Also, many country cottages are small and overcrowded, 'tied' to farm employment and lack adequate water supplies, gas, electricity and mains drainage.

(4) *Village urbanisation.* Improved transport and living standards have led many town workers to seek homes in the countryside. This can transform farming villages into commuter settlements. The newcomers are often wealthy upper- or middle-class families and professional workers who can afford to buy cottages at prices far higher than those within the reach of country folk. The resulting rise in property values causes an increase in the rate of out-migration by the original villagers. This change in population has a serious effect on the essential character and community spirit of many rural areas.

(5) *Second homes.* The urbanisation of the countryside is further encouraged by the increasingly common phenomenon of weekend or holiday accommodation. Well-off town dwellers buy homes for temporary use – caravans, houseboats, converted cottages and even, in some places, purpose-built villas and chalets. Areas of particular natural beauty, such as mountains and coastlines, are especially vulnerable to this sort of development and are suffering in consequence with inflated property prices, traffic congestion on narrow roads, and greater stress on social facilities. 'Urbanites' seek 'unspoilt' rustic communities for their rural retreats, but their very presence destroys that quality.

(6) *Tourism.* Leisure and recreational facilities now represent the most serious danger of urban encroachment into the countryside. The periodic invasion of tourists brings in its wake traffic congestion, litter and pollution, conflict between farmers and visitors, ugly camping and caravan sites, and the intrusion of petrol stations, cafés, gift shops and other such incongruous features.

authorities and to independent boards appointed by Parliamentary ministers. In this way, it was argued, planning decision-making would be brought closer to those people most likely to be affected by its provisions.

Urban planning

Urban planning has a history that goes back long before the government took responsibility for it. Mention has already been made of Bath and other spa towns as examples of planned Georgian urban settlements (Ch. 15) and of model villages built by Victorian philanthropists (Ch. 14). Even during medieval times, there were occasional attempts to control traffic movement and waste disposal in towns.

Towards the end of last century a further aspect of urban planning appeared with the 'Garden Suburb' concept. Under the influence of Ebenezer Howard, the housing reformer, this grew as a reaction against Victorian housing congestion. The notion was that towns should combine rural and urban characteristics, obtainable through low housing densities, tree-lined avenues and open gardens. The first Garden Suburb to be built was at Bedford Park (Acton) in 1875 and another appeared at Hampstead in 1907. The same concept also developed to envisage whole towns built to the same formula: a Garden City grew at Letchworth (begun 1903) and another at Welwyn (begun 1919).

Notwithstanding these developments, it could be said that urban planning did not begin in earnest until after World War 2 when it came under strict government supervision. Basically this type of planning has been instigated with two aims: to stop, limit or guide the outward spread of large urban areas and to improve the economic and social conditions that exist within towns. The former involves the establishment of 'Green Belts', the decentralisation of population and industry, and the control of urban land-use extension. The latter involves slum clearance, rehabilitation schemes and the rationalisation of urban land-use patterns.

Controlling urban spread

Green Belts encircle towns and are broad rings of countryside (perhaps 10 km wide) in which urban development is restricted. The first to be designated surrounded London (proposed in 1944 and approved between 1954 and 1958) but now others exist elsewhere, notably around Glasgow, Leeds and Bristol.

Limiting outward urban growth through Green Belts meant that excess urban populations had to be accommodated beyond the immediate town environs. This has been done either through the construction of New Towns or through the expansion of existing old towns. The latter leads to the growth of satellite settlements whose prosperity is dependent upon that of the parent cities. Usually towns that receive overspill populations are close by their donor cities, but this is not always the case. Swindon and Kings Lynn receive overspill from London, and Weston-super-Mare from Birmingham.

Such has been the extent and success of these overspill schemes that some cities are experiencing too much depopulation, causing an adverse effect on their prosperity and, sometimes, the appearance of 'dead hearts'. For this reason, policies geared towards decentralisation are now diminishing in significance (in some cases, are being reversed) and greater emphasis is being placed on planning within cities. Enterprise zones – where there are few planning controls – have been set up, for example, in order to revitalise inner city areas.

Improving urban conditions

Internal urban planning is difficult. This is because of complexities of land ownership, the constraints imposed by outdated urban structures (old buildings and narrow, winding streets) and the conflict of interests between residential and industrial land uses. Even so, much success has been achieved and many townscapes in Britain have been transformed.

Since the late 1950s, slum clearance and redevelopment has been the pivot of many planning policies. Sometimes this takes place on a piecemeal basis, sometimes comprehensively, whereby whole areas are demolished and redesigned. Certainly the existence of the Comprehensive Development Area (CDA) procedure has helped the latter. By this, authorities are empowered to take over complete urban zones, through compulsory purchase, and entirely refashion the use of land within them – building new roads, new residential areas, landscaping new parks and so on. Some towns have examples of extremely ambitious schemes indeed – the Barbican in London, the Park Hill area in Sheffield, central Birmingham and much of Glasgow (see Fig. 19.1).

Until fairly recently, redevelopment often resulted in the construction of high-rise tower blocks of flats, which were considered to be the most efficient

273

Figure 19.1   Urban renewal in Glasgow, Scotland
Large areas of wasteland and slum housing, including much of the notorious Gorbals district, have been cleared over the past 20 years. In their place have grown up high-rise blocks of flats, new office complexes, modern industrial premises and urban motorways. However, many of the social problems – vandalism, crime and violence – seem to continue.

method of housing people at high densities. Today this is no longer the case. Constructional drawbacks (brought to light by several disasters involving gas explosions), social and psychological problems (exemplified by the high incidence of vandalism, perhaps as a result of a lack of recreational facilities, and by an increase in the number of unsocialised and even mentally deranged children, possibly caused by living at high levels and in enclosed spaces), and public opposition to 'rabbit-hutch' living have, together, led to a drastic reduction in the number of tower blocks built. More commonly, redevelopment schemes now involve the construction of small terraces and the provision of private gardens.

Redevelopment, in whatever form it takes, generally results in a lower population density than existed before. This may be desirable from a sociological point of view, but it causes planners the problem of rehousing those people not accommodated by the new buildings. This rehousing can be allowed through new residential estates built on the urban fringe – for example, at Roehampton and Thamesmead in London, and at Gleadless Valley in Sheffield.

Slum clearance and redevelopment can be expensive, waste resources, destroy community life, create urban deserts and produce new, inhuman buildings. For this reason, rehabilitation schemes have become more important in recent years. By these, old buildings are repaired, given modern conveniences such as bathrooms, and are set in refurbished and more attractive surroundings. A great incentive for these schemes came in 1968 when the government issued a White Paper, *Old Houses into New Homes*, and in 1969 when the Housing Act allowed local authorities to designate 'General Improvement Areas' and to draw on government funds. In this way money can be saved, structurally sound buildings are preserved, and community life is maintained.

The rationalisation of land-use patterns usually involves segregation: the zoning of different land uses, the division of pedestrian from vehicular traffic and the separation of different types of transport movement. The first results in distinctive urban sectors, the second in such features as pedestrian precincts and the third in road hierarchies. Transport segregation was originally proposed by Sir Colin Buchanan in *Traffic in towns* (HMSO, 1963). He envisaged the subdivision of towns into *environmental units*, in each of which vehicular access is limited and pedestrians dominate. These environmental units would be linked to each other, and to the rest of the town, by a network of wide roads specially designed to carry heavy traffic. In some towns such environmental units have since appeared and, in a few, distinct road grades have been established: national distributor roads (like motorways, for heavy through-traffic), primary distributor roads (like trunk roads, for cross-country traffic), local distributor roads (used by delivery vans and other local vehicle movements) and local access roads (used only by the local inhabitants).

Where future town planning will lead is a matter of

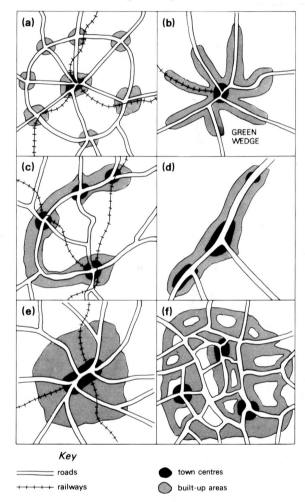

Figure 19.2 Developing urban forms
Large urban areas (conurbations and megalopoli) may grow in any of these patterns: (a) satellite or neighbourhood plan (e.g. Stockholm); (b) stellate or radial plan (e.g. Copenhagen and London); (c) circuit or ring plan (e.g. Randstad and San Francisco); (d) linear or beaded linear plan (e.g. Paris); (e) core or compact plan (e.g. New York); (f) dispersed plan (e.g. Los Angeles).

INNER CITY AREAS

Characteristics of inner cities

(1) Large areas of waste land, many empty buildings (residential and commercial), high percentage of general dereliction and decay, high number of closures amongst commercial premises because of high rates and rents.

(2) Very high unemployment, few job opportunities, limited career prospects for those still employed.

(3) Unbalanced population structure with unusually high proportions of elderly and disadvantaged people, racially mixed inhabitants with substantial ethnic minorities, out-migration of native residents.

(4) A lack of morale and confidence, high levels of crime and violence, depressed community spirit, insufficient policing, falling educational standards.

Policy proposals for inner cities

(1) *Policy for the Inner Cities*, a White Paper published in 1977, had three central elements: greater resources and priority for inner-city areas (through expanded aid programmes); a co-ordinated approach by central and local government working together; and measures to help strengthen inner areas' economies and to encourage employment. These would form the foundation to environmental improvement.

(2) The Inner Urban Areas Act 1978 gave specific powers to selected inner-city local authorities to support the creation of new employment opportunities and to improve industrial environments. The use of grants and loans would help finance the revitalisation of inner-city areas.

(3) The setting up of enterprise zones (after 1980) helped to reduce planning delays, lower tax-rate overheads and thus encourage comprehensive redevelopment within urban areas.

(4) The Scarman Report (1982) led to various social changes aimed at reducing human tensions within inner-city regions. Community policing, positive discriminatory employment agreements and the expansion of sports and leisure facilities were all gradually introduced thereafter.

---

conjecture. Some people foresee towns enclosed in tall towers (perhaps 1 km high), others see them built on ocean rafts, on the sea bed or underground. More realistically, and in the nearer future, urban forms are likely to develop into the structures shown in Figure 19.2.

New Towns

The New Town concept began in 1944 with the publication of Sir Patrick Abercrombie's *Greater London Plan* in which entirely new settlements were proposed for south-east England to accommodate the capital's overspill population. Unlike expanding or satellite towns, these New Towns were to be self-sufficient units, having a full range of manufacturing, services, shopping and entertainment facilities, providing employment for all their own inhabitants, and containing a balance of social communities.

By the 1946 New Towns Act, the building of the first of these settlements was instigated and by 1974 there were 33 in existence, with more being planned (Fig. 19.3). Today, over 1.5 million people in Britain live in New Towns. Yet these New Towns are not all the same, in either structure or appearance. Changing planning objectives and ideas have resulted in four recognisable phases of New Town development, each phase being characterised by distinctive features of form and layout. These phases are discussed below and their structures are compared in Figure 19.4.

Stage 1 (1946–50)

The first 14 New Towns, including Stevenage, Crawley, Harlow and, in Scotland, East Kilbride (see Fig. 19.5), were built to strict and inflexible plans. Neighbourhood units were central to their structures, each being a separate community containing about 5000 people and having its own school, church, shopping centre and social facilities. Low housing densities were a feature (as low as 50 people per hectare) and some attempt was made at residential–industrial zoning (the factories being positioned around the fringes of the built-up areas). Growing car ownership was allowed for, with wide streets and pedestrian precincts, but little attempt was made to establish a road hierarchy and only 25% of the houses were provided with garages.

Stage 2 (1951–60)

Many lessons were learnt from the first New Towns so that the second phase – of which Cumbernauld in Scotland is the prime example – did not repeat some of the earlier mistakes. The neighbourhood unit was less strictly adhered to and land-use zoning was less rigidly applied. Housing densities were increased (up to 200 people per hectare), a greater number of

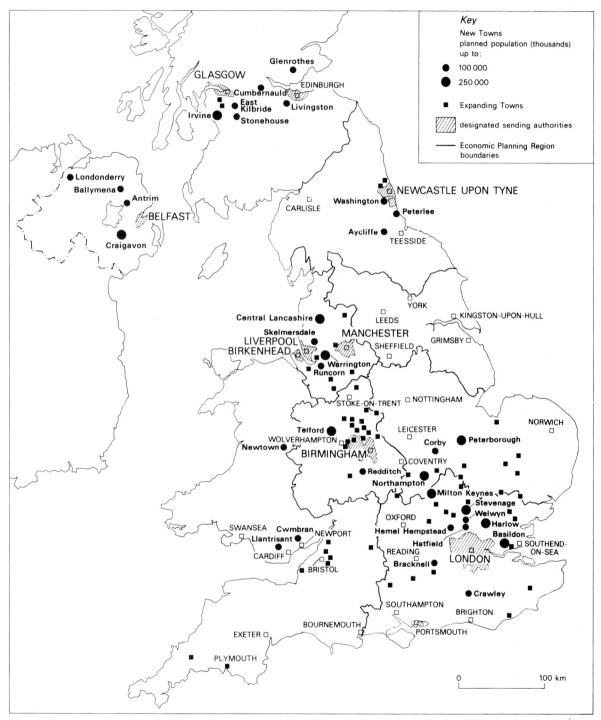

Figure 19.3 New Towns in Britain
Most of these were built on largely green-field sites and owe their origins to the 1946 New Towns Act. Some, like Welwyn Garden City, were built at the beginning of this century and have since been redesignated as New Towns. A few, like Northampton and Warrington, are merely revamped old towns.

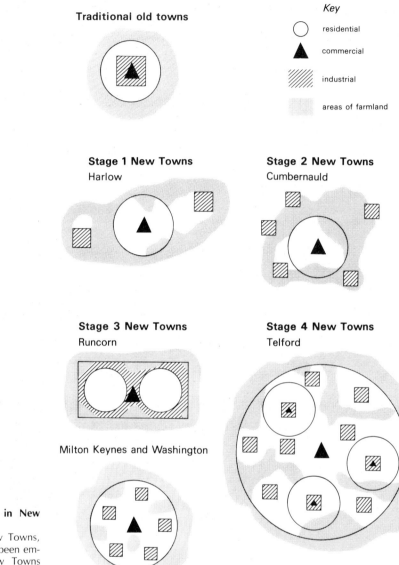

Figure 19.4 Land-use zoning in New Towns
Since the birth of the first New Towns, various internal structures have been employed. The more recent New Towns demonstrate a partial return to the pattern common in traditional towns.

flats were built and more private development was allowed. Schools, shops and social centres were dispersed more through residential areas and many separate factory estates were sited at the urban edge. More attention was also given to car ownership: 75% of the houses built with garages, there was complete segregation of pedestrian and vehicular traffic, and a road hierarchy was established.

Stage 3 (1961–70)
The third phase again represents a questioning of

former concepts. Seventeen New Towns appeared in these years, including Runcorn, Dawley, Redditch, Washington, Milton Keynes, Irvine (Scotland) and Ballymena (Northern Ireland). In general they were larger and less self-sufficient in concept than former New Towns, in some cases being socially and economically linked to existing old towns (providing, for example, commuters to nearby cities or receiving industrial workers from beyond their own boundaries). The neighbourhood unit concept made a partial reappearance and population densities were

Figure 19.5 Stage 1 New Town: East Kilbride, Scotland
This was designated in 1947 and now has well over 120 000 inhabitants. Note the low housing density, the isolation of industrial plants and the diversity of architectural designs.

reduced from those at Cumbernauld (to about 150 people per hectare). More provision was given to public transport and both traffic/pedestrian segregation and road hierarchies were continued. Although urban structures were more varied in this stage – Redditch is linear, Runcorn has a figure-eight shape and Washington is square – all show a further movement away from land-use zoning.

Stage 4 (since 1971)
Although the first three phases are the most commonly identified, a fourth is becoming apparent.

Those now being planned will be, not separate settlements, but amalgams of existing towns, in some cases housing up to half a million people. Dawley, Wellington and Oakengates are being merged into Telford, another town is emerging from Leyland, Preston and Chorley, and yet others are envisaged around the Solent and Humber estuaries. These places will be more complex in structure than their earlier counterparts and will be more integrated into the existing character of their surroundings.

Although New Towns have been praised for providing modern industrial premises, spacious homes and

279

rural surroundings, they have also been criticised. Some people complain that their social amenities and shopping facilities are inadequate for their populations; some say that their rents are too high; and many say New Towns are ugly in appearance, lack the variety of architectural styles common in older towns and have no bustle, community spirit or homeliness. Indeed, such are their faults that new settlers may suffer from 'New Town Blues' and long to return to their old homes in more traditional towns.

In retrospect, many New Towns have been only partially successful in both economic and social terms. Some faired remarkably well during the recession of the early 1980s – suffering less from unemployment and deindustrialisation than have other places – but many faired worse. Skelmersdale, Livingston and Peterlee, for example, suffered higher unemployment, more redundancies and more industrial closures than the national average. On a social level, Milton Keynes is among the worst towns in Britain for crime, vandalism and schoolchild truancy. Perhaps, with hindsight, we can argue that too much time, money and planning have been invested in New Towns and not enough on inner-city areas.

Rural planning

It was once assumed that the countryside – which covers 90% of Britain – required no special help, protection or control, and that only towns need planning. Now it is realised that this is not true. Rapid changes in the social, economic and physical environment of rural areas are making controls ever more necessary: depopulation should be stemmed, increasing urban influences accommodated, new farming technologies adopted in the context of the existing environment, and the beauty of the countryside must be protected against aesthetic spoliation.

Of course, these objectives may conflict with each other, and rural planning attempts to reconcile one aim with others. There are., however, problems inherent in this: rural planning policies are needed to produce positive, beneficial changes rather than simply to maintain existing conditions, and should conserve the natural beauty of the countryside without reducing nature to the status of a museum piece. These aims are diverse and the difficulty is to find the balance between them.

A major step towards the achievement of the aims came with the 1947 Agriculture Act. This set up machinery for controlling urban–industrial

Figure 19.6   Hedgerow removal in Gloucestershire
It is estimated that 8000 km of hedgerow are removed annually in England and Wales. These hedgerows, it is claimed, waste valuable land, hinder the use of machinery and harbour vermin. However, they are also beneficial. They prevent wind erosion, support wildlife, which is necessary to keep soils fertile, and enhance the aesthetic quality of the countryside. So questionable are the benefits of prairie farming that various farming bodies and the Countryside Commission now encourage farmers to set up 'ecological corners' – small plots of land within a farm where bushes, trees, rivers and ponds are left untouched to form oases of wildlife and unspoilt nature.

development (thereby protecting agricultural land) and helped to encourage more efficient farming methods. Today, partly as a result of this Act, Britain has one of the most efficient agricultural systems in the world.

Provision for the increasing influence of urban areas has been aided in various ways. Certain rural settlements have been designated **key villages** in which expansion has been encouraged; elsewhere the

"We're very lucky, when you think about it, working in such beautiful surroundings."

Figure 19.7 The power to destroy
Progress is a mixed blessing (From Thelwell, N., 1978. *The effluent society*. London: Methuen.)

natural decline of villages has been helped by re-settlement schemes and the integration of cottages into larger residential units. Many villages have been allowed to grow with new council or private housing estates and new light engineering factories; others have been converted into specialised functional settlements – military camps, forestry villages, holiday resorts and so on. In some places entirely new villages have been built, within the countryside, to act as separate communities: at Bar Hill (Cambridgeshire), Studlands Park (Suffolk) and New Ash Green (Kent).

Whatever form urban assimilation takes, there are likely to be drawbacks. Village expansion is often opposed by local inhabitants, it frequently involves the building of totally inappropriate development out of keeping with the surroundings, and it can cause the decline of the rural way of life.

The introduction of new farming technologies has been an especially successful aspect of rural planning since World War 2. More efficient agriculture has largely come about through government aid in the form of technical advice and financial grants. Higher yields have been achieved through the greater use of fertilisers, increased mechanisation, farm amalgama-

tion and the removal of hedgerows (Fig. 19.6). Improved marketing has been achieved through better communications and the modernisation of farm buildings and equipment.

One aspect of rural planning that poses particular problems is the provision of public services (Fig. 19.7). On the one hand, rural depopulation means that services (shopping, health and educational facilities, piped water, drainage and electricity) must be rationalised; on the other hand, the same services must be preserved since they are essential for the remaining population. This conflict is especially acute in transport. Increasingly, bus and train services are being withdrawn, but this particularly affects those without access to cars – the poor, the old and the young. The aim of the planner is to provide a regular and reliable transport system, but one which is economically viable. The use of minibuses, school buses and postal buses for public transport may help provide a solution, but there still remains no complete and satisfactory answer to the problem.

Finally, it should be noted that rural planning is becoming ever more broadly based. All aspects of the countryside – settlements, agriculture, forestry, industry, water resources and recreational facilities – must be organised in relation to each other, and policy plans must be comprehensive and co-ordinated. To this end, multipurpose planning authorities are appearing at the regional level, exemplified by the Highlands and Islands Development Board (established 1965), which covers half of Scotland and has strong and far ranging powers.

Recreation and tourism

Over the past 30 years, and for various reasons, the demands for recreational and tourist facilities have increased out of all proportion and have become more varied. Population increase, higher incomes and living standards, shorter working weeks, longer vacations, greater education and improved transport (especially the growth of car ownership) together have created an age of leisure pursuits.

Recreational activities can be passive – watching television, reading, theatre and cinema-going, and so forth – or active, being simple (driving, walking, sightseeing), requiring minimal preparation and equipment (playing sports, fishing), or requiring very specialised equipment (sailing, skindiving, rock climbing). Tourism involves the mass movement of people from home to temporary accommodation for durations ranging from a weekend to, perhaps, many months.

Both recreation and tourism require some facilities – for example in the form of amenities, transport and accommodation. Both exert great demands on the environment and both can drastically alter it. For these reasons, their planned control is necessary to provide for maximum use of the resources of recreation and tourism, to channel human activity through and to particular places and to protect nature from the excesses of increased leisure activities.

More than ever before, leisure pursuits constitute an 'industry'. As such they are facing distinct economic and social problems, creating demands for services, providing a market for manufactured goods, and helping to create significant benefits. Recreation and tourism are essentially a service industry that is labour-intensive (offering temporary or seasonal employment) and wasteful of capital (since its facilities lie idle for part of each year). Advantages and disadvantages may both ensue. On the plus side, the leisure industry can bring economic wealth and improved social facilities to individual regions and countries as a whole. On the minus side, it can bring

overcrowding, congestion, pollution and social stress. Areas like south-west England and North Wales have survived economically because of their tourist attractions, but few inhabitants in either region would view tourists as unmixed blessings. Britain attracts over 10 million foreign visitors annually, making tourism her largest dollar-earner in invisible trade, but the resulting drawbacks in terms of overpeopled sites (like the London 'sights' and such places as Stratford-upon-Avon) can hardly be ignored.

Planning for recreation and tourism involves two approaches: organisation and the provision of facilities. The former, for tourism, is usually undertaken by travel agents, tour operators and so forth. The latter – more important in the context of this chapter – includes the supply of sports equipment, catering, car parking, accommodation and other services, and undertakings requiring the work of local and central authorities, and of private enterprise.

To help policy-making it has been suggested that various grades of recreational facility areas should be identified. These are as follows:

(1) *High-density recreation areas.* These should be near towns, have maximum access, cater for heavy, short-term use (especially for sports) and, if possible, be totally planned and built from scratch.

(2) *General outdoor recreation areas.* These should be set in fairly open countryside where a wide choice of day and weekend activities is offered. They should have easy access.

(3) *Natural environmental areas.* These should be unspoilt expanses of countryside where access is limited. Provision for weekend and longer-stay visitors should be allowed through such facilities as camping sites.

(4) *Unique natural areas.* These, being regions of outstanding natural beauty, should be retained in their natural state. Human access should be restricted.

(5) *Primitive areas.* These should form isolated wildernesses in which change is avoided and human beings are barred. Often such areas might be of significant ecological value.

(6) *Historic and cultural sites.* These would provide specialised sightseeing points, access being allowed (though perhaps not encouraged) and tourist facilities such as car parks provided.

In Britain, leisure planning has been a feature of

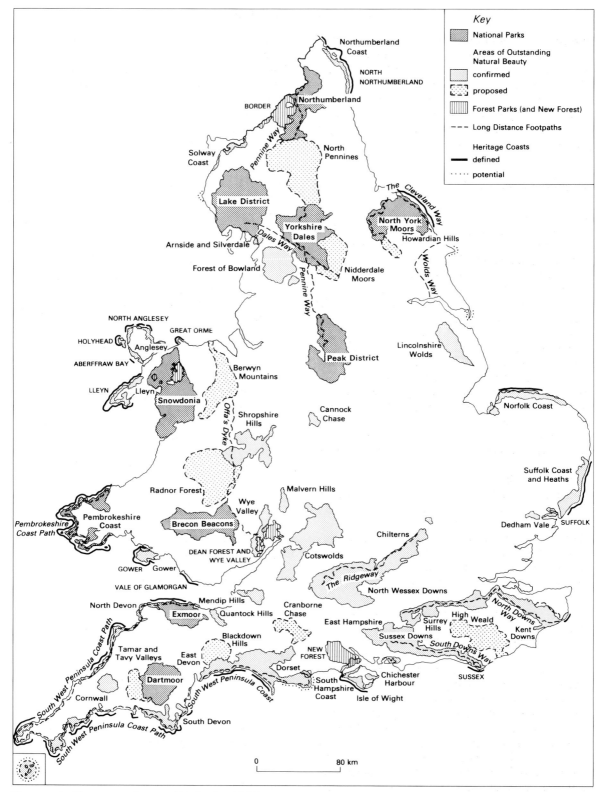

Figure 19.8 The protected areas of England and Wales
In addition to these areas there are countless other protected spots – those owned by the National Trust, for example, and the Nature Conservancy authorities.

local and central government policies since World War 2 and, to a large extent, has set up examples of all six of the area types listed above. In order these are: sports centres, country or regional parks, national parks, Areas of Outstanding Natural Beauty (AONBs), nature reserves and, finally, such places of historic interest as Stonehenge, Hadrian's Wall and the ruined monasteries of the Yorkshire Dales. The appearance of these has occurred gradually and as a result of various government Acts.

The first major planning development came in 1949 with the National Parks and Access to the Countryside Act. This set up national parks, allowed for the designation of AONBs, and provided for greater public access to rural areas. A complete survey of public rights of way was instigated and local authorities were empowered to open up new access points, either through agreements with landowners or through the imposition of 'access orders'. In the same year, the Nature Conservancy was established – an organisation primarily concerned with the preservation of ecological aspects of the countryside (achieved through nature reserves). As a result of the 1949 Act, about 20% of the total area of England and Wales was brought under official protection (Fig. 19.8).

Since then, more planning has led to further innovations. Long-distance footpaths have been set up (including the Pennine Way, Offa's Dyke and the North Downs Way); regional parks have been established (like that along the Lee Valley in Essex) and, in conjunction with the Forestry Commission, forest parks have appeared (including those of the New Forest and Forest of Dean). By the end of the 1960s, as a result of the Countryside Act and the Development of Tourism Act, there was an efficient co-ordination of planning policies and a comprehensive scheme of tourist provision, these being permitted by the Countryside Commission, the British Travel Authority and the Tourist Boards for Wales, Scotland and England. In addition to these official government bodies, Britain also possesses various private organisations that help preserve the environment: the National Trust, the Council for the Protection of Rural England, the Ramblers' Association, the Royal Society for the Protection of Birds, and numerous county Naturalists' Trusts.

Notwithstanding the overall success of the various environmental bodies, certain fundamental problems persist in planning for leisure pursuits. Central to these problems are the conflicts of interest inherent in all fields of policy formation. Nowhere are such conflicts more conspicuous than in the national parks (Fig. 19.9). These are areas designated for conservation and planned to provide for tourism. This very intention, however, may run counter to other land uses – defence installations or military training grounds, power stations, reservoirs, oil refineries, new roads, quarrying and mining. Almost by definition national parks are rural areas where population density is low and the economy sluggish, yet the cures for these conditions (farming improvements and industrialisation) may be disallowed on the grounds that they are aesthetically detrimental and would discourage tourism. Perhaps more serious still – and more insuperable a problem – is the difficulty of reconciling the conservation of the countryside with the provision of tourist facilities. The latter would involve the setting up of camping and caravan sites, car parks, public conveniences and gift shops, all of which disfigure the very beauty that tourists want to see.

Balancing such diverse conflicts is not easy and in many cases there is considerable opposition to planning policies. Plans that aim to encourage tourism may be opposed by country lovers, and those aiming to preserve intact stretches of countryside may be opposed by industrialists, tourist boards and motoring organisations. Over recent years the Countryside Commission has made a gallant and not unsuccessful attempt to satisfy all shades of opinion. In areas under its jurisdiction (such as national parks), changes have been allowed but are so controlled that their effect on the environment has been minimised. New roads are hidden under 'cuts-and-covers' or within cuttings; camping and caravan sites are shielded by belts of trees, and new buildings are constructed out of local stone and to local designs. Tourist 'honeypots' are also becoming a common feature. These are points that are deliberately planned to attract tourists who, encouraged by picnic sites, 'viewpoints', car parks, gift shops and information centres, gravitate together in masses. By concentrating visitors in a few selected points, the untidy thin dispersal of people over large areas is prevented. Areas away from 'honeypots' are preserved in their unspoilt and quiet character for the enjoyment of the few who wish to walk more than a few hundred metres from their car doors.

Socio-economic effects of planning

It should be remembered that, by controlling and determining the characteristics of the environment,

Figure 19.9 Getting away from it all
Tourism can spoil the very areas which tourists wish to see unspoilt. (From Thelwell, N. 1978. *The effluent society*. London: Methuen.)

planning has a direct effect upon the way people live: where they reside and work, how they behave and interact, what personal contentment they enjoy. Because of this, the topic of planning should be viewed not as an impersonal study of academic problems and solutions but as a real-life investigation into human conditions. Facts and figures, policy documents and decisions, objectives and concepts should not be considered alone but in the context of their social, economic and political repercussions. Such repercussions, of course, vary according to circumstances. The short-term results of a particular planning scheme may be very different from its long-term results, its impact on one section of the community very different from its impact on another section. The ways in which planning is perceived and understood by different groups of people can similarly be diverse, varying according to levels of personal education, knowledge, attainment and wealth.

The varied ways in which planning can have an impact on human society can be seen in both countryside and town. A few examples may help to demonstrate this. Since World War 2 – and especially over the past 20 years – much planning has taken place to accommodate modern developments in transport and communications: the building of motorways and airports, the closure of railway lines,

the development of teletext, computer and cable television links, and so on. Such changes have had positive effects: they have greatly improved the movement of goods and passengers (to the delight of industry and travellers); have facilitated the spread of tourism; have released certain occupations (self-employed craftsmen, businessmen in service activities and technical consultants, for instance) from urban-based locations; and have made village life more economically viable with the injection of new facilities – schools, housing estates and medical centres. On the negative side, the same changes have helped to destroy the way of life in local communities (motorways dividing cohesive districts and producing air and noise pollution) and have caused public services in country districts to be withdrawn for economic reasons (thus cutting off many rural folk from contact with local towns). Within towns, the introduction of buses-only lanes and parking restrictions has reduced traffic congestion but has also caused serious losses in turnover for many shopkeepers. The spatial segregation of residential and industrial land uses has improved urban conditions but increased commuter traffic.

Within national parks and AONBs the conflicts of planning interests (often apparent at public inquiries) are especially obvious. Proposed developments in the form of new industry and housing, road building, natural resource exploitation and the construction of reservoirs are frequently supported by locals who want to encourage job and wealth creation, but are violently opposed by occasional visitors, tourists, second-home owners, newly settled pensioners and conservation groups who wish to preserve an area's natural attractiveness. Planning controls may severely limit the enterprise and initiative of some people while maintaining the interests of others or of the country as a whole.

A further aspect of planning that should be noted is its detachment from real human issues. To a large extent the inception and execution of planning policies have been the preserve of politicians (both national and local representatives), architects, landscape designers and builders, whereas the recipients of planning policies – those intended to benefit – are businessmen and members of the general public. What the latter groups want is not necessarily what the former groups provide. The result of such a dichotomy between demand and supply is frequently failure.

Large areas of British towns have been rebuilt and redesigned as a result of mass slum clearance and the need to replace structures demolished by German air raids during World War 2. Yet the opportunity to create exciting new townscapes, of diverse and attractive appearance, seems to have been missed by all those involved in planning. The urban landscapes of Britain have been given an apparent dreariness – certainly in the opinion of many people. Everywhere, towns look similar, with high-rise blocks of flats and offices, estates of small box-like houses and bungalows, and vast expanses of glass and concrete. There are few people today who would honestly say that London's South Bank complex, Birmingham's Bull Ring, Coventry's city centre or almost any New Town is pleasing to the eye.

The truth is that urban renewal has taken place in a piecemeal fashion with little concern for overall or future considerations. Local authorities, architects, planners and builders have worked for immediate results, political expediency, and short-term financial gain. Victorian slums have been replaced by modern slums: many new housing estates – some less than 20 years old – are already empty and abandoned, rotting away and collapsing or being demolished. In many cases, such estates will continue to be paid for, by tax- and rate-payers, until the end of the century, so reducing the money available for yet new developments.

For many years, few planning authorities thought to ask the opinion of the general public. Slum dwellers were seldom asked about the kind of rehousing they preferred; office workers were rarely consulted about what sort of premises they wished to be given. The result was that families have been forced into high-rise or rabbit-hutch living against their will, and white-collar employees have been made to work in noisy open-plan offices. Planners tend to impose their own ideas on others: middle-class architects design homes for the working classes in forms that they think the latter ought to like. It is not uncommon for a planner to instigate the building of a concrete-desert housing estate yet live, himself, in an elegant Georgian home. He will design a Thamesmead but live in Hampstead, he will plan Peterlee but live in Durham.

Only very recently has planning begun to come down from Mount Olympus – begun to relate itself to the real needs and desires of the general public. Inquiries and open forums are growing more common so that individuals can have their say over projected redevelopment schemes. Still more could be done and geographers in particular should become more active in the decision-making process of planning. Not just for large programmes – the revitalisation of inner-city areas for example – but also for relatively small planning schemes, geographers ought to be able to use methods of **synthesis** (the interrelated study of real world issues and environmental changes) and help to guide the development process. For new road routes, hypermarket and supermarket site allocation, sports-hall siting, the closure of village schools and other rural services, the provision of tourist facilities and other such schemes, geographers should be asking questions and offering answers. Will the planning scheme benefit the local inhabitants and fulfil regional or national needs in the context of such present-day issues as racial harmony, party political divisions and the role of the police? Is social and economic justice maintained or will the underprivileged suffer? What opposition will be generated and whose interests are being satisfied? What will be the long-term socio-economic or political impact of a particular scheme? In all these ways, geographers should compare and evaluate different planning proposals; they should analyse their merits and drawbacks. Only in this manner can planning be brought back to the people.

Summary

1 Planning is necessary to control changes taking place in town and countryside and to improve the conditions in which people live, work and take leisure. However, there are problems involved in finance, organisation and policy decision-making.

2 Planners, politicians and geographers rarely agree since they see the environment through different eyes. Planners may see the landscape as a testing-ground for ideas, politicians may see it as a raw material for electioneering or civic manoeuvring, geographers probably see it more simply as a place where people live.

3 Town and country planning in Britain dates from 1947, since when it has widened in scope: through the setting up of Green Belts, New Towns, national parks, smokeless zones, the Countryside Commission, Economic Planning Councils and Development Corporations.

4 Urban areas need planning because of their growth, slums, traffic congestion and pollution; rural areas because of their depopulation, deruralisation (loss of social services, country crafts, village communities) and their use for tourism.

5 Inner-city areas have particularly acute problems – commercial decline, unemployment, slum housing, crime, social disintegration.

6 Planning has helped improve urban living – through redevelopment, traffic control, land-use segregation and building rehabilitation. New Towns, however, have not been totally successful – many lack social cohesion and architectural elegance.

7 Rural planning has helped countryside cope with change – through agricultural improvements, planned village growth, the building of key villages and the provision of 'ecological corners' (to compensate for loss of hedgerows).

8 The growth of tourism is the greatest problem facing the countryside since it leads to congestion, pollution and the spoliation of attractive scenery.

9 The Countryside Commission and various other organisations (e.g. the National Trust) do much good work in the conservation of the landscape. National parks, tourist 'honeypots', long-distance footpaths, nature reserves, picnic sites and nature trails have been set up to channel tourists into zones.

10 Planning can be criticised for a lack of human understanding – the general public often dislikes what planners have designed.

Data–response exercises

1 Examine the various forms in which urban renewal takes place, as indicated in Figure 19.1. Discuss the advantages and disadvantages of urban motorways.

2 Account for the regional distribution of British New Towns (Fig. 19.3). To what extent do the locations of these New Towns determine the future development of megalopoli in Britain?

3 Analyse the relative merits of the land-use zoning patterns in the four stages of New Towns (Fig. 19.4). Why should the stage 4 pattern show a partial return to the pattern found in traditional towns?

4 Discuss the environmental impact of progress on the countryside as indicated in Figures 19.6, 19.7 and 19.9. In what ways can the spoliation of the countryside be minimised?

5 Examine the location of the protected areas of England and Wales (Fig. 19.8). Are the areas that are not protected necessarily less deserving of protection?

20 Regional policy in Britain

Introduction

Regional policy is closely associated with general planning. The two are frequently coexistent and complementary: they are undertaken and administered by the same authorities; they often involve the use of the same controls and programmes. Sometimes a particular scheme of general planning – as outlined in the previous chapter – might be a component part of an overall project of regional policy.

This chapter can be viewed as a continuation of the previous chapter and also as a companion to Chapter 18. Not only may it be of interest to study the role of regional policy in the comprehensive planning scheme for Britain as a whole, but it may also be informative to compare British regional policy programmes with those being adopted in countries of the Third World.

The questions specifically to be posed – and answered – by this chapter are various:

- Why does the government deem it necessary to undertake a regional policy?
- How is such a specialised form of national planning organised and administered?
- What has been the nature of the growth of regional policy over the years?
- Which have been the most insuperable problems faced in the implementation of regional policy?
- Is regional policy necessarily advantageous to the regions it intends to help?

The need for regional policy

Just as differences in wealth exist between countries and continents, so too are there inequalities between different regions within countries. Britain is no exception. Here there are very wide spatial variations in both economic and social characteristics: in incomes, industrial output and efficiency, agricultural systems, living standards and price levels, employment and welfare services. These variations are the result of physical factors (climate, relief, soils and resources) and of human or historical factors, and are maintained through economic, social, demographic and technological interrelationships.

Productive human activity in Britain is concentrated into relatively few locations. The 'industrial coffin' (the broad rectangle stretching diagonally across England from Lancashire to Kent) together with the central Lowlands of Scotland, South Wales, industrial Yorkshire and the Tyne–Tees area account for over 80% of Britain's national industrial output. The remaining less prosperous regions generally have unused resources and underused labour supplies.

Clearly, economic activity could be redistributed more evenly over the country and it is towards this end that the government has instigated regional policy. Through its operation, and to aid the formulation of regional and national planning, three types of socio-economic regions have been officially recognised. These are as follows.

Depressed rural regions

These are large areas of countryside characterised by inefficient or small-scale agricultural systems, below average incomes, inadequate social facilities, limited potential for industrialisation (owing to lack of raw materials, capital and labour) and serious depopulation. Such areas include the Southern Uplands of Scotland, central Wales, the Pennine Hills and much of the South-West Peninsula.

Depressed industrial regions

These are normally areas where industrialisation occurred early (during the Industrial Revolution) but where, in recent years, economic decline has set in. Old industries stagnate or contract in terms of output and efficiency; labour-intensive activities are in decline; the economic infrastructure is in decay (with substandard service facilities, antiquated factory buildings and outmoded machinery), and average incomes are low. Unemployment levels are higher than the national average, social conditions are poor with a preponderance of slum housing, old hospitals and crowded schools, and overall depopulation is experienced. Such areas include South Wales, where the coalmining industry has declined, and Tyneside, where shipbuilding has diminished in importance.

Congested developed regions

These areas represent the positive side of regional imbalance. With natural and human advantages they have acquired a disproportionately high concentration of wealth, employment opportunities and population, and are usually characterised by expanding towns, prospering industries, high living standards, much 20th century development, a complex and efficient economic infrastructure and a preponderance of tertiary and quaternary activities. Such regions not only have detrimental effects on less developed areas, by drawing investment and resources away from them, but also suffer disadvantages of their own in the form of overcrowding and traffic congestion, restricted industrial expansion and greater pollution. South-east England and Avon exemplify such regions.

Reasons for government intervention

Faced with economic and social inequalities between regions, most governments now intervene in order to redress the imbalance. They do so, however, for a number of reasons and not always out of purely disinterested motives. Generally, five incentives to regional policy can be listed:

(1) *Social reasons.* Regional differences in wealth can produce social unrest. Unemployment, lack of opportunities and poor living standards create discontent – often reflected by crime and vandalism – and could upset the cultural basis of a region (perhaps being caused by the decline in a regional tongue as people move away from an area; for example, from Wales). Thus, regional policy is seen as a moral undertaking: improving the health, happiness and cultural stability of regional populations. Social reasons underlay British government planning during the 1930s.

(2) *Economic reasons.* Most governments aim to utilise fully all the resources of their respective countries and to maximise industrial output and expansion within optimal competitive levels. Encouraging the economic advancement of depressed areas and relieving congestion in developed areas would succeed in doing this, in which case regional policy will normally result in greater industrial productivity and an increase in wealth on both a regional and a national scale.

(3) *Political reasons.* Regional development is often seen as a means of placating nationalistic feelings within individual regions – in Wales and Scotland, for instance. Governments are also keen to reduce unemployment in order to gain political support, knowing that the unemployed are likely to vote for opposition parties at election time. For this reason, marginal-seat areas invariably receive greatest financial aid. A further political motive developed in Britain during the 1950s when regional policy was seen as a method of bringing the country more in line with Europe, so helping Britain's application to join the European Economic Community.

(4) *Strategic reasons.* A strong productive capacity must be maintained in case of war and this is assured through the dispersal of industry. Also the relocation of key industries into remote areas safeguards them from attack: industrial agglomerations provide obvious bombing targets, dispersed industries do not. Such considerations were especially strong in British regional policy during the 1940s, in the first half of which Britain was at war with Germany and in the second half of which the 'Cold War' between East and West was at its most volatile.

(5) *Planning reasons.* Regional wealth equalisation will aid the co-ordination of general planning policies, in housing, recreation, industry and education. If regional differences were to continue – for example, in employment levels – the success of such other planning policies as urban growth would be jeopardised. It is significant that, although comprehensive town and country planning in Britain goes back to the last war, its effects have only been widely apparent since the early 1960s when regional policy grew to be strong and effective.

Approaches to regional policy

The reduction of regional inequalities is not an easy policy to pursue. It must overcome physical differences such as climatic variations and must contend with traditional human desires, expectations and ways of life. The development of a formerly 'back-

Figure 20.1 It pays to advertise
Advertisements like these illustrate the ways in which people and industries are encouraged to move to depressed regions. (By kind permission of the Borough of Newport.)

Sit down, grab a pencil and compare Newport with your ideal site

The Need	Your Ideal	Newport
How many minutes from:		
Major East/West motorway junctions?		10
Major North/South motorway junctions?		25
Main line rail links to London and the North?		10
Container ship facilities?		10
The town centre?		5
A local airport?		35
A major international airport?		90
The centre of London?		125
Real, unspoiled countryside?		15
Beautiful, relaxing coastline?		20
What is the workforce within a ten mile radius?		169,000
How good are labour relations locally?		Excellent
What is the total industrial acreage?		450
Are there ready-made factories and warehouses to let?		Yes
Below £2.25 per square foot?		Yes
Is there a choice of small and large plots?		Yes
Is it a Development Area?		Yes

NEW COMPANY BASE? NEW FACTORY?
A big decision made simple by four key factors.

COMMUNICATIONS

Internal – No site in Newport is more than ten minutes from a motorway, railway or dock.

Road – London is just two and a half hours down the M4. Bristol is half an hour away, and the M50 North/South connection is fifteen minutes from central Newport.

Rail – Newport is just 93 minutes from Paddington, 111 minutes from New Street, Birmingham.

Air – From Rhoose airport you can fly direct to Amsterdam and most UK centres. Heathrow is a consistent two hours drive.

Sea – We have container facilities, plus regular import/export links around the world.

PEOPLE The people you take will like Newport. There's superb countryside to live in, not just visit. And all the other things that make up 'the quality of life' all within easy reach.

The people you hire have a fine track record as a workforce. In a 10 mile radius from Newport there are 170,000 workers. They are brought up on a variety of skills ranging from engineering to electronics. Skills that a number of major international manufacturers have already come to appreciate.

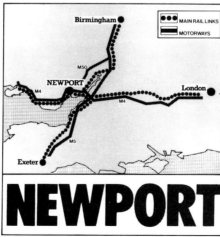

SITES A total of 450 acres is available. Factory, storage and office facilities from 750 to 40,000 square feet.   OR undeveloped plots from ½ to 24 acres. Private and Council developments are constantly in progress. Rents are extremely low in comparison with other conurbations.

AID A full time Industrial Development team offers a unique blend of business skills. And local knowledge about site availability, planning clearance, finance, health and safety details.

Newport is a Development Area. This means that there are numerous opportunities for assisted schemes.

For a 16 page colour brochure ring Gareth Isaac or Tony Parker on 0633 56906 now – or write to:
Borough of Newport,
The Civic Centre, Newport, Gwent NPT 4UR

Name:
Position:
Company:
Address:

Telephone: SL

ward' region may face all manner of problems: environmental hazards, inadequate resources and local opposition from the inhabitants.

Regional policies are difficult to undertake for other reasons also. One of these is the problem of approach: how best can a government make depressed areas grow economically and how best can the problems of congested areas be alleviated? Numerous methods have been tried in most countries and normally a combination of approaches has been used. In Britain this is certainly true.

In the early days of regional planning, the problem was largely one of technique: whether to move labour supplies to industry or industry to labour supplies. Both were attempted but it was soon realised that the former policy is the more difficult to undertake. Redirecting labour involves the break-up of social groups and the enforced movement of workers away from their friends and places to which they are attached. Moving work to the workers was found to be more straightforward and less liable to inflame opposition. Today the government employs both techniques, but concentrates more on the relocation of industry and jobs (see Fig. 20.1).

Directing workers to the work has been aided in various ways. More information about job opportunities is now distributed (through Job Centres); grants are made to help towards removal costs and, sometimes, towards the sale and purchase of property; subsidised local authority housing is occasionally provided; and there is a system whereby workers moving into new areas are given free fares between home and work and are provided with a boarding allowance for up to a year if they maintain dependants at their original place of residence.

Attempting to direct work to the workers largely entails the removal of industries and capital away from wealthy regions and into depressed regions. This may be done in two ways: by encouragement and bribery, or by compulsion. The British government has used both methods – a policy sometimes referred to as the **'carrot and stick approach'**. The 'carrot' consists of a number of government assistance schemes (economic and social aid programmes) and the 'stick' comprises the use of town and country planning controls (building permission being refused to firms wishing to develop in non-assisted areas).

The 'carrot' side of regional policy is by far the more important, and the various government incentives are now summarised.

(1) *Infrastructure improvement.* Many depressed regions (such as Mid-Wales) lack the environmental character conducive to economic development: having poor-quality transport arteries, bad housing conditions, substandard welfare facilities and so on. To rectify this, the government spends money in refurbishing old towns, building New Towns and trading estates, improving agricultural techniques, providing better medical and educational services, and clearing or reclaiming derelict land. Through these schemes, formerly depressed regions can become more attractive to businesses.

(2) *Financial aid.* As a direct encouragement to firms moving into assisted areas, the government offers a range of grants, loans and tax concessions. It provides regional development grants for new buildings and machinery, selective grants to cover capital costs incurred by newly moved industries, low-interest loans to firms wishing to expand, and long-term tax allowances on capital and labour expenditure. In addition, the government builds and subsequently sells, at below market prices, factory space, office premises and workshops (or else lets them out at low rents); gives financial aid towards technological research and the resettlement of workers; and gives active encouragement (financial help, advertising, advice) to schemes designed to increase a region's tourist trade. Much of this finance comes directly from the British government, but some percolates through from the regional development funds of the EEC.

(3) *Training schemes.* To increase the occupational mobility of labour (and to encourage incoming firms in assisted areas to employ local rather than imported labour) the government subsidises further-education and retraining programmes. Under the auspices of the Manpower Services Commission, new courses have been instigated – both at existing evening class and technical colleges and at specially set-up retraining centres. Part-time and full-time courses aim to give school leavers, and the unemployed in particular, new skills and new trades with which to further or change their careers. It is hoped that a more skilled and flexible labour supply within depressed regions will attract firms wishing to expand.

(4) *Enterprise zones.* Enterprise zones were set up after 1980 as part of an experimental policy to

boost industrialisation in areas where problems of unemployment, commercial decay and economic stagnation are especially acute. They are relatively small areas in which industrial and commercial development is encouraged without certain fiscal, planning and administrative constraints. Firms moving to or starting up in these zones are guaranteed exemption from land tax, rates and training levies; they receive full development grants, and are subject to simplified planning and administrative procedures, and quicker decision-making by local authorities. There are many enterprise zones now in existence, including those at Clydebank (Scotland), Speke (Merseyside), Corby (Northamptonshire) and the Isle of Dogs (London's dockland).

The development of regional policy

Since its conception over 50 years ago, Britain's regional policy has grown stronger and more far reaching. Yet its development has been neither constant nor consistently effective owing to the fact that it has always been subject to political and socio-economic conditions which change with the years. In consequence, the historical evolution of regional policy has been slow and erratic.

Before World War 2, some attempts were made to alleviate regional unemployment (as a result of the great recession in the 1930s), but it was not until after the end of hostilities that the government took a more definite control over industrial location. In 1945 the Distribution of Industry Act set up Development Areas, which qualified for government help in the form of financial incentives to new firms, and some success was achieved in directing light engineering industries to areas of high unemployment. The 1947 Town and Country Planning Act created the Industrial Development Certificate (IDC) policy and three years later a further Industries Act allowed for more generous government incentives.

The IDCs were introduced with the specific intention of giving the government (as opposed to local authorities) direct control over the location of economic activity. Every major industrial development scheme could take place only after an IDC had been applied for and granted. Simply by refusing to award IDCs in developed regions and granting them in development regions, the government could encourage industrial dispersal.

The following decade, however, witnessed a steady decline in government interest in regional policy: some plans were not implemented, government powers were not fully used and no additional acts aimed at relocating industries were passed. This meant that, by the end of the 1950s, serious regional inequalities still existed and, if anything, were worsening. Clearly, greater government action was necessary.

This duly came, and the 1960s saw the greatest progress yet made towards a complete and all-embracing regional policy. In 1960, the Local Employment Act designated Development Districts – small regional areas such as north-west Wales, north and west Cornwall and the Cumbrian coast, where unemployment was especially high and financial aid was readily given – and in 1963 another Local Employment Act provided for grants of 10% of the cost of machinery and 25% of the cost of buildings (more than previously) and introduced a more stringent use of IDCs in congested areas. No longer was unemployment the only criterion by which an area qualified for government aid, since other inequalities were also to be considered – low living standards and poor housing conditions, for example.

The Industrial Training Act of 1964 set up boards to review training schemes and subsidise educational courses, and in the following year there came the introduction of Office Development Permits (ODPs) in an attempt to restrict office development in Greater London.

The 1966 Industrial Development Act reconstituted the old Development Areas, but this time industries were encouraged to move, not necessarily to places of high unemployment, but to localities where there was greatest potential for economic success. In the same year the government also introduced a policy to provide lump-sum redundancy payments in an attempt to encourage workers to change jobs and move from declining to expanding industries.

Special Development Areas were established in 1967 as small pockets within Development Areas where aid was particularly necessary, and Intermediate Areas were established in 1970 in which lower levels of aid were made available (because of the existence there of less serious problems). All assisted areas were further extended in the Industries Act of 1972.

The most recent changes in regional policy began after the election of the Conservative government in 1979. With the aim of making regional planning programmes more effective and less wasteful of resources, this government made fairly wide-ranging alterations. It drastically reduced the size of the assisted areas and radically redesigned the forms of assistance it gave to industry within those assisted areas (see Fig. 20.2). Some grants were reduced or abolished; loans were more specifically tied to industrial projects; the use of the IDC control was removed; and greater emphasis was placed on retraining schemes run by the Manpower Services Commission. Later, in the 1980s, further measures were taken to change the emphasis of regional policy – to make it less directly reliant upon government and more reliant on industry. The number of enterprise zones was increased and freeports were set up – the latter being customs-free areas where foreign investment is encouraged and foreign-owned companies can be established. By encouraging the growth of small firms and abolishing many of the restrictions on industrial development and profit-making, the government successfully introduced 'regional policy through private enterprise' – a newly created philosophy of planning.

Parallel to the development of a national regional planning policy during the 1960s was the growth of local planning at a regional level. Such planning was seen as essential for the success of regional policy as a whole. In 1963 two White Papers appeared, one on north-east England and one on central Scotland, and the following year saw the publication of the *South-East Study*. Each of these proposed future growth patterns which would utilise the available resources of the areas concerned and complement the government's overall national strategy. In 1965 the *National Plan* was published, which studied in depth all aspects of the national economy with the intention of co-ordinating individual regional plans and ensuring that their proposals were consistent with the plan for the country as a whole.

Central to all regional planning have been the Economic Planning Regions. These were set up in 1964, eight in England and one each for Scotland and Wales. Each Region has an Economic Planning Council composed of industrialists, administrators and academics, and an Economic Planning Board composed of civil servants from those government departments chiefly concerned with regional policy. The task of the former is to help formulate regional plans and advise on the regional implications of national economic policies. The task of the latter is to help the Councils produce their plans and to co-ordinate the work of various government departments. Together, they are largely responsible for the

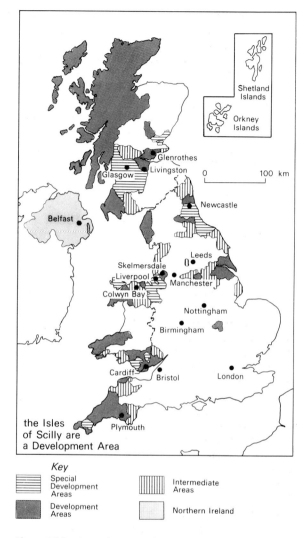

Figure 20.2 Areas for expansion
This map shows the situation before the 1984 changes when the Government further reduced the size of the assisted areas and abolished Special Development Areas altogether.

execution and success of all policies aimed at reducing spatial inequalities.

Problems of regional policy implementation

Economic and social conflicts
Encouraging economic development in depressed areas and controlling growth in prosperous areas are both likely to conflict with the provision of social welfare. Industrialisation in a region of unemployment will be economically beneficial but could also cause social stress – traffic congestion, stretching

REGIONAL PLANS

The future development of each individual region should not only be planned with regard to available resources but should also be formulated in the context of the government's overall regional policy objectives. Two areas that may exemplify the kinds of plans proposed for regions are Central Wales and the West Midlands, the former being a depressed rural region, the latter a congested wealthy region.

Central Wales has caused much concern amongst planners: the Birmingham University School of Planning made a special study of its problems and suggested certain remedies; in 1966 there was an *Industry in Wales report*, and the Mid-Wales Industrial Development Association has been set up, together with the Development Board for Rural Wales.

Overall, the development of Central Wales is taking the form of a broad-based attack. Industries are being encouraged to move there, and urban expansion is taking place at such towns as Rhayader, Brecon and Dolgellau. A New Town has been built at Newtown. In addition, communications are being improved, roads widened and straightened, and suggestions made for the construction of two new motorways, one running from north to south, the other from east to west, the two crossing near Llanidloes. Agriculture is being made more efficient through farm amalgamations and the encouragement of specialisation (stock-breeding and battery egg production, for instance). Afforestation under the auspices of the Forestry Commission has resulted in new coniferous plantations, for example on the slopes of Plynlimon, and water resources are being exploited with the building of new reservoirs in the Bala, Llanidloes and Brecon areas. Above all, it is hoped to expand the tourist industry by developing the holiday potential of the region: new

facilities for visitors are being allowed (car parks, gift shops and so on) and there is the possibility that a new national park will be designated, based on Powys and northern Dyfed.

In the West Midlands, planning aims have been to improve the urban environment of the main towns (through slum clearance, redevelopment and further land-use segregation) and to control the outward spread of the Birmingham conurbation. To these ends there was a *Regional study of the West Midlands* in 1965; a report entitled *West Midlands, patterns of growth* in 1967 and the *West Midlands transport study* in 1968.

The first named suggested that Birmingham should continue to be contained within a Green Belt and that its overspill population should be accommodated in New Towns and expanding towns further afield. In particular, it suggested further growth of towns in the 'rural west' of the region – Worcester, Ludlow, Leominster and Shrewsbury – together with the development of a 'growth pole' stretching from Birmingham to Telford.

Patterns of growth proposed corridor development: the building of urban–industrial fingers radiating from the Birmingham conurbation. Though not necessarily continuous, these corridors would be aligned along major communication routes and would accommodate all extra economic activity should any occur (Fig. 20.3). Between the corridors would be wedges of countryside preserved for agricultural and recreational purposes.

Whether these corridors will eventually come about depends on numerous factors, not least of which are the disagreement between planners and the lack of capital investment. Also, since 1973 there has been a general re-examination of regional plans and not all those once envisaged are likely to come to fruition.

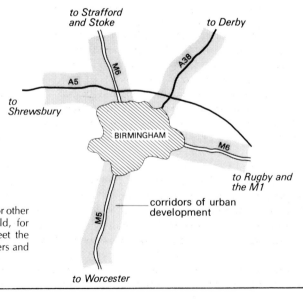

Figure 20.3 Corridor growth for Birmingham
Similar corridor growth schemes have been put forward for other major cities; London, Manchester, Leeds and Sheffield, for example. However, such regional plans frequently meet the opposition of involved parties – local authorities, planners and native inhabitants.

limited educational and medical facilities, and causing pollution. Decentralisation in prosperous areas could result in underused social capital – half-empty schools and hospitals, for instance.

Aid distribution

Governments must decide whether to supply aid equally to all regions within Development Areas or to concentrate on special places where the problems are greatest. If the latter is decided, a further difficulty arises: whether to help places that have the lowest living standards or those that have the highest levels of unemployment. Sometimes the government may help, instead, areas where economic potential is at its maximum (where success is most likely). Such decisions are hindered by the fact that cost benefit analysis is difficult to assess for alternative policies. Regional policy is not an accurate science and mistakes can often be made.

Definition of areas in need

This is problematical because no exact method exists to measure regional inequalities. Indices might be formulated to identify backwardness – incomes, living standards, social conditions and so forth – but these are subject to individual perception. What is considered poor housing or low educational opportunities in one region may be the accepted norm elsewhere.

Development Area delimitation

Boundaries between rich and poor regions are not clear cut and yet delimitation is necessary to enable the provision of aid. On one side of a line, aid might be available; on the other side it might not, yet the two sides could appear identical. There is also the problem that poor pockets of land within wealthy areas may not qualify for aid whereas rich pockets of land within poor areas do. In addition, Development Area boundaries frequently cut across existing functional or local authority boundaries, thereby making administration difficult.

Character of industrialisation

The 'footloose' industries usually directed to depressed areas tend to be 'branch plants' (often subsidiary units) and therefore would be the first to close down in times of recession. Also, many firms – like those in light engineering – employ women rather than men because of the intricate nature of the work and the preference of companies to employ shift labour at piece rates. Many other firms either take their own employees with them when they move, or else are not labour intensive in character. Therefore, industrialisation may not in fact greatly help to reduce male unemployment levels in areas of greatest need.

Inadequacies of regional plans

Planning policies and strategies are often inflexible, having few alternatives and being unable to adapt easily to changing social and economic conditions. They may also be ill conceived with little agreement between those involved in their formulation: the government, local authorities and individual planners. In many cases, regional plans are opposed by public opinion since they have been devised with minimum regard for tastes and desires.

Political influences

Regional policy is closely linked to political ideology and is therefore subject to constant change. Strategies are liable to alter with a change of government or local council. Also, because party politics is involved in such planning, some confusion and inconsistency may exist in the distribution of regional policy information.

It is perhaps because of the above problems that regional policy has not been an unqualified success. There are still marked regional inequalities and assisted areas still suffer from high unemployment rates, low incomes and depopulation.

Arguments against regional policy

Reduced national prosperity

It can be argued that regional inequalities are the result of spatial specialisation and the most efficient use of resources, and are therefore the natural consequence of economic progress in a free market. The dispersal of industry would thus lead to the suboptimal location of economic activity, a fall in the economies of scale achieved by firms (by the disintegration of industrial agglomerations), and greater inefficiency. This would reduce productivity and have an adverse effect on national prosperity.

Social upheavals

Directing industries to rural areas may destroy the aesthetic quality of the natural environment and have detrimental effects on the culture and social conditions. Encouraging overspill English populations to settle in Wales, for example, may generate hostile Welsh feeling and dilute the Welsh culture. It is partly for this reason that the Welsh language is on the decline.

Resource competition

Developing all depressed regions equally and at the same time could increase demands on the economy (on capital, labour supplies and so on) at a faster rate than increases in resource production. This could lead to wasteful competition for the acquisition of the limited resources available – competition between private and public enterprises, between different regional authorities and between central and local government.

Capital wastage

Some regions are subsidised at the expense of others; some areas receive a larger share of the national cake than others. The fact that assisted areas are receiving government aid (provided through taxation or through Common Market funds) might encourage them to ask for more aid than they actually need. If the government supplies the help requested, some regions may acquire capital they cannot use. This capital is either wasted or left idle.

Inflationary undertones

The distribution of industry into suboptimal locations will increase the costs of production through higher transport charges, more expensive marketing and the loss of external economies of scale. These increased costs, if not fully offset by government grants, will be passed on to the consumer and the resulting increase in retail prices is liable to lead to inflation. Indeed, even if the government does absorb the costs, inflation is likely to result since regional policy involves an increase in public expenditure.

The success of regional policy

It is not easy to make an objective assessment of the achievements of regional policy. Success rates simply cannot be gauged. It is not good enough just to compare the characteristics of depressed areas 50 years ago with those today. Conditions are indeed better than they were – but well might they have been in any case without national planning. All areas are relatively better off than half a century ago. To judge the impact of regional policy it would be necessary to contrast the conditions within depressed areas now

with conditions that might have occurred by now without government intervention – naturally an impossible task.

All that we can do is to consider the ways in which regional policy has had an effect on society. The degree to which industry has used government help, the extent to which inequalities between regions have been evened out, the ways in which the general public has perceived regional development – all help us in quantifying the impact of regional policy programmes.

Generally regional planning has been financed through taxation. This means, to some extent at least, that the more successful, most efficient industries (located in southern England) finance the less successful, inefficiently located businesses in depressed regions. Capital, which should be used to 'plough back', is thus creamed off from profitable companies, reducing their ability to reinvest, re-equip and compete against foreign firms.

Simply through official designation as Development Areas some regions might have been adversely affected. Once people and companies are told that they live in a depressed area, which needs special help, they perhaps feel self-consciously inferior and insecure. From northern England and Scotland, workers and companies are likely to flee south (or even abroad) to escape the inevitable blight that tends to follow official recognition. Perhaps it is no surprise that many regions appear just as poor as they always did: the North-East, Clydeside and parts of the North-West still have above-average unemployment rates – just as in the 1930s.

In this respect it can be argued that the role of the unions has not been entirely unobtrusive. One of the assets of many depressed areas has been low wage rates – these acting as a magnet to industries searching for cheap (low labour-cost) locations. However, once a new factory has opened within such areas, union demands tend to increase for wage parity with other British regions. If companies comply with these demands, and increase wages accordingly, they may be forced into suboptimal conditions, go bankrupt and close down.

Worker–management relationships, in any case, can seriously impede the success of regional policy. The 'them and us' mentality among employers and employees is breaking down but remains common within some companies and regions. It has been especially common in parts of Scotland, northern England and South Wales, and, because of this, has done much to jeopardise industrial development in those areas. Merseyside, for example, has had a long history of labour relations problems, and this has kept many firms away, regardless of government incentives.

In conclusion, then, we see that the success rate of regional policy is debatable, bedevilled as it is by sociological and political considerations. National planning, like local and regional planning, is subject to human behaviour and is likely to succeed only within the confines set by economic, cultural and political realities.

Summary

1 Regional inequalities exist in employment, social facilities and wealth: 'depressed areas' suffer from depopulation, slum housing, declining labour-intensive industries and decayed infrastructure. Overdeveloped areas suffer from congestion and pollution.

2 Government help is given to regions in order to improve social conditions, reduce unemployment and prevent crime. It is also given to secure government support at election times.

3 Regional policy pivots on the 'carrot and stick' approach. The 'carrot' includes financial incentives (grants and loans), road building, factory construction and retraining schemes. The 'stick' involves the rigid use of planning restrictions.

4 Regional policy dates from 1947, was strengthened and widened during the 1960s and was radically modified after 1979. New additions to the government armoury of planning schemes have been the Manpower Services Commission, enterprise zones and the encouragement of small businesses.

5 The implementation of regional policy is problematic: there are conflicts of regional interests and socio-economic goals, difficulties of aid distribution, inexact ways of delimiting Development Areas.

6 Regional policy has not been a total success and problem areas still contain serious problems. Even the concept of such a policy is questionable since economic inefficiency and social upheaval may result.

Data–response exercises

1 How effective do you think the advertisements in Figure 20.1 are in encouraging firms to move to a depressed area, and could they be improved? Examine the impact on the local environment if many firms were to move to this area.

2 Analyse the regional distribution of areas for expansion as shown in Figure 20.2. Are there any areas not shaded that require help to solve problems of overcrowding and stretched social services?

3 Discuss the advantages and disadvantages of corridor urban growth as shown in Figure 20.3. Which organisations in particular might oppose such a regional plan for a conurbation?

Project work

1 From fieldwork, questionnaire distribution and personal interviews the degree of success achieved by various new planning schemes can be investigated. Who benefits from a new road scheme and who suffers? Which inhabitants of a New Town enjoy their new life and which do not? Are workers and firms pleased to have moved into a Development Area? Do high-rise flats create more environmental and human problems than they solve? Such fieldwork is likely to show how most planning programmes are a mixed blessing.

2 Patterns of tourism and leisure activities can be studied through detailed surveys of holiday centres. What determines the exact location of tourist 'honeypots' within national parks and how successful have these been in preserving the overall appearance of the areas in which they are sited? How far do people travel away from their parked cars in holiday resorts? (Percentages can be worked out of those who do not leave their cars at all, those who walk up to half a kilometre away from their cars and those who walk further afield.) On average, how long do people stay at a tourist 'honeypot', at a picnic site or in a car park? What do people most look for in a holiday?

Further reading

Chisholm, M. 1982. *Modern world development*. London: Hutchinson. A stimulating, thoughtfully written book looking at world inequalities, their causes and consequences. Ways in which poor countries can develop are considered and the author ends on a surprisingly optimistic note.

Cole, J. P. 1983. *Geography of world affairs* 6th edn. London: Butterworth. An objective, factual survey of current affairs from a geographical viewpoint (though not an unbiased one). Detailed case studies from both rich and poor countries and a well argued discussion of future prospects. Well written; a good reference book.

Cullingworth, J. R. 1976. *Town and country planning in Britain*. London: George Allen & Unwin. The history of planning is outlined and the extent of government influence reviewed (and criticised). Attempts to streamline planning procedures are considered. Useful reference book.

Gilg, A. W. 1978. *Countryside planning*. Newton Abbot: David & Charles. Part of the *Problems in modern geography* series. A comprehensive study of rural planning, 1945–76, and of rural change. Readable for non-specialists and well produced. Also recommended in the same series are *Land and leisure*, *Derelict land* and *Recreation geography*.

Hall, P. 1982. *Urban and regional planning* 2nd edn. London: Penguin. Gives a historical perspective to the evolution of planning. Very readable, even for non-geographers. By the same author is *Great planning disas-*ters (1980, London: Penguin) a most readable account of some major world mistakes in urban and transport planning. Highly critical of planners and 'experts' it also discusses how future disasters might be avoided.

Mabogunje, A. L. 1980. *The development process, a spatial perspective*. London: Hutchinson. A guide to regional problems and policies in less developed countries by an author who has personal experience of African affairs. A forceful and direct approach is used, producing an effective result.

Miles, C. W. N. and W. Seabrooke 1977. *Recreational land and management*. London: Spon. Studies the pressures on Britain's countryside and investigates how they can be controlled. Emphasis on the practical application of management techniques – especially useful to those interested in planning.

Ratcliffe, J. 1981. *An introduction to town and country planning* 2nd edn. London: Hutchinson. A review of the development of planning, with a strong economic slant. Covers a wide field: planning history, survey preparation, techniques of analysis, amenity resource considerations and town planning law.

Stretton, H. 1978. *Urban planning in rich and poor countries*. Oxford: Oxford University Press. A critical account of modern planning bureaucracies and projects. A readable – if biased – text is accompanied by numerous case studies, examples and questions. Some powerful arguments put forward and some worrying conclusions.

Appendix A A guide to project work

The main aim of this book has been to provide you with a general and comprehensive guide to the subject, outlining the principal ideas, approaches and information contained within it, and setting theory in the context of real world examples. The book is not intended as a complete and exhaustive study of all aspects of human activity. You are expected to substantiate and supplement the knowledge obtained here with your own background reading, exercises, case study research and project work. There is a plethora of books to help you in this: regional geography textbooks, economic geography books and, indeed, other books on human geography which concentrate on particular subjects in greater depth than has been possible here. Suggestions for individual project work and private investigation have been given at the end of each section and a further guide is provided below for studies in agriculture and urban settlements.

Table A1 Agriculture

Hypothesis	Test-method	Follow-up
(a) That there is a correlation between land use and altitude. (Similar tests can be made of the hypothesis that land use is related either to slope or to aspect. For these it might be necessary to select and compare data from different land-use maps.)	Choose a 1:25 000 Land Utilisation Map on which there is marked variation in relief. Establish a 100 random point sample and for each point record its altitude and land use. Determine the mean altitude and altitudinal range for each of your land-use categories. (The same information can be obtained by fieldwork.)	Plot your 100 points on a scatter graph, land-use type categories along the horizontal axis and altitude along the vertical axis. Transfer your information into two tables and from these make general conclusions.
(b) That there is a correlation between land use and soil type. (More specifically, the hypothesis might be that arable farming is found on fertile soils or that pasture is found on infertile soils. Of course, in these instances fertility must be carefully defined.)	Choose two maps of a single area, one a land-use map and one a geological drift map. Draw a sketch map to show soil types and another, drawn on tracing paper, to show land use. (The same information can be obtained by fieldwork).	The superimposition of the two maps should give a basis for a conclusion. For more detailed study of a single land-use type tabulate data into six columns: (1) soil type, (2) number of hectares, (3) % total area, (4) number of hectares of land-use type, (5) % total land-use type, and (6) expected number of hectares covered by land-use type (estimated from columns 3 and 4). Work out the index of land-use type concentration (observed value ÷ expected value). Values above 1.0 show a positive correlation.
(c) That land use and intensity are related to distance from the market (as suggested by Von Thünen).	This study can be undertaken either from fieldwork or from maps and published sources of data. A single town should be taken as the market and parishes can be used as the basis of study.	Tabulate data into four columns: (1) the parish, (2) the dominant land-use type, (3) yields per hectare, and (4) distance from market. A regression line graph can be drawn, distance from market along the horizontal axis and land-use density along the vertical axis. The line must pass through the mean value of each array.

APPENDIX A

Table A2   Urban settlement

Hypothesis	Test-method	Follow-up
(a) That there are certain functions associated with the central business district and that these can be delimited.	Divide towns into sections. Plot according to classification (shops, warehouses, offices, residential, etc.).	Produce urban functions map of whole town. Delimit the CBD and draw conclusions.
(b) That the most accessible land at the town centre will be the most valuable, with decline outwards from the centre.	Rateable value per front metre. Plot rateable value of each building, then divide by frontage (information from local authorities).	Draw section along main road. Column graph – rateable value per front metre.
(c) That there will be most traffic congestion at the most accessible point and therefore most traffic management schemes at centre.	Plot traffic management on morphology map using key.	Draw neatly on morphological change map.
(d) That pedestrians will move towards the centre and that the highest pedestrian density will be at the centre.	On selected days make a static count for pedestrian flow. Make a moving count along a section for density. Mark points and section on town map.	Draw a proportional flow diagram above count point on the section of main road. Draw column graph of density above section of main road.
(e) That there is a relationship between the population and/or number of functions of a town and the size of its urban field, and that there is a hierarchy of urban fields.	Questionnaire survey. This may be used either in a town-based study or a countryside-based study. Questions should not be ambiguous.	Work out theoretical urban fields for different levels of hierarchy based on population and number of functions. Plot actual fields by desire lines (straight lines connecting each central town with the settlements linked to it). Urban field boundaries can be estimated from the points of the desire lines.

Appendix B   A guide to essay writing

Approach

Writing essays on human geography – as with writing essays on most other arts and social science subjects – involves not simply the recording of facts but the use of a skilled technique of presentation. Marks are awarded on style, approach and understanding as well as on the content of essays, and the successful candidate is the one who can 'think round' a topic. Facts alone do not produce a good essay; they provide the foundation and framework upon which an answer hangs, and should not be seen as an end in themselves.

Above all else candidates must be careful to write essays that answer the questions. Only information that is relevant should be used and it must be arranged and presented in a clear, precise and logical way. The content of any essay must not be allowed to wander off at tangents: any facts or discussion which add nothing to the answer and are not specifically pertinent to be content matter should be left out, however interesting they may seem to the candidate. Remember, the person who reads and marks an essay should be able to guess the wording of the question. If the reader cannot guess the question from the answer, then it must be a poor answer.

The wording of a question is a guide to the kind of answer required by the examiners and teachers. The writer must read every word of a question carefully and ask himself or herself, 'What exactly is being asked and how best can I answer it?'. Clear interpretation is the key to answering questions. Certain instructional words tend to appear in essay questions and these, especially, should be considered and defined. The following are the most common:

(a) *'Describe'*, *'Outline'*, *'Give account of'*, *'Write a geographical essay on'*. Each of these asks for a fairly straightforward, usually factual essay, which needs an orderly, logical presentation of information.

(b) *'Explain'*, *'Examine'*, *'Analyse'*, *'Assess'*. Each of these demands an answer that puts forward arguments, critical comment and evidence, which is judged and evaluated. The reasons both for and against particular phenomena should be covered and, normally, a well argued conclusion is required.

(c) *'Compare'*, *'Contrast'*. Both of these ask for the constant comparison of two or more geographical features. The candidate must not write separate descriptions and compare only at the end of the essay. Similarities as well as differences should be considered in every paragraph.

(d) *'Account for'*. This asks the candidate to give reasons for geographical phenomena: why something exists or occurs. Often this instruction is followed by 'the importance of' or 'the significance of', in which case the writer must consider the results and effects of the subject in hand. These can be both long-term and short-term effects, and both direct and indirect.

(e) *'Discuss'*. This term usually asks for a wide, all embracing answer which gives an exchange of opinions, judgements, reasoned comments and a general discussion of the subject from all angles. Often this word follows a quotation. The candidate need not necessarily agree with the comments or opinions contained in a quotation – the essay writer can agree, disagree or modify the comments, but must always support the answer with well informed evidence.

Essay content

(a) A plan of the major points in note form is a good way to start an essay. It enables the writer to present a logical sequence of information and helps the clarification of ideas.

(b) An essay should have a set form. The opening paragraph should introduce the subject, state how the essay title has been interpreted and summarise the way the writer intends to answer the question. The final paragraph should sum up, stressing the main points and making a conclusion. Ideally the first sentence of each paragraph should be a guide to the content of that paragraph.

(c) Avoid waffle. Unnecessary padding is not only time consuming but can destroy the flow of an essay. Also, many examiners imagine that waffle is an attempt to hide lack of knowledge, and mark down accordingly. Every sentence should add something to the answer.

(d) Be accurate, specific and precise with information. Avoid generalisations and vagueness: 'Local power supplies', 'warm temperatures', 'wet climate', 'fertile soil', 'coffee from Brazil'. As far as possible, candidates must give exact locations, exact statistics, and exact terminology.

(e) Write neatly. Use a fountain pen (preferably) and ensure that all written work is legible. Diagrams and sketch maps should be drawn in pencil and should be simple, accurate, clear and uncluttered. Labels ought not to interfere with the drawing; they should be written away from the sketch and signalled by arrows.

(f) Use correct English. Be careful with spelling, sentence construction, tenses and punctuation. In general keep words and sentences short and simple. Never use colloquialisms and slang expressions and avoid abbreviations such as 'e.g.', 'i.e.', 'etc.', 'don't'. Even accepted abbreviations (HEP, for example) should only be used after the full words have been used at least once.

(g) Avoid personal pronouns and purely personal opinions. An essay writer living in Britain should refer to that country by name and not as 'we' or 'us'. Candidates should try not to say 'I think that . . .' but instead say 'It is thought that . . .'.

(h) Avoid lists of numbered facts. All essays should be in essay style – that is, full prose composition.

(i) Use quotations where relevant, provided they can be remembered accurately. State their sources.

(j) Be topical. However modern a textbook, some information in it is likely to be out of date, especially statistics and other geographical information, which change weekly, monthly and yearly. To keep their essays topical, students should, throughout the duration of a course, read newspapers and specialised magazines and listen to radio and television programmes (news broadcasts, travelogues, documentaries). It is surprising how much human geographical information can be gleaned from everyday life. An essay that contains up-to-date information has a distinct advantage over one that contains merely textbook material.

Appendix C   Examination questions

Demography

(1) How would you define 'overpopulation' and how would you attempt to measure it? (London)

(2) Discuss the circumstances which have given rise to the existence of multiracial societies. (Cambridge)

(3) What do you understand by 'population density'? Discuss the significance of this concept in human geography. (Oxford)

(4) 'People do not move to empty lands; they move towards better opportunities.' With reference to specific examples critically examine the truth of this statement. (L)

(5) Demonstrate the different types of demographic contrast that can exist within a country. (L)

(6) With reference to specific examples discuss the causes of the rapid growth of population in developing countries and the social and economic problems which this has created. (Northern Universities' Joint Matriculation Board)

Economic activity

(1) What factors account for spatial variations in either the value of farmland or the size of farms? (L)

(2) 'To understand modern rural land-use patterns it is more important to appreciate the factors of physical geography than the factor of distance from markets.' Discuss with examples. (O)

(3) Discuss the world patterns of supply and demand for mineral oil. (NUJMB)

(4) How true is it to say that each medium of transport has a different optimum distance for the most economic movement of goods? (L)

(5) 'The exploration of the resources of the seas and sea floors is a matter of increasing political as well as economic importance.' Discuss this statement. (C)

(6) 'Patterns of traffic flow are both the cause and effect of developments in communications.' Discuss and illustrate this statement. (C)

(7) With reference to specific industries, demonstrate the variable effects of 'weight loss' on the location of manufacturing. (L)

(8) Explain the location of major centres of either ship-building or motor vehicle production. (NUJMB)

(9) Write an essay on the geographical effects of technological change in ocean-going transport. (C)

(10) Discuss the view that an abundance of natural resources is not necessarily a major factor limiting industrialisation. (C)

Settlement

(1) Give an explanatory account of the pattern of settlement in a rural area which you have studied. (NUJMB)

(2) Critically examine the criteria that might be used to distinguish between urban and rural settlement. (L)

(3) To what extent are models useful in understanding patterns of human settlement? (O)

(4) What factors have stimulated the growth of large cities in the underdeveloped countries? (C)

(5) Demonstrate the different ways in which increasing mobility in the 20th century has affected the characteristics of urban development. (L)

(6) What are the main contrasts in the processes of urbanisation between the more developed and less developed world? (O)

(7) Consider the various theories which seek to explain the grouping of similar functions within a city. Which theory do you favour and why? (L)

(8) With reference to a town or city you have studied in some detail, outline and comment on the location and structure of (a) the central business district, (b) residential areas, and (c) industrial areas. (C)

(9) 'Most cities are too complex in form for simple models of urban structure to be of relevance to their study.' Discuss. (O)

(10) Define what is meant by the term 'spatial interaction' and examine the factors which might affect the amount of spatial interaction between two settlements. (L)

Geography and planning

(1) With reference to one developing country, comment on the assertion that 'trade, not aid, is what the country requires'. (L)

(2) The conservation of landscape may frequently be desirable – but what is to be conserved and at what cost? (C)

(3) 'An advantage of the tourist industry is that it does not rely on non-renewable resources.' Discuss. (L)

(4) Outline the problems of regional development and planning in any one country you have studied. (C)

(5) 'The dual use of land for farming and recreation is good in theory but difficult in practice.' Discuss. (L)

(6) 'The use of land in Britain has increasingly to compete with urban demands for housing, water supply, transport and even recreation.' Comment on this statement. (C)

Appendix D   Glossary of terms

bastide   A town built for military or strategic reasons – usually fortified or centred on a castle.

bid-rent   The amount users are prepared to pay for land or accommodation; a sum offered for using a facility.

climax   The final result of a sequence of steps or stages; the culmination of a process.

concept   An assumed idea, a theoretical construction based on experience.

diffusion   The spreading out of a geographical feature or process; a broadening distribution.

ecosystem   The set of life forms existing in an area; the interdependent features of the living environment.

enterprise   A scheme; bold or spirited effort. Management or administrative skill; a business venture.

entrepôt   A commercial centre where goods are collected, stored and transhipped for re-export.

eutrophication   Rapid bacterial activity and oxygen removal, which causes the eventual extinction of plants and animals; especially common in water.

exponential model   A mathematical plan which explains or describes a phenomenon; an analogy chosen to fit an observed relationship employing the principle of geometric progression.

faubourg   An encampment or settlement especially for foreigners, located outside a town's perimeter.

gavelkind   The equal distribution of wealth or land amongst heirs.

ghetto   A cultural, racial or religious enclave within a city, which has distinctive characteristics.

gravity model   A theoretical structure that employs the concept of natural pull or attraction.

hierarchy   A list in which elements are ranked in importance; a layered structure.

hinterland   The zone around a settlement, which relies on that settlement for trading facilities. A district of urban influence.

inertia   The state of continued existence, a lack of movement. Passivity in the face of change.

infrastructure   Non-productive assets; facilities that support or indirectly produce industrial or agricultural development.

innovation   The original introduction of a geographical feature; the first production of a landscape element.

intermediate technology   Labour-intensive, often small-scale, manufacturing activity that does not require advanced expertise or elaborate inputs.

lapse rate   The degree of change over a given space or time; a rate by which an entity diminishes or increases.

latifundia   Large agricultural estates in which landlord–tenant or management–worker relationships are traditionally strict. Common in the Iberian Peninsula.

law   A postulated relationship between geographical phenomena; a general explanation applied to observed occurrencies.

linkage   A physical or functional bond – an economic tie that binds elements together.

marginal land   Land which, physically, is near the bounds of economic agricultural use.

matrix   A set of figures laid out in grid form to show or summarise information; a rectangular array of data which can be manipulated arithmetically according to strict mathematical rules.

model   Simplified structure (physical or theoretical) which generalises about real world complexities.

monoculture   The cultivation of a single agricultural product; specialist farming. Often used synonymously with plantation agriculture.

multiplier effect   An economic snowball effect by which a single event leads to several further events.

optimum   The most favourable; the best or most balanced.

paradigm   A set of ideas or behaviour patterns; a conceptual framework.

perception   A personal view, a way of seeing or understanding that provides an image.

pioneer advance   Movement into new, and often uncharted, territory.

plural society   A culturally or racially mixed group of people within a given region. A society with many ethnic categories or sources of authority.

primogeniture   The inheritance of wealth or land by the eldest son only.

quotient   A numerical value – normally a ratio – which aids comparisons; a number obtained by dividing one number by another.

rationality   Assumed normal behaviour; logical thought processes, based on common sense.

shanty town   A rude, ill-equipped, poor assemblage of shacks where public utilities are meagre. A collection of slums or huts.

spatial analysis   The study of distribution – how factors are located in horizontal space.

synthesis   A collective study of comprehensive information; the integration of knowledge.

system   A topic area comprising many interrelated elements.

systems analysis   A study whereby a topic is considered through a detailed investigation of its composite parts.

theory   A set of statements that attempts to account for relationships and real world phenomena.

transhumance   The movement of animals and/or people to temporary (or seasonal) accommodation; a system of farming that involves this.

utility   Degree of usefulness; the benefit derived from a person or object.

Author index

Index of place names

307

INDEX OF PLACE NAMES

INDEX OF PLACE NAMES

General index